Gardening

FOR

DUMMIES®

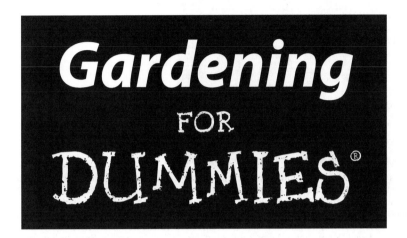

Gardening FOR DUMMIES®

by Sue Fisher, Michael MacCaskey, Bill Marken, and the Editors of the National Gardening Association

JOHN WILEY & SONS, LTD

Gardening For Dummies®

Published by

John Wiley & Sons, Ltd
The Atrium
Southern Gate
Chichester
West Sussex
PO19 8SQ
England

WILEY

About the Authors

Sue Fisher is a lifelong plant enthusiast whose main aim is to make gardening as user-friendly and approachable as possible. After training at Oaklands College, St Albans, the first ten years of her career were spent in the nursery and garden centre industry, including five years as plant buyer for a group of top garden centres and a landscape company. In 1990 Sue decided to bring her enthusiasm for plants to a wider audience and became a freelance writer and broadcaster. To date she has written ten books, including *Garden Colour, Essential Plants for Small Gardens,* and *Fast Plants,* as well as co-authoring *Ground Force Garden Handbook* and *Geoff Hamilton's Gardening Year,* and contributed to several of the Reader's Digest gardening books. Her gardening features have been published in many magazines and newspapers, including *Gardeners' World, Gardens Monthly*, and *Garden News.* Sue currently gardens in Buckinghamshire where her two young children are fast making her an expert on family gardening.

Michael MacCaskey began his college career as a creative arts student at San Francisco State University in 1969, but in the process became instead a passionate gardener. By 1976 he received a Bachelor of Science degree in ornamental horticulture from California State Polytechnic University, San Luis Obispo. Since then, he's had the good fortune to work for and learn from garden editors such as Walter Doty, Richard Dunmire, Joe Williamson, and Bill Marken. A second-generation Los Angeles native (zone 9), he was appointed Editor-in-Chief of Vermont-based *National Gardening Magazine* (zone 4) in 1994. Since then, he's been learning about gardening in a short-season, cold-winter region. His magazine writing has been honoured by both the Western Magazine Publishers Association and the Garden Writers of America.

Bill Marken is the editor of *Rebecca's Garden Magazine,* a new publication from Hearst Magazines Enterprises based on the popular television show. A lifelong resident of California, Bill served as editor-in-chief of Sunset, the *Magazine of Western Living,* from 1981 to 1996. Earlier in his career, he wrote for the magazine's garden section, pitched in on several editions of the best-selling *Western Garden Book,* and generally nurtured his interests in subjects related to gardening, landscaping, travel, and other aspects of the good life in the West. A vacation garden at 6,200-feet elevation gives him insight into cold-winter climates with 100-day growing seasons.

The National Gardening Association is the largest member-based, nonprofit organisation of home gardeners in the US. Founded in 1972 (as 'Gardens for All') to spearhead the community garden movement, today's National Gardening Association is best known for its bimonthly publication, *National Gardening* magazine. Reporting on all aspects of home gardening, each issue is read by some half-million gardeners worldwide. For more information about the National Gardening Association in the US, see its Web site at www.garden.org.

Dedication

We dedicate this book to new gardeners, individuals who sow a packet of seeds, plant a tree, or otherwise nurture a plant for the first time.

Publisher's Acknowledgements

We're proud of this book; please send us your comments through our Dummies online registration form located at www.dummies.com/register/.

Some of the people who helped bring this book to market include the following:

Acquisitions, Editorial, and Media Development

Project Editor: Rachael Chilvers

(Previous Edition: Kyle Looper, Patricia Yuu Pan, Melba Hopper)

Content Editor: Simon Bell

Commissioning Editor: Alison Yates

(Previous Edition: Holly McGuire, Sarah Kennedy)

Copy Editor: Sally Lansdell

(Previous Edition: Diane L. Giangrossi, Diana R. Conover, William A. Barton)

Proofreader: Sue Gilad

Technical Editor: William G. Denne, Principal Horticultural Advisor, RHS Garden Wisley

(Previous Edition: Deborah Brown, John R. Dunmire, Denny Schrock)

Executive Editor: Jason Dunne

Executive Project Editor: Amie Jackowski Tibble

Cover Photo: © Photographer's Choice/ Getty Images

Cartoons: Ed McLachlan

Composition Services

Project Coordinator: Maridee Ennis

Photography: David Cavagnaro, Dwight R. Kuhn, Jerry Pavia, Positive Images, Michael S. Thomson

Layout and Graphics: Stephanie D. Jumper, Barry Offringa, Julie Trippetti

Proofreader: Dwight Ramsey

Indexer: TECHBOOKS Production Services

Special Help
Jan Withers

Publishing and Editorial for Consumer Dummies

Diane Graves Steele, Vice President and Publisher, Consumer Dummies

Joyce Pepple, Acquisitions Director, Consumer Dummies

Kristin A. Cocks, Product Development Director, Consumer Dummies

Michael Spring, Vice President and Publisher, Travel

Kelly Regan, Editorial Director, Travel

Publishing for Technology Dummies

Andy Cummings, Vice President and Publisher, Dummies Technology/General User

Composition Services

Gerry Fahey, Vice President of Production Services

Debbie Stailey, Director of Composition Services

Contents at a Glance

Table of Contents

Introduction

The more you discover about gardening, the more satisfying it is. Gardening is all about a process that delights the eye and fuels the soul with a connection to the earth. As countless teachers and community workers have learned, gardening is one of the quickest (and cheapest!) ways to reduce vandalism and crime, and to increase community pride. Gardening is good for the body. An hour or two of weeding, harvesting, or cultivating provides just the right kind of light exercise we all need. Responsible gardening also does good things for the environment: materials get recycled and certain habitats attract wildlife, for example.

The point is, gardening has moved out of the vegetable patch and the flower bed. Gardening now encompasses our lives – if you have a garden, even a very tiny one, you are a gardener. If you have a sunny windowsill, you are a gardener. National surveys show that gardening has become the most popular, least exclusive hobby of all. Everybody's doing it.

People are simply enjoying their time outdoors and striving to make their little corner of the world more peaceful and beautiful – a better place to live. And that's what this book is about.

About This Book

You have in your hands a gardening encyclopedia in miniature – all you need to know to get off to a good start. No matter what area of gardening interests you – growing roses or perennials or just cutting the grass – you'll find good advice here. In every chapter, our basic goal is to give you the information you need to go out and plant or prune what you want. But novices aren't the only ones who'll find this book useful. Gardening is such a huge topic that no one ever comes close to knowing everything about it. (That's one reason why gardening has become one of the most popular hobbies of all time.) If, for example, you are a seasoned rose grower but know almost nothing about starting a salad garden or pruning trees, you can find excellent advice in Chapters 18 or 15, respectively.

This book offers lists of plants that you can choose from to create a beautiful garden. We list the plants by the common name first, followed by the botanical name. The lists are alphabetised according to the botanical name.

Conventions Used in This Book

To help you navigate through this book, we've set up a few conventions:

- ✔ *Italic* is used for emphasis and to highlight new words or terms that are defined.
- ✔ **Boldfaced** text is used to indicate the action part of numbered steps.
- ✔ Monofont is used for Web addresses.

Foolish Assumptions

In this book, we make some general assumptions about who you are:

- ✔ You've bought a place with a garden and suddenly realise that you don't know your begonias from your buttercups. You want to know the basics on how to get started on creating an outside space that you'll love spending time in.
- ✔ You need a helpful reference guide to answer all those questions you have about when exactly to plant bulbs, how much room certain plants will take up when they mature, and how to improve your soil.
- ✔ You want easy-to-understand information that explains exactly what you need to know about raising plants from seed, pruning, weeding, and controlling garden pests.

How This Book Is Organised

Gardening For Dummies is organised into seven parts, each covering a general topic. The chapters within each part go into more detail so you can easily find the information you need.

Part 1: Getting Going with Gardening

Before you buy your first six-pack of bedding in spring, you need to decide just where and when to start digging.

Chapter 1 begins at root level, guiding you through what your plants need to what you want from a garden.

Chapter 2 gets into the details of designing or planning a garden, with emphasis on making a plan that you can work to as your plot develops.

Chapter 3 is all about planning your plantings, how to choose the right plants for your garden and those that work best for you.

Part II: Designing with Plants

Chapter 4 goes over the garden's skeleton – the trees, hedges, and shrubs that form your garden's foundation and frame your plot.

Chapter 5 goes down to ground level and discusses lawns and ground covers, while the vertical dimension (climbers and wall shrubs) gets similar treatment in **Chapter 6**.

Part III: Colour Your World

Here's where the real fun starts! This part is the heart of the book because, for most people, the essence of gardening is putting in colourful plants and watching them grow.

Chapter 7 tells you about those comets of the garden, flowering annuals.

Chapter 8 is about the colourful stalwarts, the perennials. We also talk about ornamental grasses.

Chapter 9 deals with bulbs for all seasons – not just spring.

Chapter 10 covers the world's most famous flower, the rose.

Part IV: At Ground Level

This section is the nitty-gritty of gardening – literally. The three chapters in this part are about working with soil and getting your plants started.

Chapter 11 helps you understand and improve your soil.

You find the basics of starting seeds in **Chapter 12**, and planting methods for a whole range of seasonal, permanent, and other plants in **Chapter 13**.

Part V: Caring for Your Plants

In a nutshell, this section covers long-term garden maintenance.

Chapter 14 covers everything you need to know about the basics of plant care: watering, feeding, and composting.

Chapter 15 covers pruning, **Chapter 16** common sense pest control, and **Chapter 17** all those tools you need to help you.

Part VI: Special Gardens

It's back to the fun stuff – plants and planting – in this section!

If you want to grow at least some of your own food, check out **Chapter 18**. In **Chapter 19**, discover what it takes to create a moveable feast with containers.

In **Chapter 20**, you figure out how to achieve one of the most important gardens of all: the kind that's made with wildlife in mind.

Don't worry if you have just a small patch of garden; **Chapter 21** lets you in on some limited-space gardening secrets.

Chapter 22 is all about creating a fragrant garden.

Part VII: The Part of Tens

No *For Dummies* book is complete without the Part of Tens, so we offer a compendium of expert tips for ten quick projects **(Chapter 23)**.

Chapter 24 gives you ten hints on how to make your garden even more attractive to wildlife.

Icons Used in This Book

Icons are a handy For Dummies way to draw your attention to special bits of information.

Bear these important nuggets of information in mind as your green fingers develop.

Flags information that can save you time and effort in the garden.

Demystifies gardening lingo. Although we've made this book as jargon-free as possible, you need to know some terms.

This icon alerts you to avoid bad gardening experiences, including some that may cause injury.

Where to Go from Here

This book is organised so you can skip to wherever you want to find complete information about a topic. Mad about roses? Dive straight into Chapter 10. Want to prune that shrub that's taking up half your lawn? Find out how to tame it with the help offered in Chapter 15. You can use the table of contents to find broad categories of information or use the index to look up more specific topics.

Of course, you can always start with Part I – what a novel idea!

Part I

Getting Going with Gardening

"For heaven's sake, Ernest - we've only got a window box!"

In this part . . .

You've probably heard about the green thumbs and the brown thumbs. Some people seem to have an almost magical ability to raise beautiful, healthy plants, whereas others seem to turn out only withering brown husks.

No matter which group you identify with, take note: Anyone can become a gardener. Like any other interest that's worth pursuing, gardening requires knowledge, experience, attention, and enthusiasm. If you're willing to dedicate some time and attention to gardening, you can move from the brown thumb camp into the green thumb camp. If you already consider yourself to have a green thumb, you undoubtedly know that gardening never ceases to surprise you, and you never finish learning.

Part I gives you a basic understanding of some of the key issues that gardeners face: what plants require in order to thrive, how to plan your garden to suit your lifestyle, what to do to cut down on maintenance, how to choose the best plants for your garden, and how to take the space you have and maximise it.

Well, what are you waiting for? Get going!

Chapter 1

Just a Few Ground-Level Questions and Answers

. . . .

In This Chapter

▶ Understanding what plants need from you

▶ Knowing what your garden can do for you

▶ Speaking the garden language

. . . .

*I*f you want to learn more about gardening – and you must if you're reading this – just where do you start? We could start with some heavy-duty science, tossing around terms like *cotyledon*, *cambium*, and the ever-popular *pith*. Or we could start talking about beautiful gardens like critics of fine paintings – employing words like *composition*, *energy*, *focal point*, and the like.

We don't mean to suggest anything but respect for scientists and artists. In fact, the chance to combine science and art is what draws many of us to gardening in the first place – especially if you throw in a little farming and a few old wives' tales (of course you shouldn't plant sweet peas at the full moon).

All we really want to do here is to get you through a few basic principles of plant growth and garden planning so that you can rush out into the garden when the weather's right for planting and the soil's ripe for digging.

First, any questions?

How Do I Make My Plants Grow Rather than Die?

Like other living things, plants have certain requirements for good health. For example, they require the right amounts of light, temperature, moisture, and nutrients.

When selecting plants, you can meet their requirements in one of two ways. The first (which we don't recommend) involves selecting your favourite plants and then doing your best to alter the growing conditions at the planting site to meet their needs. You can change the growing conditions by adding irrigation, incorporating fertiliser, hauling in fresh topsoil, pruning some trees, or covering plants with blankets in winter. But this is the backward approach that costs you loads of time, money, and hassle.

By far the best approach is to work with what you have. Get to know the conditions at the planting site first and then choose plants that will thrive there. The better you match plants to the planting site, the longer the plants live, the better the plants look, and the less work (watering, pruning, fertilising, and controlling pests) you have to do to care for them. Your garden looks great, and you have more time and leisure to enjoy it – a win:win situation all round.

Your climate and microclimates

You need to match a plant to a planting site on both a large and a small scale. On a large scale, a plant needs to adapt to the general climate of the area in which it lives. Can the plant withstand winter's low temperatures and summer's high temperatures? Is the annual rainfall enough to keep the plant alive, or will it need watering? Understanding your climate is a huge step towards successful gardening.

The plant pioneers

The plants you can buy at garden centres today originate from countries all around the world, from as far afield as the United States, New Zealand, South Africa, and China. Even if you didn't pay much attention in geography classes at school, it's not hard to realise that climates vary enormously in all these countries and the plants have adapted to suit.

If you fancy learning a bit more about the origins of some of your garden plants, the history of the 'great plant hunters', as they're known, makes for gripping reading. Men (sorry, ladies, it was usually men in days of old) who, as the world was explored over the last 400 years, travelled to these new countries to bring back plants never seen before. Theirs are stories of bravery, endurance, and even death: Robert Fortune single-handedly fought off a band of pirates; Joseph Hooker was taken prisoner in Tibet and nearly executed; and David Douglas met a horrible end by falling into an already occupied bull pit in Hawaii. You see plants in a whole new light with centuries of history stretching behind.

On a smaller scale, can the plant grow well in the localised climate of your garden or the particular spot where you want to plant? Smaller climates, called *microclimates*, can be quite a bit different from the overall climate of your area. For example, because of the shadows that your house casts, the northern side of your house is cooler and shadier than its southern side. Or a planting site located beside a white, west-facing wall can be several degrees warmer than the rest of the garden because of the reflected heat from the wall.

Sun and shade

All plants need light to grow properly. However, the amount of light that plants need varies. The main terms to determine a plant's needs are *full sun*, *partial shade*, and *shade*.

- Plants that require *full sun* need at least six to eight hours of sun per day. Plants that don't get enough sunlight become *leggy* (develop long, spindly stems), as if stretching out for more light. Sun lovers that don't get enough sunlight also tend to flower poorly. Sites that get full sun face south or south-west.

- Plants that prefer *partial shade* need to grow in sites that face east or west to north-west, where they have sun for several hours but not enough to bake. Other plants also create partial shade – trees and large shrubs.

- Some plants prefer to be out of the sun entirely, growing in *shade*. Heavy, all-day shade appears on the north side of buildings, and under trees. Note one obvious rule for gardening in the shade: Put *shade-loving* plants in the shade. Sun-worshipping plants just won't make it. Don't fret. Hundreds of incredible shade-loving plants (some with showy flowers and others with attractive foliage and form) are available to choose from.

To make matters just a little complicated, a plant's shade tolerance may vary both by region and by specific garden conditions. For example, many plants that need full sun in cool climates tolerate or require some afternoon shade when growing in warm southern climates. The label on the plant, or the information in this book, can help you figure out where to put your plants.

Soil and water

The kind of soil in your garden – heavy clay or porous sand, for example – is closely related to soil moisture. Chapters 11 and 14 detail the importance of these two factors and the ways in which they affect plant growth. Those chapters also cover cultural practices such as cultivating, watering, and fertilising. Wet, soggy clay soil is very difficult to correct, but certain *moisture-loving* plants can grow, and even thrive, under those conditions.

Similarly, if your soil is *free draining* (sandy or stony, not holding water for long), you're well advised to go for *drought-tolerant* plants that have developed various strategies for conserving water, such as waxy or narrow leaves, or fleshy leaves that store water. Choosing plants to fit existing soil conditions is a great deal easier than altering the soil conditions themselves.

What Can I Use My Garden For?

A garden can make your life more comfortable, healthier, more colourful, and more convenient. A garden lets you expand your living area to the outdoors, harvest fresh food, and pick your own flowers. Take a look at the different ways that a garden can enhance your life.

- ✔ **A private getaway.** Imagine taking a break in your own back garden or relaxing in a shady spot, secluded from the hustle and bustle of daily living. This dream can be yours, if you begin by creating a private area for your own pleasure.

- ✔ **A place for entertaining.** Whether you like large get-togethers with family and friends, or a quiet dinner *à deux*, your garden can provide an ideal atmosphere. You need a few key ingredients to make your garden perfect for entertaining, such as comfortable seating, shade provided by a pergola or parasol, screening to create a secluded atmosphere, fragrant plants, plus lighting and heating for evening use.

- ✔ **A site for children and pets.** Everyone in the family has a stake in the garden, so take account of all their interests. A garden isn't just for the grownups. If you tell your kids to keep off the garden they may just obey you – for life – and miss out on a fascinating and absorbing hobby that can give them a lifelong interest in gardening and the environment. Not to mention art, science, and an excuse to get joyfully grubby.

- ✔ **A way to get close to nature.** Unless you live in a treehouse, your garden is the nearest and probably the best way of getting in touch with your environment. Gardens are increasingly vital for the survival of wildlife, with natural habitats disappearing fast. Feeding the birds, watching the butterflies, and listening to the bees is a fabulous way of de-stressing, and high on the feel-good factor too – you know you're doing a bit for the environment. Research has shown that walking barefoot on the grass significantly reduces heart rate and blood pressure!

- ✔ **Your own flower stall.** Cutting a bunch of flowers from your own garden and arranging them in a vase indoors is hugely satisfying. Some flowers are better for cutting than others, so be sure to include a few in your borders. If you have enough space, consider having an out-of-the-way patch for a 'cutting garden' so you won't feel guilty about robbing the borders.

✔ **Harvesting the fruits of your labours.** A delicious aspect of your garden is that it can produce wonderful vegetables, fruits, and herbs. No shop-bought produce can ever beat the taste of your own crops, picked and eaten straight away, like crisp crunchy salads, and strawberries still warm from the sun. Mmm. You can grow gourmet produce, or rare and special crops, and grow them organically.

✔ **A practical work area.** Being outdoors means more than fun and games. You're likely to need a place in your garden to keep your garden tools, barbeque, firewood, clothesline, or rubbish bins. If possible, organise all of these less than attractive outdoor necessities in the same out-of-the way location – separate from your entertaining and play areas. Ideally, the location should be handy, near the garage or driveway, but screened from view.

✔ **A haven to relax.** Anywhere that seems cosy and pleasant is a great place to put a secluded seating area. The area doesn't have to be fancy, just a place for you to relax. If you put in an all-weather surface – gravel, paving, or mulch, for example – you can sit outside regardless of the soil conditions.

The possibilities for your garden are almost endless. Take some time to jot down everything you may possibly want in your garden. Chapter 2 shows you how to pull together all your needs and wishes in a garden plan.

Do I Have to Learn a Foreign Language?

The language spoken in gardening circles can be a little odd at first. For example, dirt isn't just *dirt*, it's *soil*. Dirt is what you make mud pies with; it's the stain on your shirt. Soil, on the other hand, is full of promise and good nutrients. And some gardenaholics tend to go on and on about plant names. You may catch them at the nursery asking 'Which Latin name is *most* correct, the old one or the new one?' or 'What is the proper pronunciation for that plant?' Real garden snobs even get into heated debates about how to spell a particular plant name. Don't be too hard on these people. Not only can they not help themselves, but you may find yourself behaving the same way someday.

Plants usually have tongue-twisting scientific names and easily-pronounced common names.

The fancy name

The proper (scientific) *botanical name* of a plant consists of two or more parts, much in the same way that people have a first and a last name. However, in plant language, the last name comes first.

The most important name is the *genus* – the 'Smith' of Joe Smith, if you will. (The genus name always begins with a capital letter when part of a multipart name.) A genus is a group of closely related plants. Just as in your own family, some of the plant cousins look a lot alike, while others don't bear much resemblance at all. Also like your family, some closely related individuals have very different comfort levels. One uncle lives in the sun and warmth of the south coast, the other loves the cool damp Scottish climate. It's the same for plants.

The second name, the 'Joe' part of Joe Smith, is the *species* name. The species name usually describes some feature of the plant or its native origin, or serves as a tribute to whoever discovered the plant. But the species name is in Latin, of course, just to keep things interesting. Consider, for example, *Hosta undulata*. *Hosta* is the genus name. The species name, *undulata*, describes the undulating shape of the leaf.

The plain old-fashioned, natural species of some plants acquire new status in face of prodigiously hybridised plants – tulips, for example. In those cases, the norm for the plant is some kind of hybrid of indeterminate botanical origin. That's why when gardeners finally have in their gardens an actual natural, nonhybridised type of tulip they say something like, 'And this is my species tulip.' Gardeners are funny, aren't they? (In this book, we use the abbreviation *sp.* for *species.*)

Occasionally, a third name follows the species name – the *variety*. Varieties are members of the same species but are different enough to deserve their own name. Just as you may have one redhead in a family of brunettes, some plants are quite dissimilar to their siblings. For example, *Lychnis coronaria* bears magenta flowers. Her sister *Lychnis coronaria alba*, however, wears a white (*alba*) flower.

Another part of a botanical name is the 'cultivated variety', or *cultivar*. Whoever discovered or created the plant decided that it was special enough to have its own name. The cultivar name appears after the species or variety name. The cultivar name is the only part of the botanical name that isn't in italics but is always enclosed with single quotation marks. For example, a very nice form of *Lychnis coronaria* with a pink blush is called *Lychnis coronaria*, 'Angel Blush'.

The common name

Of course, ordinary people don't go around using long Latin botanical names in everyday conversation. Instead, they use a sort of botanical nickname, called a *common name*. Common names are less formal and easier to pronounce than botanical names. They're also less precise. Just as your Aunt Betty calls you 'pet' and Uncle Bob calls you 'bruiser', many plants have several nicknames.

Often, the common name describes some distinguishing characteristic of the plant. For example, the plant called blue star has starry blue flowers. Sometimes, the origin of the name is lost in the mythology of a former time. Does anyone have a clue just who was the Susan of black-eyed Susan fame?

Finding that several unrelated flowers share the same common name isn't unusual at all. Unfortunately, regular English flower names are often just as silly as their highfalutin Latin cousins, if for different reasons. For example, two distinct plants share the name 'mock orange', while 'flowering cherry' refers to literally dozens of different varieties. At least three unrelated perennials are called coneflowers: *Echinacea purpurea*, the *Rudbeckia* genus, and the *Ratibida* genus. On the other hand, many plants have no common name! Figure that one out.

The long and short of it is that you do need to pay some attention to plant names – if only to avoid buying and planting the wrong plant.

Chapter 2

Planning Your Garden

. . . .

. . . .

*W*hether your garden consists of a brand new bare plot, an overgrown jungle, or any situation in between, your property is the canvas on which you create your garden masterpiece – your place to relax, entertain, welcome visitors, watch your children play, hold barbecues, and so on. A well-planned and planted garden becomes an extension to your home and creates a relaxing environment in which to unwind and enjoy getting in touch with nature. A good garden not only adds value to your home, it can also solve problems such as bad views, noise, and lack of privacy.

We strongly recommend that you tackle your garden by making a plan. Most gardeners benefit from planning a design on paper to a lesser or greater degree, but it's possible (although unlikely) that a loose mental plan may suffice. In any case, the goal is to figure out the best ways to make use of your outdoor space. Base your decisions on what looks good to you, how you plan to use the space, how much maintenance you want to do, and what you can afford. This chapter should give you enough information to assess the strengths and weaknesses of your site, and sketch out a plan for a garden that suits your lifestyle.

Your garden is likely to be a large investment of your time and money, so it's well worth considering the benefits of professional advice and calling in a landscape architect or garden designer. Their input can vary from a one-off advisory visit to a full and detailed garden design and planting plan (with varying costs to suit, obviously). If you just want some advice, you can show the professional your own plan and ask for suggestions or confirmation of your good sense. However, even if you go down the route of a complete plan, we recommend reading through this section to put your thoughts in order.

Taking Stock of Your Existing Garden

The results of your landscaping work depends, to some extent, on what you have to work with, so you should begin your plan by assessing the current condition of your garden. This up-front *site analysis* is an important starting point in planning your garden.

Recording your thoughts and observations on paper is always best, unless you're blessed with a memory that gives you total recall. Start your site analysis by pencilling out a rough drawing of your garden on a large piece of paper (at least A4 size). Be sure to include important existing features of your property such as the outline of your house (including windows and doors), existing hard landscaped areas such as the patio, paths, and driveway, and permanent structures like the garage and garden shed. Remember to add general compass directions to your sketch. The sketch doesn't have to be very precise at this stage. Take lots of photographs right from the start too; as well as serving as memory boosters, they're also great morale boosters later on when you look back at the changes you've made.

Put your drawing on a clipboard and walk around your house and garden. Note the following:

- **Views.** Note the good and bad views that you want to preserve or block. Good views are easy to recognise, but what about the neighbours' views of your garden or your view of theirs? Envisage what you're likely to see if you add new features too; if you put in a raised deck, what will you see then?

- **Prevailing winds.** Make a note of exposed areas that may benefit from screening. Filtering the wind with a hedge or 'gappy' fence is better than trying to block it completely, because a solid barrier creates turbulence on the lee side (facing away from the wind).

- **Slope and drainage.** Draw in some arrows that give you a rough idea of the contour of the land. Sloping ground or uneven terrain can become an interesting part of the design, especially if you accentuate it with retaining walls or dry streambeds. But sloping ground also can present erosion or drainage problems that can threaten your house or garden. Record any areas that seem overly wet or where moss or algae grows. Watch where excess rainwater flows. Some plants not only live in wet or soggy soil but also thrive in it; these are the plants you find in bog and water gardens. Drainage problems are sometimes complicated – consider consulting with a landscape architect or engineer who has experience with water drainage problems.

- **Soil.** The soil in your garden provides nutrients, moisture, and support for plants. But soil types differ, sometimes even within the same property. Soils come in a huge range of textures and pH levels (the measure of acidity or alkalinity) and contain different amounts of organic matter, nutrients, and moisture. See Chapter 11 to find out more about soil characteristics so that you can choose plants that will thrive in your garden.

✔ **Interesting natural features.** If you're lucky enough to have rock outcroppings or a small stream, they can become special landscape features.

✔ **Noise, smells, lights.** Open up all your senses and then write down anything else you notice – lights at night, noise from next door, and even unpleasant odours. You may be able to mask or conceal such nuisances to some degree.

✔ **Existing plants.** Draw in plants, such as shrubs and large trees, that you want to preserve. Make a separate note of other, smaller plants like shrubs and perennials that you want to keep but that you can move to a new spot.

✔ **Sun and shade.** Note areas that are sunny or shady and at what times of day. Different plants prefer different conditions, and matching the right plant to the right place is always best for an easy life and a successful garden. This information may also give you ideas about creating a more comfortable living space. Sunlight changes direction and intensity dramatically according to the season. For example, in midsummer, the south and west sides of the house are sunniest and warmest. If you live in a cool summer area, you may want to take advantage of the warmth in those areas, but if you live in a hot summer area, these may be places where you want to create shade with a plant-covered pergola or arbour.

✔ **Views from indoors.** When you look out of your windows, what do you see? Can you improve your view out by removing or reducing plant growth, or even removing walls or fences? Also consider who can see into your home via the windows from the street or next door, and if you're happier blocking such views.

To help you organise the different areas of your garden, you can draw *goose eggs*. Drawing a goose egg refers to pencilling in roughly circular areas that you think work well for specific purposes, as shown in Figure 2-1. After you finish the first goose egg, draw several more to consider alternatives and decide which works best.

Don't forget to use your property's natural strengths to your advantage and take time to get to know your garden before making any changes. If at all possible, after moving to a different property, wait a full year to see the changes that take place in the garden and to find out exactly what plants are growing there. You soon get a feel for the most sunny or sheltered spot for a patio; the location of the best flat lawn for ball games; where's the most discreet place to hide the compost heap, dustbins, and other essential but ugly paraphernalia; where the sun beats down on late summer afternoons – perfect for the herb garden – and where the neighbour's oak tree casts a pool of shade.

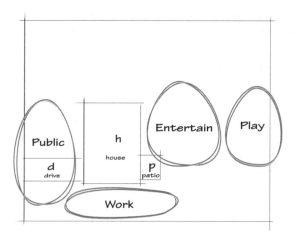

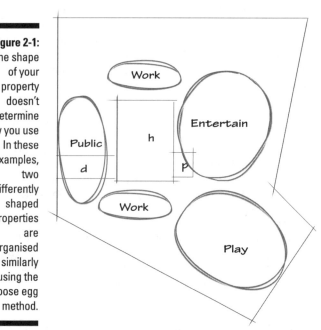

Figure 2-1:
The shape
of your
property
doesn't
determine
how you use
it. In these
examples,
two
differently
shaped
properties
are
organised
similarly
using the
goose egg
method.

Tackling an Overgrown Garden

Unless your house is brand new, it's unlikely that you're starting with a blank
slate. Indeed, sometimes the slate is cluttered up to such a degree that it's
hard to see through all the overgrown plants and out-of-date garden features.
Inheriting someone else's garden can be a mixed blessing indeed.

First, try to live with your garden for a while before making any major decisions – for a full year, if at all possible. The tree that looks so overwhelming in autumn, for example, may cast much-needed shade in summer; a tall hedge or bank of shrubs could screen a grotty view of a factory, or shield you from the neighbours' prying eyes. Bear in mind that certain plants only reveal their full glory in certain seasons – bulbs are a prime example – and by bringing in a digger during autumn you could be ruining a wonderful spring display. As the seasons turn, make notes and take photos of what is happening in your garden.

Existing plants can be a puzzle too, particularly if you're new to gardening and one plant looks like another. Although overgrown shrubs may well have passed their 'sell-by' date and you need to dig them up, others may be worth saving and rejuvenating with some careful (or even brutal!) renovation pruning. Here's where a little expert knowledge can go a long way. If you have a knowledgeable friend or relative, fantastic, but if not then you can pay a garden consultant for a one-off advisory visit. Ask at your local garden centre for a recommendation.

Dreaming Up the Perfect Landscape

To get the most from your property, you need a design that meets the requirements of your lifestyle. A good way to start is to develop a wish list of everything that would go into the garden of your dreams. Be sure to consider the needs of all members of the household. Take a look at some of the things you may want to add to your wish list:

- ✔ **Patio.** No rules say you have to site your patio bang next to the house, or that you're limited to having just one. Think outside the box and have a look at the sunniest, most sheltered spots around your garden that you can use at different times of day. Maybe a little paved spot for breakfast or morning coffee, a large patio for lunch and evening gatherings with family and friends, or a secluded little arbour where you can sit with drink in hand to watch the sun go down. If you're lucky enough to have a good view, make that your prime patio spot.

- ✔ **Conservatory or summerhouse.** Location tends to be obvious for immediate build, but if this is somewhere down the road in your five-year plan, remember to allow space in your design.

- ✔ **Lawn.** Again, no rule book says you have to have a lawn (though most people want one). In a very small garden where a lawn would get lots of wear and tear, and be a hassle to mow, hard landscaping may be a better alternative.

- ✔ **Water features.** From a half-barrel mini-pond to a small lake, you can make water fit any size of garden. Remember that moving water, such as a fountain or waterfall, requires access to electricity and needs to be close to a power source.

Gardens have to serve a wealth of practical purposes too, so along with the features you'd *like* to have, remember to include those that are boring but essential.

- ✔ **Extra living space.** Garden buildings such as existing sheds can improve your lifestyle in all sorts of ways should you need a home office, summerhouse, hobbies' room, or kids' playroom, yet without the bankbreaking costs and hassle of building an extension.

  Garden buildings generally don't need planning permission, but it's always wise to check with your council first.

- ✔ **Storage.** Essential to a lesser or greater degree for gardening equipment, furniture, bicycles, and children's toys. For winter furniture storage, bear in mind that you can use tough plastic covers rather than investing in a huge shed.

- ✔ **Dustbins and compost bins.** You can hide them behind screens of trellis, plants, or woven willow hurdles. Always make space for compost if at all possible – it's a great way of recycling your garden and kitchen waste back into improving your soil and making a better garden, for little or no cost. And, from an eco-friendly point of view, you reduce the amount of waste going to landfill.

- ✔ **Washing line.** You need an open, sunny spot to dry washing, which, in a small garden, is probably the one earmarked for your patio. However, nothing stops you from having several sunken sockets in different sites for a rotary line, which can be put out of the way when necessary. Pull-out, retractable washing lines are great for small gardens.

- ✔ **Paths.** All-weather access is essential for garden entrances and highly recommended for frequently used spots like sheds and washing lines.

- ✔ **Watering.** Set up a water butt (several, if possible) to collect rainwater. Not only is it good for the environment, it's also fantastic for reducing water bills.

Who will use your garden?

Plan your garden so that it gets maximum use and provides plenty of enjoyment. Make sure that you think about issues like the following:

- ✔ If you have young children, safety, as well as fun, is a consideration. Avoid all but covered water features if children are very young. Play equipment is best set in a fenced back garden, close to the house if children are small; further away for big kids. Think about a storage area for all those toys, too. Older children who you don't need to supervise can probably make use of any garden at the front and sides of the house.

✔ If food production is high on your agenda, perhaps you can keep the back lawn smaller so that you have room for a big vegetable garden. Or even space for a few chickens? (Check the deeds to your house in case you're not allowed to keep livestock before counting your chickens.)

✔ Keen gardeners may want to include a greenhouse. Allow enough room for a cold frame and a little 'nursery' area for growing plants on.

✔ Do you barbecue enough to warrant a built-in barbecue? The ideal place is close to the kitchen door.

✔ What about Fido? A dog run is a great idea if you're worried about what he may do to the new landscape.

When will you use your garden?

Think about the time of day and the time of year in which you plan to use your garden. Consider the following tips when planning your landscape and when you're going to use it most.

✔ If you like having breakfast outside, create a sheltered little seating area that gets the morning sun.

✔ If you plan to be outdoors after work in the late afternoon, where will you be most comfortable at that time of day? Maybe that shady spot under the big tree out back, or somewhere that catches the last of the evening sun? On the other hand, if summer sunshine heats up the patio area, maybe you need an overhead structure or a patio umbrella for shade.

✔ If you like to use the garden at night, good outdoor lighting and heating are a must. Create a sensory evening garden with plants that give off their perfume late in the day (see Chapter 22 for plants to delight your senses).

Creating a garden with a sense of place

Most neighbourhoods have a distinct character created by gardens and homes in similar styles. When you dream up your new garden design, remember to keep any regional or neighbourhood character in mind. Try not to be so different in your landscaping that you disrupt the overall continuity of the community, particularly in front gardens, which often tend to blend together (save any wild ideas for the back).

Don't forget that little thing called 'resale value'. Lots of people find themselves landscaping simply to enhance the overall appearance of their home for potential buyers. If you're landscaping for resale, play it safe. Go for the gardening equivalent of the 'warm neutrals' so often advised for use indoors.

Matching your garden to the style of house and area is an easy jumping-off point. Consider an old-fashioned cottage garden for a charming cottage, a minimalist contemporary style for a modern house, a smart formal look for a town garden, or an informal mix of lawns and borders for a new estate.

Cutting down on maintenance

All gardens need a certain amount of regular maintenance, but how much depends a great deal on your garden design. If you love gardening and pottering outside, skip this section right now. But if, like many garden owners, you want to relax and enjoy looking at your garden rather than working on it, then plan for low maintenance right from the start. Here's how:

- Design your garden with lots of hard surfaces like paving and gravel and relatively little in the way of lawns or planting.

- Avoid planting too densely, which, although it gives immediate impact, requires more pruning and replanting later.

- Permanent plants are low maintenance, particularly if you're careful to select varieties that need little or no annual pruning. Avoid having lots of annuals, which, although they add brilliant colour, need replanting every year.

- Choose plants that like your garden environment and they need virtually no attention once established. By contrast, if you put plants where they're not happy it means more work for you (moisture lovers in dry soil, for example, mean you spend a large portion of your spare time attached to a hosepipe).

- Instead of a lawn that needs regular mowing, consider alternatives such as a meadow or ground-cover plants for some or all of your garden (see Chapter 5).

- Use paving rather than decking to cut down on future work. If you plan to include wooden decks and fences, you have to paint or apply preservatives every two to three years. Consider some of the recycled plastic wood look-alikes for fences and decking, which look quite acceptable and are more environmentally friendly into the bargain.

- Containers are very labour intensive, especially if you use bedding plants that need replanting every year. However, permanent plants in containers are a whole lot less work. Or do away completely with patio containers and have raised beds instead. They still need some watering, but much less often.

✔ If you have to water essential plants in containers, set up an automated irrigation system (as explained in Chapter 14), which can water even when you're away from home. Otherwise, it's down to watering by hand.

What Goes Where: Designing the Plan

After adding the elements from the wish list to your sketch, you may want to create a more accurate and specific site analysis, drawn exactly to scale. (Check out this section's sidebar, 'Making a scale drawing of your property'.) You may be able to get exact dimensions of your garden from the building plan if it's a recently built property, or from the title deeds.

Figure 2-2 is a sample of what your site analysis may look like after you transfer the details of your inventory to the plot plan.

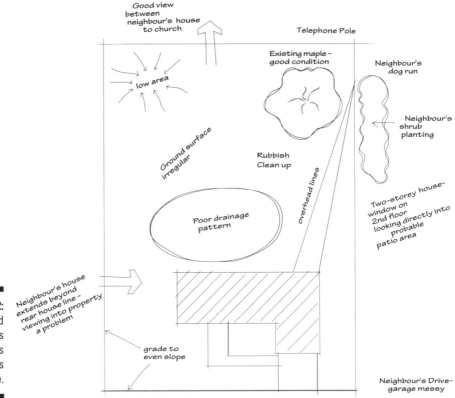

Figure 2-2: A completed site analysis that includes problems to solve.

Good view between neighbour's house to church

Telephone Pole

Existing maple – good condition

Neighbour's dog run

low area

Neighbour's shrub planting

Ground surface irregular

Rubbish Clean up

overhead lines

Two-storey house– window on 2nd floor looking directly into probable patio area

Poor drainage pattern

Neighbour's house extends beyond rear house line – viewing into property a problem

grade to even slope

Neighbour's Drive– garage messy

Using your space effectively

Make sure that you think of the entire garden as living space. Overcoming the traditional approach – back gardens are where we actually live, front ones are for show, and any bits round the side are mostly ignored – can be difficult. Why not make your whole plot into your living area? The following are some off-the-beaten-track ideas that allow you to make good use of all your space.

- ✔ **Front garden.** If you shield the front with walls of greenery or a privacy-creating fence or hedge, then you can do what you like with your front garden. Bear in mind that you may cut down the amount of light reaching your front rooms, though. If you're inspired to plant a prairie or a meadow out there, talk to the neighbours first so that they know what you're doing, and keep paths neat and tidy so that the landscape looks intentional instead of frighteningly wild.

  Some areas, such as housing estates, may have restrictions on what you can do with your front garden. Be sure to check before embarking on any do-it-yourself makeovers.

- ✔ **Ornamental edibles.** You don't need to relegate your vegetable patch to the furthest corner of the garden, but grow your crops wherever the light, soil, and convenience are best. Edible plants can look as good as they taste; a well-tended patch out the front, planted in an interesting design of diagonals or squares that intersperses veggies with flowers and herbs, can look as grand as its posh name, a _potager_.

- ✔ **Side areas.** The land around the side of a house is often narrow, usually shady, and generally seen as nothing more than a through route between the front and back. Create a feeling of light and space with crafty touches such as painting a fence in a pale shade; adding containers or a seat to make more of a feature and a reason to linger; and for the ultimate illusion of space, incorporate outdoor mirrors (using mirror-finish plastic rather than breakable types). Or add a surprise to be discovered – such as a whimsical garden ornament.

Creating garden boundaries and pathways

Try to imagine decorating a living room with no walls. You'd have a hard time putting your furniture in the right place. Outdoor living rooms work the same way, except now you need to work out where to put the flowerbed instead of the sofabed.

Structures and plantings can define the boundaries of your landscape, creating 'walls' to set off different areas of your garden. For example, surround your herb garden with a hedge of lavender and install a gate at the entrance. Add a trellis screen to your patio and grow flowering and foliage climbers on it if you need a bit of seclusion. See Chapter 6 for suggestions on climbers for privacy.

Making a scale drawing of your property

If you don't have a plot plan, consider these tips for drawing your property to scale.

✔ Use graph paper (large sheets, A2 or A1 size) and a scale rule.

✔ Find a proportional scale suitable for your drawing and garden size. Do this by roughly measuring the width and depth of your plot (the front and back gardens are usually best drawn up separately). A scale of 1:50 is generally a good one to choose for small to medium gardens, and 1:100 for larger ones.

✔ Start by measuring the house, including the exact location and size of doors and windows. Accuracy is very important, as the house is the focus for all the surrounding areas of garden. Always use a measuring tape to calculate distances. Eyeballing or estimating is not precise enough. Measure from each side of the house to the garden boundaries. This creates a single 'base line' from which to measure other features and parts of the garden.

✔ Measure your garden boundaries. Don't assume that the sides are straight and the width constant, even if they appear so to the eye. Use a measuring technique called *triangulation* to make sure that your measurements are accurate, as shown in the diagram below.

✔ Using the same technique, plot the location of all other features that you want to keep.

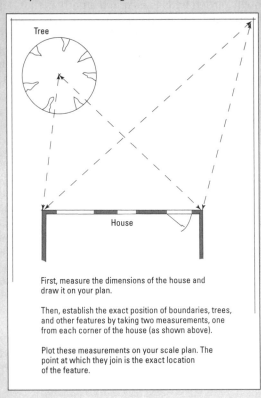

Tree

House

First, measure the dimensions of the house and draw it on your plan.

Then, establish the exact position of boundaries, trees, and other features by taking two measurements, one from each corner of the house (as shown above).

Plot these measurements on your scale plan. The point at which they join is the exact location of the feature.

After you establish the boundaries of your garden, both internal and external, turn your attention to the pathways. Make pathways simple and practical. Everyone who uses the paths frequently goes as the crow flies, so any curves or meanders should only be slight or they'll ignore the path. You also want an easy-access path for getting to your car in the morning or lugging in groceries after work. Plan a wide, flat, solid path for where you need to trundle wheelbarrows full of compost, manure, or grass clippings.

Exercise your artistic side by planning scenic routes through the rest of your garden. Guests can enjoy wandering along paths that go through flowerbeds and meadows – space permitting. When you start playing with paths, you find that they're a great design trick for making your garden seem bigger. Obscured by shrubs, ornamental grasses, or other tall plants, paths can double back, twist and turn, and proceed for much longer than you'd think in a limited space.

The width of paths affects the speed at which people walk them. Wide paths are not only practical for two people to stroll along side by side; the width encourages lingering. Narrow paths make your feet speed up.

You don't have to make paths of paving materials. A swath of lawn that wends through garden beds is as much a path as that beautiful brick herringbone you lay through the herb garden. Crafty tricks with simple, cheap materials can give you a great-looking path for very little cash too (see the next section). If you plan to include fenced areas in your design, make sure that they don't block access to other parts of the garden. Include gates where they make sense, or leave sections open for easier access.

Hard landscaped areas

The hard areas of your garden – patios, decks, paths, fences, trellises, garden buildings, and other features – form the true 'skeleton' of your garden that you live with a long time. Most importantly, don't be tempted to skimp or cut corners on the construction; the results of poor workmanship or too-cheap materials are likely to stare you in the face for years. Remember that you'll be looking at these structures unadorned for months in winter, when leaves are down and many plants are dormant, although all these hard features can be softened and moulded into the garden using seasonal planting. This is one area of gardening where getting the work done by the professionals can really pay off, in terms of a smart finish that will last and last. Unless, that is, you're very handy at DIY.

If you're starting with a new garden or giving your old one a total revamp, you're probably going to have to do a fair bit of hard landscaping. Any construction job involves a lot of mess and upheaval, so it makes sense to complete these jobs before moving on to the planting.

Shopping for hard landscaping materials is not for the budget squeamish. Take your time to look around the huge selection of materials at vastly differing prices to see what's on offer. Most garden centres and builders' merchants tend to offer a limited range of materials and then only from certain manufacturers. Paving specialists (you can find details in *Yellow Pages*, local directories, and the classified ads section of your local paper) generally stock a good range. Find out which suppliers have materials laid out on display – a far better way to view products than just slabs stacked on pallets. Buy sample slabs to look at in your garden before ordering. Observe how the slab colour and texture go with your house, if the paving will be close by, and water the slab to see if you like the colour when both wet and dry. Ask for the material price *per square metre* because this gives you an easy means of comparison.

Consider combining different materials for a more decorative look (but don't go too mad – a maximum of three different materials in one area is a good rule to work to; more, and the garden may look too 'busy'). Combinations are a great way to make cheap materials look a million dollars. For example, cheap slabs interspersed with a crisp edging of brick pavers, or blocks of bricks laid in a decorative pattern, look extremely smart.

Designing with repetition and unity

Unity refers to the overall feeling that a landscape creates – a whole greater than the sum of its parts. In a unified landscape, the eyes and feet of visitors flow from one part to another. Clearly defined pathways are a first step towards unifying your landscape.

Repetition refers to a theme or element that crops up in different parts of your landscape. Repetition and unity go hand in hand – repeating elements often helps create a feeling of unity in your landscape.

Repetition of hard landscaping materials – including brick, wood, stone, concrete, wood chips, and fencing – is a simple way to give your garden a unified look, even if the areas are distinctly different. Man-made materials carry great weight in the landscape, because they draw human eyes like a magnet. If your hard landscaping materials match the style of your garden, you can quickly unify the various elements of your garden. For example, you can use a single section of diagonal, framed trellis to support a climbing rose along the wall of your house.

Attach a few sections to form an L-shape to shield the compost heap from view; or add three or four linked sections to serve as a privacy screen along the patio.

Repeating shapes helps pull elements together, too: curved outlines of beds, undulating paths, and mounds of plants; or yardstick-straight bed edges, spiky plant forms, clipped hedges, and vertical-board fences.

Repetition of plants themselves is another way to achieve unity. Sticking the same plants here and there is an easy trick. Simply repeat backbone plants that perform well most of the year – like hostas, evergreens, ground-cover plants, and shrubs – to tie your garden areas to each other.

Repeating colours also helps to unify your landscape. Plant clumps of yellow flowers in various beds, pots, or plantings across your garden, and you find that your eye travels from one patch of yellow to the next in a satisfying way. You can combine colours of plants with colours of the house or hard landscaping, too, for unity's sake.

New materials aren't the only ones to consider for the garden. By searching out reclaimed materials, you can come up with a beautiful hard landscape without breaking the bank. You can find reclamation yards that deal in all manner of reclaimed materials for the home as well as the garden (but, as recycling gets more trendy, prices are creeping up, so old doesn't always mean cheap). Keep your eye out for demolition sites, dumps, and other likely bonanzas, too. (Don't assume that construction debris is headed for the dump. Always ask permission before loading your car.) Most contractors are happy to give you their refuse so that they don't have to pay to put it in a landfill. But again, builders are more aware of the value of their 'rubbish' so some cash may need to change hands – particularly if you have your eye on a choice old chimney pot, for example.

Frugal substitutes are fun to come up with and can give you even more satisfaction when you gaze on your finished work. Jog your ingenuity with these starters:

- Instead of making a stone wall out of expensive natural stone, stack chunks of old concrete slabs.

- Can't afford an all-brick path? Use a strip of brick (one or two bricks wide) along the sides and fill the centre with inexpensive slabs or pavers. Edge with railway sleepers for a finished look for straight paths, or use 15 x 2.5 centimetre (6 x 1 inch) gravel boards where you want gentle curves. Slabs set in 10 mm gravel look great too.

- Dress up plain grey concrete with dyes. Or use the small stones called *aggregate* in the mix so that the finished surface has a pleasant pebbly look (call in the pros for this work).

- Customise your patio by making your own art pavers for corners and accents. Make handprints (wear latex gloves if you have sensitive skin), press in and peel off leaves to make impressions, make a pebble mosaic, or stud with bits of smooth coloured glass for a one-of-a-kind look.

- Visit architectural salvage dealers for good-value fencing, arbours, ironwork, and neat decorative touches. (Many people have sussed out the bargains to be had here, so prices may not be cheap – a lot depends on where you live.)

- Brick for buildings (that's usually covered with plaster and paint) deteriorates in the garden, but unless you're laying miles of paths, it can be a fine and frugal choice until you can afford the heavy-duty, high-fired exterior grade you want.

Creating a Final Plan

Think of your final plan as a tool to help determine the price tag of your project, to establish your priorities, and to ensure that all the separate parts of your garden are present and accounted for.

If you have an outline plan of your plot, this is a good basis on which to start your garden design, sketching in existing landscape features that you intend to keep, using your site analysis as a reference point.

On paper (or computer: see the following section), you can eliminate the existing features that you no longer want – you create a blank slate on which to draw new features. You can adapt, change, and reorganise with a flick of an eraser. To help you visualise your new garden layout, make tracing paper overlays to show different scenarios for your design, moving your patio behind the garage or close to the kitchen door, for example. Set overlays on top of the original plot plan and secure them with masking tape so that you can move and change them easily. Other overlays can show the colour of the garden as it changes by season or the size of trees and shrubs as they grow.

Follow these steps to create a final plan (assuming you have a plot plan).

1. **Take the graph paper and measuring tape out into the garden with you.**

   Note on the paper which directions are north and south and the scale you're using.

2. **Plot each landscape feature that you intend to keep.**

   Find its depth in the length of the garden by measuring from either the house or the street. Make a pencil mark to show its location. Then measure its distance from the side of the property. Move the pencil mark to indicate the correct spacing from the side property line.

   If the landscape feature is a tree, measure the limb spread of the tree and indicate it with a circle around the mark. If the tree is young, you may want to use a dotted line to show the ultimate shady, mature spread.

   If you plan to eliminate existing features, don't bother to sketch them in. Not including them saves you time and trouble as you plan new developments for your garden.

3. **After you pencil in the entire garden, check the accuracy of the drawing.**

   When you eyeball the plan and look at the garden, does everything appear to be in the right place? Pull out your measuring tape and check several sample distances. Redraw as necessary.

4. **Add new features and plants.**

Draw in the plants and areas for all those special activities you will enjoy eventually. Add any paths you have planned, drawing lines to indicate their shape and width. Draw in fences, arbours, hedges, a patio or deck, and other elements you've chosen. After you have all the parts of the design in place, ink over your pencil lines with different coloured markers; you can see at a glance which lines are paths, which are fences, and so on. See Chapter 3 for how to draw up a planting plan.

Using your computer

A number of landscaping software programs are now available that can help you design your dream garden. After you have your scale plot plan, you can input it into your computer and develop your design electronically.

Using landscaping software

- ✔ Saves you the time and trouble of drawing all changes and updates by hand.

- ✔ Lets you explore the way a landscape may look when viewed from different angles, at different times of the year, or at any time in the future.

- ✔ Helps your decision making. The software may include a detailed plant encyclopaedia. You may be able to indicate your landscaping needs and have the program select suitable plants.

Try the Royal Horticultural Society's online plant selector at www.rhs.org.uk/rhsplantselector/index.aspx and the BBC's online virtual garden design at www.bbc.co.uk/gardening/design/virtualgarden_index.shtml.

Field testing

If you want more of a real-life picture of what your landscaping will look like, go outside and play make-believe:

- ✔ Outline paths with a water hose or rope, or sprinkle a path of flour or sand so that you can see the direction paths take.

- ✔ Put garden chairs where you want to add shrubs or young trees.

- ✔ Put bamboo canes into the ground to show the future homes of roses or large perennials in your flowerbeds.

- ✔ Rake leaves or straw into the outlines of your new beds.

- ✔ Use a stepladder as a good fool-your-eye representation of an arbour.

Chapter 3

Planning Your Planting

- -

- -

*W*ith hundreds of beautiful plants available, deciding just which ones to buy and where to start can seem completely bewildering. This is where a bit of advance planning really pays dividends. Do not, we beg you, stroll along to the garden centre and hope that the right plants will somehow find their way into your trolley. They won't. And you'll come home in need of a long lie down.

The solution to successful planting lies in concentrating on getting the basic framework right and building up a good balance of permanent planting. Then you can move on to the 'pretties' – all those tempting flowering plants that colour the seasons. After you have a firm foundation, your garden can look good right through the year, and with the minimum of maintenance too.

Choosing a Garden Style

Selecting a distinct style of planting really helps to make your mark on a garden and gives it a definite air of harmony. Don't be swayed by whatever the current fashion for gardens may be (let's face it, fashions can be pretty odd). Let your preferences come first and foremost.

One of the most important aspects of choosing a garden style is matching design with location. In a small town garden, for example, a formal layout really looks in keeping, whereas a garden in the country is perfect for a more relaxed, informal, even cottagey look. A larger garden has the potential to be divided into separate areas, each with its own distinct style of planting if you wish.

The *aspect* of your garden – the amount of sun and shade it receives – influences the plants you choose. A sunny, sheltered garden is perfect for Mediterranean-type plants, full of fragrance and aromatic foliage, whereas a shady site can be planted with lush foliage plants to create a jungle look.

Here's a thumbnail guide to the most popular garden styles and their plants:

- ✔ **Formal.** Ideal for town gardens, small spaces, and courtyards. Formal gardens are characterised by straight lines and a strong degree of symmetry, usually with a fair bit of hard landscaping such as patios, paths, and paved areas forming the 'skeleton' (the basic layout) of the garden. Key plants are usually those that are naturally formal in appearance (conical, pyramid or upright trees, and shrubs with an architectural shape. You're likely to come across the word 'architectural' a fair bit in planting – see below for an explanation). Low hedges are excellent to edge borders and paved areas too. If your wallet can stand the strain, ready-grown *topiary* plants – plants trimmed and trained into shapes from the simple and elegant to the weird and wonderful – are great for instant impact.

- ✔ **Oriental.** Also ideal for a small space, and perfect if your taste is more for foliage and form rather than masses of flowers. Hard materials such as rocks, gravel, and pebbles make up a substantial part of an Oriental garden, so it's low maintenance too. Plants to suit the Oriental style include Japanese maples, bamboos, ornamental grasses, and conifers.

- ✔ **Informal.** Just about any garden can take an informal style, characterised by sweeping curves and plants in irregularly shaped groups or *drifts*. Mixed borders of different types of plants (trees, shrubs, perennials, ornamental grasses, and ground-cover plants) are perfect for this style. A couple of formal touches can still go down a treat, like a low, clipped hedge enclosing a border that is a riotous mix of flowers, or pairs of clipped box balls or pyramids flanking a path or gateway.

You can go for variations on the informal style:

- ✔ **Cottage garden.** In the old days a cottage garden served a thoroughly practical role, growing crops of fruit, vegetables, and herbs to sustain a family through the year. Flowers were a luxury to many people and were jumbled in between the crops as space permitted. Today, flowers are the stars of cottage gardens. Choose either genuinely old or heirloom varieties of plants, such as pinks, foxgloves, lilac, or Michaelmas daisies, or newer ones like the range of English roses that have been bred to look old-fashioned. Edible plants can be grown cheek by jowl with ornamentals, though it helps to choose good-looking varieties like ruby-leaved Swiss chard, and lettuce with red-tinged or frilled leaves.

  Although spring and summer are the seasons when a cottage garden looks its best, be sure to include some evergreens for a bit of all-year structure and interest.

- ✔ **Mediterranean.** If your garden (or part of it) gets the sun all or most of the day *and* has well-drained soil, you can have plantings redolent of foreign holidays, brimming over with colour and fragrance. Plants from a Mediterranean-type climate include those from the south and west of North America and from South Africa, as well as from the Mediterranean itself. Think lavender and rosemary, rock roses and Californian lilac, pergolas (arched trellises) clothed with jasmine and scrambling vines . . . ahhh.

Before you get too excited about this planting style, we can't emphasise enough that good drainage is essential, as Mediterranean-style plants detest having wet feet, especially in the cold of winter.

Matchmaking: Right Plant, Right Place

Successful gardening is all about matchmaking. Although you can find lots of good-natured plants that thrive almost anywhere, many are choosy about their site. The way to have an easy-care, great-looking garden is to match the plants' preferences to the conditions in your garden. Plants that like the same conditions tend to look good together, so you're already well on the way to creating some really great-looking plant combinations.

Remember these points when you're thinking about planting:

- **Do** check out whether the area for planting is in shade all day or is sunny most of the time, as most plants have distinct preferences for one or the other. However, a site that gets sun for several hours a day is suitable for plants that like partial shade.

- **Do** inspect your soil thoroughly to see what type you have (see the nearby sidebar ' Ground force' and Chapter 11). Then you can choose plants that suit your soil type.

- **Don't** be tempted to fight nature and grow plants that aren't suited to your garden, regardless of however much you love them. They're likely to struggle and look sickly for years, take up far too much work, and end up being chucked out. Always remember that however awkward the conditions may be, at least a handful of other plants can thrive there.

Changing climate

As well as assessing conditions within the garden itself (see Chapter 2), the climate and location of your garden are tremendously important when it comes to choosing plants. In the warmer parts of the United Kingdom such as the south, many plants that thrive outside would be killed by the cold further north. In coastal areas the sea has a tempering influence that keeps winter temperatures higher than just a few miles inland. In exposed, coastal sites it's vital to choose plants that tolerate salt-laden winds. Town gardens tend to be warmer than country gardens, as the shelter created by industry and buildings makes for a slightly hotter environment.

Ground force

Choose plants that like what your garden spot can offer them and you're on to a winner straight away. So, first check out the card you've drawn in the soil stakes. Take a fork or spade and dig a few test holes in your garden. If the soil is heavy and sticks together in large lumps it's likely to hold moisture well, whereas sandy, stony, or chalky ground that breaks up easily dries out quickly.

When selecting plants to suit your soil, bear in mind that plants need a similar environment right through the year. It's no use growing drought-tolerant plants if your soil is only dry in summer but is heavy, cold, and wet over winter. Similarly, moisture-lovers need ground that's damp all year. Soil can be acid, alkaline, or neutral, the level of which is called pH. A cheap and simple test kit can determine the exact level and this is well worth doing, as certain plants are picky about their soil. The chief plants to note are camellias, azaleas, rhododendrons, and pieris, all of which hate alkaline (limey soil), but they can always be grown in pots if the ground isn't suitable. See Chapter 11 for more on getting to know your soil and using a pH test.

 Find out what grows well in your area by doing a bit of local research. Walk around your neighbourhood to see which plants are thriving, visit gardens open to the public, and talk to knowledgeable neighbours and staff at nearby nurseries and garden centres. Most garden centres and nurseries have trained staff who are only too happy to help, so don't be backward about coming forward if you need advice on finding the right plants. If you want help at a garden centre, avoid the busiest times at weekends and go during the week (day workers take note – many garden centres stay open late on selected nights) or first thing Saturday, when staff are less likely to be rushed.

Creating Year-round Colour and Interest

Year-round good looks are particularly important for those bits of the garden that are on view all year. You may not get out in the garden much in the winter months, but you want to enjoy it from your window seat or the kitchen sink!

Creating a year-round garden requires a two-pronged attack:

- ✔ Choose larger structural plants to form the long-lasting 'backbone' of the garden.
- ✔ Select plants that flower at different times of year for a succession of colour through every season.

Mixed borders that blend different types of plant give the most bang for your bucks. Trees, shrubs, conifers, roses, herbaceous perennials, and ornamental grasses work incredibly well together, and to this heady mix you can add seasonal splashes of colour with bulbs, and short-lived plants such as annuals (plants that only flower for the summer), and tender perennials (summer-blooming plants that won't tolerate frost).

A bit of advance planning is the key to success, for it's all too easy to go down to the garden centre and buy whatever's looking good at the time, and then find out that your garden only looks great for the season in which you went shopping (usually spring or summer). But choose your plants with care and you can have something looking good in every month of the year.

Start by selecting plants for winter and early spring when good-looking plants are at their most scarce, then autumn, spring, and summer – in that order.

Drawing Up a Planting Plan

Sketching out a rough planting plan on paper is the best starting point when creating new planting (jump to Chapter 2 for how to draw up a plan). In a large garden you may find it easier to make separate plans for each border rather than doing the whole plot in one go. Select your plants in the order described below to build up a framework of permanent plants infilled with a succession of seasonal colour.

1. Trees are the largest and most dominant occupants of the garden. Those with green or softly coloured leaves are the safest choice, as golds and purples can look rather overpowering when big. Consider how different-shaped trees will fit into your garden, as well as how many seasons of interest they provide.

2. Evergreen shrubs and conifers can make up around a third of all the medium to large plants to give year-round structure and long-lasting colour. Include several bold and architectural shrubs with large or spiky leaves or a striking shape.

3. Deciduous shrubs with attractively shaped or coloured foliage look good from spring to autumn and make a wonderful backdrop to flowers, too.

4. Next, choose flowering shrubs to bloom at different times of year to create a succession of interest.

5. After all these key plants are in place, infill with ornamental grasses, herbaceous perennials, and small shrubs.

6. You can plant bulbs in the spaces between groups of plants for splashes of colour.

7. You can leave a few gaps to fill with seasonal flowers such as annuals, biennials, and frost-tender perennials, which provide spectacular and long-lasting summer colour.

Permanent Plants for Structure

The key plants that form the 'backbone' of your garden planting are primarily the medium-sized and large ones – shrubs, conifers, and trees. Choose these first. Because of their size larger plants really need to pull their weight and look good for as long as possible, so try to see beyond the immediate appeal of flowers and instead look for attributes such as evergreen foliage, attractively shaped or coloured deciduous (non-evergreen) leaves, colourful bark, or two seasons of interest such as spring flowers followed by autumn fruit.

Trees and shrubs

Start with the biggest plants: Trees. Trees come in a number of forms including columnar, upright, wide-spreading, or weeping. Choose the right-shaped tree for your garden: A tall, thin tree such as Prunus 'Amanogawa' takes up less room in a small garden than a wide-spreading one such as Prunus 'Tai-Haku'. Height varies enormously too: always bear in mind that the root spread of a tree is roughly equivalent to its height, and make sure the tree is sited far enough away from buildings and mains drainage pipes. However, as the smallest trees reach around 2.5 metres (8 feet) in height, even a tiny garden should be able to incorporate at least one tree.

After choosing your trees, move on to evergreen shrubs and conifers, which are wonderful for year-round structure and really come into their own in winter. These should make up around a third of all the medium to large plants, but don't increase that proportion because too many evergreens make a garden appear to be stuck in a time warp, changing little from season to season, even year to year. Include a few evergreens that are bold and architectural, with large or spiky leaves or a striking shape, to introduce some strong form and impact.

Good evergreens to choose include

- Bamboos
- Holly (*Ilex*)
- Golden privet (*Ligustrum ovalifolium* 'Aureum')
- *Mahonia*
- New Zealand flax (*Phormium*)
- Evergreen viburnums such as *V. davidii* and *V. tinus*.

Incorporate deciduous plants with attractive foliage that looks good from spring to autumn and makes a fantastic backdrop to lots of different flowers.

Place all these larger plants first, allowing plenty of room according to their eventual height and spread.

Given that flowers are a relatively temporary occurrence in the yearly life of a plant, concentrating on getting the best combinations of plant shapes and foliage really pays off in terms of the long-lasting interest you get from your borders. Plenty of dramatic plants and bold foliage also make a striking backdrop for flowers in any season, particularly if the flower size contrasts with the accompanying foliage.

Architectural plants

Plants with bold or striking leaves or shapes are often called *architectural plants*, and give a touch of real style to any garden. A few look fabulous; just don't choose too many. A stage full of prima donnas never works too well. The main shapes are:

- ✔ **Vertical.** Bamboos, tall ornamental grasses (such as *Miscanthus sinensis* varieties).

- ✔ **Narrow and upright** (correctly called fastigiate, if you want to impress your friends). *Berberis thunbergii* 'Helmond Pillar', *Juniperus scopulorum* 'Skyrocket', *Malus* 'Van Eseltine', *Sorbus aucuparia* 'Fastigiata'.

- ✔ **Spiky.** Cabbage tree (*Cordyline*), New Zealand flax (*Phormium*), *Yucca*.

- ✔ **Weeping or arching.** Japanese maples (*Acer palmatum* 'Dissectum' varieties), weeping crab apple (*Malus* 'Royal Beauty'), weeping purple willow (*Salix purpurea* 'Pendula').

Infilling for Colour through the Seasons

After you put in the backbone plants, move on to the smaller ones such as perennials, ornamental grasses, small shrubs, and roses. While a few of your smaller plants should have long-lasting attractive foliage – either evergreen or deciduous – many of these infill plants can be seasonal performers that give shorter but showier bursts of colour. For the most part, place larger plants farther back and grade down to the small ones towards the front, although it pays to have the occasional tall plant at the front so long as it has a light, airy, see-through habit, such as giant oat grass (*Stipa gigantea*) or *Verbena bonariensis*.

In a small garden, or where you want to pack in loads of plants for maximum colour, go for the technique of 'lasagne planting' – layering plants of different sizes together in tiers. Here's how it goes:

1. Start with the biggest plant such as a tree or a large shrub, perhaps a birch or sorbus that only casts a light, dappled shade rather than dense gloom, so plants that you pop underneath get plenty of light.

2. Next, put in medium-sized shrubs that thrive in this dappled shade, such as ornamental elder, *Sambucus,* and viburnums.

3. Under the deciduous shrubs, plant low-growing, shade-tolerant perennials or other plants that look good in winter or spring, before the larger shrub leafs up. Good plants include epidemiums, winter heathers (*Erica carnea*), Lenten rose (*Helleborus orientalis*), lungwort (*Pulmonaria*), and lesser periwinkle (*Vinca minor*). Bulbs (see below) can be packed in for bursts of bloom.

After several years the shrubs become well established and you can have even more flowers by planting climbers to grow through these living supports. Choose with care though, as some climbers are ultra-vigorous and anti-social, and would soon overwhelm their hosts. Well-behaved climbers that you can plant with a clear conscience include large-flowered hybrid clematis; *Clematis viticella* varieties; and perennial pea (*Lathyrus latifolius*).

Bursts of Bloom with Bulbs and Annuals

Since you may enjoy your garden most in summer, consider leaving a few bare spaces to fill with seasonal flowers that bloom for months on end. Hardy annuals and biennials are tolerant of frost and you can sow them directly into the ground, while you can plant half-hardy annuals and tender perennials once all danger of frost is past. See Chapter 7 for lots more on these summer stars.

Bulbs are fantastic infillers; you can cram them in just about anywhere. You can plant spring-flowering bulbs under deciduous trees and shrubs to bloom before a canopy of leaves shades them out; similarly, you can plant them in borders between clumps of perennials and under roses; and to pop up through carpets of ground-cover plants.

Leave your bulbs to die back naturally after flowering (without tying the leaves into knots either), because this is how they build up energy to perform again next year. (Even better, give them some food and water too.) Take a stroll to Chapter 9 to find out just how much bulbs can do for you.

Planting for Privacy

Lack of privacy can be a big problem in gardens, particularly in towns and new developments where close-packed houses stare in on one another. Now gardens are increasingly used as extensions to the house, it's even more important to have a bit of privacy and seclusion where you can eat meals, socialise, read, and relax without being observed.

Although the immediate response to prying eyes may be to put up a tall fence or plant a hedge of rampant conifers, think again. Not only does a high boundary make the garden feel gloomy and unwelcoming, but in most cases the law limits the height of boundary fences to around 1.8 metres (6 feet) high. And Leyland cypress, that scourge of the suburbs and cause of numerous neighbourhood disputes, needs pruning three times a year to stay within bounds. So, take a good look at exactly where you need privacy by concentrating on what you see as you walk through or sit in the garden.

You may only need screening at certain points in your garden, so making an entire high boundary is rather like using a sledgehammer to crack a nut when just the odd tree or group of tall plants would do. Give priority to screening the patio and any other seating areas, where an internal screen of fencing, trellis, or plants is effective. Make sure you still keep good views of your own garden while blocking out neighbouring properties.

To screen out overlooking upstairs windows, put up a pergola and clothe it with vines, wisteria, or clematis, which look gorgeous after the plants are established.

Where screening is only required in certain spots, small groups of tall plants are the perfect solution. Good garden trees that grow to between 4 and 7 metres high include birch, crab apple, cherry, and sorbus. You find numerous different varieties of varying shapes and eventual heights, so check the small print before buying. Evergreen shrubs that quickly grow to 2–3 metres high include *Elaeagnus x ebbingei*, *Viburnum rhytidophyllum*, and airy, rustly bamboos such as *Fargesia murieliae* and *Phyllostachys nigra*. When buying bamboos, watch out for the words 'invasive' or 'spreading' in the description – some varieties do just that! If you're desperate for instant privacy and have plenty of cash to spend, you can buy mature specimens of shrubs, climbers, and trees. With trees available in excess of 5–7 metres high, your budget is likely to be the limit rather than the sky!

Hedges make gorgeous living screens that become more beautiful as time passes, whereas fences inevitably deteriorate. Bear in mind that hedges take up much more room than a fence – around a metre in depth – a less appealing option if your garden is small. Even the fastest plants take several years to provide a good degree of privacy. In exposed sites a temporary shelter of windbreak netting for the first couple of years makes the world of difference to how well your hedge grows. Go to Chapter 4 to find out more about hedges.

How Many Plants, How Far Apart?

Larger plants need to be spaced sufficiently far apart to allow for their eventual height and spread. Correctly spaced plants may look gappy at first, so for the first year or so fill the spaces with annuals or perennials and grasses that are quite happy to be moved later on. In small to medium-sized gardens, plant the largest plants singly, while smaller ones such as small shrubs, perennials, and grasses look most effective in groups of three to five. Bulbs look wonderful in big numbers, particularly if you limit the number of varieties to create a real impact.

Although a border needs a variety of different plants to give plenty of interest, beware of seeking constant change. The most attractive effects are created by planting some repeated groups of the same plants, setting up a rhythm of colour that looks tremendous and is easy on the eye.

Part II
Designing with Plants

"When Norman said he wanted to put in some hedges for a bit of privacy, I thought . . . ."

In this part . . .

We live in a three-dimensional world, so naturally you want your garden to be interesting and functional in all dimensions. For example, give your garden a sense of perspective – and a feeling of privacy – by using trees, shrubs, and hedges. Or go horizontal with lawn and ground covers, which also are the best way to protect and enhance your garden's soil. And get out of the rut of looking at eye-level: Use climbers to put your garden up over your head!

This part brings your garden into fine perspective. You'll find our favourite trees, shrubs, and climbers here, so you can do a little designing of your own.

Chapter 4

Trees, Hedges, and Shrubs

. . . .

In This Chapter

▶ Choosing the right tree for your garden

▶ Looking at our favourite trees, hedges, and shrubs

▶ Using hedges and shrubs in your garden design

▶ Organising your shrubs

. . . .

Trees, hedges, and shrubs are the most fundamental types of plants. They may not be the most exciting or colourful in your garden (although they can well be), but they're the ones you typically count on the most – for shade, scale, background planting, property dividing, screening, and all sorts of other landscape functions (not to mention tree houses). Think of trees, hedges, and shrubs as the skeleton of the landscape – the bones that you build beauty around by using other plants such as flowering annuals and perennials.

But don't limit these plants to workhorse-duty only. As you discover in this chapter, trees, hedges, and shrubs can themselves add beauty and interest to any garden.

Tree-mendous: The Benefits of Trees

All but the very smallest of gardens should have at least one tree. Trees bring a home into scale with the surrounding landscape and give a neighbourhood a sense of place. Deciduous or evergreen, trees provide protection from the elements by buffering strong winds and blocking the hot summer sun. In a crowded environment, trees can also provide privacy by screening you from neighbours or unpleasant views. However, more than anything else, trees offer beauty: Beauty in flowers held high among the branches, or simply beauty in their leafy green canopy. Beauty in colourful berries and seed pods dangling among the limbs. Beauty in dazzling hues created by autumn leaves. Even beauty in winter, when the texture of bark and the structure of branches add strength and permanence to the landscape. Beauty in diversity, too – after all, without trees, where can the birds perch or the squirrels scuttle?

In our fast-paced world of concrete, tarmac, and hazy skies, trees are the great equalisers. They shade our streets and cool our cities and neighbourhoods, they cleanse the air, and their roots hold the soil in place and prevent erosion.

Choosing the Right Tree

Before you buy and plant one, you need to learn everything you can about the tree you're considering; both the good and the bad. Many trees get big and live a long time (probably longer than you), so if you make a mistake and plant the wrong one in the wrong place, it may be very costly to remove or replace. Removing the tree may even be dangerous to people and property. The overall shape of a tree influences its suitability for a particular site. A weeping or wide-spreading tree is great in a lawn or meadow where it has plenty of space to grow (underplanted with shade-tolerant plants rather than grass), whereas an upright or columnar tree can be grown in a border and underplanted with shrubs and perennials. Figure 4-1 shows the general shapes that trees come in.

Concentrate on the practical aspects of a tree before being seduced by its good looks. Consider the following points:

- How fast does it grow?
- How tall and wide does it get?
- Is it adapted to the climate and the sun, soil, and water conditions at the proposed planting site?
- Is it likely to have any problems – invasive roots, weak limbs, insects, or diseases?
- Does it need any special maintenance, such as pruning?
- How does the shape of the tree fit into your overall landscape?
- How messy is it? Does it drop excessive amounts of flowers, fruits, or leaves?

A local nursery is a good place to find out how a tree performs in your area. Botanical gardens and arboretums are especially good places to observe a wide variety of trees at maturity, as are gardens open to the public (a good excuse for an enjoyable day's garden visiting, too).

Columnar

Cone

Fastigate

Globe

Horizontal Spread

Open Irregular

Vase

Weeping

Informal Globe

Figure 4-1:
Choose a
tree shape
that suits
your
landscaping
needs.

After you decide on the kind of tree you need in terms of size, shape, and suitability, you have a wealth of ornamental characteristics to choose from. Think about:

- ✔ **Seasonal colour.** Many trees bloom in spring, some in midsummer, and a very few even in winter. Choose from a wide range of colours and blooms that vary from tiny and delicate to huge and showy. Trees such as maples, sweet gum (*Liquidambar*), and snowy mespilus (*Amelanchier*) also give marvellous autumn leaf colour.

- ✔ **Attractive foliage.** Trees with colourful or attractively shaped foliage look good from spring to autumn (even all year in the case of evergreens). Their appeal is more subtle than that of flowering trees, but much longer lasting.

- ✔ **Colourful fruit.** Trees such as crab apples and hawthorns follow their blooms with colourful fruit, which can (if the birds don't eat it) hang on the tree into winter after the leaves have fallen. Birds tend to prefer red and orange fruit, which nearly always get eaten first, whereas yellow, pink, and white fruit remain until later in the season and, if the winter is mild, sometimes don't get eaten at all. Don't overlook trees that produce edible fruit when you're making your choices. Although they're less ornamental, the pleasure of having a crop of fruit to harvest can more than outweigh lack of looks.

- ✔ **Attractive bark.** The white bark of birch trees is familiar to most people, but many other trees have handsome peeling or colourful bark.

If your garden is small with only room for one tree, make sure it really 'pays its rent' and looks good for as long as possible. Ignore any three-week wonders that just bloom in spring and do nothing else for the rest of the year. Instead, go for a tree like a crab apple that has spring flowers and long-lasting ornamental fruit, or a tree that has attractive foliage for months of colour.

Don't Try This at Home

The following sections point out some things that you should *not* do when planting a tree, for practical and aesthetic reasons. (See Chapter 13 for more about the process of planting trees.)

- ✔ **Planting too close to buildings.** Even the smallest trees should be planted well away from buildings while larger trees should be much farther away. Otherwise, the trees don't have room to spread and develop their natural shape. Also, aggressive roots can damage the building's foundations, or falling branches can damage the house. The all-important point to remember is that in most cases, the root spread of a tree is approximately equivalent to its height or canopy spread. Certain trees, notably the popular weeping willow (*Salix x chrysocoma*), have wide-spreading root systems and must be planted well away from buildings and drains.

✔ **Planting a tree that's too big at maturity.** Some trees can get huge – more than 15 metres (50 feet) tall and almost as wide. These trees belong in parks and open spaces where they can spread out. But even smaller trees can be too big for a planting site, eventually crowding houses or shading an entire garden. Choose a tree that, when mature, will be in scale with your house and won't crowd out the rest of your garden. To avoid falling foul of neighbours or your local council, the safest course of action is to plant a tree in a site where its eventual spread will remain within your garden boundary. Once a tree overhangs a neighbouring property, the owner of that land is legally entitled to cut back the branches to your garden boundary. See Figure 4-2 for an illustration of how large some trees get at maturity.

✔ **Don't plant trees where they can grow into power lines or drains.** Pruning such trees is costly and results in misshapen trees; and fallen limbs can cause power cuts. Pruned trees look unsightly, too, their natural grace and beauty spoilt.

✔ **Planting too close to paving.** Almost any tree, especially larger species, can cause problems if you plant it too close to paving. Leave at least 1–1.2 metres (3 or 4 feet) between the trunk and the paving. To encourage roots to grow deep rather than near the surface, insert several pieces of drainpipe around the rootball when planting so that the lower ends are level with the bottom of the rootball and the tops are just above soil level. Water via the pipe a couple of times a week during its first year during active growth only and during any long, dry spells in the following couple of years.

✔ **Planting a messy tree in the wrong place.** All trees shed some leaves at one time or another, but certain species are messier than others. Don't plant trees that drop fruit or bear large crops of blossom near patios or pavements. They not only make a mess (and more work for you) but can also make the surface slippery, causing a passer-by to fall.

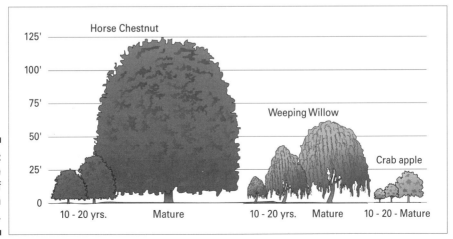

Figure 4-2: The mature height of certain trees.

Horse Chestnut

Weeping Willow

Crab apple

125'

100'

75'

50'

25'

0

10 - 20 yrs.   Mature   10 - 20 yrs.   Mature   10 - 20 - Mature

Tree-buying tips

A tree should last for many years, so take care to purchase and plant one that's healthy to begin with. Here are some tips for buying a healthy tree:

✔ Avoid trees that have been growing in a container for too long or are unhealthy and growing poorly – they'll probably perform badly once in the ground.

✔ Examine the top of the rootball. Avoid specimens that have large, circling roots near the surface, a sign that the tree has been in the container too long.

✔ Avoid trees that are the smallest or largest of a group. Select ones that are well proportioned from top to bottom.

✔ Choose trees that can stand on their own without being tightly tied to a stake. (Watch out for trees tightly tied to tall stakes which can be like crutches, preventing a tree from developing a strong trunk.) Younger trees establish more quickly than older ones.

✔ Ideally, pick a tree that has an evenly tapered trunk from bottom to top.

✔ Look for healthy, even-coloured foliage.

✔ Pick a tree that's free of insects and disease. (See Chapter 16 for more about common pests and diseases.)

Our Favourite Trees

Here are a few of our favourite trees. All trees are deciduous unless stated otherwise. Heights given are approximate and are those reached after 10–15 years. This is by no means a complete list of all the trees available, just a selection of our favourites. We organise our favourite trees by botanical name as this is how you're likely to find them organised in garden centres and plant catalogues; however, we list the common name first because this is far less offputting.

✔ **Maple.** *Acer* species. Maples are grown for their attractive foliage, a few for their good-looking bark, and they comprise a large number of species and varieties.

The 'snakebark' maples (*A. grosseri* var. *hersii, A. davidii,* and *A. pennsylvanicum*) are grown primarily for the year-round appeal of their attractive bark, patterned and striated with white (like that of a snake's skin). Their large, lobed leaves have good autumn colour. Height and spread to 6 metres (20 feet).

The Japanese maple is one of the most popular small trees (ranging from 1.5–7.5 metres [5–25 feet]) high, depending on the variety). It comes in dramatic weeping forms with finely cut leaves and bright autumn colour, mostly in shades of red, orange, and yellow. Some varieties, like 'Bloodgood', have purplish leaves the entire growing season. Japanese maples are best planted in partial shade, in a retentive soil, and in a site sheltered from the wind. Unless you have a lot of cash for a well-grown specimen, be prepared to start with a small plant in a two- or three-litre pot and wait for it to grow.

✔ **Snowy mespilus.** *Amelanchier.* A top choice for small gardens, the snowy mespilus gives months of interest yet is compact and attractive. It bears masses of white flowers in spring, followed by handsome, rounded leaves that colour well in autumn (the leaf tints are best on acid soil). Height 3.5 metres (12 feet).

✔ **Birch.** *Betula.* Grown for their attractive bark and autumn colour, most birches are excellent garden trees as they are slender and upright with a light covering of leaves that doesn't cast a dense shade, so you can grow other plants beneath them. One of the most popular is the Himalayan birch (*Betula utilis* var. *jacquemontii*), which has dazzling white bark. Birches can be grown as single-stemmed trees or as multi-stems (with three or more young trees planted together in a clump). Birch prefers well-drained soil. Height to 10 metres (33 feet).

✔ **Conifers.** The pines, junipers, spruces, firs, hemlocks, and cedars form a diverse group of evergreens, most with needlelike leaves. They are widely grown throughout the world and are especially valuable for year-round greenery and as windbreaks and screens. Most are large trees and need room to grow, but many dwarf forms are available. The overall appearance of these varieties is often similar, but foliage density, colour, and texture vary.

✔ **Judas tree.** *Cercis siliquastrum.* Grown for its showy purple-pink flowers in spring and attractive foliage, the Judas tree grows to around 5 metres (15 feet) and is excellent in small gardens. As with Japanese maples, you need to start with a small plant unless your budget is large. Prefers well-drained soil. Best avoided in cold areas.

✔ **Hawthorn.** *Crataegus* species. These small trees – most are 6–7.5 metres (20–25 feet) high – offer a long season of colour, with white, pink, or red flowers in mid-spring, bright orange-to-red fruit in autumn and winter, and usually orange-to-red autumn leaf colour. While varieties of *C. laevigata* such as 'Paul's Scarlet' are common, it's worth seeking out the less common *C. x lavallei* 'Carrierei', which is much more decorative, with fruit and foliage lasting well into winter.

✔ **Gum tree.** *Eucalyptus.* Several of these Australian natives make excellent garden trees and, unlike most of the trees mentioned here, are evergreen. One of the best is the snow gum, *Eucalyptus paucifolia* subsp. *niphophila*, which grows to around 6 metres (20 feet). It has large, silvery leaves, and its bark becomes patterned with age. The most widely available gum is Eucalyptus gunnii, but this species is very fast growing and soon forms a tall, rather spindly tree. However, you can keep it as a large, bushy shrub by hard pruning every spring, which also encourages production of the more attractive, rounded, young foliage rather than the sickle-shaped mature leaves. Gum trees prefer well-drained soil.

✔ **Sweet Gum.** *Liquidambar styraciflua.* Tall (12–15 metres, 40–50 feet, and higher), narrowly upright trees put on bright autumn colours, in shades of yellow, orange, red, or purple.

✔ **Magnolia.** *Magnolia* species. Magnolia has a foot in the shrub as well as the tree section, starting as a small plant but attaining tree size in time. The deciduous magnolias bloom stunningly on bare branches in early spring. Flowers are huge, often more than 25 centimetres (10 inches) across, and come in shades of white, pink, and purple. Some are bicoloured. The leaves are large and leathery. Magnolia trees usually grow 4.5–7.5 metres (15–25 feet) high, and are often multistemmed. One of the best types is the *M. soulangeana*, which bears large, cup-shaped flowers, usually white on the inside, purplish on the outside. 'Lennei' and 'Rustica Rubra' are good named varieties. Although it's hardy, it's best to grow magnolias only in sheltered areas as late spring frosts can spoil the blooms.

✔ **Flowering crab apples.** *Malus* species. Superb garden trees that offer lots of interest. Crab apples differ from apples in that the fruit measures less than 5 centimetres (2 inches) in diameter. You have many species and varieties to choose from, ranging in tree size and shape. Spring flowers come in white, pink, or red. Colourful red, orange, or yellow edible fruit often hang on the bare branches into winter. A few of the many good varieties include 'Evereste', 'Golden Hornet', 'John Downie', 'Red Jade', and 'Red Sentinel'.

✔ **Flowering cherry.** *Prunus* species. The large family of early spring-blooming trees includes flowering cherries and plums. Flowers are sometimes fragrant and come in shades of white, pink, or red. Most range in height from 4.5–10 metres (15 to 30 feet). Most varieties give an exceptionally showy display of bloom but this only lasts for a short time – maybe just a couple of weeks if a strong spring wind whips off the blossom early. Pick out those varieties with a longer season of interest, like the Tibetan cherry (*Prunus serrula*), which has beautifully glossy, mahogany-coloured bark, or the winter cherry (*Prunus x subhirtella* 'Autumnalis') that blooms through the winter.

✔ **Sorbus.** An extensive group of excellent garden trees that includes the native rowan or mountain ash, *Sorbus aucuparia*. With spring flowers, attractive foliage and autumn fruits, sorbus have an enormous amount of ornamental value. Varieties range in size from the compact, columnar *Sorbus aucuparia* 'Fastigiata', which grows to around 3 metres (10 feet), to taller varieties such as S. Americana and S. aria at around 10 metres (30 feet). Particularly worthy of mention is the Kashmir sorbus, *S. cashmiriana*, with blush-pink flowers and white, pink-tinged berries.

✔ **Weeping purple willow.** *Salix purpurea* 'Pendula'. Unlike its much larger and ultra-vigorous cousin, this variety of weeping willow remains small and is a well-behaved tree, growing to around 1.8–2.4 metres (6–8 feet). This willow has slender, dark green leaves, and purple-green catkins in early spring. It prefers a moist soil.

Hedging Your Bets: Choosing the Right Hedge

A hedge makes a superb living screen and becomes more beautiful with the passage of time, compared to a wooden fence or screen that will inevitably deteriorate. Many types of hedge also help to mitigate traffic noise and pollution. However, a hedge occupies a lot more room than a fence; an important consideration depending on the size and shape of your garden. Hedges also require a bit of patience because plants take several years to start forming a well-established screen, but in the long run you have an attractive boundary that complements your garden hugely.

You can choose between formal and informal hedges. The difference is that a formal hedge is close-clipped on the top and sides to create a neat shape maintained by trimming two or three times a year (remember the two to three times a year bit – it's rather important). An informal hedge is more loose and open in design, with the plants allowed to grow naturally and pruned every second year, so it takes up more room than a formal hedge. You grow a formal hedge solely for foliage effect, whereas you grow an informal one for other ornamental attributes such as flowers and fruit as well as its leaves.

If your garden is in the country, yet another option is a mixed hedge of native plants. It's fabulous for wildlife, providing flowers for bees, plenty of fruits and berries to feed the birds, and shelter in which they can nest. Deciduous plants such as hawthorn, blackthorn, field maple, and hazel should make up about three-quarters of the hedge, with the remainder made of evergreens such as holly and yew. Plant this type of hedge in a double staggered row.

If security is a consideration, choose prickly plants such as holly and berberis. These hedges are viciously spiny and certainly put off would-be intruders (or make life extremely uncomfortable for persistent ones at least).

Choose your hedge with care because you'll be living with it for many years. Conifers are a popular choice; Leyland cypress (*x Cupressocyparis leylandii*) is the fastest plant and is fine if pruned two to three times a year, but often the best option is something a little slower and much better looking. A better conifer is Western red cedar (*Thuja plicata* 'Atrovirens'), which has handsome foliage that responds well to trimming and has a lovely aroma, and

Lawson cypress (*Chamaecyparis lawsoniana*) varieties are also attractive. Favourite evergreen shrubs include golden privet (*Ligustrum ovalifolium* 'Aureum'), which is much more handsome than its green-leaved cousin, and cherry laurel (*Prunus laurocerasus*), which, although bulky, has glossy, light-reflecting leaves.

A stylish and space-saving option is a *pleached* hedge – a hedge on legs – which you train to have around 1.8 metres (6 feet) of clear stem with the branches trained on a framework made of wood, metal, or stout bamboo canes (you can remove the framework after around 4 or 5 years when plants are well established). Plant young trees of beech, lime, or hornbeam about 1.6–1.8 metres (5–6 feet) apart – preferably during the winter months when cheaper field-grown plants are available. Although it takes time to grow, a pleached hedge is a great way of creating high-level privacy without the claustrophobic feel of a tall, solid barrier, and the space beneath gives loads of room for other plants, too.

Growth rates

Different plants grow at dramatically different rates, so this has to be a prime consideration when you decide which one to plant. The list of our favourite hedge plants outlines the approximate rates of growth, but be aware that this is only a general guide, as other factors influence the speed. These include how well you prepare the soil; the amount of watering and feeding you do after planting; climate; and local weather conditions such as exposure to wind.

Hedges as windbreaks

In exposed sites, and especially near the coast where the wind is laden with salt, hedges are essential for shelter. A hedge makes an excellent windbreak because the air filters through, compared to a solid barrier that creates turbulence. Exceptionally windy sites benefit from more than one line of protection, such as an informal belt of trees outside a tall hedge.

Create coastal windbreaks from salt-tolerant plants. *Elaeagnus x ebbingei* and tamarisk (*Tamarix ramosissima*) make lovely informal hedges, as does *Escallonia*, which is widely grown for its colourful flowers. You can trim *Escallonia* to make a more formal hedge but one that flowers less freely. *Griselinia littoralis* can be close-trimmed to a formal shape. In mild areas, *Fuchsia magellanica* and tall hebes such as *Hebe salicifolia* make excellent flowering hedges.

Low hedges

Low hedges can be immensely attractive within the garden in a wealth of ways – along paths, fronting borders, and as dividers between different parts of the garden. While box (*Buxus sempervirens*) has long been a favourite for low hedges, the spread of the fungal disease *Cylindrocladium* to which box is susceptible may make alternatives more appealing. These alternatives include *Berberis thunbergii*, Atropurpurea Nana, Hyssop (*Hyssopus officinalis*), Japanese holly (*Ilex crenata*), lavender (most varieties except slightly tender ones such as *Lavandula stoechas*), and cotton lavender (*Santolina*).

Our Favourite Hedge Plants

Here's a list of our favourite formal and informal hedges. We've simplified the growth rates:

- ✔ **Slow** means up to 23 centimetres (9 inches) of growth per year
- ✔ **Medium** means 23–45 centimetres (9–18 inches)
- ✔ **Fast** means over 45 centimetres (18 inches)

The spacing given for each plant applies for standard size plants. Should your budget allow for buying larger plants, ask for advice on spacing.

Plants for formal hedges

Here's a list of our favourite plants for formal hedges.

- ✔ **Hornbeam.** *Carpinus betulus*. Slow. Grow this for its dense, fresh green foliage. A good plant for heavy soils. Space plants 45 centimetres (18 inches) apart. Deciduous, although the leaves hold well into winter.

- ✔ **Lawson's cypress.** *Chamaecyparis lawsoniana*. Medium. An attractive conifer with foliage in greens, golds, and blue-greens, depending on variety. Space 60 centimetres (25 inches) apart. Evergreen.

- ✔ **Hawthorn or May.** *Crataegus monogyna*. Medium. An excellent native plant for a mixed hedge, with white blossom in spring and red fruit in autumn. Space plants 30 centimetres (12 inches) apart. Deciduous.

- ✔ **Leyland cypress.** *x Cupressocyparis leylandii*. Fast (actually very fast – should carry a health warning for small gardens). Mid-green foliage. An excellent hedge if you trim it regularly right from the start. You can also find several golden-leaved varieties. Space 75 centimetres (30 inches) apart. Evergreen.

✔ **Beech.** *Fagus sylvatica*. Slow. An excellent foliage hedge with dense, twiggy growth and fresh green leaves. A purple-leaved form, *F.s.* 'Atropurpurea', is also available. Dislikes heavy, poorly drained soil. Space 30 centimetres (12 inches) apart. Deciduous, although the dead leaves remain on the plant well into winter and often until spring, giving good cover (and looks better than it sounds).

✔ **Holly.** *Ilex aquifolium*. Slow. Glossy, dark green, prickly leaves borne on dense, bushy growth. Good to add evergreen interest to a mixed hedge of native plants. Space 45 centimetres (18 inches) apart. Evergreen.

✔ **Privet.** *Ligustrum ovalifolium*. Fast. Useful if you need a quick, vigorous hedge, but privet is a very hungry plant, making it difficult to cultivate other plants nearby. The golden-leaved form *L.o.* 'Aureum' is a more decorative choice. Space 30 centimetres (12 inches) apart. Evergreen.

✔ *Lonicera nitida*. Medium. Tiny, oval, dark green leaves on twiggy stems. The golden-leaved variety 'Baggessen's Gold' is slower growing but more attractive. Space 45 centimetres (18 inches) apart. Evergreen.

✔ **Laurel.** *Prunus laurocerasus*. Fast. Bushy and vigorous, with large, oval, light-reflecting leaves. Space 60 centimetres (25 inches) apart. Evergreen.

✔ **Blackthorn or sloe.** *Prunus spinosa*. Medium. A useful native plant for mixed hedges, with white spring blossom and purple-black autumn fruits on thorny stems. Space 30 centimetres (12 inches) apart. Deciduous.

✔ **Yew.** *Taxus baccata*. Medium. A classic hedging plant, this handsome conifer has very dark green, needle-like leaves. Poisonous, so don't grow near grazing animals. Space 60 centimetres (25 inches) apart. Evergreen.

✔ **Western red cedar.** *Thuja plicata* 'Atrovirens'. Medium. An attractive conifer with lustrous green foliage that deserves to be used more widely. Space 60 centimetres (25 inches) apart. Evergreen.

Plants for informal hedges

Many shrubs are suitable for informal hedges. Here's a selection of the best ones.

✔ **Berberis.** Medium. Many species, such as *B. x stenophylla* and *B. darwinii*, make excellent hedges. It has yellow or orange-yellow flowers in spring. Space 45 centimetres (18 inches) apart. Evergreen.

✔ *Elaeagnus x ebbingei*. Medium. An upright shrub with silvery-green leaves. It has tiny, creamy-white, sweetly scented flowers in autumn; their piercingly sweet scent often has passers-by looking round, puzzled, for the source of the perfume. Space 60 centimetres (25 inches) apart. Evergreen.

✔ **Escallonia.** Medium. With summer flowers and evergreen foliage, escallonia makes an attractive if rather untidy hedge. Tolerant of salt winds so excellent for coastal areas. Space 45 centimetres (18 inches) apart. Evergreen.

✔ **Firethorn.** *Pyracantha.* Medium. Vigorous and thorny, firethorn makes a good boundary hedge and looks attractive too, with clusters of white spring/early summer flowers and colourful autumn berries. Select varieties such as the 'Saphyr' series, which have good to scab disease. Space 60 centimetres (25 inches) apart. Evergreen.

✔ **Flowering currant** (*Ribes sanguineum*). Fast. Masses of brightly coloured pink flowers in spring. People tend to either love or hate flowering currant; it all depends on how your nose perceives its smell, which to some has a distinct similarity to that of tomcats. Space 45 centimetres (18 inches) apart. Deciduous.

✔ **Rosa rugosa.** Fast. You can find a number of varieties of this vigorous, thorny, bushy rose, with colourful summer flowers and large, showy, red-to-orange hips in autumn. Space 90 centimetres (35 inches) apart. Deciduous.

✔ **Laurustinus.** *Viburnum tinus.* Medium. Lovely for its clusters of white/pink flowers in winter to early spring, against dark foliage. Space 60–90 centimetres (25–35 inches) apart. Evergreen.

The Workforce of the Garden: Shrubs

Both versatile and hardworking, shrubs are the backbone of the garden. They tie the garden together, bringing unity to all the different elements, from tall trees to low-growing ground covers.

The term *shrub* covers a wide variety of woody plants. They can be deciduous or evergreen, and they provide a variety of ornamental qualities, from seasonal flowers to colourful fruit to dazzling autumn foliage colour. But equally important, shrubs offer diversity of foliage texture and colour, from bold and dramatic to soft and diminutive. As the backbone of the landscape, shrubs are always visible, whether or not they're in bloom. Always consider the foliage and form of the plant when selecting shrubs and deciding how to use them.

Technically, a *shrub* is a woody plant that branches from its base. But that's too simple a definition. Shrubs can range from very low-growing, spreading plants that are ideal ground covers (see Chapter 5) to tall, billowy plants that gradually attain the size of a small tree. In general, shrubs cover themselves with foliage from top to bottom.

What Shrubs Can Do for You

Most shrubs are long-lived plants, many reach a substantial size, and the choicer shrubs can cost a fair bit, so you need to select ones that can thrive at your specific site. Consider the points we make in Chapter 3 regarding climate and hardiness, and on designing with plants. Also be mindful of your soil type and the quantity of light or shade in your garden.

So many shrubs are available that you're sure to find plenty that can thrive no matter what the condition of your soil. However, if you make even modest improvements to your soil, such as improving the drainage of heavy soils or the moisture retention of sandy soils, or increasing the fertility of poor soils, you can dramatically increase the number of shrubs that grow well. You can read more about improving your soil in Chapter 11.

You can buy shrubs in containers, bare-root, or balled-and-burlapped (see Chapter 13). The vast majority of shrubs are sold in containers. Examine container-grown shrubs carefully to be sure of choosing a healthy plant. Avoid any that look *potbound* (the container packed with roots that are visible on the surface of the compost); with yellowing, discoloured, or distorted leaves; or with damaged or broken stems. If you want to inspect the roots, ask a member of staff at the garden centre or nursery to take the pot off the plant for you. See the section on choosing container-grown trees and shrubs in Chapter 13 for more information.

Design considerations

Shrubs serve many functions in gardens. As you consider your garden design, use these following categories to understand how best to use shrubs.

- ✔ **Foundation plantings.** As most shrubs are long-lived and many of a substantial size, shrubs form the skeleton of the garden's planting. Evergreen shrubs provide structure and all-year appeal.

   Go for variety to achieve maximum good looks. Choose a range of shrubs with attractive foliage – both evergreen and deciduous – and select shrubs that bloom in every season of the year for a succession of colour. As a general rule of thumb, evergreens should make up no more than a third of all your larger shrubs, or the garden is likely to look static and dull, changing little from season to season. Try mixing groups of plants with different sizes and textures. And don't plant too closely to the house. Bring the plantings out some distance to gain a smoother transition and to give the shrubs more growing room.

✔ **Harmony.** Repeating small groupings of plants in different parts of a garden ties everything together and gives the garden a feeling of order and purpose. Similarly, shrubs serve well when planted among shorter-lived perennials in border plantings. Because shrubs are usually larger and more substantial, they provide a foundation for the more extravagant flowers like bulbs, annuals, perennials, and ornamental grasses, and give structure to the garden when these plants are dormant.

✔ **Accent.** Some shrubs, such as azaleas and rhododendrons, are spectacular bloomers. Others have stunning berries or autumn colour. Just a plant or two in a special place can light up a whole garden. And don't forget the foliage – a bold New Zealand flax (*Phormium*) with large leaves can make a stunning statement among plants with smaller leaves.

As you select shrubs for your garden, be sure to note the season of the shrub's peak interest. For example, many shrubs produce flowers in early spring, but others – such as several of the hollies – are showy in winter. By mixing shrubs with different seasons of peak interest, you can be sure to have plants worth admiring in your garden any time of the year.

✔ **Hedges, screens, and ground covers.** Many types of shrubs can form hedges or screens when you plant them close together and maintain them as such. For example, you can clip some shrubs, including box and euonymus, into the rigid shape of a formal hedge to give a garden a very organised look. Let other types grow naturally to create screens for privacy. Many prostrate (low-growing) shrubs make excellent ground covers. (For more information about ground covers, see Chapter 5.) If you want to keep pets (or people) out of a certain area, plant a line of thorny pyracantha or berberis. The interlopers will get the 'point'.

✔ **Background.** Shrubs can be the perfect backdrop for flowers. For the most decorative effects, choose foliage of varying colours to make a contrast with other flower and foliage colours – golden-leaved shrubs with blue flowers and purple foliage, for example. Remember to include plenty of green foliage, the most restful of nature's colours.

Organising shrubs by height and shape

When planting a mixture of different shrubs or when planting shrubs with other plants (such as flowering perennials), consider the mature height of the shrub. You can follow the old gardening axiom: Place low growers in front, medium-sized plants in the middle, and tall plants at the back. With that approach, you don't block anything out and you can see all the plants. This is a rough guide only; don't stick rigidly to this rule or you could end up with a rather formal and artificial-looking border. Remember that mature heights of plants are, at best, only generalisations. Plants often grow taller in areas with long, warm growing seasons than they do in areas with short summers.

For the best-looking borders that look attractive all year, group shrubs so that their shapes contrast – spiky leaves against rounded shrubs with carpet or mat-forming ones in front, for example.

Our Favourite Shrubs

The following shrubs are easy to grow (given their preferred conditions, of course) and require the minimum of care. Included in this section are bamboos and phormiums, which you'll find on display with shrubs in garden centres.

- **Abelia grandiflora.** Evergreen. This handsome, arching plant has bright green, glossy foliage. New growth is bronzy red. Leaves turn reddish purple in winter. Small, fragrant, white flowers appear in summer. Plant in full sun or light shade.

- **Bamboos.** *Fargesia* and *Phyllostachys* species. Wonderful plants for structure and screening, forming upright clumps of handsome canes and attractive foliage. Their leaves rustle in the slightest breeze too, adding yet more appeal to the garden. There are many different bamboos in sizes ranging from tiny to huge, so do check the eventual size. Also, be wary of certain invasive species whose apparent aim in life is the domination of your entire garden. Our favourite tall bamboos are both well-behaved and good-looking, and all have green leaves – they include *Fargesia murieliae* (yellow-green canes); golden bamboo, *Phyllostachys aurea* (yellow canes); and black bamboo (*P. nigra*), dark green to black canes. Height to 3 metres (10 feet). Plant in sun or shade.

- **Barberries.** *Berberis* species. Evergreen and deciduous. These shrubs are known for their thorny stems, brightly coloured berries, and tough constitution. Some have showy yellow or orange flowers and colourful foliage. Upright-growing barberries make excellent hedges and barriers. The deciduous Japanese barberry, *B. thunbergii,* is generally 1.2–1.8 metres (4–6 feet) high with arching stems. However, you have many varieties from which to choose, varying in height and foliage colour. Most have good autumn colour. 'Atropurpurea' has reddish-purple foliage during the growing season. Evergreen barberries include *B. x darwinii, B. gagnepainii,* and *B. candidula.* Most barberries can grow in sun or shade and tolerate all but the most extreme of growing conditions.

- **Butterfly bush.** *Buddleia davidii.* Deciduous. This much-loved, summer-flowering shrub has long, arching clusters of lightly fragrant flowers that attract butterflies. The blooms come in shades of purple, blue, pink, or white flowers. Buddleias grow very fast, reaching up to 3 metres (10 feet) high. Cut back severely in early spring to keep the plant compact and attractive. If you prefer smaller plants, several varieties only grow to 1.5 metres (5 feet), including 'Adonis Blue', 'Camberwell Beauty', and 'Purple Emperor'. Plant in full sun.

✔ **Box.** *Buxus sempervirens*. Evergreen. The boxwood is one of the finest plants for clipping to form topiary shapes and low hedges. Small, dark green leaves densely cover the branches. Plant in sun or part shade.

✔ **Camellias.** *Camellia* species. Evergreen. Not the easiest of shrubs to grow, but many people fall in love with camellias. With glossy, deep green leaves and perfectly formed flowers, camellias are one of the finest shrubs for early spring flowers. Flowers come in shades of red, pink, and white, with some bicolors. However, camellias dislike limy or chalky soils, need a good moisture-retentive soil rich in organic matter, and a site that doesn't get the early morning sun (which can damage their showy blooms). You can grow camellias in large containers in *ericaceous* (lime-free) potting compost. Never allow camellias to go short of water during summer, as this is a common cause of bud drop before flowering the following spring.

The Japanese camellia, *C. japonica* and *C. x williamsii*, are most commonly grown, usually reaching 1.8–3.6 metres (6–12 feet) high (much less in a container). Many hundreds of varieties are available, varying by colour and flower form. A few of our favourites include 'Adolphe Audusson' (red), 'Anticipation' (rose-pink), 'Donation' (clear pink), 'Jury's Yellow' (white with pale yellow centre), 'Lady Vansittart' (light pink striped with rose), 'Leonard Messel' (deep pink), and 'Nobilissima' (white).

✔ **Flowering quince.** *Chaenomeles*. Deciduous. Among the first shrubs to bloom in early spring, flowering quince are tough, reliable plants that never let you down. The flowers are borne on bare stems in shades of mostly red and pink, but also white. Plants range in size and shape depending on variety, but generally grow 1.5–3 metres high (5–10 feet), are upright, and have thorny branches. You can train the plants against a wall or fence, and look best with regular pruning. Bring cut branches indoors in late winter to force into early bloom. Many named varieties are available, differing mostly in flower colour. Plant in sun or shade.

✔ **Rock roses or sun roses.** *Cistus* species. Evergreen. Particularly well adapted to dry soils, rock roses are tough, colourful plants. Several species and hybrids are available. Most grow between 90–150 centimetres (2–5 feet) and bloom early to mid-summer. The round, silky blooms are 2.5–5 centimetres (1–2 inches) wide, come in shades of white, red, and pink, and are often spotted or marked. Avoid growing rock roses in the coldest parts of the country. Plant in full sun.

✔ **Cotoneaster.** *Cotoneaster* species. Evergreen and deciduous. You can choose from many types, which range from low-growing ground covers to tall, upright shrubs. Most share a profusion of white spring flowers followed by berries – usually red but some varieties have yellow, white, or pink berries – and are tough, widely adapted plants. Deciduous kinds often have good autumn colour. Taller types include *C. lacteus* that reaches about 2.4 metres (8 feet) high and equally as wide. Deciduous *C. divaricatus* has stiff, arching branches to 1.8 metres (6 feet) high and bears a heavy crop of berries.

Plant in sun or shade. Head to Chapter 5 for more on ground-cover types of cotoneaster.

✔ **Euonymus.** *Euonymus* species. Evergreen and deciduous. Euonymus are workhorse foliage plants, tolerant of tough conditions and thriving in sun or shade. Deciduous kinds include winged euonymus, *E. alata*, which has stunning red autumn colour. The European spindle tree, *E. europaeus* 'Red Cascade', grows to about 1.5 metres (5 feet) high and produces attractive red, orange-seeded berries in autumn.

Euonymus fortunei varieties are easy and excellent ground-cover plants, with glossy foliage that looks handsome all year, but are particularly useful for winter interest. Varieties include 'Blondy' (bright gold and green), 'Emerald 'n' Gold' (green and yellow), 'Emerald Gaiety' (green and white, tinged pink in winter), and 'Harlequin' (white and green speckles).

Euonymus japonicus forms an upright bush with handsome, glossy leaves. Most showy is 'Ovatus Aureus', which has bright yellow leaves with narrow green margins. Height to 1.5 metres (5 feet).

✔ **Hebe.** A large and invaluable group of long-flowering, evergreen, summer-flowering shrubs, many of which are grown more for their coloured or variegated foliage than their flowers. Plants range in size from dwarves to taller shrubs up to 1.8 metres (6 feet) high. Not reliably hardy in cold areas, although the small-leaved forms tend to be hardier than the large-leaved ones. Plant in sun on well-drained soil.

✔ **Hydrangea.** *Hydrangea* species. Deciduous. The big, bold leaves and huge summer flowers of these unique plants put on a great show in shady gardens. The mophead hydrangea, *H. macrophylla*, is most commonly grown. Flower clusters are 15 centimetres (6 inches) or more across and are white or light to deep blue in acid soil, pink to red in alkaline soil. Plants usually grow 1.2–2.4 metres (4–8 feet) high and you need to prune them heavily to encourage compactness and heavy bloom.

H. arborescens 'Annabelle' has large, white flowers. 30 centimetres (1 foot) wide.

H. paniculata grows to 3 metres (10 feet) high and produces large flower clusters in late summer. The oakleaf hydrangea, *H. quercifolia*, is notable for its large leaves that colour well in autumn. Height 1.2–1.5 metres (4–5 feet).

H. villosa is handsome in both flower and foliage, with pointed grey-green leaves and china-blue and mauve flowers borne in late summer. Height to 1.8 metres (6 feet).

✔ **Hollies.** *Ilex* species. You can find many kinds of hollies, all notable for their glossy foliage, and many bear red berries in autumn. Because holly plants are either male or female, both types must be present in order for female plants to produce berries.

Most hollies are evergreen, although there are a few, such as *I. verticillata*, which are deciduous. Evergreen hollies have bright-red berries and clean-looking, spiny, often variegated leaves. Many make excellent hedges. Most familiar is the native holly, *Ilex aquifolium*. It generally grows slowly to form a tree 4.5–6 metres (15–25 feet) high, but it responds well to trimming and training to form hedges, pyramids, and lollipops. Variegated varieties are superb for winter interest, such as 'Argenteo-marginata', 'Golden King', and 'Silver Queen'. Hollies prefer well-drained soil and grow well in sun or shade, although variegated varieties produce the best leaf colour in a reasonable amount of sun.

✔ **Junipers.** *Juniperus* species. Evergreen. The low and wide-spreading growth pattern of most junipers makes them most useful as ground covers. (See Chapter 5.) However, many more upright, shrubby types exist, including forms of the Chinese juniper, *J. chinensis*, such as 'Blauuw' and 'Obelisk'. Slender, columnar varieties are also available, such as *J. scopulorum* 'Skyrocket'. Plant in full sun.

✔ **Lavender.** *Lavandula* species. A favourite garden plant for its fragrant summer flowers and aromatic, grey-green foliage. Height 30–60 centimetres (1–2 feet). Lavender bears flowers in shades of white, pink, blue, and purple, although the latter two shades are by far the most popular. Grow on well-drained soil in full sun. Species such as *L. dentata* and *L. stoechas* are slightly tender and should be grown in a sheltered site.

✔ **Tree mallow**. *Lavatera* hybrids. Easy, fast growing, and long flowering, the drawback is that tree mallows tend to live only for several years. However, they're well worth growing for their masses of large flowers in shades of pink that can be borne from late spring right until the end of autumn. Prune hard in mid-spring. Plant in sun and well-drained soil.

✔ **Sacred bamboo.** *Nandina domestica*. Evergreen. Light and airy in appearance, sacred bamboo has divided leaves and the straight, erect stems of a small bamboo, but is much more ornamental. New growth is bronzy red when the plant is grown in full sun. The entire plant turns red in winter. White spring flowers turn into bright red berries. Grows 1.8–2.4 metres (6–8 feet) high, but dwarf forms are available, such as 'Fire Power', that grow to 90 centimetres (3 feet) high. Grow in a sheltered site.

✔ **New Zealand flax** (*Phormium*). Forming bold, upright clumps of sword-shaped leaves, New Zealand flax is a handsome architectural plant. You can get many varieties with leaves in different colours – bronze, purple, variegated, and multicoloured. Size ranges from 0.6–1.8 metres (2–6 feet). Plant in sun and fertile, well-drained soil.

✔ *Photinia x fraseri* '**Red Robin**'. Evergreen. A handsome foliage plant, the large young leaves are brilliant red, contrasting sharply with the dark green mature foliage. Plant in sun or light shade. Height 2.4 metres (8 feet).

✔ **Shrubby cinquefoil.** *Potentilla fruticosa.* Deciduous. Particularly valuable for its long flowering period, shrubby cinquefoil is a handsome little shrub with bright green, fine-textured foliage and colourful, wild-roselike flowers. Plants bloom from early summer into autumn in shades of red, yellow, orange, and white. Yellow varieties, such as 'Katherine Dykes', are most popular. Heights range from just under 60 centimetres (2 feet) up to 1.5 metres (5 feet). Plant in full sun.

✔ **Cherry laurel, Portuguese laurel.** *Prunus laurocerasus, P. lusitanica.* Tough, quick-growing, and hardy evergreens with white spring flowers and handsome foliage. Upright varieties are useful as tall screens, but their smaller varieties are more appropriate for borders and as tall ground cover. 'Zabeliana' and 'Otto Luyken' are compact forms that grow to around 1.2 metres (4 feet) high and wide. Plant in sun or shade.

✔ **Firethorn.** *Pyracantha* species. Evergreen. Colourful and dependable, firethorn comes in a wide range of forms, from low-growing spreading types to upright shrubs that you can train against a wall. All cover themselves with clusters of small, white flowers in spring followed by showy, yellow, orange, or red berries that last into autumn and winter. Branches are sharply thorned. Plant in sun or shade.

✔ **Azaleas and rhododendrons.** *Rhododendron* species. Evergreen and deciduous. This is a huge family of much-loved flowering shrubs. You can choose from many types, but all need acid soil in order to thrive. If your soil doesn't suit, you can grow compact varieties in containers in lime-free compost. In the garden, most rhododendrons and azaleas prefer moist, shady conditions and soil rich in organic matter. Some can take full sun, but most prefer a woodland environment of light, dappled shade.

Azaleas are generally lower-growing, compact plants that cover themselves with brightly coloured spring flowers in shades of pink, red, orange, yellow, purple, and white. Some are bicoloured. Rhododendrons generally have larger flower clusters. They come in the same colour range but in a wider range of sizes, from compact dwarfs to tall species and hybrids that can attain small-tree size in favourable locations.

✔ **Roses.** *Rosa* species. Deciduous. Many roses are outstanding garden shrubs. So many roses exist for so many garden situations, we've set aside an entire chapter for them, so skip to Chapter 10.

✔ **Sambucus.** The 'ornamental elders' are superb quick-growing foliage shrubs with colours that make wonderful contrasts to many flowering and foliage plants. Purple varieties (*S. nigra* 'Black Beauty' and 'Black Lace') have intense purple leaves and pink summer flowers; the leaves of 'Black Lace' are more deeply cut to give a ferny appearance. Most striking of the golden forms is *S. racemosa* 'Plumosa Aurea', with deeply cut golden foliage. Height and spread to 2.1 metres (7 feet). Prune in early spring to encourage vigorous, more brightly coloured leaves. Deciduous.

✔ **Cotton lavender** (*Santolina*). A useful small shrub for border edges and low hedges, cotton lavender has attractive, aromatic foliage in silver, grey, or green, and button-like flowers on slender stems in summer. Plant in full sun and in well-drained soil. Evergreen.

✔ **Spiraea.** *Spiraea* species. Deciduous. You have many types of spiraeas to choose from. Many are mounding, fountainlike shrubs with an abundance of tiny, white flowers in mid-spring to late spring. Included among these is the bridal wreath spiraea, *S. arguta,* which grows to about 1.5 metres (5 feet) high and wide. Other spiraeas, like *S. bumalda* 'Anthony Waterer', have clusters of pink-to-red blooms later in summer. Some are grown for their golden foliage, such as 'Firelight', 'Goldflame', 'Gold Mound' and 'Magic Carpet'. Plant spiraeas in full sun or part shade.

✔ **Common lilac.** *Syringa vulgaris.* Deciduous. Their season may be short, but wonderfully fragrant clusters of spring flowers make lilacs a favourite wherever they grow. Flower colours include shades of lavender, purple white, cream, and rosy pink. Plants usually grow 2.4–4.5 metres (8–15 feet) high and have dark green leaves. *Syringa microphylla* 'Superba' has rosy-pink flowers and is smaller, to about 1.5 metres (5 feet). Plant in full sun or light shade.

✔ **Viburnum.** *Viburnum* species. The viburnums represent a large family of evergreen and deciduous shrubs that are wonderful additions to the garden. They offer great variety and their ornamental characteristics include colourful flowers, brightly coloured berries, and sometimes evergreen foliage. Favourite evergreen types include the neat-growing *V. tinus*, which grows up to 3 metres (10 feet) and has white winter flowers. The variety 'Eve Price' is more compact, as is 'Variegatum', which has leaves coloured with white and creamy yellow, but is less hardy and needs a sheltered site. All make good unpruned hedges. *V. davidii* is a useful low evergreen that makes good, taller ground cover, with dark, ridged, evergreen leaves and clusters of white spring flowers. It sometimes produces turquoise-blue berries. Height 90 centimetres (3 feet).

Several of the deciduous types of viburnum bear large clusters of wonderfully fragrant flowers in spring and early summer. These include *V. burkwoodii, V. carlesii, V. x carlcephalum,*and *V. x juddii.* These grow from between 1.2 to 2.4 metres (4–8 feet) high. The horizontal-branching *V. plicatum* is also distinctive, with rows of white spring flowers and red autumn colour. It grows about 2.4 metres (8 feet) high.

Plant viburnums in full sun or partial shade.

Chapter 5

Lawns and Ground Covers

- -

In This Chapter

▶ Deciding on size and grass variety

▶ Making a lawn from seed

▶ Laying turf

▶ Taking care of your lawn

▶ Planting a meadow

▶ Choosing the right ground-cover plants

- -

*F*or most people, a garden isn't complete without at least some lawn. The lush colour and smooth, uniform look are a practical and attractive way to complement your home, garden features, and surrounding planting. Not a lot can beat a grassy area as a place for family and pets to relax and play. Many grasses can handle heavy foot traffic, and some even thrive in moderately shady areas, so lawns solve certain landscaping problems.

If foot traffic is not an issue, you may decide on an alternative surface instead of a traditional lawn. Ground-cover plants can offer your garden a natural look and are relatively low maintenance, while a meadow is a rewarding and easy-care alternative to part or all of a lawn.

This chapter guides you through the options and gives loads of helpful hints on maintaining your lawn so that it looks its best all year round.

Lawn Decisions

Do a little homework before you run down to the local garden centre and purchase a load of seed or turf. First, work out how much space you need for a lawn. Then determine which type of lawn you want to have – a fine 'bowling-green' type or just a tough utility lawn? Your final choice is whether to plant from seed or turf.

Size matters

If you have a newly built home and you're starting from scratch with the landscaping, think seriously about how much weekend time you want to spend pushing the lawn mower. Consider the costs of water, irrigation system, fertiliser, and perhaps paying someone to mow and maintain your grass. Although a large lawn may seem like an easy-care option, permanent plants such as shrubs and ground covers can be a better low-maintenance choice in the long term.

Seed vs turf

The most popular and certainly the cheapest way to make a lawn is to sow seed, but you need bucketloads of patience as you wait for several months before you can use the lawn. Proper soil preparation and follow-up care are the keys to success here.

The fastest way to put in a new lawn is by *laying turf* – like laying a carpet outside. The idea of an instant lawn certainly has its appeal, and is nearly always the best choice if you only want a small lawn. A turf lawn can be used within several weeks of laying, as soon as the grass has rooted down. However, turf is an expensive option, and you still have to prepare the soil thoroughly and maintain the newly planted area as carefully as you would a lawn from seed.

Preparing the Ground for a New Lawn

Regardless of whether you decide on seed or turf for your new lawn, ground preparation is all-important, particularly as your lawn will be a central feature of your garden for many years to come. Groundwork can be hard work, but bear in mind that it's easier and cheaper to sort out problems now, rather than trying to remedy them later. Ideally, allow at least a couple of months between starting to prepare the ground and sowing or turfing, in order to clear the ground of weeds and to give the soil time to settle. It's vital to clear every bit of *perennial* weed root – this term means these pesky weeds come back year after year.

Tackling weeds

Before digging, raking, or rotovating the soil, check the site for perennial weeds such as bindweed, dandelions, couch grass, and creeping buttercup. These annoying weeds regrow from tiny bits of root, so don't even think of running a rotovator over weedy ground or you'll get hundreds more plants to tackle! If your garden only has a few weeds, it doesn't take long to carefully dig them out by hand. If the problem is more widespread, spray with a systemic weedkiller and leave for several weeks to be sure the weeds have been killed (see Chapter 16 for more on tackling troublesome weeds).

Checking soil pH

The soil pH, or its level of acidity or alkalinity, is unlikely to need adjusting, but check just in case. Use a cheap and simple soil test kit, available from garden centres, to assess the level. If the soil is extremely acidic (below pH 5) you need to add lime to the soil and mix it in well. *Lime* (ground limestone) reduces the acidity of the soil; it comes in powdered form and you can buy it from your local garden centres.

Getting to grips with the ground

Follow these steps to get the ground in tiptop condition for your lawn:

1. **Dig over the area to around one spade's depth (about 30 centimetres) and remove any large stones.** A small area can be dug by hand, but otherwise hire a rotovator (available from tool-hire stores).

    You can improve light and free-draining soil by adding well-rotted organic matter such as compost or manure, which should be dug or rotovated in. Improve heavy, poorly drained clay soils by adding coarse grit to open out the soil structure and to aid drainage. If the ground is very poorly drained and becomes waterlogged on a frequent basis, get the professionals to put in a drainage system.

2. **Rake the soil so it's roughly level and leave the ground to settle for several weeks.** This process also allows annual weeds to germinate so you can kill them off at the seedling stage (using a hoe is easiest, done on a dry day so weeds die fast) and you can hoick out any surviving perennial weeds too.

    If the soil is very shallow (less than 15 centimetres, or 6 inches deep), you need to add topsoil to your existing soil. Spread the topsoil smoothly over the lawn area, mixing some of it in with the native soil below to prevent a water barrier. Make the topsoil layer 2.5 centimetres (1 inch) below the final level of the lawn if you're installing turf, or 1 centimetre (½ inch) centimetre below if you're sowing seed. Make sure that the soil for the lawn area slopes slightly away from the house for proper drainage.

3. **When the soil is reasonably dry and workable, tread over the whole area to ensure that the soil is firm all over.** For a large lawn, use a roller or a wheel, as in Figure 5-1. For a smaller lawn, rope in your family and friends to spend an hour or so marching over the ground, weight on the heels. (This method is guaranteed to raise a laugh and is great for entertaining the neighbours.)

4. **Rake the ground to ensure it's absolutely level, repeating the treading process if necessary.** Your soil must have no bumps or hollows, and have a fine crumb texture. (If you're tempted to skimp on the levelling, just imagine the hassle of mowing a bumpy lawn later.)

5. **A few days before you lay the lawn, apply a general fertiliser and rake it over the soil very lightly.** After all this hard graft, you're ready to sow or turf your new lawn!

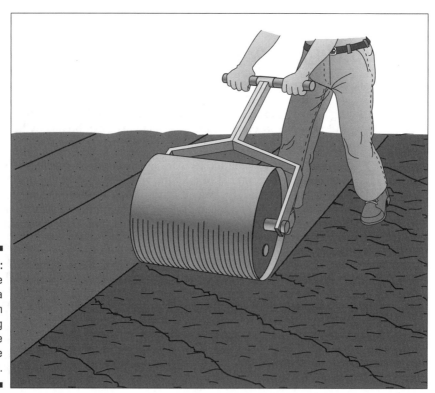

Figure 5-1:
For a large
lawn, use a
roller to firm
the planting
surface
before
seeding.

Going to Seed: Making a Lawn from Seed

To choose the right grass seed for your lawn, think about how much wear and tear your grass will get; the site and soil conditions; and how much time you want to spend on maintenance. 'Bowling-green' type lawns may look gorgeous, but they need one heck of a lot of work and can't be used a great deal into the bargain. Most people need practical lawns, so choose a seed mix containing some hard-wearing grass such as rye grass.

Working out how much seed you need

To determine how much seed you need to purchase, start with a pretty close estimate of the size of the area you aim to plant. For example, if you have a rectangular lawn area measuring 6 x 15 metres (20 x 50 feet), you have a 90-square-metre (1,000-square-foot) area. You can measure the area of an irregularly shaped patch by dividing it into separate shapes and then adding them all together at the end.

Measure with your stride: An adult stride is usually around 1 metre (3 feet). Measure your stride with a yardstick until you know what a 1-metre (3-foot) stride feels like before heading out onto your lawn.

The label on the grass seed specifies the coverage.

Sowing your seed

Autumn is the best time of year to sow lawn seed, when the soil is still warm from the summer yet moist from autumn rains. The next best time to sow is spring, although the soil is colder then and so the grass won't grow so readily. You can sow seed in summer provided that you can keep the soil moist using a sprinkler.

Follow the steps below to sow your seed.

1. **Spread seed by hand, or with a drop spreader or a hand-held broadcast spreader, as shown in Figure 5-2.** Small, basic spreaders aren't expensive to buy. If you're tackling a large area, hiring a good-sized machine is a better bet.

   Don't be tempted to oversow; if you do, the grass won't develop properly. Although a mechanical spreader helps spread the seed uniformly, spreading seeds by hand is also practical, especially with larger seeds, such as ryes and fescues. Whichever way you spread the seed, coverage is more even if you apply half the seed moving in one direction across the lawn area, and the other half moving in the opposite direction.

Figure 5-2:
Using a drop
spreader or
a hand-held
broadcast
spreader to
sow seed.

2. **Rake the surface lightly, barely covering about half the seed and leaving the rest exposed.** Birds love a meal of lawn seed, so keep them off with a few homemade bird scarers of strips of foil fluttering from canes. You can cover a small area of lawn with netting or twiggy prunings (but this option isn't practical on a larger scale).

3. **Give the newly seeded area a thorough initial soaking with a hose or sprinkler, shown in Figure 5-3, and then keep it well watered until the grass is established.**

   Water more deeply but less frequently as the grass becomes more established. Each watering should penetrate the soil to a depth of several inches to promote good root growth.

When the grass reaches a height of around 5 centimetres (2 inches), you can give it its first cut. Aim to remove just the tips of the grass to encourage bushy growth, taking the grass no lower than 2.5 centimetres (1 inch). A newly seeded lawn is vulnerable to wear and tear, so use it as little as possible during the first few months.

Figure 5-3:
Giving the
newly
seeded
ground a
good
soaking.

Making a Lawn from Turf

Turf has two important advantages over seed: The results are immediate and, climate and aftercare permitting, you can get away with laying turf almost any time of year. However, for the best results and the minimum of aftercare, lay turf either in early to mid-spring or in early autumn. At these times of year the grass grows strongly enough to establish and put down roots quickly, and the weather should be warm with a reasonable amount of rain. You can lay turf in summer, but regular watering is absolutely essential – you must never allow the turf to dry out. In very mild areas, you can even lay turf in the middle of winter.

Buying turf

Turf is expensive, so buy from a quality supplier. Inspect samples of turf before ordering, and also check the quality when your load is delivered. Look for turves about 2–3 centimetres (1 inch) thick, free from weeds, and with no brown patches or dried-out edges.

Have the turf delivered on planting day so that it doesn't sit in a pile and heat up (a stack of fresh turf literally cooks itself to death, just like a compost pile). Keep the turf covered or in a shady location until you plant it to prevent it from drying out. If you have to leave the turf for more than a couple of days, unroll the turves (grass-side up, at the risk of stating the blindingly obvious!) on a paved surface or plastic sheeting – not earth, as the turves would start to root. Keep well watered.

Laying turf

To lay turf you need:

- ✔ Rake
- ✔ Wooden plank
- ✔ Large, old knife or half-moon edger
- ✔ Lawn roller (for large areas)
- ✔ Sieved mix of 50:50 sieved soil and sand
- ✔ Stiff broom
- ✔ Hose with sprinkler attachment or lawn sprinkler

Follow these instructions for laying turf:

1. **Roll out a piece of turf and press it into position.** Fit the next section against it tightly but don't overlap, as shown in Figure 5-4.

Figure 5-4:
Roll out turf so the pieces don't overlap.

2. **Continue laying sections, staggering them slightly like bricks.**

Lay a wooden plank across the turf to spread your weight and avoid damaging the turves, as shown in Figure 5-5. Trim odd-shaped sections with a heavy utility knife or half-moon edger, as shown in Figure 5-6, and fill gaps with small cut sections, as shown in Figure 5-7.

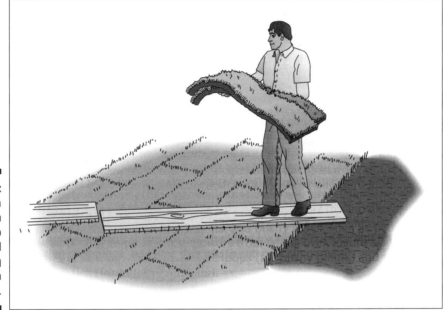

Figure 5-5:
Use a wooden plank to avoid damaging the fresh turf.

Figure 5-6:
Trim turf with a knife until it fits curves, odd shapes, and around obstacles.

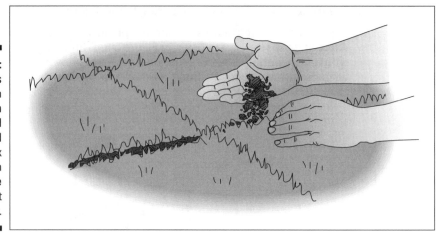

Figure 5-7:
Fill in gaps
between
turves with
the sieved
soil and
sand mix
which
ensures the
turves knit
together.

3. **Use the back of a rake to tamp down the turf to get rid of any air pockets underneath.** Use a roller for large areas (the roller on the back of a mower is fine to use too).

4. **Where the turves join, spread a thin layer of the soil and sand mix and brush into any cracks.** This helps the turves knit together quickly.

5. **Water thoroughly, and keep the soil moist until the turf is well established.**

Keeping Your Lawn Happy

It's no secret that your lawn requires some regular maintenance to keep it looking its best. Basic lawn care consists of weeding, mowing, and fertilising. Take care of those things and you may avoid more complex chores like pest and disease control. The following sections give you some tips on performing the basics.

Weeding

The best technique for keeping weeds under control in your lawn is to grow the right kind of grass and take good care of it. Weeds can't get established in a thick patch of healthy turf.

If you want to yank out the prime offenders, you can find tools for this purpose at most garden centres. But you don't need to be obsessive – a few weeds won't spoil the overall look or purpose of the lawn, and a stretch of daisy-spangled turf has a charm all of its own.

Garden centres offer an array of weedkillers, sometimes mixed with fertilisers, that you can spray or spread over your lawn. However, spreading chemicals on a lawn where children or pets roll about and play may not appeal to you. See Chapter 16 for more about weeds and herbicides.

Mowing

The lawnmowers available today make the inevitable task of mowing the lawn easier and more enjoyable. If you're in the market for a new mower, read about some of your options in Chapter 17.

Here are some tips to keep your grass healthy:

- Mow regularly from spring to autumn. Letting the lawn grow long and then chopping it down all at once weakens it.

- Mow in winter if the grass is long, but only when the grass is dry and free from frost. Go over the lawn first with a stiff broom to scatter the little earthy casts that worms deposit, then set the mower blades high.

- Mow when the grass is dry. If you mow when the grass is wet it's likely to get torn and ragged.

- Mow in a different direction each time – north–south one week, east–west the next. You can even mow at a diagonal. Changing the mowing pattern prevents uneven soil compaction and helps the grass grow upright.

- Remove the clippings (they're great for compost heaps and mulching). If left on the lawn, clippings clog up the lawn surface and can encourage disease problems.

- Don't cut long grass in one go. Take it down in two or three cuts, starting with the mower blades at their highest setting and then reducing the height of the cut down to normal.

- Never cut the grass really short to try to stretch out the time between mowings. You weaken the grass and give an open invitation to weeds.

Fertilising

Fertilising lawns is a whole science, and you really don't need to know much about it unless you're the head greenskeeper at St Andrews golf course – in which case, we're surprised and flattered that you're reading this book. All you need to know is that your lawn needs a spot of lunch twice a year, in spring and in autumn. Some gardeners are reluctant to fertilise, thinking that the grass will grow even faster and need mowing more often. Bad move. A well-fertilised lawn is healthier, denser, and more weed free than a poorly managed one, so you save work in the long run.

When buying fertiliser, simply look for one that's suited to the time of year you feed your lawn. Always stick to the right fertiliser for the right season. Never use a spring fertiliser in autumn, for example, as you encourage lots of lush growth that frost is likely to damage. Most lawn fertilisers are helpfully labelled, for example 'spring lawn feed', so choosing the right one is pretty easy. Many fertilisers also include weedkiller or mosskiller, so check the small print to make sure you're buying what you want.

Read the label directions for how much to apply. You can use a fertiliser spreader (they're pretty cheap) to get an even application, or your lawn may end up patchy.

For more detail about fertilisers, see Chapter 14.

Watering

Unless you're hooked on the idea of a velvety green lawn, you don't need to bother watering your lawn. A hard-wearing utility lawn is surprisingly resilient to drought, and although the grass goes brown during long, dry spells, it greens up really quickly after rain. With many people on water meters, and with water becoming increasingly scarce too, don't waste it on the lawn – save it for thirsty plants instead. The only type of lawn that does need regular watering is one made of fine grasses.

Tune-ups and face-lifts

You've got too many thin spots, weeds have got the upper hand, or the wrong type of grass is struggling to survive: What do you do? Relax. This section offers solutions to some common lawn problems.

Bare patches and thin lawns

As long as your lawn is at least 50 per cent grass (as opposed to weeds), you can give it a face-lift by seeding right on top. The process is called *overseeding* and is best done in autumn or, failing that, spring.

1. **Mow your lawn closely and thoroughly rake out the mat of dead grass and stems called *thatch*.** Fertilise the lawn if you haven't already done so that season.

2. **Sow seed at the rate recommended on the package.**

3. **Sprinkle a light layer of sieved soil mixed with equal parts of sharp sand over the lawn.** This mixture is called *topdressing* and you can buy it in large bags if you don't want to bother mixing your own.

4. **Water thoroughly.**

Alternative surfaces

If you have a small garden, or if the thought of maintaining a lawn really doesn't appeal, you have plenty of other options. Hard surfaces like paving or decking may be costly to install but need very little care. For a more informal look (and cheaper too), you have a choice of gravel, stone chippings, slate, smooth glass, chipped bark, and even coloured rubber mulches. When you lay any of these loose layered materials, always use a thick landscaping fabric to prevent the stones mixing with the earth beneath, and to prevent weeds growing through.

Bumps and hollows

These are a nuisance when mowing: Hollows fill with coarse, uncut grass, and the mower scalps bumps. Use a spade to cut under the affected area, roll back the turf, then add or take away soil until the level is correct.

Moss and drainage problems

Lawns get trampled on, year in, year out, so it's no wonder that the surface becomes compacted, resulting in less air getting to the grass roots and water draining away too slowly. *Aerate* your lawn if you notice water lying for a while on the lawn after rain. (Puddles = no air = dead grass = lots of moss.)

To aerate your lawn, insert a digging fork into the lawn right up to the top of its tines. Rock it backwards and forwards to enlarge the holes and repeat in a line, making each line about 15 centimetres (6 inches) apart. If you have a large lawn you can hire or buy a *coring machine* to take out plugs of soil. To make a really pukka job of your lawn drainage, brush sharp sand into the holes so that you end up with a honeycomb of little drainage channels.

Don't simply treat your lawn with a mosskiller without improving the drainage – you need to tackle the cause, not treat the symptom! Aerate your lawn every couple of years whether you have drainage problems or not.

Going for Ground Covers

Perhaps you don't want a lawn, maybe you have an area too shady for grass, or possibly you want something in addition to lawn. You may be considering a lawn alternative for one of many reasons. That's where ground-cover plants come in. *Ground covers* (low-growing, spreading plants) come in many varieties, and they fill in enough to give solid coverage when you plant them close together. Some ground covers are less demanding than lawns, but others aren't as tough or as forgiving as a lawn. And you can't walk or play on a ground cover like you can a lawn.

Ground covers range from very low-growing plants that are just a few inches high to more shrubby types that are several feet high. Some of the lowest-growing ground covers, such as chamomile and creeping thyme, can take a little foot traffic; you can plant these types between stepping-stones or in other areas where people occasionally walk.

Ground covers have an artistic side, too. You can create a nearly infinite variety of contrasts with ground covers, and you can mix in other shrubs, vines, annuals, and perennials for a variety of effects. Foliage textures range from grassy to tropically bold, and colours range from subtle shades of grey to vibrant seasonal colours. Ground covers provide a natural appearance, so look to your local wild areas for ideas. Choose plants that mimic what you see in wooded areas, in unmown fields, in meadows, or on steep slopes.

Planting and caring for ground covers

The spacing between ground-cover plants is very important. If you space the plants too far apart, they take a long time to fill in, which gives weeds more time to gain a foothold. If you plant them too close together, the plants can quickly become overcrowded. We include recommended plant spacings in the plant descriptions later in this chapter. For best results, plant ground covers in rows. Staggering the rows gives even more complete coverage.

As with all plantings, you need to attend to soil needs (see Chapter 11) before introducing your plants to your landscape. Newly set-out plants need adequate watering to help get established; after the plants are growing well, many types need only minimum maintenance.

 If you're planting a ground-cover plant on a steep slope, set the plant on its own terrace (with the top of the rootball slightly above the soil level) and make a hollow or sink an empty pot into the ground behind the plant to create a watering basin.

Control weeds between plants until the ground cover is established. We like to use an organic mulch or, for shrubby ground covers, *planting membrane* (also known as *landscape fabric*, see Chapter 16) to control weeds. Planting membrane is also excellent on slopes, to prevent soil being washed away. An occasional cutback can rejuvenate or freshen up many spreading, non-woody ground covers such as ivy and periwinkle. Cut the plants back to just several inches above the ground in spring and then fertilise them. Within a few weeks, the plants regrow and look full, clean, and healthy. You can use shears, a brushcutter, or a strimmer for this job.

Top ground-cover choices

The following common ground-cover plants are tough and easy to grow, given their preferred site and soil requirements.

✔ **Bugle.** *Ajuga reptans.* Evergreen. This plant forms a low-growing, spreading ground cover with attractive dark green or purplish-green foliage reaching 5–15 centimetres (2–6 inches) high. Bugle has blue flowers in summer. Plant in partial to full shade (some types with coloured foliage do best given some sun), 15–30 centimetres (6–12 inches) apart.

✔ **Chamomile.** *Chamaemelum nobile.* Chamomile has fine-textured, aromatic evergreen foliage and small yellow flowers in summer. Chamomile stays low and compact in full sun, rarely getting over 15 centimetres (6 inches) high. You can mow chamomile or plant it between stepping-stones. Plant in full sun, spacing plants about 15–30 centimetres (6–12 inches) apart.

✔ **Cotoneasters.** *Cotoneaster.* Deciduous or evergreen. Cotoneasters are a large family of shrubs that includes many dependable ground covers known for their bright-green foliage, small flowers, and red berries. Favourites include the evergreen bearberry cotoneaster, *C. dammeri* (which grows only 20 centimetres or 8 inches high and spreads up to 3 metres, or 10 feet); the deciduous rock cotoneaster, *C. horizontalis* (which grows 60–90 centimetres, or 2–3 feet, high and has orange-to-red autumn colour); and the evergreen rockspray cotoneaster, *C. microphyllus* (which rarely exceeds 60–90 centimetres, or 2–3 feet, in height). Plant at least 90 centimetres (3 feet) apart in full sun. (Some of the widest-spreading types should be spaced 1.5 metres, or 5 feet, apart.)

✔ *Euonymus fortunei.* This very hardy, evergreen plant comes in many fine ground-cover varieties. 'Colorata' has bright green foliage that turns purple in autumn and winter. 'Emerald Gaiety' has green and white leaves that become pink-tinged in winter. 'Emerald 'n' Gold' has bright gold and green foliage. All these varieties grow about 61 centimetres (2 feet) high. 'Kewensis' grows only 5 centimetres (2 inches) high and makes a very dense ground cover. Plant in sun or shade, spacing the plants from 30–90 centimetres (1–3 feet) apart.

✔ **Blue fescue.** *Festuca glauca.* Silver-blue foliage highlights this mounding, grassy ground cover. It grows 10–25 centimetres (4–10 inches) high and gets by on little water. Plant in full sun, spacing the plants 15–30 centimetres (6–12 inches) apart.

✔ **Ivy.** *Hedera helix.* With its dark green, lobed leaves, English ivy is one of the most popular ground covers. This evergreen grows well under many conditions, including sun or shade. Many varieties (differing in leaf size, texture, and colour) are available. Ivy can be invasive, climbing into trees and over structures if not kept under control. Space plants 30–45 centimetres (12–18 inches) apart.

- ✔ **Junipers.** *Juniperus.* Many prostrate junipers (differing in height and foliage colour) are available. Junipers are tough, evergreen plants that get by with little care but must have well-drained soil. *J. chinensis* 'San Jose' has greyish-green leaves and grows 60 centimetres (2 feet) high. *J. horizontalis* 'Bar Harbor' grows about 30 centimetres (1 foot) high and spreads up to 3 metres (10 feet); the grey-green leaves turn bluish in winter. *J. h.* 'Wiltonii' is only 15 centimetres (6 inches) high and has silver-blue foliage. Plant junipers in full sun. Space most 60 –150 centimetres (2–5 feet) apart, depending on the variety.

- ✔ **Lily turf.** *Liriope muscari.* A grasslike plant makes attractive evergreen ground covers in shady situations. *L. muscari* grows up to 60 centimetres (2 feet) high and has purple late summer flowers that are partially hidden by the foliage. Some varieties have variegated leaves. Space these plants 15–20 centimetres (6–9 inches) apart.

- ✔ **Japanese spurge.** *Pachysandra terminalis.* Japanese spurge is an attractive spreading, foliage plant for shady, moist conditions. This evergreen features rich green leaves on upright 25-centimetre (10-inch) stems, with fragrant white flowers in summer. Plant in partial to full shade and space them 15–30 centimetres (6–12 inches) apart.

- ✔ **Creeping thyme.** *Thymus serpyllum.* This low-growing, creeping evergreen herb is especially useful between stepping-stones. It can take foot traffic and can even be grown as a lawn alternative. Creeping thyme grows 8–15 centimetres (3–6 inches) high and has white-to-pink flowers in summer. Plant in full sun and space the plants 15 centimetres (6 inches) apart.

- ✔ **Lesser periwinkle.** *Vinca minor.* This spreading, evergreen ground cover is good for shady conditions. It grows from 15–30 centimetres (6–12 inches) high and has violet-blue flowers in spring. You can find white and purple-flowered varieties, and some with variegated foliage. Space the plants 30 centimetres (12 inches) apart.

Musing on Meadows

Instead of a grass lawn or ground-cover plants, consider using native wild flowers to create a natural-looking meadow, or drifts of perennials and ornamental grasses to form a 'prairie' planting. You get masses of beautiful flowers for months, spend far less time on mowing, and provide a much-needed haven for insects and wild creatures, which are losing their habitats to development and intensive farming.

If you have a large garden, try creating more than one of the meadows below to give colour from spring to autumn. You can always retain an area of close-mown lawn near to the house for sitting out, as well as making mown grass paths that meander through the flowers.

Wildflower meadows

To be of greatest benefit to wildlife, use a good proportion of native flowers, because the insects in your area have evolved to feed and breed on native plants. The delicate beauty of butterflies and the soothing hum of bees are part and parcel of the enjoyment you get from your meadow, and even those less welcome insects like aphids have their uses in providing food for birds.

Make a note of the mowing regime that each type of meadow requires as detailed below, because cutting at the right time is crucial to success, allowing the plants to bloom unhindered by long grass and then set seed for next year. Always take away the clippings to avoid smothering the flowers and raising soil nutrient levels, which encourages lush grass growth at the expense of flowers.

Your meadow can contain many different types of bulbs, annuals, and perennial flowers, so long as they look natural enough to be in keeping with the meadow environment.

Show off your meadow at its best by regularly mowing grass paths and any adjacent lawn area to create a sharp and attractive contrast between long and short grass. It also shows that your meadow is intentional, rather than somewhere you've not got round to cutting, and you avoid awkward questions about whether the owner of the house has died recently!

Spring meadows

The freshness of spring flowers looks enchanting against a backdrop of vivid green, just-opening leaves. A spring meadow is ideal if you want to have a good-sized area of grass that's useable for the summer; for children to play on, for example. Once the flowers have set seed, mow the area from around late June to mid July onwards.

Wild daffodils (*Narcissus pseudonarcissus*) and pools of azure bluebells (*Hyacinthoides non-scripta*) spangled with gleaming white greater stitchwort (*Stellaria holostea*) are a delight; clumps of golden cowslips (*Primula veris*) and blue self-heal (*Prunella vulgaris*) thrive in sun; and for damp soil use elegant snake's head fritillaries (*Fritillaria meleagris*) with their chequered flowers alongside deep pink ragged robin (*Lychnis flos-cuculi*) and paler lady's smock (*Cardamine pratensis*).

Summer meadows

The tangled, glorious abundance of a summer meadow comes alive with butterflies and insects during the day, and takes on an ethereal beauty in the early morning and evening when lit by the low rays of the sun. Grasses look surprisingly lovely when in flower and provide the perfect foil for masses of colourful blooms. These include greater knapweed (*Centaurea scaboisa*), lady's bedstraw (*Galium verum*), field scabious (*Knautia arvensis*), oxeye daisy (*Leucanthemum vulgare*), yarrow (*Achillea millefolium*), and musk mallow (*Malva moschata*). Mow your summer meadow occasionally in spring until late May or early June, then cut again in autumn around late September or early October when flowering has finished.

Converting a Lawn to a Meadow

You need a couple of years to change from a lawn to a meadow if the soil is rich and the grass is fertilised. In such a situation the grasses thrive so well that they would outperform all but the strongest wild flowers.

The slow and easy way to convert your lawn to a meadow is to stop applying fertiliser and to cut the lawn regularly, taking away the clippings so that they don't rot down and return nutrients to the soil. After a year or so the grass won't grow so strongly and you can plant pot-grown or plug wild flowers.

A quicker but tougher way to create a meadow is to strip off the turf along with the top 5–8 centimetres (2–3 inches) of soil. You can do the job yourself, by hiring a turf-stripping machine that quickly cuts and lifts the turf, or get a contractor in. Never throw away the turf, but stack it in a heap, grass-side down, where it will rot down in a year or so to make wonderful crumbly topsoil.

Preparing soil for meadow planting

Lowering soil fertility is important when preparing bare soil, unless the ground is already poor, stony, or sandy. A useful way to do this is by growing a crop of hungry vegetables such as potatoes or cabbages, which uses up a good proportion of the soil nutrients (but not beans or peas, which add nitrogen to the soil). Most importantly, get rid of existing weeds that would smother the slower-growing wild flowers, particularly perennial weeds such as bindweed and ground elder. You can kill all weeds using a systemic weed-killer while plants are in active growth, then lightly dig over the ground after several weeks once the weeds are dead. Alternatively you can dig over the ground and remove all the roots of perennial weeds.

Rake the soil to break down lumps, and level the ground ready for sowing. In both cases it's worth delaying sowing for several weeks after cultivating the soil so that weed seeds can germinate and you can hoe them off while they're small.

Sowing meadow seed

Most meadow seed mixtures are a blend of grasses, quick-growing annual flowers such as field poppy (*Papaver rhoeas*), corn marigold (*Chrysanthemum segatum*), and corncockle (*Agrostemma githago*), and perennial wild flowers. The ideal time to sow is late summer to early autumn, soon after rain when the soil is still moist. Raise more choice and delicate plants, like cowslips, in pots and plant them out rather than sow direct.

Either buy a pelleted 'throw and sow' seed mix, or blend ordinary seed with four times its volume of sand, to ensure an even distribution of fine seed. Broadcast the seed evenly and rake very lightly to cover with a thin layer of soil. Water during dry spells of weather until the seed germinates.

Yee-hah! Prairie Planting

Also known as a modern meadow or a natural herbaceous border, *prairie planting* unites the naturalistic style of planting popular in some European countries with the natural prairie planting of North America, to create a tapestry of summer and autumn colour. Plant tough and easily grown perennials and ornamental grasses in clumps or drifts to look as natural as possible, achieved by repeat planting of the same varieties in informal groups.

A wide range of perennials and grasses is suitable for prairie gardens. You can include bulbs and hardy annuals for colour in spring and early summer; but you need to cut down and clear the border in late winter so as not to damage the growth of these earlier blooms.

Choose prairie plants with a natural look that thrive on neglect. Our favourite plants include:

 ✔ Ornamental grasses: *Calamagrostis x acutiflora, Deschampsia x cespitosa, Helictotrichon sempervirens, Miscanthus sinensis, Stipa tenuissima.*

 ✔ Perennials: *Achillea, Aster latifolius, Echinacea purpurea, Helianthus, Helenium, Salvia x sylvestris, Solidago.*

After plants are established and weeds kept down in the first couple of years, your prairie requires little maintenance. Your chief job is the mass cutting down of all plant growth during the dormant season, which you need to do in late winter to early spring in order to enjoy the dramatic effects of frost on the dead foliage and flowers, and so that beneficial insects have somewhere to hibernate. A brushcutter makes light work of a large area. You can clean out dead foliage of ornamental grasses using a rake. Later in spring, hoe out any unwanted self-sown seedlings to avoid the more vigorous plants becoming dominant over others.

Chapter 6

Climbers and Wall Shrubs

· ·

In This Chapter

▶ Understanding how climbers work . . . and work for you

▶ Getting to know some climbing dos and don'ts

▶ Providing necessary support

▶ Looking at our favourite climbers

▶ Exploring a few annual climbers

· ·

Climbers are fantastic plants that give us the chance to garden upwards into a whole new dimension. Every garden has a wealth of vertical surfaces such as walls and fences, trellises and screens, plus all kinds of decorative garden features can be clothed with climbers, like pergolas, arbours, arches, and obelisks. And you can get even more bangs for your buck by festooning colourful climbers through big plants such as trees and shrubs.

If your garden is tiny, you can grow plants upwards. If your garden is chockfull of plants but, addicted, you want more – grow up. If you need privacy from prying eyes, a cover-up for an ugly building, or a sheltered screen from the wind – grow up. The versatility of climbers is well-nigh endless.

In this chapter, we help you understand how climbers work and how to put them to work for you. We also share some of our favourite climbers – permanent types as well as fast-growing annuals.

Playing Twister

All climbers need to grow on something, be it a wall, fence, trellis, arch, or another plant. Before deciding what kind of support to provide for your favourite climbers, you need to know exactly how the climbers hold on. Plants divide into several groups, according to the way they climb, as shown in Figure 6-1.

✔ **Self-clinging climbers.** These plants are the Spidermen of the plant world, securing themselves by using the aerial roots or little suckers along their stems that can cling onto any surface they touch. Examples are ivy and Virginia creeper.

✔ **Twining climbers.** These plants have stems that spiral upwards. You need to grow them on wires, set vertically or in a fan shape, on trellis, or through established plants. Twining plants include Actinidia, golden hop (*Humulus*), honeysuckles (*Lonicera*), jasmine, and wisteria.

✔ **Winding tendrils or leaf stalks.** These plants need closely spaced trellis, mesh, or wires to scramble up, hand over hand. They're also ideal for growing through other plants. This group includes clematis, passion flower (*Passiflora*), sweet peas, and vines (*Vitis*).

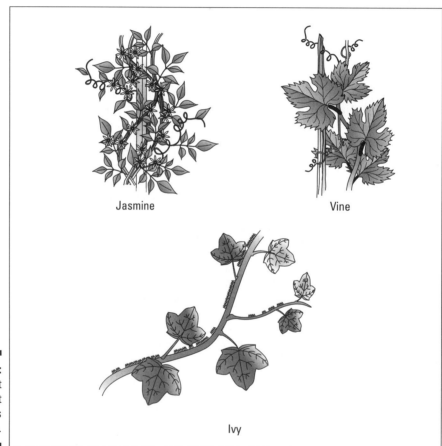

Jasmine

Vine

Ivy

Figure 6-1: Different ways that climbers attach.

Two more types of plant you can use in a similar way to climbers are:

- ✔ **Sprawling plants.** In the wild these plants would naturally scramble up through trees and hedgerows; you can let them perform similarly in the garden or train them on trellis or wires. An example is a climbing rose that has long, sprawling stems.

- ✔ **Wall shrubs.** Such shrubs are naturally upright in habit, but are best supported against a wall, fence, or trellis. Depending on how neat you like your plants, you can prune the outward-growing stems to keep the plant growing closely against its support. Examples include *Chaenomeles* and *Pyracantha*, and we cover these plants in Chapter 4.

Advice for Climbers

Like other plant groups, climbers offer a variety of ornamental characteristics, including seasonal flower colour, evergreen foliage, bright berries, and autumn colour. And, like other plants, different varieties of climber have distinct preferences for sun or shade. Only a couple are tough, go-anywhere plants. The influence of sun or shade is most pronounced in sites like on house walls and high fences, so it's really important to match the right plant to the right place. You'll find our favourite climbers are marked with their preferences for full sun, partial shade, or shade.

- ✔ **Full sun.** A south or south-west facing site is hottest of all, and indeed a wall will have a storage-heater effect, making it possible to grow a slightly tender plant that is likely to die if grown just a few metres out in the garden.

- ✔ **Partial shade.** A site that faces east, south-east, or west, which receives sun for only part of the day.

- ✔ **Shade.** A north-facing site that gets no sun at all.

Because of their rapid growth rate and the way they attach to structures, some climbers have the potential to cause problems as they mature. The following sections give you tips on avoiding problems with climbers.

Don't let climbers grow where they shouldn't

Self-clinging climbers, particularly ivy and Virginia creeper, attach firmly to walls. This is fine where the brickwork and mortar are sound, but keep plant growth trimmed away from roof tiles, drainpipes, and paintwork. Avoid planting self-clingers on a wall where the brick, stone, or cement is starting to crumble, because the plant growth speeds deterioration. Avoid planting self-clinging climbers on fences, because the stems force their way through slats or planks and eventually cause damage.

Provide sturdy support

As climbers grow, the branches enlarge, and the plant gets heavier. If the supports aren't strong enough, they can buckle under the weight. Build supports that are sturdy and long-lasting. (See the section 'Lean on Me: Choosing a Support and Plants to Match' later in this chapter for more information.)

Prepare the ground

Thorough soil preparation is even more important for climbers than for other plants because they have only a small area of ground from which to support lots of growth. Make sure you add loads of organic matter to the soil next to walls, as the ground here is drier and poorer than elsewhere (see Chapter 11).

Prune for healthy plants

Pruning prevents climbers from getting out of control, becoming too heavy, or growing into places where they're not wanted. (For more information on pruning, see Chapter 15.)

The timing of your pruning is important to get the best from your plants, but bear in mind that you can prune in any season to keep a rampant plant in check. The time to prune flowering climbers is dictated by when they bloom. Prune those that flower in spring or early summer immediately after the plants drop their blooms, whereas with those that flower later in the season you prune in early spring.

Wisteria is an exception; prune in mid-summer by shortening side shoots to 5–6 buds from the main stem, and again in mid-winter by further shortening these shoots to 2–3 buds. The best time to do your major pruning of vigorous-growing fruiting plants, such as grapes and kiwi, is during their dormant season (winter). But you can nip back plants of any kind whenever they begin to grow out of the bounds that you set for them.

Lean on Me: Choosing a Support and Plants to Match

You have many ways to support a climber, from pergolas to trellises to wires strung between secure anchors. The important thing is to plan the supporting device in advance, make it strong, and design it to fit the growth habit of the climber.

Heavy fences or the walls of outbuildings are another place to plant climbers, and these supports require little work from you. You can also choose trellises, obelisks, and other special supports for vines.

Although the chief purpose of supports is to hold up climbing plants, trellises and their kin also add height to the garden and maximise ground space. These structures can be decorative, as well as practical, when they turn a plain wall into a vertical garden, frame a view, or create a privacy screen.

The most important guideline for choosing a structure is that it is large and sturdy enough to support the plant when fully grown. Choose a simple garden structure that harmonises with your home and existing garden features. And remember that some climbing plants naturally cling to their supports, but others must be trained and tied.

Recycled nylon tights or stockings, cut into strips, make one of the very best materials for tying plants to their supports. Nylons are strong yet stretchy, so they don't bind and cut plant stems.

You can grow most types of climbers on one or more of the supports described here. (The exception is self-clinging climbers, which grow best on stone or brick walls.) When choosing a support for your garden, first consider the type of plant that you're growing and how it will fit and look on the structure. After that, your choice is a matter of personal taste, maintenance considerations, and budget. (See Figure 6-2.)

Wire and trellis supports

Walls and fences tend to be the first places in the garden to be clothed with climbers simply because, as climbers say about Mount Everest, they're there. All climbing plants, apart from self-clingers, require some form of support, and the main choice is between wire or trellis.

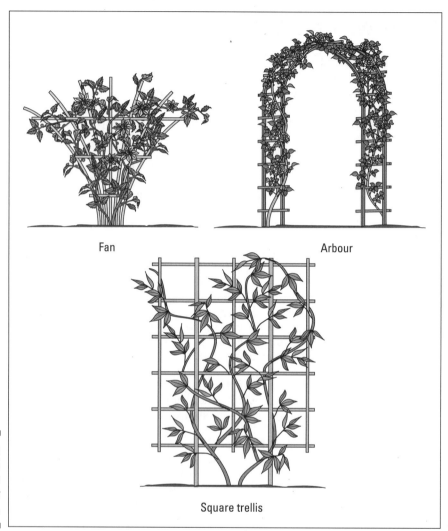

Fan

Arbour

Square trellis

Figure 6-2:
You can find
a trellis to
suit every
need.

You can create a sturdy support system with galvanised wire, which you can buy from your local garden or DIY shop. Follow these steps:

1. **Attach vine eyes (screws with an 'eye' at the end) to the wall or to fence posts, and then thread stout galvanised wire through the holes.** Don't use thin green garden wire, because it's not strong enough.

2. **Arrange the wires horizontally, vertically, or in a fan shape, depending on the space and the plant you're growing.** If you use horizontal wires on a brick wall, run them parallel with the mortar so they won't be very visible.

A wire system is sturdy and supports heavy climbers like roses and wisteria. Another, although less versatile, alternative is simply to attach *plant ties* (any flexible material used for tying plants – your nursery sells several types) through the screws, and eliminate the wires.

Trellis is a decorative form of support, but more expensive than wire. Just how much more expensive depends on the design and material of trellis you choose. The less substantial, squared trellis is fairly economical (and you can give it a very classy look by treating the wood with a smart, colourful wood stain), while chunky lattice trellis is more expensive. Avoid using flimsy, plastic-coated wire trellis. You can also buy trellis made from recycled plastic, which looks less natural but has the great bonus of not having to be stained or treated.

Whichever trellis you use, space the trellis 5–10 centimetres (2–4 inches) away from the wall or fence so that the plant has room to grow. Use wooden battens or blocks as spacers between the wall and trellis. On a house wall, take care that the trellis doesn't go below the level of the damp-proof course.

You can add a section of trellis to the top of a wall or fence to create privacy and more growing space for plants. This top trellis is up there in the wind, so fix it firmly, using posts at least 7.5 centimetres (3 inches) square that extend a good way down the wall, or even right into the ground.

 Fasten the trellis panels to hinges at the bottom so that you can lay the trellis back for easy access to the wall in case you need to paint it. Use metal hooks and eyes to attach the trellis to the wall at the top. Many climbers, including star jasmine (*Trachelospermum jasminoides*) and winter jasmine (*Jasminum nudiflorum*), are flexible enough to bend as you raise and lower the trellis.

Fan trellises

Made from wood or plastic, shop-bought fan trellises come in many sizes. Each fan trellis generally supports a single climber. You can use fan trellises in much the same way as you would use a standard trellis panel. A fan trellis also can support a climber in a container. Secure the fan trellis to the inside of the container, or wedge it in using a couple of bricks. In a large container you can grow a permanent climber that stays fairly compact, such as one of the many patio clematis or a miniature climbing rose, or annual climbers such as sweet peas.

Trellis screens

Trellis can be used as a stand-alone screen in many ways – on boundaries; as dividers within the garden to create privacy and shelter from wind; and to screen off ugly bits like compost heaps and storage areas. Choose well-made, substantial trellis, especially in a windy position, and make sure that you put the supporting posts in firmly.

Complementing your colours

Choose climbing plants with flower and foliage colours that are shown off well by their background. Dark backgrounds such as red brick walls and dark-coloured fences look superb with golden or variegated foliage and pale flowers, while lighter backgrounds like pale stone and wood, or whitewashed brick, make a fabulous contrast to rich, vibrant flower colours and purple foliage.

Choose climbers and wall shrubs for trellis screens that aren't too vigorous, or the support will eventually be swamped by the plant. The following plants all do well: *Chaenomeles*, *Clematis* (except *C. armandii*), climbing roses, smaller ivy varieties, golden hop (*Humulus lupulus* 'Aureus'), jasmine (*Jasminum officinale*), perennial pea (*Lathyrus latifolius*), honeysuckle (*Lonicera*), passion flower (*Passiflora caerulea*), and all annual climbers.

Bamboo wigwams

Bamboo wigwams are popular in vegetable gardens for supporting climbing beans. You can also use them for any annual climbers. Wigwams are quick and easy to make, and you can reuse the bamboo stakes for years.

To make a wigwam, arrange at least three or four 2.4-metre (8-foot) bamboo stakes around a 1–1.2-metre (3–4-foot) circle. Space the stakes at least 45 centimetres (18 inches) apart. Push each stake into the ground at least 30 centimetres (12 inches) deep. Lash the top of the stakes together with twine.

Plant beans (or other annual climbers) at the base of each stake. As the beans start to grow, direct them up the stakes; once started, the plants don't need additional training or tying. At the end of the season, clean off the bamboo and store it indoors.

Free-standing wigwams made of hazel and willow are widely available and are useful supports for annual climbers in containers or in your borders. Try planting sweet peas, morning glory, or climbing nasturtiums.

Chain-link fences

Okay, so chain-link fence is not the most attractive plant support, but such fencing is strong and durable. You may be stuck with it as a shared boundary belonging to your neighbour. Chain link's industrial appearance practically screams to be cloaked in greenery. For an attractive barrier or privacy screen, plant evergreen honeysuckle at the base of a chain-link fence. Or cover the fence with a dense climber like ivy or an annual type such as sweet peas.

Pillars

Simply put, a pillar is a sturdy, rot-resistant wood or metal post set in the ground. (Perhaps you have a lamp post or telegraph pole just waiting for a climber.) Pillar dimensions can vary, but bury the pillar's base at least 60 centimetres (24 inches) in the soil. A permanent climber needs a sound support; a few turns of wire to climb up is not enough, because the plant ends up slouching around the base like a sock that's lost its elastic.

If you plant roses, make a framework of stout wire through vine eyes. Clematis and honeysuckle are excellent pillar plants, and these are best supported with wire or plastic mesh wrapped in a cylinder shape around the post.

Arbours and pergolas

Decked with wisteria, honeysuckle, climbing roses, or clematis, an arbour or pergola raises the garden to new heights. A plant-clad pergola can shade a hot, sunny patio or make an inviting entrance to your garden. Most enjoyably, a fragrant plant-clad arbour with a seat makes a gorgeous little retreat where you can hide away from the demands of doorbell and telephone (so long as you leave the mobile indoors). These structures can be works of art in their own right, or they can be simple designs that highlight plants without competing with them. A heavy-duty arbour or pergola makes a major landscape feature, creating a feeling of permanence as well as a feeling of comfort. You make your own arbours and pergolas, or buy them in kit form. Above all else, they must be sturdy.

To avoid damaging the growing plant while working, put the trellis or support in place before planting.

Growing climbers through other plants

Well-established hedges, shrubs, and trees can look even better with a garland of extra summer colour. Against the background of well-established plants, climbing plants can weave their way through and add brilliant splashes of seasonal flowers. Matching a climber to its host is really important, as a vigorous climber would soon smother a small tree, for example. Partner hedges and shrubs that need regular trimming with climbers that are herbaceous in habit or tolerate hard pruning, like *Clematis viticella* varieties or golden hop. A large, well-grown tree can support a vigorous climber such as *Clematis montana* or a rambler rose.

A climber planted to grow through established plants faces stiff competition in ground already well colonised with roots. Plant at the edge of the larger plant's canopy of branches, from where you can train the climber upwards with canes or wires. Dig a planting hole at least 45 centimetres (18 inches) square and fill it with fresh topsoil mixed with lots of organic matter. To be really sure of success, frame the inside of the planting hole with a bottomless wooden box to protect the roots until the climber is well established.

Climbers We Love

You can choose from dozens of climbers to adorn the sides of buildings or fences and vertical structures, as well as ramble through your shrubs and trees. If your space is limited, look for varieties of climber that offer more than one benefit, such as those with handsome foliage as well as beautiful flowers or delectable fruit. Some climbers also offer superb autumn colour. Following are a few of our favourite climbers.

- **Trumpet vine.** *Campsis.* Bring an exotic touch to hot, sunny walls with the large and vividly coloured blooms of trumpet vine, which grows to around 5 metres (18 feet). Flower colours include red, orange, and yellow. The bold, divided leaves look attractive too. Plant in full sun and on well-drained soil.

- **Clematis.** Clematis species. Justly known as the 'queen of climbers', this diverse, mostly deciduous family of eye-catching twining climbers is available in hundreds of varieties. Large-flowered hybrids, with summer blooms up to 25 centimetres (10 inches) across in shades of white, pink, red, blue, and purple, are showiest of all, but the drawback is that this group is most choosy about its growing conditions. Plant where the roots are cool and shaded but where the top can grow into full sun. For example, set the plant at the base of a large shrub and let it ramble through to the sunny top. Large-flowered hybrids also need rich, fertile soil that doesn't dry out or become waterlogged. Oh, and they prefer to be sheltered from strong winds too!

  Give up on those requirements? Opt for the many gorgeous clematis species which, although their blooms are smaller, are much more tolerant of less than ideal conditions. Some of the most popular ones are *Clematis alpina* and *Clematis macropetala* varieties for early tomid-spring (height to 3 metres, or 10 feet); the ultra-vigorous *Clematis montana* for late spring (height to 9 metres, or 33 feet); and the many delightful *Clematis viticella* varieties for late summer bloom (height to 3 metres, or 10 feet). This short list is a mere tempting taster of the numerous different varieties and species available.

- ✔ **Evergreen clematis.** *C. armandi.* Masses of fragrant white flowers appear in mid-spring. The leaves are handsome, shiny, and dark green. In cold areas, grow against a sheltered wall in full sun. Height to 6 metres (20 feet).

- ✔ **Ivy.** *Hedera colchica, H. helix.* Evergreen, fast-growing, tenacious, and adaptable, ivy comes in many varieties differing in foliage size, shape, and colour. The species has deep green, heart-shaped leaves and is very vigorous. It clings with small aerial rootlets and takes over in next to no time – you have to keep your eye on this one! Choose between varieties of the small-leaved ivy (*Hedera helix*) or the larger-leaved Persian ivy (*Hedera colchica*). Plant in sun or shade.

- ✔ **Golden hop.** *Humulus lupulus* 'Aureus'. Fast-growing, very vigorous, yet herbaceous in habit, dying back to the ground in winter and regrowing in spring, the large golden-yellow leaves make a handsome splash of colour. Grow in sun or partial shade.

- ✔ **Climbing hydrangea.** *Hydrangea anomala* subspecies *petiolaris*. Wonderful for shady walls, the climbing hydrangea clothes its support with lush green foliage and big heads of lacy white flowers in summer. As a bonus, the leaves turn butter-yellow in autumn before falling. This plant is self-clinging yet not as rampant as ivy or Virginia creeper. Although slow to start growing strongly, climbing hydrangea eventually reaches around 3.6 metres (12 feet) high.

- ✔ **Honeysuckle.** *Lonicera species.* Beloved for their sweetly scented summer flowers (although beware – a few honeysuckle varieties aren't scented). This twining climber grows to around 3 metres (10 feet). You have lots of different honeysuckles to choose from; most popular are *Lonicera periclymenum* varieties, which do best in a part-shaded site and on retentive soil. The evergreen honeysuckle *Lonicera japonica* 'Halliana' is more vigorous and tolerates sun.

- ✔ **Virginia creeper and Boston ivy.** *Parthenocissus species.* These two deciduous climbers are known for their dramatic red and gold autumn colour. Virginia creeper, *P. quinquefolia*, has leaves divided into five leaflets. Boston ivy, *P. tricuspidata*, has glossy, three-lobed leaves. Both climb vigorously, clinging to surfaces with their small adhesive discs. Plant in sun or shade.

- ✔ **Passion flower.** *Passiflora caerulea.* A fast-growing tendril climber that bears unusually shaped blue and white flowers, which may be followed by egg-shaped orange decorative fruit after a hot summer.

✔ **Climbing roses.** *Rosa species*. You can use many types of vigorous-growing roses the same way as climbers. (Climb to Chapter 10 for more details on roses.)

✔ **Star jasmine.** *Trachelospermum jasminoides, T. asiaticum*. The evergreen star jasmine is one of the most attractive and well-behaved climbers, although not reliably hardy in cold areas. Clusters of delectably fragrant white flowers are borne against shiny, dark green foliage in from mid-summer into autumn. Twining stems reach up to 3 metres (10 feet). Plant in full sun and in a sheltered site.

✔ **Grape vine.** *Vitis species*. The sprawling grapevine is one of the best choices for covering an arbour or wall. In addition to interesting gnarled trunks, good-looking leaves, and autumn colour, you may get edible fruit if you live in a mild area. 'Wine not' start your own mini vineyard? For attractively coloured foliage opt for the purple leaves of *Vitis vinifera* 'Purpurea'.

✔ **Chinese wisteria.** *Wisteria sinensis*. Purely elegant – that's about the best way to describe one of the finest deciduous climbers you can grow (if you have enough space for it). Beautiful, large (often over 30 centimetres, or 12 inches long), dangling clusters of fragrant purple blooms hang among bright green, divided leaves in spring. The twisting, twining shoots keep growing almost indefinitely. As the shoots mature, they take on the classic 'muscular' appearance.

For a more limited space, choose the smaller *Wisteria floribunda*. Casting just the right shade, wisteria is the perfect cover for a sturdy arbour or pergola. It also looks great on walls. Wisteria requires pruning twice a year to look its best and to bloom prolifically. Plant in full sun and, in cold areas, in a sheltered site.

Annual Climbers

Want a really fast but temporary climber? Consider an annual one. Like a petunia or other annual flower, an annual climber grows quickly and blooms in one growing season, which may be just fine for screening off a summer eyesore. (We're not talking about your neighbour mowing his lawn with his shirt off.) Annual climbers give you masses of glorious summer flowers.

Annual climbers are second to none for speedy summer cover on all sorts of vertical features like screens, walls, obelisks, and other supports. Although some nurseries and garden centres sell ready-grown plants in spring, often the only way to enjoy these ultra-quick scramblers is to grow your own. Sow the seed in pots under cover in early spring, plant out by early summer, and by mid to late summer just watch them go.

Patience is the watchword to be sure of success with tender plants. Never put plants outside until all danger of frost is past, because even a light frost can kill or severely check the growth of annual climbers. Plants raised under cover need to acclimatise to the outside environment for a couple of weeks first – see *hardening off* in Chapter 7. Hardening off involves putting plants out for increasing periods during the day and then at night, protecting them if frost is forecast.

Here are five favourite annual climbers that are easy to grow:

- ✔ **Canary creeper.** *Tropaeolum peregrinum*. This fast-growing climber can reach 3 metres (10 feet) in one season. The name comes from the bright yellow flowers that look like they have wings. Plant on trellis or netting for support.

- ✔ **Cup-and-saucer plant.** *Cobaea scandens*. So called for its unusually shaped flowers, which are deep purple and trumpet shaped with a 'ruff' or saucer at the base. This tendril climber rapidly grows long stems up to 4 metres (13 feet) long, and blooms in late summer. Sow seed in pots indoors in early to mid spring, and plant out in a sunny, sheltered site.

- ✔ **Morning glory.** *Ipomoea tricolor*. Sumptuous, but a bit tricksy to grow, this twining climber is not for totally new gardeners. Sow seed in pots on the windowsill in spring, and put out plants in a sunny, sheltered spot in June. All the faff is worthwhile when the massive trumpet flowers appear, up to 10 or 13 centimetres (4 or 5 inches) wide and in a rich range of blues, pinks, and purples. 'Heavenly Blue' is an all-time favourite. Newer varieties stay open for longer, not just the 'morning' suggested by the name.

  The seeds have a hard coat and don't sprout easily. Help seeds to start growing by notching them with a knife or file, or soak them for a couple of hours in warm water before planting.

- ✔ **Nasturtium.** *Tropaeolum majus*. Nasturtiums make themselves right at home in a casual garden. Edible, bright flowers in orange, yellow, cream, red, or pink bloom abundantly through the summer. The only drawback is that these plants are a gourmet feast to the caterpillars of cabbage white butterflies; inspect the leaf undersides regularly and pick off any caterpillars (a good pocket-money job for small children).The bright green, round leaves make a thick low carpet that's attractive in its own right. You can train climbing varieties, which trail up to 1.8 metres (6 feet), on a trellis, or use nasturtiums as a ground cover.

  Sow seeds directly in the ground in full sun or part shade in spring after all danger of frost has passed. Thin seedlings to stand 30 centimetres (12 inches) apart. Nasturtiums are easy to grow in well-drained soil, and are quick about it.

✔ **Sweet peas.** *Lathyrus odoratus*. If you appreciate old-fashioned charm and heady fragrance, find a sunny spot for sweet peas.

Tall climbers are the most familiar sweet peas, scrambling to 1.5 metres (5 feet) or so, and are the best for cut flowers. Colours include blue, pink, purple, red, and white. You need to provide something for sweet peas to climb on; wigwams, trellis, or wire mesh are all fine.

You can sow sweet peas either directly where they are to flower, or you can steal a march on the season and sow seed under cover in autumn or early spring. To hasten seed germination, soften the seed coat by soaking seeds in water for at least a few hours (and up to 24 hours) before planting. Germinate the seeds in a warm spot indoors until the shoots appear, then move the pots to a cool spot such as an unheated conservatory or greenhouse.

Sweet peas do best in full sun in a fertile, moisture-retentive soil. Feed regularly with a liquid fertiliser. Remove the faded flowerheads a couple of times a week, because if sweet peas are allowed to set seed they stop producing new flowers.

Michael S. Thomson

Early spring-blooming Dutch crocus

Yellow spears of lupine accentuate the brilliant blue perennial catmint.

Garden acid test: Does the cat approve?

Sweet alyssum softens the edges of a walkway.

Each daylily flower lasts only one day, but they are produced in such abundance that you'll have plenty for cutting.

Positive Images

Morning glory is a beautiful annual climber. In cold areas, grow against a wall for best results.

Michael S. Thomson

Verbena is excellent in containers and hanging baskets.

Michael S. Thomson

Miniature rose thrives in a pot.

Part III
Colour Your World

"Our neighbour is going to start keeping bees to pollinate his garden – hope they don't spoil our Sunday barbecues."

In this part . . .

Once the permanent layout and larger plants are in place, you can choose from heaps of smaller plants to incorporate into your garden. Of all the wonderful benefits that flowers bring to a garden, their vibrant and beautiful colours mean the most to us. We get excited just thinking about mixing and matching flowers of different colours to create striking effects, but actually seeing them is the real payoff.

Think of your garden as your canvas, and the colours of the various annuals, perennials, flowering bulbs, and roses as your palette. Now stretch out with your imagination: Can you see that little clump of yellow over there? Can you see those purple bunches here and there? How about splashes of red in the corners and there in the middle?

In this part, we tell you about our favourite annuals, perennials, grasses, flowering bulbs, and roses. Enjoy the colours!

Chapter 7

Annuals

. . . .

In This Chapter

▶ Understanding annuals and their needs

▶ Buying annual plants

▶ Using annuals' colour, shape, and fragrance in your garden

▶ Taking care of your annuals

▶ Looking at favourite annuals

. . . .

Annuals are the workhorses of the flower garden. If you want summer colour that is virtually guaranteed, if you want your borders or containers to be bright and showy, and if you want your garden to look good right from the start, annuals are the answer.

What's an Annual?

Annuals are the shooting stars of the garden universe. They burn very brightly indeed, but briefly.

To be technical for a moment, an *annual* is a plant that undergoes its entire life cycle within one growing season. You plant a sunflower seed in spring, the seedling sprouts quickly, it starts blooming in summer, frost kills it in autumn, seeds scatter and (we hope) sprout the next spring to start the process again. Figure 7-1 shows the life cycle of an annual.

In some instances, however, our definition of annual gets a bit dicey. Annuals and *perennials* (which we formally introduce in Chapter 8) have a way of overlapping – in definition, as well as in the garden. Frost-tender perennials (usually known as tender perennials) are best treated like annuals in most parts of Britain but grow year round in the mildest areas such as the south-west of England. You find perennials that act like annuals listed as annuals in this book.

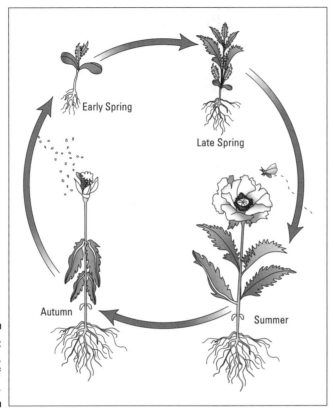

Early Spring

Late Spring

Summer

Autumn

Figure 7-1:
The short,
happy life of
an annual.

Breeding annuals

Because annuals grow so easily and quickly – and are so popular – you can find an overwhelming number of varieties. Plant breeders have been busy with annuals for more than a hundred years, and look what they've done: A plant that in nature had yellow flowers with four petals may now produce a bloom with sixteen white petals.

Many of the breeding efforts have gone into producing smaller, more compact plants (dwarfs). You can also find annuals developed to trail from hanging baskets (trailers). You can also find an amazing array of flower types, as described here:

✔ A *single* flower, the type most often found in nature, has a single layer of petals.

✔ A *double* flower has additional layers of petals.

✔ A *fully double* flower has many layers of petals.

✔ A *bicolour* flower has two prominent colours in its petals.

✔ A *star* flower has a colour pattern in the petals that is remarkably star shaped.

✔ A *picotee* flower has petal tips in a colour different to the rest of the petal.

Analysing Annuals

Annuals broadly divide into three groups: hardy, half-hardy, and biennials.

✔ **Hardy annuals** are tough enough to cope with frost so you can sow them in the garden in early spring, or even in autumn if your garden has well-drained soil so the seeds won't rot. Popular examples include sun-flower, sweet peas, and love-in-a-mist. Just look for the letters 'HA' when you're browsing through seed catalogues and packets. Hardy annuals are dead easy to grow because you can sow seed directly in the ground. Most hardy annuals give a good few weeks of bloom, but won't flower for anything like as long as half-hardy annuals.

✔ **Half-hardy annuals** (also called *bedding plants* or *patio plants*, and listed as HHA on seed packets) are the real summer stalwarts. These plants don't tolerate any frost, so you must grow them under cover at first. If you wait until the weather is warm enough to sow outdoors, the plants won't flower until late in the summer. Plant out half-hardy annuals in late spring or early summer when all danger of frost is past, and they flower their socks off right through the summer and often through the autumn too. Examples include marigolds, cosmos, begonias, antirrhinums, and salvias.

Just to muddy the waters a bit more, some of the plants you find under the banner of bedding or patio plants are *tender perennials* because, although they won't tolerate frost (hence *frost* tender), they can grow for years in a frost-free environment. In milder parts of Britain, tender perennials often survive if left outside; elsewhere, you can bring plants into a heated porch, greenhouse, or conservatory for the winter. Many tender perennials are very colourful and exotic looking, such as African daisies (*Gazania*, *Osteospermum*, and *Arctotis*), and also many popular bedding plants like geraniums, fuchsias, and busy lizzies, which are actu-ally tender perennials as well as being half-hardy annuals. But, unless you're keen to keep your plants for next year, don't worry about the dif-ference and just chuck them all on the compost heap in autumn after the frost turns their growth to mush.

✔ **Biennials** take 12–15 months to complete their life cycle, and you sow the seed in late spring to mid-summer. Popular examples include fox-gloves, forget-me-nots, and sweet Williams. While a few are good in con-tainers, most make excellent filler plants for borders and are very easy to grow.

Sunny sunflowers

Giant sunflowers are children's favourite hardy annual. Sunflowers grow so fast that both their rate of growth and their huge flower faces are fascinating. A sponsored sunflower-growing competition is great fun for siblings, a pre-school group, or a school class. Sow the seeds outside where they flower in April or May (sow a few seeds in pots at the same time in case slugs and snails do their worst to the seedlings outside). Sunflowers come in a huge range of varieties, so be sure to choose tall ones like 'Russian Giant' or 'Giant Single'.

Hardy annuals

If you've never grown anything from seed before, start with hardy annuals. You don't need any special equipment because you can sow seed straight into the ground, and most varieties are really easy to grow. Hardy annuals are absolutely great for new gardens because you can use them to fill the gaps between newly planted permanent plants, and they look fantastic in a border on their own (Chapters 5 and 12 have lots more on growing hardy annuals). Although the blooms don't last as long as those of half-hardy annuals and tender perennials, you still get a good couple of months of colour for very little money, time, and effort. Best of all, plants often sow themselves for the next year if you leave the seeds to ripen and fall, with absolutely no input from you whatsoever – which makes them pretty good plants to our way of thinking!

Half-hardy annuals and tender perennials

Nothing beats a riot of summer flowers at the time of year when you're most likely to be outside enjoying your garden to the full. Half-hardy annuals are virtually guaranteed to provide a fantastic show for months, and although you need to put in new plants each year, the results are more than worth the time and money.

Patience is the watchword to be sure of a successful display: The terms 'half-hardy' and 'frost tender' mean that even a light frost may damage or kill these plants. Although garden centres have plants on sale from early spring, only buy early if you can grow the plants somewhere warm and under cover – don't plant them outside until all danger of frost is past (usually early May for the mild south and early June for the north).

While it used to be the fashion to plant up or 'bed out' entire borders with half-hardy annuals – hence their other name of bedding plants – most people now prefer their borders to have a fair amount of permanent plants for all-year interest and lower maintenance. Have the best of both worlds by leaving a few spaces within your borders to fill with summer flowers, so your garden has loads of summer colour plus lots of interest at other times of year too.

Stacks of different plants are available, so order a few seed catalogues in winter to browse through at your leisure. Most companies supply catalogues free or for just a small charge to cover postage. That way you avoid being bamboozled by the bewilderingly large range of seeds on sale at your local garden centre.

Biennials

Biennials are often called spring bedding plants because some varieties such as wallflower, forget-me-not, and double daisy make a really spectacular show along with bulbs. However, others like foxglove and sweet rocket offer a gorgeous (and very easy) splash of colour in early and mid-summer. Biennials grow from seed sown from late spring to mid-summer and flower the following year. Biennials are tough as old boots and dead easy to grow from seed: Either sow where you'd like the plants to flower or, if you have a spare bit of ground, sow plants in nursery rows to transplant in early to mid-autumn. Alternatively, you find plenty of ready-grown plants on sale in autumn, though this works out a lot more expensive than buying a few packets of seed. Once flowering is over let the seed pods ripen and turn brown, then scatter the seed to grow of its own accord for next spring.

Planting on the Sunny Side

Most annuals are sun worshippers. After all, to grow as quickly as they do, their leaves need to collect all the energy they can, especially early in the season. Here's where it pays to be an observer: Watch how the sunlight falls in your garden and use that information to decide which annuals to plant and where to plant them. Watch the patterns of sun and shade in your garden. The patterns change with time and the seasons, as the sun moves higher and lower in the sky, as trees grow taller and develop and lose leaves, and as neighbours build or tear down buildings.

Most annuals need sunlight for at least half the day in order to perform well. Where a site gets sun all day, or receives a thorough baking from the sun from midday onwards, you need to pick out plants that can stand the heat. These include several plants all known as African daisies (*Arctotis*, *Felicia*, *Gazania*, and *Osteospermum*), golden daisies (*Bidens*), and geraniums. Just a few annuals like to be out of the sun in a shady spot, notably fuchsias, busy lizzies, and lobelia.

Buying and Growing Half-hardy Annuals

You have three choices when it comes to buying or growing half-hardy annuals.

You can grow your own plants from seeds from your own existing flowers or from packets, which is great if you want something really different. Ensure that you have a warm place to grow plants from seed: Sunny windowsills can suffice for a small number of plants, but you need a heated greenhouse or conservatory if you want to grow plants in any quantity. A heated propagator is very useful for good results when germinating seed too.

Alternatively you can buy ready-grown plants from your local garden centre; seedlings and 'tots' (young plants), available from late winter to mid-spring, or bigger plants ready to pop in the ground at planting time.

Table 7-1 covers the pros and cons of the different ways of producing gorgeous annuals.

Table 7-1	Weighing Up Whether to Buy or Grow Half-hardy Annuals	
	Advantages	*Disadvantages*
Grow your own plants from seed	Very satisfying Lots of plants for relatively little cash outlay You can choose from a huge selection of seeds	Unsatisfying if seed fails to grow You need somewhere warm and well lit to grow plants
Buy pots of ready-grown seedlings	Satisfaction from bringing your own plants to maturity Cheaper than buying finished plants	You need somewhere warm and well lit to grow on plants Choice of varieties is not extensive
Buy ready-grown plants	No hassle at all – just shop, buy, and plant Great for instant colour	Costs a lot

Transplant yourself to Chapters 12 and 13 to find out all you need to know on raising seeds, young plants, and planting out.

What You Can Do with Annuals

Inexpensive, fast-growing, and long-blooming, annuals are perfect plants to have fun and experiment with. Try out wild colour combinations, carpet an entire bed, or fill pots to overflowing. Even after a hideous mistake (perhaps red and lavender together makes your dog howl) you may have time to replant during the same growing season.

Annuals are versatile and just about foolproof. You don't need to be born with a silver trowel in your hand to achieve some beautiful effects in your garden:

- Plant entire beds and borders in swathes of colour.

- Create a combination of annuals for your pots and window boxes that bloom all summer long.

- Mix annuals into borders of permanent plants to add seasonal colour, fragrance, and texture.

- Grow annual climbers up trellis or free-standing supports for extra colour and privacy.

- If you have any spare plants, pot them up into cheap plastic pots or reuse leftover black pots from trees and shrubs. Then, come late summer when your borders may look a bit tired, simply drop in a few of these annual pots.

Playing with colour

Try different combinations of colour to find what you most enjoy in your garden. Experiment with mixing colours, and trust your own eye. One gardener's favourite combination, such as purple petunias with scarlet geraniums, may be another gardener's worst colour-clash nightmare.

Also remember that a great many garden plants now come with multi-coloured leaves (known as *variegated*), which creates a tapestry of colour and pattern even when the plant is not in bloom. Yellow-foliaged plants, or those with leaves splotched in cream or white, can brighten a dark corner as effectively as white flowers. Such foliage gives the effect of dappled sunshine on leaves. Coleus (*Solenostemon*) is a classic foliage plant with leaves mottled in every colour from near black to lime green, white, and bright fuchsia pink.

 An easy way to deal with colour is to think of all colours as falling within the ranges of *hot* or *cool*. Hot colours, such as yellow, orange, bright purple, and red, are lively and cheerful. Most cool colours, such as pink, blue, lavender, and cream, blend well together, creating a feeling of harmony and serenity.

Using shape, height, and structure

A plant's form is every bit as important as its colour and too often gets overlooked.

Need an almost instant privacy screen from neighbours? Annuals offer the perfect remedy. Annuals can add height to a garden, with towering sunflowers creating screening, or providing colour at the back of the border. Take a walk through a wood or a well-planted garden and notice how plants grow in layers – tall trees; small or *understorey* trees, large shrubs, and ferns; and then ground-cover plants that carpet the shaded ground beneath. Such complexity pleases the eye, and you can blend annuals with other plantings to create this same effect in your garden beds. Use different heights, from a tall sunflower or ornamental corn to diminutive sweet alyssum.

No rule exists about planting the shortest flowers in the front, with the taller at the back! Tall, airy annuals, such as *Verbena bonariensis*, with its skinny branches topped with tiny purple flowers, is virtually see-through and adds a whole new dimension to a border. A few tall 'dot' plants in the centre, such as spider flower, *Cleome*, or tobacco plant, *Nicotiana sylvestris*, can make a dramatic impact.

Texture adds another element to the garden. The droopy, chenille-like softness of love-lies-bleeding (*Amaranthus*) adds a striking note to a planting scheme, while the feathery foliage of love-in-a-mist (*Nigella*) can knit together varied plantings in the front of a border. Frilly China asters or the soft seed heads of annual grasses add fluff and interest. The spiky spires of foxglove or the candelabra-like heads of the giant tobacco plant (*Nicotiana sylvestris*) accent the more rounded forms of lower-growing annuals, perennials, and shrubs.

Designing for fragrance

Of all the senses, smell most strongly evokes memory. The strong perfume of sweet peas or the spicy smell of nasturtiums can bring back an acute longing for a favourite garden from the past.

The flower fragrances you prefer are as personal as the perfume or aftershave lotion you choose to wear. Plant generously so that you have plenty of flowers and leaves to pick for bouquets and bowls of potpourri. Even a few sprays of the unassuming common mignonette (*Reseda odorata*) can scent a room or front porch. As a rule, choose the more old-fashioned varieties of flowers, which tend to be more fragrant than modern hybrids; you may need to order seed packets from companies specialising in heirloom flowers to find the older, most strongly scented varieties.

Add a few fragrant blooms to every pot, window box, or hanging basket. Concentrate sweet-smelling flowers near pathways, gates, patios, and decking so that you and your guests can enjoy them often. Some plants don't waste their scent on the daylight hours; they reserve their allure for night-flying moths and their pollinating ways. For instance, flowering tobacco (*Nicotiana*) and night-scented stock release their sweet scent on the evening air and so are an ideal addition to planting beds or pots near bedroom windows or on patios that you use in the evening.

Here are some favourite easy-care annuals that add fragrance to the garden:

- ✔ **Heliotrope.** Dark, crinkly leaves show off cherry-pie-scented purple or dusky-white flowers.

- ✔ **Mignonette.** This little plant is easy to grow from seed and has an amazingly strong, sweet fragrance.

- ✔ **Nicotiana, or flowering tobacco.** The white flowers have a nearly tropical scent that is particularly strong in the evening.

- ✔ **Night-scented stock.** This old-fashioned, early-blooming favourite has the scent of cloves.

- ✔ **Scented-leafed geraniums.** Fuzzy, splotched, and streaked leaves come in a wide variety of scents, from chocolate to cinnamon, lemon, and mint.

- ✔ **Sweet alyssum.** Masses of tiny, scented flowers make this a favourite edging plant.

- ✔ **Sweet peas.** A childhood favourite for many people, the older varieties of sweet peas retain the sweetest of scents all day long.

- ✔ **Sweet William.** Gardeners have grown this plant since Elizabethan times for its spicy, sweet fragrance.

Getting annuals together

For the brightest blast of colour, plant annuals en masse. Either go with just one colour or mix a number of colours, although we prefer to choose a definite scheme to avoid ending up with a 'liquorice allsorts' jumble of colours. Plant lots of annuals and plant them close (usually 10 to 15 centimetres, or 6 to 8 inches, apart). Start with well-grown plants grown in cellular trays or individual pots and space them evenly in staggered rows (see Figure 7-2). The plants grow quickly and fill in the spaces to give you a solid bed of bright colour.

Low-growing annuals, such as ageratum and some lobelia, are very useful as edgings. You can plant these low growers along pathways or in front of other annuals, in front of perennials, or even in front of flowering shrubs, such as roses.

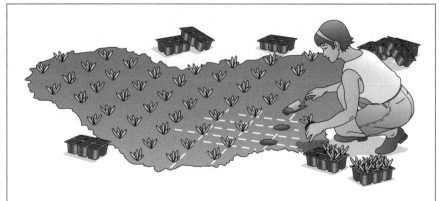

Figure 7-2:
Plant
annuals in
staggered
rows, evenly
spaced.

Containing annuals

Annuals are especially at home in containers, making it easy for you to insert a touch of colour into visible, highly used areas. Match the plant's habits with the pot. Spreading plants, such as lobelia, *Bidens*, *Plectranthus*, and *Helichrysum petiolare*, cascade over the sides of containers and look really nice in hanging baskets or window boxes. Lower-growing, compact varieties are most suitable for container growing, but you can use taller types as well. By planting many pots with many different annuals, you always have some at peak bloom to put in your most visible spots, such as doorways or patios. For details on growing plants in containers, see Chapter 19.

Taking Care of Your Annuals

Maintenance, especially proper watering, greatly affects how annuals behave. Unlike many plants, annuals aren't forgiving if they don't get the water they want when they want it. Fast, consistent growth is critical with annuals. If plant growth stalls, you may lose a good part of, if not all, of the blooming season.

Watering requirements vary with the weather, seasons, and garden conditions. (You knew we were going to say that!) If you garden on sandy or chalky free-draining soil, select those annuals that really thrive in dry conditions to save yourself a heap of work (not to mention money, if your water is metered). Take a look at these ways to tell when your annuals need water:

- ✔ **Study your plants.** When an annual starts to dry out, the leaves look droopy, start to wilt, and may lose their bright green colour.

- ✔ **Dig in the ground.** Annuals don't have time to reach down deep in the soil. Most need water when the top 5–8 centimetres (2–3 inches) of soil dry out. Dig around with a small trowel or shovel to check how moist the soil is.

Fertiliser is also critical for first-rate blooming. For best flowering, you want to keep plants growing vigorously, never stalling. Here's a simple fertiliser method that works for most annuals in most gardens:

- ✔ When you are preparing the planting bed, spread a general-purpose fertiliser evenly over the bed at the rate recommended on the package. Work the fertiliser into the soil along with a 5–8-centimetre (2–3-inch) layer of organic matter such as packaged planting compost, home-made garden compost, or well-rotted manure.

- ✔ About halfway through the growing season, apply a second dressing of fertiliser.

- ✔ Towards the end of summer, keep your annuals growing strongly with an application of liquid fertiliser every couple of weeks.

The other essential step is deadheading: Cut or break off flowers as they fade. Doing so encourages even more blooms because the plant doesn't expend energy producing seeds. This is vital with sweet peas, which stop blooming if you leave the seed pods on (other plants aren't so temperamental, luckily).

Our Favourite Annuals

Everyone has his or her favourite flowers, and we have quite a few ourselves. This section details some of the most reliable, colourful annuals, though this is by no means an exhaustive list of all the gorgeous plants available! We divide the list into hardy annuals, and half-hardy annuals and tender perennials. All plants need sun for at least half the day to do well, unless stated otherwise.

Hardy annuals

Choose among these favourites for low-maintenance flowers:

- ✔ **Pot marigold.** *Calendula officinalis*. Vivid yellow or orange (or sometimes white) daisylike flowers highlight this easy-to-grow annual. Pot marigold is a nice cut flower. The compact plants reach 30–45 centimetres (12–30 inches) high.

- **Cornflower.** *Centaurea cyanus.* Once one of our native cornfield weeds and now a popular garden plant, particularly in its vivid true-bloom forms. Other flower colours are pink and white. Cornflowers love dry, sun-baked sites. Height 30–60 centimetres (12–24 inches).

- **Clarkia.** *Clarkia elegans.* Colourful blooms in a wealth of colours, freely borne on slender, upright spikes. Both single and double flowers are available. Colours include many shades of pink and purple as well as white. A lovely plant of informal habit that's ideal for mixing with other plants in borders.

- **California poppy.** *Eschscholzia californica.* The silken-petalled California poppy blooms mostly in shades of yellow and orange (or sometimes pink or white, borne above clumps of attractive ferny foliage), and self-seeds readily. The plants reach 25–60 centimetres (10–24 inches) high. Loves a sun-baked spot.

- **Sweet peas.** *Lathyrus odoratus.* Intensely fragrant blooms make this a much-loved annual. The climbing plant comes in single colours and multicolours. Sweet peas make a wonderful cut flower. Most varieties need support such as a fence or trellis. However, bushier, low-growing types, such as 'Knee-Hi', do not need supports. Plant in full sun and in good, fertile soil.

- **Poached egg flower.** *Limnanthes douglasii.* Aptly named, for the blooms of this little annual have a bright yellow centre with a wide white surround. Ideal for border edges. Height 15 centimetres (6 inches).

- **Sweet alyssum.** *Lobularia maritima.* This ground-hugging annual (usually under 15 centimetres, or 6 inches high) covers itself with tiny, bright white, purple, or pink blooms. Alyssum is one of the finest edging and container plants.

- **Love-in-a-mist.** *Nigella damascena.* An old favourite, with intense blue flowers shown off by a green ruff around each bloom. Has the bonus of attractive feathery foliage and showy, inflated seed pods too. Self-seeds very freely. Height 30– 45 centimetres (12– 18 inches).

- **Nasturtium.** *Tropaeolum majus.* Quick-growing nasturtiums come in many varieties, with neat, round leaves and bright orange, yellow, pink, cream, or red flowers. Some varieties trail (or climb if given support) while others are bushy. All parts of the plant are edible. Check the leaf undersides regularly for signs of the pesky cabbage white butterfly and squash any eggs or young caterpillars.

- **Sunflower.** *Helianthus annuus.* Few annuals make a statement the way sunflowers do. Many sunflowers reach 2.5–3 metres (8–10 feet) high, topped with huge, sunny, yellow blooms. Some dwarf varieties, such as 'Teddy Bear', stay under 60 centimetres (2 feet). All sunflowers have edible seeds.

Half-hardy annuals and tender perennials

Following is a list of summertime annuals that we like the best. You can raise plants from seed, as seedlings or starter plants, or use ready-grown at planting time after frost is past.

- **Snapdragon.** *Antirrhinum majus.* These plants produce wonderfully coloured spikes of white, yellow, orange, red, purple, and multihued flowers. The common name comes from the hinged blossom, which opens and shuts like jaws when you squeeze the sides (children love them). Varieties range from 30–100 centimetres (12–36 inches) high.

- **Bedding begonia.** *Begonia semperflorens.* These versatile annuals thrive in a reasonable amount of sun, but dislike hot, sun-baked sites and tolerate a bit of shade. The flowers of bedding begonias come in shades of white, pink, and red. Leaves can be shiny green or bronze-red. Most varieties grow about 30 centimetres (12 inches) high. Look out for the dramatic begonia 'Dragon's Wing', which is taller, with large, attractively shaped leaves.

- **Coleus.** *Solenostemon* hybrids. Grown for its intensely coloured foliage, coleus comes in a variety of colour combinations and different leaf shapes. This plant grows best in shade for part or all of the day. You can also grow coleus as a houseplant. Pinch off the flowers to keep the plant compact.

- **Cosmos.** *Cosmos bipinnatus.* Bright green, airy plants bear brilliant blooms of white, pink, lavender, purple, or bicoloured daisylike flowers for a long period, with the bonus of attractive, feathery, green foliage too. *C. sulphureus* has red, yellow, or orange flowers. This is a taller annual, growing to around 60–120 centimetres (2–4 feet). With a more informal habit than many annuals, cosmos is a lovely plant to use in borders mixed with permanent plants.

- **Geranium.** *Pelargonium* species. These old-time favourites can last for years if overwintered in a frost-free place. Geraniums have huge clusters of white, pink, red, purple, orange, or bicoloured flowers in spring and summer. The plants grow 20–100 centimetres (8–36 inches) high; some have variegated or aromatic leaves. Grow in full sun to light shade.

- **Impatiens.** *Impatiens wallerana.* These plants are the stars of the shady garden and one of the most popular annual flowers. The 2.5–5-centimetre (1–2-inch) wide blooms come in bright shades of white, red, pink, salmon, orange, and lavender. You can also find bicoloured varieties of impatiens. Impatiens have dark green or bicoloured leaves and grow 30–75 centimetres (12–30 inches) high. Plant in part or full shade.

- **Lobelia.** *Lobelia erinus.* Deep to light blue blooms cover this dainty little plant that comes in bushy and trailing varieties. Few blues are as bright as those of lobelia; you can also get white- and pink-flowering forms. Look out for the tender perennial *Lobelia richardii*, which has more vigorous growth than the annual varieties. All lobelias reach about 10–15 centimetres (4–6 inches) high. Plant in sun or shade.

- **Flowering tobacco.** *Nicotiana alata.* Small, tubular, often fragrant blooms come in shades of white, pink, red, lime green, and purple. Flowering tobacco plants grow 30–90 centimetres (12–36 inches) high, depending on variety. Plant flowering tobacco in full sun or light shade.

- **Petunia.** *Petunia hybrida.* This much-loved annual has single or double, usually trumpet-shaped flowers in a myriad of single and bicoloured shades. Petunias are compact plants that range from 25–60 centimetres (10–24 inches) high.

- **Sage.** *Salvia* species. Tall spikes of bright white, red, blue, or purple flowers top these compact, sun-loving plants. Some types of sage are perennials in mild winter climates. Sages range in height from 25–100 centimetres (10–36 inches).

- **Marigold.** *Tagetes* species. Marigolds are one of the most popular summer annuals, with blooms in the sunniest shades of yellow, orange, and red. You can get many varieties. Blossoms can be big or small, as can the plants.

Biennials

The life cycle of biennials differs from that of annuals in that you raise the plants from seed one year and they flower the following year. Biennials are great for colouring your garden from spring to early or mid-summer, and many plants self-seed readily. Biennials are easy to grow from seed, sown outside in mid to late summer, or you can buy ready-grown plants to plant out in autumn. Here are some of our favourites:

- **Foxglove.** *Digitalis purpurea.* Tall spires of summer flowers are excellent for brightening up shady spots. Pink and purple are the most common colours, but other shades include white, pale yellow, and apricot. All parts of the plant are poisonous. Height up to 1.2 metres (4 feet).

- **Sweet rocket, dame's violet.** *Hesperis matrionalis.* A delightful if rather untidy cottage garden plant, developing tall and slightly floppy stems of mauve or white flowers, up to 1.2 metres (4 feet) high. Grow it if you like scented flowers – the fragrance is strongest in the evening.

- **Forget-me-not.** *Myosotis sylvestris.* Lovely for spring colour in borders and containers, forget-me-not is most popular in its blue forms, but you can also get white and pink varieties. Height 30–45 centimetres (12–18 inches).

Chapter 8

Perennials and Ornamental Grasses

....

In This Chapter

▶ Getting to know perennials and grasses

▶ Using perennials and grasses in beds and for borders

▶ Putting plants in the ground

▶ Getting into some can't-miss perennials

....

Perennials are the phoenixes of garden plants: Every winter they die, only to rise from the ashes the following spring, fuller and more beautiful than before, to bring a bounty of colour throughout the garden. Perennial plants, grown for their flowers, their foliage, or both, are with us like the seasons – perennials return with their beauty year after year. Compared with annuals (which you need to replant every year), perennials stay in place to grow, to look better, and to bloom more, season after season.

Perennials encompass some of the best-loved flowering plants, such as daisies, chrysanthemums, and carnations. Spectacular foliage plants, such as hostas, cardoons, and plume poppy, are also perennials. We include ornamental grasses in this chapter because you treat them in the same way as perennials.

Pondering Perennials

A *perennial* is a plant that can live for several years or more, sprouting new growth and making new blooms cyclically year after year. If you start a typical perennial, such as columbine, from seed in spring, it spends the summer growing foliage and dies back completely to the ground when winter arrives. The following spring it starts growing again, blooms that summer, dies back again, and repeats the pattern of blooming and dying back for years. Some varieties of perennial bloom in their first year from an early sowing.

Perennials have soft, fleshy stems. Herbaceous perennials bloom with worthwhile flowers or have attractive foliage. Most perennials are *deciduous*, meaning that they die back completely to the ground. Other perennials are evergreen. Perennials generally have one main flowering season, mainly in spring, summer, or autumn, although a few even bloom in winter. The season can be as brief as a few weeks or last a couple of months or even more.

Perennials are interesting for a variety of reasons: The range of their flowers – from tiny, fragrance-packed pinks, *Dianthus*, to towering blue delphiniums; their sheer numbers and variety – thousands of kinds are available; and the challenges they present – how to cut back, how to divide, what to do with them in the winter. You don't just relegate them to the compost pile at the end of the season as you do with annuals.

Perhaps perennials' most appealing aspect – particularly if you're new to gardening – is that they are both versatile and moveable. While woody plants such as shrubs, trees, and climbers prefer to stay put once you plant them and tend to sulk if you move them, nearly all perennials thrive on a bit of upheaval from time to time and so you don't need to get too hung up about putting plants in the wrong place. In fact, after several years a clump of a perennial plant starts to get a bit congested and performance begins to decline. Rejuvenation is simple – and drastic – dig up the clump when dormant and chop it into pieces, then replant all but the old woody centre. You get lots more plants to spread around your garden (and your friends' and neighbours' gardens), and your plants have loads more living space. A win:win situation all round.

Beds and Borders

The classic use of perennials is to combine many of them in a large planting bed, known as a *herbaceous border*. A well-designed perennial border has something in bloom right through the year. This type of border not only has a well-thought-out colour scheme, but also relies on plant texture for visual interest.

A perennial border is constantly evolving, which is part of the fun of creating it. If certain plants don't work, you can replace them with something else. If the border has some downtime when nothing is in bloom, add some flowering annuals to fill in the gap or plant some flowering shrubs, such as floribunda roses, which bloom over a long season.

When your border consists of a medley of plants, including small trees, shrubs, bulbs, annuals, herbs, and even vegetables, you have a *mixed border*. Perennials and grasses are fantastic plants for mixed borders, as they can be woven between and under other plants to introduce a wealth of colour through the seasons. Use shade-tolerant perennials to get even more interest from your garden by planting them in drifts under trees and large shrubs. Not all perennials are infillers: Some have real personality of their own with bold foliage or a tall, architectural shape, and are great as key plants in a scheme.

Designing a Border with Perennials

Even though individual experience is the best teacher, here are some pointers that we've found useful in designing a perennial border:

- **Start with a plan and keep records.** Draw your bed on paper, making sure to give plants the room they need to grow. Work with a simple colour scheme, such as three of your favourite colours, and use plants that bloom only in those colours.

- **Plan for a succession of bloom.** Think seasonally, aiming always to have something in bloom. Keep records of blooming times so that you know which gaps to fill in during the next planting season. And don't forget winter.

- **Prepare the soil carefully.** You won't be remaking this bed every year. Dig deep, add organic material, and, most important, eliminate perennial weeds. Chapter 16 gives the lowdown on how to battle weeds.

- **Plant in groups.** One plant, alone, gets lost in the masses. We find that grouping plants in odd numbers (whether it's three, seven, or nine) looks the most natural. The exception is with those perennials that are real giants, which can be planted singly. But don't get hung up on such rules. If you have room for only two of something, go right ahead and plant with confidence.

- **Don't forget the foliage.** Use plants with dramatic foliage to set off the flowers. Ornamental grasses or bold-textured shrubs make excellent contrast and focal points.

- **Use silvers and whites.** Silver-foliaged plants (such as lamb's ears) and plants with white flowers highlight other colours and can tie everything together visually. These plants also reflect light and look great on those nights when the moon is bright.

- **Consider the background.** A dark green background enriches the colour of most flowers. Consider planting a hedge (possibly of flowering shrubs or evergreens) at the back of the border. Or, if you have a fence there, stain it dark brown.

Beyond borders

Perennials and grasses are ultra-versatile and can be used in other ways all around the garden too. Don't feel that you have to limit them to beds and borders.

Perennials and grasses in pots

Plants with long-lasting good looks make perfect easy-care fillers for containers. They require very little attention apart from watering, plus feeding and *topdressing*, or mulching with a fertile mulch such as well-rotted manure, in spring, yet make a great display for years. Shade-loving plants are perfect for brightening gloomy, soil-less spots too. Containers are a great place for growing plants that slugs and snails are likely to ravage, such as hostas, because you can protect plants more easily in pots than in the ground. In cold areas, grow plants vulnerable to frost in containers and move them into a sheltered spot for the winter.

Grow one variety of plant per container – depending on the pot size – either putting in one plant, or three, or even five, rather than combining different plants in the same pot that are likely to grow in an unbalanced way. Pick out plant varieties that are naturally compact in habit, and that look good for a long period, rather than those that only bloom for a short while. Be sure to buy a good-quality soil-based potting compost, because this type has plenty of 'body' for long-lived plants, rather than a less substantial multipurpose compost.

The following perennials and grasses are all good choices for container life:

- Japanese painted fern (*Athyrium niponicum pictum*)
- *Carex hachijoensis* 'Evergold'
- Japanese golden grass (*Hakonechloa macra* Aureola)
- Euphorbia (compact varieties with attractive foliage, such as 'Redwing', 'Blackbird', or 'Silver Swan')
- Coral bells (*Heuchera*)
- Plantain lily (*Hosta*)
- Joseph's coat (*Houttuynia cordata* 'Chameleon')
- Purple fountain grass (*Pennisetum setaceum* 'Rubrum')

Perennials for cutting

You can grow perennials specifically to cut them for indoor use – usually in rows or beds like a vegetable garden. Or work favourite bouquet makers into your regular flower beds. Either way, the following perennials are long lasting and striking as cut flowers:

✔ Yarrow (*Achillea*)

✔ Pinks (*Dianthus*)

✔ Coral bells (*Heuchera*)

✔ Peonies (*Paeonia*)

✔ Black-eyed coneflower (*Rudbeckia fulgida* 'Goldsturm')

✔ Pincushion flower (*Scabiosa*)

✔ Goldenrod (*Solidago*)

✔ Stokes' aster (*Stokesia laevis*)

✔ Speedwell (*Veronica*)

Planting Perennials . . . and Afterwards

Plants are on sale in containers right through the year.

You can plant container-grown perennials any time that you can work the ground, but bear in mind that you need to water plants put in during spring and summer during dry spells, because they won't have had time to make much root growth. The best times for planting are in the autumn or early spring, so the plants have time to get established before hot weather begins. In cold regions, plant in early autumn or early spring to avoid the worst effects of the winter weather on your garden's new residents.

For more details about planting, see Chapter 13.

Raising perennials and grasses from seed

If you need lots of plants to fill a new border or garden and you're prepared to wait a few months, consider raising your own plants from seed. Lots of varieties are easy to grow, and growing your own saves you a heap of cash. Choose plants from mail-order seed catalogues, because garden centres rarely offer a wide selection of perennials and grasses. You find an increasing range of *first-year flowering perennials* too; this means plants will bloom in their first year if you sow them early, in late winter or early spring.

Caring for your plants

With all permanent garden plants, you need to choose the right plant for the right place. Get the matchmaking right and, once plants are established, watering is only required rarely, if at all. You can find out a lot more about the whens, whys, and hows of watering in Chapter 14.

Fertilising perennials is simple. One application of a complete fertiliser (see Chapter 14) to your perennial bed in early spring should be enough. If you think that plants are lagging (weak or pale growth), follow up with another shot or two of the same fertiliser during the growing season. If you've forgotten to fertilise and your plants have developed discoloured leaves, apply a liquid or foliar feed as a quick pick-me-up, then apply a complete fertiliser. Keep the soil in good condition by mulching the bare ground between clumps with well-rotted manure or garden compost, in late winter to early spring.

Many perennials benefit from being cut back at various times during their growth cycles. To stimulate branching on lower stems and to make the plant bushier, pinch out new growth at the top of the plant. (See Figure 8-1.)

Deadheading is the process of pinching or cutting off faded flowers while the plant is in bloom. Deadheading forces the plant to spend its energy on developing more flowers instead of setting seed. The result of deadheading is usually more flowers produced over a longer period. (See Figure 8-2.)

Figure 8-1:
Pinching out new growth at the top of the plant helps it develop lower branches and become bushier.

Figure 8-2:
Deadhead spent flowers to offset seed production and divert plant energy into producing new blooms.

Some perennials, such as coreopsis, delphinium, and gaillardia, produce another flush of flowers if you cut them back by about one-third after flowering.

Taller perennials, such as delphiniums, and bushy types, such as peonies, may need staking to prevent the flowers from falling over. Figure 8-3 shows two types of staking – thin metal wire loops (for bushy plants) and bamboo stakes and ties (for taller perennials).

Figure 8-3:
Support plants as they grow with either wire loops or bamboo stakes and ties.

At the end of the growing season, allow plant growth to die back. Cut back the dead growth to ground level, any time between autumn and early spring. However, leaving dead stems on through winter has several benefits: The plant has some useful protection against frost; stems look glorious on misty autumn days strung with dew-pearled spiders' webs and in winter when silvered by frost; and beneficial insects such as ladybirds and lacewing flies have somewhere to hibernate. The exception is fleshy-leaved plants, such as hostas, which benefit from having their dead leaves removed as soon as possible because their foliage soon goes brown and mushy.

If older plants become overcrowded or bloom poorly, rejuvenate them by *dividing.* In fact, division is a good way to increase plant numbers. (For more about plant division and other propagating methods, see Chapter 15.)

Our Favourite Perennials

Everyone has a list of favourite perennials, so here's a look at ours.

- **Yarrow.** *Achillea* species. Yarrow is a useful group of easy-care, summer-blooming perennials with ferny grey foliage and tight, upright clusters of yellow, red, or white blooms. Yarrows range in height from low-growing ground covers to tall plants – up to 1.5 metres (5 feet) high. One favourite is *A. filipendulina* 'Moonshine', with bright yellow flower clusters atop 60-centimetre (2-foot) stems. Plant in full sun.

- **Artemisia.** *Artemisia* species. This very useful group of mounding, silver-foliaged plants is great for highlighting other plants. One of the best is the hybrid 'Powis Castle', with lacy, silver foliage on a plant about 90 centimetres (3 feet) high. Plant in full sun.

- **Columbine.** *Aquilegia* species. These widely adapted perennials have fern-like foliage and beautiful, spurred flowers. Columbine bloom in spring and early summer in a number of single colours and multicolours. Wildflower seed mixes include many native forms of columbine. The plants range in height from about 15–90 centimetres (6–36 inches). Columbine are easy to grow from seed, and they reseed (with enthusiasm – if you don't want lots more plants, cut off the seed pods before they ripen). Plant in full sun to light shade.

- **Aster.** *Aster* species. Colourful, late-blooming perennials with daisylike flowers, which appear mostly in shades of blue, purple, red, pink, and white with yellow centres. Asters usually bloom in the late summer to autumn. Some begin flowering in early summer or late spring. Asters range from 15–180 centimetres (6–72 inches) high, depending on the species. Plant in full sun.

✔ **Basket-of-gold.** *Aurinia saxatilis.* Brilliant gold blooms cover the grey foliage in spring. Basket-of-gold grows about 30–40 centimetres (12–15 inches) high and spreads. The plant also withstands drought. Plant in full sun.

✔ **Bellflower.** *Campanula* species. The much-loved family of mostly summer-blooming perennials produce bell-shaped flowers in shades of blue, purple, or white. You can choose from many species that vary from low-growing spreading plants to taller types, some of which are 1.8 metres (6 feet) high. Flower size and shape also vary.

Favourite species include the Serbian bellflower, *C. poscharskyana* – a low, mounding plant, 10–20 centimetres (4–8 inches) high, with blue flowers. Another favourite is the peach-leaf bellflower, *C. persicifolia*, which is also spreading, can reach up to 90 centimetres (3 feet) high, and has blue or white blooms. Campanulas grow best in sun or light shade.

✔ **Coreopsis.** *Coreopsis* species. Sunny yellow, daisylike flowers top these easy-to-grow plants. The flowers appear from spring through summer. *C. grandiflora* is one of the most common. This variety grows to about 90 centimetres (3 feet) high and has single or double flowers. Plant in full sun.

✔ **Dianthus.** Cottage pinks are hybrids that have very fragrant, frilly, rose, pink, white, or bicoloured flowers on stems reaching about 45 centimetres (18 inches) high above a tight mat of foliage. Plant in full sun.

✔ **Purple coneflower.** *Echinacea purpurea.* Tall, purple or white, daisylike flowers top this fine, long-lasting perennial. Purple coneflower reaches 90–150 centimetres (3–5 feet) high and blooms in summer. Plant in full sun.

✔ **Blanket flower.** *Gaillardia grandiflora.* The petals on these sunny-coloured, daisylike flowers are either red or yellow or a combination of the two. The plant blooms heavily in summer and grows 30–90 centimetres (1–3 feet) high. Plant in full sun.

✔ **Geranium.** This is a large group of fine perennials. Dainty-looking, purplish-pink, red, blue, mauve, and white flowers appear in abundance above good-looking, deeply cut leaves. Most grow to around 45 centimetres (18 inches) high. You can find many varieties. Plant in full sun to light shade. The species *G. maccrorhizum* and *G. cantabrigense* prefer to be grown in part or full shade.

✔ **Daylily.** *Hemerocallis* species. A dependable group of summer-flowering perennials, daylilies produce stalks of large, trumpet-shaped flowers. Blooms appear in single and bicoloured shades of yellow, orange, pink, red, and violet. Some daylilies are fragrant. Daylilies have grassy foliage that reach 30–60 centimetres (1–2 feet) high. The flower stems of some daylilies are 90 centimetres (3 feet) tall or more. Plant in full sun.

- *Heuchera varieties.* Grown for their attractive foliage, heucheras have lobed leaves in many shades of purple and green. Wiry spikes of tiny, bell-shaped, white, pink, or red flowers are held 30–60 centimetres (1–2 feet) high. Plant in sun or light shade.

- **Plantain lily.** *Hosta* species. These very useful foliage plants make a nice contrast to shade-loving flowers. Plantain lily leaves are usually heart-shaped and often crinkled or variegated. Flower spikes appear in summer. Plants and leaves range from small to large. One favourite is the blue-leaf plantain lily, *H. sieboldiana*, which has large 25–38-centimetre (10–15-inch), crinkled, blue-green foliage and pale purple flowers; it grows 90 centimetres (3 feet) high. However, slugs and snails love to munch hostas, so protect plants as soon as the leaves emerge.

- **Candytuft.** *Iberis sempervirens.* In early spring, snow-white flowers completely cover this dainty, compact plant. Candytuft grows from 10–30 centimetres (4 to 12 inches) high and makes a wonderful edging. Plant in full sun.

- **Garden penstemon.** *Penstemon hybrids.* These summer-blooming, mounding plants grow 60–120 centimetres (2–4 feet) high and bloom for months. Garden penstemon features spikes of tubular flowers in many single and bicoloured shades of white, pink, red, and purple. Plant in full sun.

- **Summer phlox.** *Phlox paniculata.* Large clusters of small white, pink, red, salmon, and purple fragrant flowers bloom in mid- to late summer. The plants grow 60–120 centimetres (2–4 feet) high. Plant in full sun and in fertile, moisture-retentive soil.

- **Gloriosa daisy; black-eyed Susan.** *Rudbeckia hirta.* This is a free-blooming, easy-to-grow perennial or biennial. These plants have large yellow, orange, maroon, or mahogany daisylike flowers with dark, domelike centres. Some kinds are bicoloured. These plants bloom from summer to autumn. The plants grow 60–120 centimetres (2–4 feet) high, grow easily from seed, and reseed themselves heavily. The plants can be invasive. Plant in full sun.

- **Salvia.** *Salvia* species. You can find so many excellent perennial salvias that we could write a book about them alone. Most are best adapted to areas with dry summers and mild winters. Many are shrublike; others are perennials that usually grow as annuals. (See Chapter 4.) Still others are valuable herbs. Favourite flowering types include *S. superba*, with violet-blue summer flowers reaching 60–90 centimetres (2–3 feet) high, and *S. azurea grandiflora*, with high 1.2–1.5-metre (4–5-foot), rich gentian-blue flowers in late summer. Plant in full sun.

- **Lamb's ears.** *Stachys byzantina.* This is a lovely, low-growing foliage plant with soft, fuzzy, silver-grey leaves. Lamb's ears grow 15–30 centimetres (6–12 inches) high and have insignificant purplish-white flowers in summer. This perennial is a fabulous edging plant for flowering perennials. Plant in full sun.

Gorgeous Grasses

Here's our selection of the most gorgeous grasses for your garden.

Certain grasses, such as *Phalaris arundinacea* var. picta and *Leymus arenarius*, can become invasive – avoid them or grow them in containers.

- ✔ **Feather reed grass.** *Calamagrostis acutiflora*. Great for vertical interest within a border to contrast with other plants, this grass forms upright clumps of slender plumes atop attractive foliage. Grow in sun and any reasonably fertile soil. Height to 1.2 metres (4 feet).

- ✔ **Blue fescue.** *Festuca glauca*. Neat, evergreen, and excellent for edging, this grass forms a little 'hedgehog' of blue leaves and bears blue-green spikelets on short stems. Varieties such as 'Elijah Blue' have the most intense colouring. Grow in sun and well-drained soil.

- ✔ **Japanese golden grass.** *Hakonechloa macra* 'Aureola'. Forming arching clumps of bright gold-and-green striped leaves, this compact grass is fabulous in containers or raised beds where you can fully appreciate its shape. Sun or part shade. Height 45 centimetres (18 inches).

- ✔ **Japanese blood grass.** *Imperata cylindrica* 'Red Baron'. Most people see a picture of this striking and unusual grass with brilliant red leaf tips and it goes straight on the 'must-have' list, but be aware that it's not a go-anywhere plant. Blood grass is only hardy down to about minus 10 degrees Celsius (14 degrees Fahrenheit), and it also needs moisture-retentive soil and partial shade. However, if you can satisfy those requirements, it looks outstanding. Height 45 centimetres (18 inches).

- ✔ *Miscanthus sinensis*. Tall, slender, and upright, these bamboo lookalikes make fantastic back-of-the-border plants. Numerous varieties exist, some whose prime attraction is variegated or coloured foliage, such as 'Morning Light', 'Zebrinus', or 'Gracillimus', while others such as 'Silberfeder' are noted for their plumes of decorative flowers. Grow in any reasonable soil, in sun or part shade. Height 1.2–1.8 metres (4–6 feet).

- ✔ **Black grass.** *Ophiopogon planiscapus* 'Nigrescens'. Although actually a perennial, you nearly always find this unusual grass-like plant sold with ornamental grasses. It forms compact clumps of slender black leaves and bears small spikes of white flowers. Grow in sun or part shade. Height 15 centimetres (6 inches).

- ✔ **Switch grass.** *Panicum virgatum*. Another eye-catching tall grass for borders, this one looks at its best from mid-summer when it bears many heads of open spikelets on slender stems. Height to 1.8 metres (6 feet).

✔ **Fountain grass.** *Pennisetum* species. One of the most tactile grasses, its numerous flower heads look just like furry caterpillars that are irresistible to touch. Looks best in a raised bed where its growth can sprawl over the edge. Grow in sun and well-drained soil. Height to 60 centimetres (24 inches).

✔ **Giant oat grass.** *Stipa gigantea.* An invaluable plant for creating height without claustrophobia, because the ultra-tall and airy stems have a 'see-through' quality that you rarely find in garden plants. The tall, slender stems are topped with open heads of yellow spikelets that look wonderful when backlit by the sun. Prefers sun and well-drained soil. Height to 1.8 metres (6 feet).

✔ **Pony-tail grass.** *Stipa tenuissima.* Slender, upright clumps of green foliage look nondescript in spring, but come summer and the plant transforms into an airy mass of spikelets that catch the light. Plant in groups for the best effect. Prefers sun and well-drained soil. Height 45 centimetres (18 inches).

Chapter 9

Bulbs

· ·

In This Chapter

▶ Understanding bulbs

▶ Caring for bulbs

▶ Dividing and propagating bulbs

▶ Taking stock of our favourite bulbs

· ·

*B*ulbs are a dream come true for many people, especially for those who have never had much luck growing any plants. Think of bulbs as flowering powerhouses – plants that pack most of what they need for a season's worth of growth into an underground storage device, the bulb. The great thing about bulbs is that they hardly take up any space at all and can be packed into all sorts of spots around the garden to give magnificent bursts of bloom. Plant a bulb at the right time of year and at the proper depth, and you're almost guaranteed a spectacular bloom – true, you have to wait a few months, but the wait is worthwhile.

Throwing Some Light on Bulbs

When you think of plant bulbs, you probably envision daffodil or tulip bulbs – brownish things that look like onions. The term *bulb*, as used in gardening, refers to a great number of different types of plant bulbs. Other terms you'll come across include corms, rhizomes, and tubers, which all act in a similar way and which, in this book, we refer to as bulbs. But don't worry overmuch about what they all *are* – just what they can *do* for you.

All bulbs have a growing period and a resting time. But there the similarity ends. For one thing, bulbs don't all grow and rest simultaneously. Some early spring bulbs – the familiar snowdrops, tulips, daffodils, hyacinths, and such – blossom early in the year when nothing much else is growing and then rest while the majority of other plants are growing. Lots of different varieties of the same type of bulb bloom at different times through the spring – so you can colour your garden for a long time if you pick your varieties with care. Other bulbs – lilies, alliums, and gladioli, for example – bloom later on, when all sorts of other plants are busy growing. Some bulbs, like autumn crocus, flower in autumn when lots of plants are packing up shop for the year.

When and How to Buy Bulbs

The best time to buy and plant bulbs depends to a great extent on their flowering times, and whether the bulb is frost hardy or not.

Spring-blooming bulbs

Hardy, spring bloomers are the major-league bulbs that most people know: Crocus, daffodils, hyacinths, and tulips are most common. You plant these bulbs in autumn and they bloom in spring. As a general rule of thumb, plant all spring-blooming bulbs except tulips as soon as you have them in your hands in the autumn. The earlier the bulb flowers, the earlier you need to plant it in order for the bulb to develop a good root system.

Plant daffodils and narcissi by the end of September (although, if you're reading this in October with a bag of daffs by your side, don't panic. Bulbs can be remarkably resilient. Just go and plant them *right now*!). Tulips are prone to rotting, and the longer the bulbs are in the ground, the more likely they are to succumb. So aim to plant tulips in November.

The difficulty with autumn planting is that, in an established garden, it's hard to decide just where to plant while all the garden is in full growth. You have two solutions. The first belongs to the school of 'it's a great idea if I'd thought of it earlier'. Go round the garden in spring and make a detailed note or sketch of all the bare spots that you'd like to brighten with bulbs. The second solution, for the vast majority of people who don't think that far ahead, is to plant bulbs in plastic pots or planting bags made of plastic mesh. Come spring, you can simply plant your thriving clumps of bulbs in just the right spots.

Success with snowdrops

The snowdrop, *Galanthus nivalis*, is beloved by many for its dainty white blooms borne in the depths of winter. However, unlike most other bulbs, snowdrops generally don't grow well from autumn-planted dry bulbs. The best way to get a thriving display of snowdrops is to buy and plant the leafy bulbs just after they've flowered, round about February, which is called *in the green*.

Nurseries get the bulk of their spring-blooming bulbs at the end of August to early September. Here are some tips for getting the pick of the crop:

- ✔ Buy early, and buy everything you intend to get. Supplies of a popular, sold-out item may or may not be replenished.

- ✔ Store your bought bulbs with care, in a cool, frost-free place in paper bags or cardboard boxes – never, never, in rot-inducing polythene.

- ✔ Order in advance. If some bulbs are in limited supply, an early order reserves them for you. Orders are often despatched in rotation – early order, early shipping; later order, later shipping.

- ✔ Specify a despatch date for mail-order suppliers. Most, if not all, mail-order sources promise to ship at the appropriate time.

Summer-blooming bulbs

Summer-blooming bulbs broadly divide into two main types. You can get hardy bulbs, the most popular of which are alliums (or ornamental onions), which you plant in autumn because they need a long growing season; and lilies, which you can plant in autumn or spring. These hardy bulbs stay put in the garden and (hopefully, pests permitting) come up year after year. You can also get frost-tender bulbs, such as dahlias, cannas, and begonias, which you plant in spring. In all but the mildest areas, pot up the bulbs in mid-spring and grow them under cover on a windowsill or in a greenhouse for a few weeks, then plant out at the end of May when the frosts are past. Frost-tender bulbs need a long growing season: You can plant bulbs straight in the ground in late spring, but they may not start blooming really well until the autumn – just in time to be clobbered by frost if you're unlucky. In mild regions, you can plant some summer-blooming bulbs once and leave them in the ground all year round. Be extra safe by putting a thick 'eiderdown' of bark mulch over the top of the plant for the winter.

Retailers often start selling summer-blooming bulbs in winter. Instead of thinking about your snow shovel, dream about your hoe and rake as you seek out your summer bulbs. Just follow these tips:

- ✔ **Don't wait.** Buy dormant, summer-blooming bulbs when you see them. If you wait to decide later, the bulbs may already be gone.

- ✔ **Aim for early blooms.** You can pot up your summer-blooming bulbs a month or two early – before frost-free weather arrives – if you have the appropriate indoor space to grow them. Doing so gives you a jump-start on the season.

- ✔ **Cheat a little.** Once the weather is mild and settled, some tender bulbs may be available as potted growing plants – dahlias, canna lilies, and begonias in particular. You can buy, plant, and enjoy all on the same day – no waiting!

Shopping tips

Always purchase fine-quality bulbs – they give you more bang for your buck. Never forget that with bulbs, bigger is better. Larger bulbs, although more expensive, give you more bloom. Bargain bulbs are often poor performers. Keep the following advice in mind as you shop:

- ✔ A good bulb is plump and firm. Reject any that are shrivelled up or soft and mushy.

- ✔ A good bulb is healthy – no mouldy patches growing on it. Judge a flowering bulb just like you would an edible one, like an onion.

- ✔ Size is relative – you never see a crocus corm as big as that of a gladiolus – but within a category, bigger is better. A large daffodil called *double-nosed* has more flowers than a smaller, single-nosed one of the same variety.

If you buy your bulbs through a mail-order catalogue, you should rely on a reputable dealer to send you good-quality bulbs. A specialist nursery can offer a wider selection of particular bulbs by mail than local nurseries can afford to stock. Take a look at some pointers for mail-order shopping:

- ✔ A good catalogue gives lots of information – more than just when a bulb flowers, its colour, and size.

- ✔ Be cautious about the truth of claims of fabulous displays that grow anywhere and everywhere. If it sounds too good to be true, it probably is.

- ✔ If prices in one catalogue are significantly lower than in other catalogues or local sources, then smaller bulb sizes can explain the difference. Undersized bulbs are inexpensive, and their flowering display is correspondingly small.

- ✔ Go large and save money. Buying 50 or 100 of one variety of bulb is usually much better value than buying 10 or 20, simply because the packaging and handling costs are almost the same regardless of quantity. So, rather than going for variety with loads of different bulbs, think about big drifts of just a few varieties, which looks better than little patches of different varieties.

Planting Bulbs

You can plant bulbs in spaces where you don't even think you have space. Their fragile-looking but oh-so-tenacious stems can shove their way through carpets of ground-covering plants, and through grass. Cram bulbs in the spaces between clumps of herbaceous perennials and ornamental grasses, both to colour bare spots in spring and, for summer, where the tall stems of lilies and alliums can rise gracefully above drifts of smaller plants. Plant bulbs wherever you want to see them bloom: In the smallest little spot by the front door, in pots, or in large swathes under trees or in grass. Think about the look you want to create, too (see 'What's your style?' a bit further on in this section). Some bulbs, such as the English bluebell, look particularly good in woodland settings, while others, such as tulips, do well in formal gardens.

One of our favourite designs involves planting large beds of tulips. We then plant low-growing annuals or perennials (such as forget-me-nots, sweet alyssum, pansies, violas, or iberis) right on top of these bulb beds. The bulbs come up through the other flowers and create wonderful combinations. After the bulbs have finished blooming, the other plants cover up the dying foliage of the bulbs.

Many bulbs grow fantastically well in containers and are great for cheering up the patio and other soil-less spots. With containers, you can really pack bulbs tightly for a spectacular bloom (but the tighter you pack the bulbs, the less likely they are to bloom the following year, though feeding and watering help to ensure future flowers).

If you really want to have fun, try a bit of lasagne planting (in layers) or forcing bulbs to bloom indoors. (See 'Growing Bulbs in Containers', later in this chapter.) Planting bulbs is straightforward, but you can break into a serious sweat if you're doing mass plantings. The two most important points that you need to know about planting a bulb are

✔ **Set the bulb at the correct depth.** The chart in Figure 9-1 shows the recommended planting depths and proper positioning for common bulb types. As a general rule, most bulbs should be planted at a depth equal to three times their height. For example, plant a 5-centimetre (2-inch) bulb 15 centimetres (6 inches) deep. Remnants of roots on the bottom of the bulb tell you which side of the bulb points down.

✔ **Place the bulb right side up in the hole.** If you see no sign of root remnants, plant the bulb so that the most pointed, narrow part points up. If you have any doubts, ask your local garden centre.

Although digging lots of deep holes can be a blister-provoking chore, don't be tempted to cut corners; shallow-planted bulbs are more likely to be *blind* (producing leaves but no flowers).

Bulbs for year-round colour

With a bit of planning you can get pleasure from bulbs in most months of the year. The earliest bulbs of all are snowdrops and winter aconites that bloom in winter. You can then enjoy a glorious spectacle of spring colour from familiar bulbs such as daffodils and tulips. Lilies, dahlias, and colchicum bloom in summer and autumn, completing your colourful year.

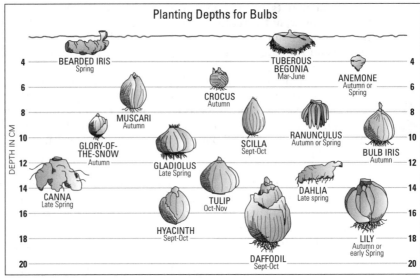

Figure 9-1:
Use this
bulb-
planting
depth chart
as a guide
when you
plant your
own bulbs.

You can plant bulbs individually by using a hand trowel, or the slightly easier option is a bulb planter that takes out a core of soil. If you're planting many bulbs, dig several big trenches or shallow holes and place the bulbs in the bottom. If you have loads of bulbs to plant, or if you're planting in grass, a long-handled bulb planter is a very worthwhile investment that's likely to save wear and tear on your hands.

Most bulbs require well-drained soil. (Bulbs can rot in soggy, overly wet ground.) If your soil is heavy and poorly drained, put a thin layer of coarse grit in the bottom of the planting hole to prevent the bulb from sitting in water.

Bulbs carry their own store of energy, but you can help them along a little bit. Before planting your bulbs, mix a slow-release, complete fertiliser into the soil in the bottom of the hole, then add a little more soil so that the bulb itself doesn't come in contact with the fertiliser granules. You can find appropriate fertilisers in nurseries and garden centres. After planting the bulbs, water them thoroughly if the soil is dry.

What's your style?

The planting method and type of bulb you choose depend on the design style you want to achieve – natural or formal. In a formal design, bulbs are set out in a distinct pattern with the same distance between each one (tulips are top choice for this style of planting). In most other styles of garden, bulbs are best in a more natural-looking clumps or drifts. *Naturalising* refers to the planting of bulbs in grass and meadows, choosing varieties that come back year after year. Good bulbs for naturalising include snowdrops, most crocuses, and many daffodils.

Beware the creatures

A gardener can be pretty perplexed when the 200 bulbs he or she planted last autumn make just a meagre showing in the spring. Yes, the reason could be inferior bulb quality or improper planting depth, but a likely culprit could be an animal. Squirrels and mice forage for and feast on newly planted bulbs. But don't despair – you can still grow beautiful flowering bulbs. Consider the following:

- ✔ Most creatures leave daffodils and snowdrops alone, one big reason that many of these plants naturalise so well.
- ✔ Use a fertiliser that doesn't contain bone meal, which can attract some animals.
- ✔ After planting your bulbs, lay wire mesh just below the surface of the soil. (On the surface is fine, but it's a bit ugly.)
- ✔ Avoid tulips if deer visit your garden; they love to nibble off the flowers.
- ✔ Use humane traps, barriers, or scare tactics such as motion-sensor water jets or ultrasonic deterrents.

Caring for Bulbs

With many bulbs (especially those bulbs that bloom in spring) you won't have much else to do; simply plant the bulbs and forget about them. The bulbs grow, bloom, die back, and come back again the following year. Summer-blooming bulbs, like dahlias and begonias, however, need regular watering and fertilising during their growth cycle. Most bulbs, in fact, benefit from a once-a-year application of a balanced fertiliser during their growing season.

Pinch off faded blooms just as you would for most flowers (see Chapter 15 for the how-to on pinching). Doing so steers the plant's energy into building food reserves rather than producing seed. After the bloom finishes, don't cut down the bulbs' foliage. The foliage provides the food for the bulb, preparing for next year's bloom. Let the foliage die down naturally and then trim off the withered leaves or just let them die back into the soil. In the same vein, don't tie or bundle up the leaves either. Doing so impedes the food-gathering process and results in poor blooms the following year.

You need to lift and store tender bulbs such as canna and gladioli in all but mild areas. Wait until the first frost, then gently dig the bulbs up (take care to dig deep to avoiding spearing the bulbs). Gently shake off surplus soil, cut off the stems (leaving a couple of centimetres of stem), and stand the tubers upside down in a cool, frost-free place for several days. Discard any damaged or rotting bulbs and dust the remaining bulbs with sulphur or another fungicide. Some bulbs, like gladioli, need to be stored dry, whereas tubers such as dahlias need to be kept just moist in trays of coir or peat. Pots of tender bulbs can be left intact and moved into a frost-free place (a dark garage is fine so long as it doesn't freeze).

If digging and storing tender bulbs is too much work, take a chance and leave them in the ground, ideally with a thick covering of bark mulch or garden compost for security. Or just treat them like annuals and plant new ones every year.

Dividing and Propagating Bulbs

Some bulbs, particularly smaller types of bulbs (such as crocuses and daffodils), can remain undisturbed for years. Such naturalisers just get better year after year. But other bulbs multiply so rapidly that they become too crowded and deplete the nutrients in the soil around them. And others, notably tulips, make smaller and smaller flowers over time. If your bulbs are vigorous and crowded, they need dividing. If they produce fewer and fewer blooms, dig them up and discard them.

Dividing occurs just after the foliage turns yellow and begins to die back. Dig up the clump by using a garden fork, being careful not to injure the bulbs. Next, break off the individual bulbs, keeping the roots intact. Replant the bulbs immediately, in pots or in the ground, at the same depth they were growing before. Water the area well and allow any foliage to mature and die before removing it. The newly planted bulbs should bloom the following spring.

Larger bulbs (for example lily) or corms (for example gladiolus) develop small, immature offspring at the base of the bulb. Remove these offsets after the plant has bloomed and the leaves have died; then plant the offsets in an inconspicuous area where they can grow until they're big enough to blossom (usually after a year or two).

Growing Bulbs in Containers

Many bulbs are ideal for containers, providing bursts of bloom and sometimes heavenly fragrances too. Tulips, narcissi, and crocus are especially good for spring, whereas lilies, cannas, and dahlias give stacks of bloom in summer and autumn. Lilies are particularly good for containers because you can grow them in shade (or, in a sunny spot, place pots of lilies among other containers to keep their roots cool), and many varieties are wonderfully scented into the bargain.

Good drainage is the key to success with bulbs in containers, because the bulbs can rot in waterlogged compost. Put a 2.5–5centimetre (1–2 inch) layer of *crocks* (broken bits of terracotta pot), large stones, or gravel in the base of the pot to aid drainage. Use a soil-based compost such as John Innes no. 3 – this has more 'body' than soil-less types and can keep bulbs going for several years. Plant bulbs at the recommended depth, and for a good display, put in lots of bulbs so that they're almost touching each other.

Stand the pots in a sheltered spot outside for the winter. Against a house or garage wall is ideal, because the building keeps off a lot of rain and maintains the temperature a little higher than elsewhere in the garden. In very cold areas, keep pots of bulbs under cover for the winter, in an unheated green-house or cold frame.

Lasagne planting, or planting in layers, is fun to try and a great way to get loads of colour if space is limited. Plant bulbs of different sizes at varying depths, and the shoots of the lower ones work their way around the bulbs above to make a glorious display. Tulips on the bottom layer, narcissi in the middle, and crocus on top is a mixture that works particularly well. Use a large container (a deep pot at least 30 centimetres [12 inches] across), around 10 each of the tulips and narcissi, and around 25 crocuses. Beautiful!

Forcing Bulbs for Indoor Colour

Forcing bulbs means bringing them indoors and getting them to bloom before their normal season. Several spring bulbs – hyacinths, daffodils (especially the ones called paperwhites), and some tulips – are good choices for indoor flowering. Generally, the larger grades of bulbs are better for forcing because they produce more and bigger flowers. (Avoid bargain bulbs.)

Shallow clay or plastic pots called *bulb pans* are the best containers for forcing bulbs because they require less potting mix than ordinary pots and are less likely to tip over. The general rule for forcing bulbs is to have the pot at least twice as deep as the bulb is tall.

Either use *bulb fibre*, a special mix for forcing bulbs, or ordinary multipur-pose potting compost. In the autumn, fill the chosen pot three-quarters full with fibre or compost and place the bulbs 1.25 centimetres (half an inch) apart on top of the mix, with the bulb's pointed end facing up. Gently press the bulbs into the mix so that the tips of the bulbs are level with the rim of the pot. Then fill the pot with more of the soilless mix, and water the pot until the soil is evenly moistened.

Set the potted bulbs in a cool (40–45 degrees Fahrenheit or 4–7 degrees Celcius), dark place such as a garage, shed, or attic for 8 to 15 weeks to allow the bulbs to grow roots. Smaller bulbs may need a little less time; larger bulbs may need slightly more time. During this time, check the compost every couple of weeks, and water if necessary to keep the compost moist but not waterlogged.

Once the shoots are around 2.5 to 5 centimetres (1 to 2 inches) high, it's time for some light. To gradually reintroduce the pots to light and warmth, place the pot in a cool room with indirect sunlight. By the end of one week, move the pot into a warmer room with temperatures to 65°F (18°C). Within a month of being brought into the warmth, the bulbs should begin to flower. After flowering has finished, stand the pots in a sheltered spot outside for the foliage to die back, then plant in the border where they may flower in future years (although they're not guaranteed to). Or just add them to your compost pile after the blossoms fade.

Favourite Bulbs

Whether it's stately lilies, fragrant hyacinths, or cheery daffodils, everyone has a favourite bulb. Following is a list of a few of our favourites.

- **African Lily.** *Agapanthus*; summer bloom. Bears large heads of showy, bright blue flowers that reach from 0.6–1.2 metres (2–4 feet). In cold areas, grow agapanthus in large pots and move under cover to an unheated greenhouse, cold frame, or dry spot against the house. You can also find varieties with white flowers. Plant in full sun.

- **Begonias.** *Begonia tuberhybrida*; summer bloom. Begonias are one of the most beautiful of all flowering plants. You have many varieties to choose from. Some have large flowers (up to 20 centimetres, or 8 inches across) and an upright habit, whereas others have smaller flowers borne on a trailing plant. Few begonias grow more than 20–45 centimetres (12–18 inches) high. Begonia flowers come in almost all shades except blue and green. Foliage is good-looking and succulent. Begonias make ideal container plants and grow best in light shade. Dig up and store the bulbs over winter.

✔ **Canna.** Summer bloom. This handsome, dramatic plant produces showy flowers in shades of yellow, orange, salmon pink, and red. Some have bicolour flowers. The plants have large, tropical-looking leaves that in some cases are multicoloured themselves. Some canna lilies grow more than 1.5 metres (5 feet) high, but many are shorter. Plant in full sun and grow in a sheltered spot to avoid the leaves being damaged by wind. Lift and store cannas over winter, or grow in pots to move into a frost-free spot under cover.

✔ **Lily of the valley.** *Convallaria majalis*; spring bloom. Small, dainty clusters of white, very fragrant, bell-shaped white flowers appear in spring. The plants grow from 15–20 centimetres (6–8 inches) high. Growth is fast and dense, so the plant works well as a ground cover. Plant the root sections (called *rhizomes* or *pips*) in light shade and acid soil and keep the soil moist.

✔ **Crocus.** Spring bloom. These popular and reliable dwarf bulbs bear cupped, upward-facing blooms in white, blue, yellow, and purple. Those that flower in late winter to early spring are best known, although several species produce flowers in autumn. The species crocus have smaller, more delicate blooms, while those of the Dutch crocus hybrids are larger and mostly brighter coloured. Height 10 centimetres (4 inches). Plant in sun or partial shade.

✔ **Dahlia.** Summer bloom. This huge, diverse family of hybrids offers an incredible array of flower forms and sizes. Some dahlia blossoms are tiny balls; other blossoms are huge showy blooms more than 20 centimetres (8 inches) wide. Available in almost every colour but blue, dahlia plants range in size from 15 centimetres (6 inches) high to more than 1.5 metres (5 feet) high. Plant in full sun and water regularly. Lift and store dahlias over winter in all but the mildest areas.

✔ **Snowdrops.** *Galanthus* species; winter or spring bloom. Lovely, drooping, bell-shaped white flowers punctuate this plant, which naturalises well. Snowdrops grow 20–30 centimetres (8–12 inches) high. Plant in full sun or partial shade. Snowdrops are great under trees. Plant bulbs 'in the green' (see the sidebar 'Success with snowdrops' earlier in this chapter).

✔ **Gladiolus.** Summer bloom. This much-loved cut flower bears tall spikes of trumpetlike flowers. Blossoms come in almost all colours except blue. Most grow to around 1 metre (3 feet), but smaller types are available. Plant in full sun. Lift, dry, and store the bulbs over winter and replant in spring.

✔ **Bluebell.** *Hyacinthoides non-scripta.* The common bluebell is one of the most glorious sights of spring in our native woodlands, carpeting the ground with azure blooms and filling the air with fragrance. Bluebells are vigorous, so only plant them in your garden if you have a woodland area. Avoid planting the Spanish bluebell, *Hyacinthoides hispanica*, because this bulb is escaping from gardens and hybridising with the native bluebell.

- **Common hyacinth.** *Hyacinthus orientalis*; early spring bloom. Wonderfully fragrant spikes are composed of white, red, pink, yellow, blue, or purple bell-shaped flowers, to about 30 centimetres (12 inches) high. Hyacinths look best when planted in masses or in containers. Plant in full sun or light shade. After flowering, remove the faded florets from each stalk but not the flower stem itself, as the fleshy stem has the same function as a leaf and helps the bulb build up food for next year. Hyacinth bulbs that are treated for indoor forcing can cause skin irritation, so handle bulbs with gloves or tongs.

- **Iris.** Iris species; spring to summer bloom. A huge group of elegant plants, you can choose from many different types. Favourites include the bearded iris, which has huge blooms and gracefully arching petals. Irises come in many colours and reach from 15 to 60 centimetres (6 to 24 inches). Plant in full sun or light shade.

- **Snowflake.** *Leucojum* species; early spring bloom. This plant is sometimes described as a large and elegant snowdrop, with white, drooping flowers. Plant in full sun or light shade.

- **Lilies.** *Lilium* species; mostly summer bloom. Lilies are a large family of beautiful bulbs. Most have large, trumpet-shaped flowers, but a great diversity of lilies exists. Blossoms come in almost every colour but blue, and plant heights range from 60 to 120 centimetres (24 to 48 inches). Many, but not all, varieties have strongly scented flowers; one of the easiest scented lilies to grow is the regal lily, *Lilium regale*. Plant lilies so that the roots are in the shade but the tops can reach for the sun. A mulch or low ground cover helps. You can also plant the bulbs among low shrubs, or in containers.

- **Grape hyacinth.** *Muscari* species; spring bloom. These wonderful little bulbs form carpets of fragrant, mostly blue flowers and grassy foliage. Grape hyacinths grow from 15–30 centimetres (6–12 inches) high and naturalise freely. Plant in full sun or light shade.

- **Daffodils and narcissus.** Narcissus species; spring bloom. With cheerful yellow flowers synonymous with spring, these easy-care bulbs are a firm favourite. If you plant only one type of bulb, plant this one! While, botanically speaking, all this group of plants are called Narcissus, the term 'daffodil' describes those tall varieties with large flowers. The blooms of narcissi are clusters of small, often fragrant flowers and, although more expensive than daffodils, narcissi perform much better in the garden because their blooms are more fragrant, longer lasting, and stand up better to poor weather. Plant daffodils and narcissi in full sun to light shade.

✔ **Tulips.** *Tulipa* species; spring bloom. These much-loved bulbs with the familiar cup-shaped flowers come in almost all colours (including multi-colours) except blue. Tulips usually grow from 25–60 centimetres (10–24 inches) high and are best planted in full sun and in well-drained soil.

✔ **Calla lily.** *Zantedeschia* species; summer bloom. Spectacular, tropical-looking plants bear large, usually white, cup-shaped flowers and bright green, arrow-shaped leaves. You can also find yellow, pink, and red shades. Calla lily plants generally grow from 60– 90 centimetres (24–36 inches) high, but dwarf forms are also available. Best grown in light shade, these plants can also take sun in cool areas. Keep plants in a frost-free place over winter.

Chapter 10

Roses

· ·

In This Chapter

▶ Speaking the language of roses

▶ Choosing varieties for you

▶ Buying and planting

▶ Pruning and other mysteries

▶ Facing up to rose problems

· ·

For a gardener, falling in love with roses is easy. As if their sumptuous petal colours and shapes weren't enough, many roses seduce with an intoxicating scent designed precisely, it seems, to snag a susceptible gardener. But even from the most pragmatic gardener's point of view, a rose holds even more power of allure.

The diversity of roses means that almost surely one fits your needs and suits your taste, no matter where you live or how you define beauty. Do you prefer roses short or tall? Do you like your flowers simple with 5 petals, or complicated with 60? Is a strong rose scent more important or less important than colour and shape? Do you want a rose bed or just a few rose bushes to mix with other plants; roses to tumble down a bank, to scramble up into a tree, or to climb over a pergola? You can find roses for pretty much every part of the garden.

To guide you through all these choices, this chapter boils things down a bit for you. If you want to grow roses successfully, pay special attention to the following two points:

✔ **Know something about the various types of roses.** Don't buy a rose just because you like the picture – you may find it to be a variety that doesn't suit the spot you have in mind or that it blooms only once a year and perhaps briefly. Remember that in winter all you'll be looking at is a mass of thorny stems, so think carefully before filling your entire front garden with roses.

> ✔ **Learn a few of the quirks about rose care.** Pruning is easier than you think but it is important. The same is true for fertilising. And it's a fact that roses run into a few more problems than typical, tough landscape plants, so be prepared to deal with common maladies. Don't worry: We show you how.

Roses by Many Names All Smell As Sweet

The entire northern hemisphere came equipped with several hundred species of roses. Over the centuries, growers have selected, crossed, and recrossed those species to form numerous types, or *classes*, of roses. If you aspire to become a rabid rose enthusiast, you need to learn about polyanthas and noisettes and other historical strains; but if you just want to grow some roses, jump right into the following pool of varieties in this section.

Time for hybrid teas

The blossoms of hybrid tea roses look like the roses that come from a florist, yet usually smell much better. The plants are upright and rather angular, and their distinctive flowers and buds on long stems have come to typify what a rose is for most people. The hybrid tea is one of the most popular roses today. The big plus of hybrid teas is that they're *repeat flowering*, meaning that they bloom all summer. (Though some varieties come close to being in bloom all season, most bloom in flushes.)

The best way to grow hybrid teas is in a special rose bed. These roses dislike competition from other plants the same size or larger, although you can underplant them with low-growing herbaceous perennials, or short-lived seasonal flowers like annuals and tender perennials.

Here are a few favourite, top-performing hybrid tea roses and their colours:

- ✔ **'Alexander'.** Bright vermillion.
- ✔ **'Blessings'.** Salmon pink.
- ✔ **'Just Joey'.** Copper-orange. Fragrant.
- ✔ **'Peace'.** Light yellow with pink blush. Light fragrance.
- ✔ **'Royal William'.** Deep crimson. Strongly scented.
- ✔ **'Silver Anniversary'.** Pure white.
- ✔ **'Silver Jubilee'.** Pink flushed with apricot and cream. Fragrant.

Fun with floribundas

Floribunda roses, which are crosses of polyantha roses (cluster-flowering roses) with hybrid teas, were developed in an attempt to achieve larger flowers and repeat bloom. Roses in the floribunda class have blossoms shaped like those of hybrid teas, but the flowers are usually smaller and are often grouped in loose clusters. Floribundas are comparatively rugged, more so than hybrid teas, and make great shrubs in mixed borders, or even as hedges.

The following are just a few of the fantastic floribundas available.

- ✔ **'Amber Queen'.** Clear amber-orange.
- ✔ **'Arthur Bell'.** Bright yellow fading to cream. Scented.
- ✔ **'Golden Memories'.** Bright yellow, good scent.
- ✔ **'Iceberg'.** Pure white.
- ✔ **'Orange Sensation'.** Bright orange. Good fragrance.
- ✔ **'Queen Elizabeth'.** Clear pink, tall, and very vigorous.
- ✔ **'Margaret Merrill'.** White flushed with pink. Strongly scented.
- ✔ **'Mountbatten'.** Golden yellow. Tall and vigorous.
- ✔ **'Rhapsody in Blue'.** Mauve-blue flowers make this the closest yet to a blue rose.
- ✔ **'Sexy Rexy'.** Light pink.

Climbing high with roses

Climbing and rambler roses are very long-branched roses that you can tie onto or weave into a support structure so that the roses look as if they're climbing. Climbing roses can be old-fashioned roses, hybrids, or chance variants of hybrid teas. The supporting structure can be anything from a chain-link fence to a fancy iron archway. Both climbing and rambler roses can be grown on all sorts of vertical structures, but to matchmake the right rose to a particular place, you need to know the difference between the two.

Climbing roses

Climbing roses form a permanent framework of branches and bear flowers on side shoots that come from these main stems. Most varieties repeat flower through the summer. Climbing roses are best suited to walls, fences, and trellis where the main branches don't get disturbed. For sites with little room, like arches, pillars, and small areas of wall, choose compact climbers, the smallest of which are *miniature* or *patio* climbers that grow to around 1.8 metres (6 feet) (find these under 'Using smaller roses').

Where possible, train the branches fan-wise or horizontally to encourage better flowering.

Most roses prefer sun but you can grow some in shade. Here are a few excellent climbers:

- **'Aloha'.** Rose-pink, strongly scented. Can grow in shade.
- **'Climbing Ena Harkness'.** Red.
- **'Gloire de Dijon'.** Buff-yellow flushed pink. Scented. Can grow in shade.
- **'Golden Showers'.** Bright yellow. Scented. Can grow in shade.
- **'Madame Alfred Carriere'.** White flushed pink. Scented. Can grow in shade.
- **'Penny Lane'.** Scented. Buff-yellow.
- **'Schoolgirl'.** Orange-apricot. Scented.
- **'Zephirine Drouhin'.** Deep pink, strongly scented. (These have thornless stems and are susceptible to mildew.) Can grow in shade.

You can train some *English roses* (covered below) as climbers, where they grow to around 1.8–2.4 metres (6–8 feet) high. These include 'Crown Princess Margareta' (apricot-orange), 'Gertrude Jekyll' (deep pink), 'Graham Thomas' (deep yellow), 'Tess of the D'Urbervilles' (bright crimson), and 'William Morris' (apricot-pink).

Rambler roses

Rambler roses produce long, unruly stems and scramble over their support. They are perfect for growing over pergolas, round arbours, through large trees or conifers, or even over small buildings. Ramblers bear masses of small flowers in large clusters, and all but a few varieties bloom once only in a spectacular display over several weeks.

Read the small print and check the eventual size when you buy rambler roses, because some ramblers grow very, very large indeed.

Here are some of our favourites:

- **'Alberic Barbier'.** Yellow fading to white. Scented.
- **'Albertine'.** Pink flushed with yellow. Scented.
- **'Bobbie James'.** Creamy white. Scented.
- **'Crimson Shower'.** Bright crimson.
- **'Debutante'.** Rose pink.
- **'Emily Gray'.** Golden yellow. Scented.

✓ **'Felicite-Perpetue'.** Cream flushed with pink. Light fragrance.

✓ **'Goldfinch'.** Pale yellow. Scented.

✓ **'Pauls Himalayan Musk'.** Pale pink. Scented.

✓ **'Sander's White'.** Pure white. Scented.

Using smaller roses

For small gardens, raised beds, and containers, you have some gorgeous smaller roses to choose from (see also 'Ground-cover roses', below). Miniature roses have small leaves, short stems, and small flowers; they usually grow between 30–60 centimetres (1–2 feet) tall. Just a little larger are *patio* roses, which are between a miniature and a floribunda in size and character. *Patio* or *miniature climbers* are neat little climbing roses that grow to a maximum of around 1.8 metres (6 feet) high. The big bonus of these small climbers is that you can grow them in large containers (wooden half-barrels or similar), unlike other, larger, climbing roses that need to be in the ground.

Miniature roses

✓ **'Jingle Bells'.** Bright red.

✓ **'Magic Carousel'.** Red edged in white.

✓ **'Mr Bluebird'.** Lavender blue.

✓ **'Party Girl'.** Apricot yellow and salmon pink.

✓ **'Pour Toi'.** White flushed with yellow.

✓ **'Rise 'n Shine'.** Yellow.

✓ **'Starina'.** Orange-red.

✓ **'Yellow Doll'.** Soft yellow.

Patio roses

✓ **'Anna Ford'.** Orange-red.

✓ **'Cider Cup'.** Deep apricot.

✓ **'Peter Pan'.** Dark red.

✓ **'Queen Mother'.** Pale pink.

✓ **'Sweet Dream'.** Peachy-apricot.

✓ **'Top Marks'.** Orange-red.

Find that rose!

Thousands of different rose species and varieties are available to choose from. If you're searching for a particular rose, take a peek at an invaluable annual publication entitled *Find That Rose*. The booklet lists over 3,000 varieties of rose in the UK and where to find them. Write to Find That Rose, Royal National Rose Society, The Gardens of the Rose, Chiswell Green, St Albans, Hertfordshire AL2 3NR. Alternatively you can call 01727-850461, or visit www.rnrs.org/find_that_rose.html. The leaflet costs £3.50 post paid (make cheques payable to 'RNRS (Sales) Ltd').

Miniature patio climbers

- ✔ **'Climbing Orange Sunblaze'.** Deep orange.

- ✔ **'Laura Ford'.** Golden yellow.

- ✔ **'Little Rambler'.** Blush pink.

- ✔ **'Nice Day'.** Soft pink.

- ✔ **'Warm Welcome'.** Orange.

When a rose is a tree

Another fun trick that rosarians have played on the hapless rose is turning it into a tree. These trees are called *standards*, and you can buy a range of popular roses this way. Imagine a regular rose such as the hybrid teas, floribundas, and miniature varieties described previously, but on stilts. Standards cost more because it takes more time and effort to create one, but they're worth it. The secret? Growers graft desired roses on top of a tall trunk. We like standards because they raise the flowers to nose height. So-called patio or miniature standards are the same idea, but smaller.

Shrub roses

You don't need to confine roses to a rose bed. Hundreds of kinds of roses serve as colourful garden shrubs, ground covers, and climbers. Shrub roses as a group combine some of the best traits of the toughest roses with the most beautiful. Ideal features of shrub roses are:

- ✔ Profuse, sometimes repeated bloom

- ✔ Good companions with other plants in a mixed border

- ✔ Need minimal pruning

✔ Attractive plant shape

✔ Good fragrance

English roses

Rose breeder David Austin creates English roses that combine the best characteristics of old and new, mixing the blossom shapes and scents of old garden roses with the disease resistance and repeat-flowering qualities of newer types. Most English roses are strongly scented and come in a range of sizes. Visit the nursery's display gardens in the Midlands (Bowling Green Lane, Albrighton, Wolverhampton) or order a catalogue online at www.davidaustinroses. com. Here's a taster of a few English roses:

✔ **'Eglantyne'.** Soft pink. 1 metre (3 feet).

✔ **'Falstaff'.** Rich, dark crimson, fading to rich purple. Scented. 1.2 metres (4 feet).

✔ **'Geoff Hamilton'.** Warm, soft pink fading to white. 1.5 metres (5 feet).

✔ **'Gertrude Jekyll'.** Strongly fragrant shell-pink blossoms on a plant that you can prune into a bush or train as a climber. 1.2 metres (4 feet).

✔ **'Glamis Castle'.** White, myrrh scented. 1 metre (3 feet).

✔ **'Golden Celebration'.** Pinkish buds open to fragrant yellow blossoms on a big plant that likes to sprawl and demands elbow room. 1.2 metres (4 feet).

✔ **'Graham Thomas'.** Rich yellow. Scented. Can also train it as a climber. 1.2 metres (4 feet).

✔ **'Heritage'.** Extremely well-behaved pink rose with a citrus scent; perfect as a specimen shrub in a mixed border.

Ground-cover roses

Ground-cover roses are a relatively new development and are ideal for small gardens. They produce long, wide-spreading canes, but grow no higher than about 60 centimetres (2 feet). They make excellent plants for raised beds, border edges, containers, even hanging baskets – and the more vigorous varieties make fantastic ground cover for large borders or banks. Look for the 'Flower Carpet' series of varieties, the 'County' series of varieties, plus a number of good individual ones. The 'Gamebird' series (including 'Grouse' and 'Partridge') are very vigorous, spreading up to 2.4 metres (8 feet), and are ideal for large banks and borders.

Here are a few of the best ground-cover roses:

✔ **'Cheshire'.** Light pink. 45 centimetres x 1 metre (18 inches x 3 feet).

✔ **'Flower Carpet'.** The original variety with bright pink flowers. 0.6–1.2 metres (2–4 feet). 'Flower Carpet' also comes in varieties of white, red, pink, and yellow.

> ✔ **'Hertfordshire'.** Pink. 60 centimetres x 1.2 metres (2 x 4 feet).

> ✔ **'Raubritter'.** Deep pink. Larger than most, forming a spreading mound 1 metre x 1.5 metres (3 x 5 feet).

> ✔ **'Suffolk'.** Bright scarlet with yellow stamens. 55 centimetres x 90 centimetres (1.8 x 3 feet).

> ✔ **'Worcestershire'.** Bright yellow. 0.6–0.9 metres (2–3 feet).

Hybrid musk roses

Hybrid musk roses are large, 1.8–2.4-metre (6–8-foot) shrubs that have good repeat-flowering characteristics. They descend in large measure from the musk rose, *Rosa moschata*, and many have a musky fragrance. Flowers are typically pink, and many produce bright orange hips, or fruits, in the autumn. Compared to most roses, hybrid musk roses grow well in light shade.

Some of the best varieties are

> ✔ **'Buff Beauty'.** Light apricot.

> ✔ **'Cornelia'.** Light pink.

> ✔ **'Felicia'.** Pink.

> ✔ **'Penelope'.** Shell pink.

> ✔ **'Prosperity'.** Ivory white.

Old garden roses

When we talk about an *old garden rose*, we usually mean old in the sense that the rose was popular among Victorians. And some types, such as the centifolias, have been grown for centuries. The plants you buy are, of course, only a couple of years old, the same as any rose you purchase. Here are just a few of the most popular old roses. If you want to check out a wide range of old rose varieties, go to a specialist nursery such as Peter Beales Roses, London Road, Attleborough, Norfolk, www.classicroses.co.uk

> ✔ **Alba.** All descended from *Rosa alba*, the White Rose of York, and made famous during the fifteenth-century War of the Roses. They make tall, vigorous, and thorny plants; flowers are fragrant and usually pale coloured. Blooms once per season. Varieties include 'Alba Semi-plena', 'Great Maiden's Blush', and 'Queen of Denmark' ('Königin von Dänemark').

> ✔ **Bourbon.** Tall, vigorous plants. Blooms more than once per season. The first Bourbons in the early 1800s were hybrids of *R. chinensis* and *R. damascena* 'Semperflorens'. Many forms evolved, shrubs and climbers, and most are very fragrant. One of our favorites is the pink-flowered shrub/climber 'Souvenir de la Malmaison'. Also consider the red and fragrant 'Madame Isaac Pereire'.

> ✔ **Centifolia.** Favored by Dutch painters of the 1700s, all are varieties of *Rosa centifolia*. All have flowers with so many thin, overlapping petals

that early on they were compared to a head of cabbage (thus their nick-name 'cabbage rose'). Centifolias have arching, thorny stems. Pink 'Fantin-Latour' is typical.

✔ **China.** Descendents of *R. chinensis*, these are the roses that came back to Europe from China via the tea trade in the early 1800s. Their capacity to bloom more than once quickly created a sensation, and the genes of these plants are prominent in most modern roses. The originals are delicate plants with lots of twiggy growth. Good varieties include 'Cecile Brunner' with tiny, dainty, pale pink blooms, and creamy-apricot 'Perle d'Or'.

✔ **Damask.** These roses descend from *R. damascena*, the rose of the perfume industry. Damask roses have thorny, arching stems. Flowers are usually pink and very fragrant, although 'Mme. Hardy' is white.

✔ **Gallica.** Many varieties of the French rose *R. gallica* exist. Plants are mostly compact, 90–120 centimetres (3–4 feet) high with arching stems. Fragrant roses come in clusters once per season. Varieties include *R. g.* 'Officinalis', the Apothecary Rose.

✔ **Hybrid perpetual.** Just prior to the advent of modern roses in the early twentieth century, these were the garden roses to have. Large bushes produce huge and often strongly fragrant flowers. One of the most popular varieties is 'Ferdinand Pichard' with pink flowers striped with crimson and purple.

✔ **Moss.** Roses with moss-like fur over their flower stems and buds are called moss roses. Two species of roses produce moss roses: *R. centifolia* (softer moss) and *R. damascena* (stiffer moss). Flowers are white, pink, or red and often very fragrant. Most bloom once per season.

✔ **Portland.** These small shrubs are also known as *Damask perpetuals*. They were among the first hybrids to combine the new China roses with the old European types, in this case *R. damascena* 'Semperflorens'. Fragrant flowers are typically pink. Good varieties are bright pink 'Comte de Chambord' and 'Jacques Cartier'.

Rugosa roses

These roses are all descendants of *Rosa rugosa*, a species of rose noted for its hardiness, vigorous growth, and disease resistance. Rugosa roses have a distinctive deeply quilted pattern in their leaves. Most repeat flower and some are strongly fragrant. Plants produce large hips that are well suited to jams and jellies. Height and spread are approximately 1.5 metres (5 feet). The rugosas make good, informal, intruder-deterring hedges.

✔ **'Fru Dagmar Hastrup'.** Flesh pink.

✔ **'Pink Grootendorst'.** Rose pink.

✔ **Rosa rugosa 'Alba'.** Pure white.

✔ **'Roseraie de Hay'.** Rich red-purple.

A rose without thorns

Looking for roses without the thorns? Now you can find a type of rose called 'Smooth Touch'. Remarkably, they are absolutely thornless. Flowers are about 8 centimetres (3 inches) wide and nicely shaped. Various colours are available including red, pink, and white. See also 'Zephirine Drouhin' under 'Climbing roses' in this chapter.

Modern shrub roses

A catch-all heading for a variety of relatively new shrub roses. All are strong growers and repeat flower to a reasonable extent. Good varieties include:

- ✔ **'Ballerina'.** Clusters of many small, pink and white flowers. 1.2 metres (4 feet).

- ✔ **'Bonica'.** Clusters of rose-pink flowers. 1.2 metres (4 feet).

- ✔ **'Fruhlingsgold'.** Large, pale yellow flowers. Scented. 1.8 metres (6 feet).

- ✔ **'Jacqueline du Pre'.** Large, blush-white flowers. 1.2 metres (4 feet).

- ✔ **'Nevada'.** Large, creamy-white blooms with golden stamens. 1.8 metres (6 feet).

- ✔ **'Rhapsody in Blue'.** An unusual colour, purple fading to mid-blue. 1.2 metres (4 feet).

Gardening with Roses

Roses in formal rows are a typical sight in public gardens, but the plants are a lot more versatile than that. You can use roses in many more ways in your own garden.

You can put several roses together in a special rose bed, plant a group of the same kind of rose in a line to create a hedge, or work your roses into a mixed bed or border with other flowers. In all three of these situations, you soon discover that roses are not beautiful all the time. Solve this problem by using companion plants that look great when your roses aren't blooming.

- ✔ **For winter allure.** Keep the scene lively with small evergreen shrubs, ground-cover junipers, or ornamental grasses.

- ✔ **For spring excitement.** Punctuate your rose planting with small clumps of daffodil, muscari, or crocus bulbs; spring bedding such as double daisy (*Bellis*) and forget-me-not (*Myosotis*); or an edging of pansies.

> ✔ **For midsummer colour and contrast.** Many herbaceous perennials make excellent partners to roses, such as lady's mantle (*Alchemilla*), geraniums, blue salvias, dwarf daylilies, thymes, artemisias, and lamb's ears (*Stachys*).

Buying Roses

The best selection of roses hits the garden centres in mid to late autumn, when the new season's crop of roses have been lifted and put into containers or sold *bare root* with their roots tightly wrapped in plastic. Bare-root roses look dead, but they're merely dormant, or sleeping. Specialist rose nurseries despatch bare rooted plants during the dormant season, though it's worth ordering well beforehand if you're after particular varieties in case stock sells out. At other times of year, roses are available in containers; treat and plant them like you would any other shrub you bring home from the garden. (See Chapter 13 for how to plant.)

If you want your roses to hit the ground running, spend the little extra money for top-quality plants, which have more stems and roots than less expensive plants. Whether bare root or in a container, a top-grade rose has several fresh, moist (green, not shrivelled) stems. Most roses are really two plants – the first plant is the hardy, vigorous root, and the second plant is the fancy rose variety grafted onto that root. The graft or *bud union* should look like a solid bulge just above the roots (see Figure 10-1).

What do you want your rose to do?

Here's a thumbnail guide to the various sites around a garden that are suited to different types of roses.

✔ **Formal beds and borders:** Floribundas, hybrid teas

✔ **Hedges:** Rugosa roses, tall floribundas

✔ **Perennial and shrub borders:** All classes, but especially ground covers, floribundas, or shrubs

✔ **Edging and low borders:** Miniatures, ground covers, small shrub roses

✔ **Containers:** miniature, patio, and compact ground covers, plus miniature/patio climbers in large containers.

✔ **Formal rose garden:** Hybrid teas, floribundas

✔ **Cutting:** All roses

✔ **In arrangements:** All classes, but especially hybrid teas for long stems

✔ **Fragrance:** Many new and old roses

✔ **Walls or trellises:** Climbers

✔ **Low fences:** Miniature patio climbers

✔ **Low-maintenance gardens:** Modern shrub roses, ground covers

✔ **Long flowering:** Hybrid teas; floribundas; many shrub roses; miniatures and patio roses; ground covers.

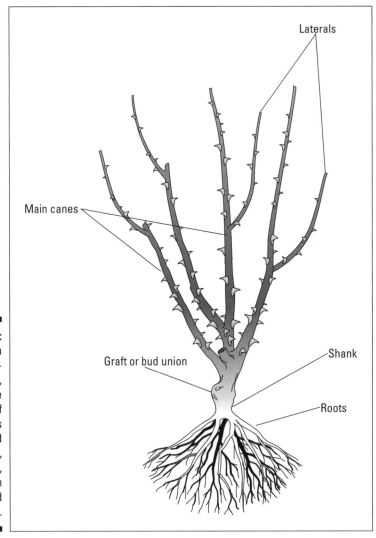

Laterals

Main canes

Graft or bud union

Shank

Roots

Figure 10-1:
When you buy a bare-root rose, familiarise yourself with its parts: bud union, shank, roots, main canes, and laterals.

The latest and greatest roses are usually registered under *plant breeders' rights*. Having breeders' rights is fair because if the rose is successful, a royalty from the patent rewards the hybridiser who invested years of cross-breeding into its development. Older, non-registered roses are often a bit cheaper.

Planting Roses

Roses are sun-loving plants, so place your roses where they can get at least six hours of sun each day. In cool, cloudy climates, roses grow best with all-day sun; in really hot regions, afternoon shade gives them a much-needed break. Only one type of rose, the hybrid musks, are notable for shade tolerance and even these prefer full sun.

Roses need sufficient air circulation to help their leaves dry quickly whenever they get wet – don't crowd the plants in close quarters. Also, make sure that you can reach your roses easily when the time comes to cut flowers, trim, and prune them.

Roses really love a fertile soil and thrive on heavy soils like clay where nutrients don't get washed away in a hurry. If your soil is light (sandy or stony), dig in loads of organic matter such as well-rotted manure, and mulch every spring with more of the same. Roses prefer a near-neutral soil pH of 6.5 to 7.0 (see Chapter 11 for details on testing and adjusting your soil pH).

To plant a bare-root rose in good, rich topsoil, dig a hole wide enough to extend the roots without bending them and create a cone of soil in the middle of the hole. If the roots are damaged, trim them as needed. Adjust the depth of the hole and the height of the soil cone until the graft union is just at or slightly above the soil level. Spread the roots over the low cone of soil in the centre of the planting hole. (See Figure 10-2.) Backfill with the soil removed from the hole, firming the soil in place with your hands. Finally, water thoroughly to settle soil and eliminate air pockets.

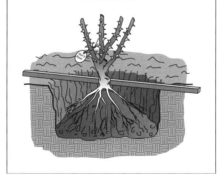

Figure 10-2: Spread the bare roots over a cone of soil.

To plant a rose in poor or light soil, dig a roomy planting hole about 45 x 60 centimetres (18 x 24 inches) square, and put the excavated soil in a wheelbarrow. Mix the excavated soil with 25 per cent composted bark and 25 per cent bagged compost, or 50 per cent composted manure, and a couple of handfuls of slow-release fertiliser. Partially refill the hole with the enriched soil, spread out the roots of your rose, add some more soil, and water well. Then finish dumping in your enriched soil.

Fertilising and Watering

Most roses need frequent applications of fertiliser to keep them growing vigorously and blooming repeatedly. To keep the process simple, go to the nursery and buy fertiliser labelled 'Rose Food', and follow the directions on the package.

Make your first application about four to six weeks before growth begins in spring, and repeat every eight to ten weeks through summer until about mid-August. Then stop, otherwise you encourage the rose to produce lots of soft, fleshy growth that can be damaged by frost.

Watering is the other key to productive roses. Of course, all kinds of variables (your climate, soil, and much more) can affect how you water. Consider a few major guidelines:

- ✔ Roses need more water more often in hot weather than in cool weather.
- ✔ Even if it rains often where you live, rainfall alone may not provide enough moisture for your roses.
- ✔ When you water, do it deeply enough to wet the entire root zone – to a depth of at least 45 centimetres (18 inches).
- ✔ If you want to be sure that the root zone is wet enough, dig into the soil. If the top 5–10 centimetres (2–4 inches) are dry, you probably need to water.
- ✔ To reduce disease problems, water the soil, not the leaves, by using soaker hoses or drip irrigation.
- ✔ Mulch to conserve moisture in the soil.

For more tips and ideas about watering, meander over to Chapter 14.

Cutting Through the Mystery of Pruning

Know which type of rose you have, and it's easy to find the right method of pruning. You don't need to get too hung up on the finer points of pruning. A pruning trial carried out by the Royal National Rose Society showed that roses pruned with a hedgetrimmer actually bloomed better than those pruned slowly and with care! They just looked a bit less tidy.

Almost all roses need to be pruned in late winter/early spring, round about March time. The exception is rambler roses, which need pruning in summer after flowering. With any pruning job, first remove all dead, diseased, or damaged stems, and then look at tackling the remainder. Buds grow in the direction they're facing, so cut to an outward-growing bud where possible to encourage an open-centred plant. Cut back weak shoots hard to increase growth, but less hard with vigorous growths. After pruning, feed and mulch to encourage lots of new growth.

Type of rose	*How to prune*
Hybrid tea and floribunda bush roses	Cut strong shoots back to within 5–7.5 centimetres (2–3 inches) of last year's growth (last year's growth is thicker, and a different colour). Cut weaker shoots to within 2.5 centimetres (1 inch).
Shrub roses	On older bushes, remove a quarter to a third of the oldest and thickest branches, as near to the base as possible.
Climbing roses	The main stems remain as a permanent framework and the flowers are produced on side shoots. Cut these side shoots back to 2–3 buds from the main stems.
Rambler roses	Prune in late summer once flowering has finished. Remove all the branches that have borne flowers. You should see lots of new, young stems developing, which you can tie in to the support afterwards.

When it comes to knowing exactly how to prune a rose, you must discuss the matter with your plant. The first year with any rose is like a blind date – you don't know what the rose thinks of you; you don't know what you think of it. Here are some things to look for when you think that your rose is subliminally telling you that it wants to be pruned:

- **Long, skinny canes with a tuft of leaves at the end:** Carefully examine the canes for tiny, pinkish, pointed bumps called leaf buds. Find a good leaf bud that faces away from the centre of the plant and is no more than halfway down the cane. Prune about 1 centimetre (¼ inch) above that bud.

- **Branches that come up out of the ground below the graft union:** These are suckers – and they're not wanted! Gently dig down to where these branches begin and then, with a sharp tug, sever them from the roots (rather than cutting, which encourages lots more suckers to grow). Suckers are shoots from the rootstock, usually an ultravigorous but unattractive type of rose. If you don't cut them out, they can take over the rose plant.

Some roses are grown *on their own roots* (that is, not grafted), in which case there's no problem in keeping any canes from below ground. The lumpy graft union, or joint, is pretty obvious to spot.

✔ **Sickly looking branches where most of the leaves show black, circular freckles:** This combination of symptoms indicates a common disease called *black spot* (see Chapter 16). Prune off badly affected branches to keep black spot from spreading out of control.

✔ **Dead or damaged stems:** Prune them out as shown in Figure 10-3.

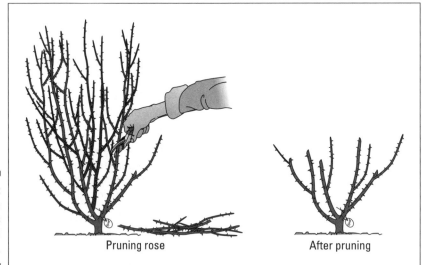

Figure 10-3: Prune out suckers and dead branches.

Pruning rose   After pruning

O Rose, Thou Art Sick: Keeping Roses Healthy

How perfect do you want your roses to be? We recommend a commonsense approach. Live with a few bugs. But if they begin to wipe out your plants, you can take some steps to control problems. However, use only products that have the least impact on the environment. See Chapter 16 for details on pest-control products.

You can do a number of things to keep potential pest and disease problems to a minimum:

✔ **Grow healthy roses.** Feed, water, and prune on a regular basis.

✔ **Plant problem-free varieties.** As you shop, pay attention to the descriptions that cite resistance to diseases, especially black spot.

✔ **Encourage beneficial insects.** The good guys include ladybirds, green lacewings, and hoverflies.

✔ **Keep your garden clean.** Doing so reduces the number of hiding places for pests and diseases.

Be prepared for the inevitable. No rose is totally immune to the insects that typically prey on them – aphids, rose sawfly, and spider mites. Typical diseases are black spot, mildew, and rust. For descriptions of these pests and diseases and how to control them, see Chapter 16.

Part IV
At Ground Level

"They may be slow but they're eco-friendly
and they also fertilise the lawn at the
same time."

In this part . . .

This is the part where you get your hands dirty. (If you have an aversion to getting a bit of soil on your hands, now is your chance to take up stamp collecting.) Even though it's the stuff that happens above ground that draws all the ooohs and aaahs, most of the important action that determines whether your plants will flourish takes place below ground.

Here you find out how to improve your soil so that your garden has its best chance to succeed, how to recycle your garden and kitchen waste, have fun raising your own plants, and how to get plants off to the best start in life.

Chapter 11

Understanding and Improving Soil

. . . .

. . . .

*P*reparing your soil is probably the most important step towards bringing your garden to life. The reason? *Roots.* This underground lifeline makes up half of every plant – sometimes more. You may often forget about roots, however, because you don't see them – except for the occasional tree root that the lawn mower keeps hitting. But the roots are there, spreading, digging, and searching for nutrients and moisture.

Trouble is, soil preparation just isn't an exciting part of gardening, and it's likely to involve a fair bit of work, so it's all too tempting to skimp this stage and head straight for the planting. Don't. Please. Imagine trying to build a house without any foundations; it's the same trying to grow a garden without any decent soil.

Before you plant, take some time to get acquainted with your soil. (It's more interesting than you think!) Chances are, you'll find out that you need to make some improvements – typically by adding organic matter and perhaps a few other goodies as well. Your goal, as you discover in this chapter, is to create an airy soil, rich in oxygen and nutrients that enable your plants to thrive.

Clearing the Ground

The perfect spot for your garden may already be occupied. Whether it's a sweep of lawn, a patch full of weeds, or a border of plants in the wrong place, you need to clear your site of existing vegetation before improving the soil in readiness for new planting. Follow these steps for clearing a site where you intend to place your garden:

1. **Outline the area where to go to work.**

   If you're developing a border, mark it out clearly first. For a square or rectangular area, you can establish straight-edge lines by stretching a string between two sticks. Leave the string in place or mark the line with a trickle of sand, spray paint, or flour. For curved areas of the garden, use a garden hose or rope to lay out the line. Adjust the hose position until the curve looks smooth.

2. **Use a flat spade to dig a small trench that establishes the outline of the garden plot.**

3. **Clear the surface by removing weeds, bushes, and large stones.**

4. **Mow the site to clear rough, grassy ground.**

5. **Cut down woody plants and dig out the roots.**

6. **When the vegetation is down to a manageable level, you can remove the turf and other low vegetation.**

You can use several techniques for clearing the site. If the garden is currently lawn, you can strip off the turf, roots and all, by using a flat spade or mechanised turf cutter.

Stripping turf

Your site-clearing process may very well involve getting rid of a lawn. Here's how to clear a small area by hand:

1. **A couple of days prior to digging, water the area that you want to clear if the ground is dry.**

   Stripping turf is easier when the soil is lightly moist.

2. **If you haven't done so already, mark the edges of the plot.**

3. **Starting at one side of the plot, slip your spade under the grass and slide it under the turf.**

   Don't dig too deep; you want to remove merely the turf and a few centimetres of roots.

   Another system is to precut the turf into square or rectangular sections and then loosen each section with the spade.

4. **Pivot the tool up, letting the turf flip up over the spade.**

5. **Slice off the turf section and toss it into a wheelbarrow to take to the compost pile.**

If you have a large area of turf to clear, then renting a turf cutter is by far the best approach. These machines are large and heavy, so unless you have a pick-up truck or trailer to get one home, you'll need to arrange for the tool hire shop to deliver and collect the machine.

Another approach is to get rid of grass by spraying it with a total herbicide (weedkiller). When the grass is completely dead, you can rotovate into the soil, adding organic matter to the soil in the process! However, most gardeners are better off avoiding weedkiller if at all possible, even considering the promise of saving time and energy, because all chemicals have some impact on the environment. The exception is if you're faced with tenacious perennial weeds. Read on for more on tackling weeds and clearing the ground.

Composting turf

Never, ever, chuck out unwanted turf; these uninspiring slabs of grass rot down to make fantastic and nutritious soil that you can return to the garden and really help your plants to thrive. If you have just a few turves, add them to the compost heap. Larger quantities are best stacked separately, sandwiching the turf in layers with the grassy side face-to-face in each one. Finish with the top layer stacked soil-uppermost. Ignore the heap for a year, after which you'll find a mound of wonderful, crumbly soil.

Other soil-clearing methods

Clearing the ground of weeds is an important part of soil preparation. Bringing a weedy patch under control need not be a hard slog, and indeed may take hardly any work at all if time is on your side (see 'The big cover-up' later in this chapter). First, get to know your enemy! Weeds divide into two groups: annuals and perennials. Annual weeds grow fresh from seed every year and aren't too much of a problem, because they only need killing once. Perennial weeds are the real nightmare because they regrow from even a tiny piece of root left in the soil. Left unchecked, they run riot and become very hard to get rid of. See Chapter 16 for more on weeds.

It's hugely important to clear the ground thoroughly *before* you do any cultivating or planting. If you're not in any hurry to get planting, the easiest way is to slowly smother your weeds for a year. Otherwise, choose your method of control from the following list.

> ✔ **Hoeing.** Done regularly, this is a wonderfully easy way to control all annual weeds and the seedlings of perennial ones. Hoe during dry weather every few weeks whilst weeds are young, sliding a sharp hoe vigorously along the soil's surface to chop off top growth, and walking backwards so you don't tread on newly-worked ground. (See Chapter 17 to find out more about hoes.)

✔ **Digging.** When clearing weedy ground, dig out every scrap of perennial weed root. Don't compost this waste, as the roots will continue to grow, but bag it up and take it to the green waste section of your local tip Or, spread out the roots in the sun until they're completely dried up, then add them to your compost heap.

✔ **Weedkillers** (Herbicides). The fewer chemicals you use in a garden, the better it is for the whole environment, but in some cases weedkiller is the only resort. Often the best approach is to use a combination of methods, hand-weeding first and then applying chemical to any stubborn weeds that continue to grow. Weedkillers divide into two main types:

• **Contact weedkillers.** Only effective against annual weeds, because this chemical kills the growth it touches but not the roots.

• **Systemic weedkillers.** Used to combat perennial weeds, you spray the chemical onto the leaves and the plant then takes the poison right down to the roots. You may need several applications on well-established weeds. Take great care not to accidentally spray garden plants because they'll die too, so apply on a windless day and shield nearby plants with wood or cardboard.

The big cover-up

You need to do almost no work to get rid of weeds by the cover-up method – just time and patience. By depriving them of light, even the toughest weeds eventually die.

First, choose any readily available light-excluding material. A waste material is best, being both free and recyclable. These include old carpet, carpet underlay, or flattened cardboard boxes. Alternatively, you can buy a bulk roll of landscaping fabric or heavy-duty black polythene.

Mow or cut down the worst of the weeds, then cover the ground with your chosen material. Ensure a good overlap at any joins, and weigh down or bury the edges to keep out all light.

After about a year everything underneath should be completely dead and the ground should be fairly easy to dig over. Leave the ground bare for a couple of months after digging and before planting so annual weed seeds can germinate and you can hoe off the seedlings.

Getting to Know Your Soil

Taking time to create a healthy underground environment before you plant goes a long way toward ensuring a healthy, productive garden. You need to know only a few basics and perform some easy tests to determine the characteristics of your soil, and you're ready to start improving your soil like an expert!

To understand your soil, keep in mind what plants need from soil: moisture, air, and nutrients.

Soil texture

Soil comprises air spaces, organic matter, and, mostly, mineral particles. Soil minerals come in three types: sand, silt, and clay. Sand is the largest particle in most garden soils. Silt particles are smaller than fine sand and larger than clay. Clay is the smallest particle. The relative proportions of these particles in the soil determine its texture.

The ideal soil texture is *loam*, which is composed of sand, silt, and clay. Loam soils have the properties of all three mineral types in roughly equal proportions – enough sand to allow good water drainage and air circulation, but enough clay to retain moisture and nutrients. (See Figure 11-1.)

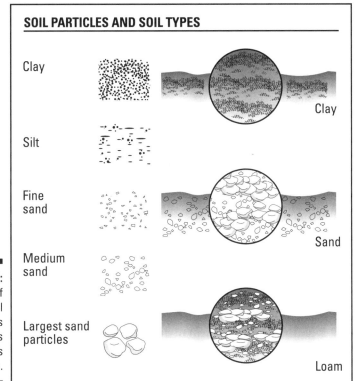

SOIL PARTICLES AND SOIL TYPES

Clay

Clay

Silt

Fine sand

Sand

Medium sand

Largest sand particles

Loam

Figure 11-1: The size of the mineral particles determines a soil's texture.

Most garden soils are best understood as either sandy, clay, or loam.

- **Sandy.** Water drains through sandy soils fast, so it dries quickly. Nutrients also pass through sandy soils quickly. Plants in sandy soils often need lighter, more frequent applications of water and fertilizer.

- **Clay.** Soils dominated by clay particles are heavy and tend to pack tightly. Clay soil sticks to your shoes and shovel when it's wet, and cracks when dry. Water enters and drains slowly from clay soils, which can make them difficult to manage. On the other hand, clay soil's ability to retain moisture and nutrients makes them very fertile.

- **Loam.** Loam soils come in many types, but all combine the properties of sand, silt, and clay. A 'perfect' loam soil contains 40 per cent sand, 40 per cent silt, and 20 per cent clay. Loam soils have such a good reputation because they're ideal for most plants. But many plants grow well in non-loam soils.

A quick test for texture: Ribbons and bows

You can use two methods to identify your soil's texture: the *ribbons-and-bows method* and the *jar method*.

Get a general idea of your soil's texture by taking a handful of moist soil, squeezing it into a ball, and working it out in a ribbon between your thumb and your forefinger. Stand the ribbon straight up in the air.

- If you can't form a ribbon, the soil is at least 50 per cent sand and has very little clay.

- If the ribbon is less than 5 centimetres (2 inches) long before breaking, your soil has roughly 25 per cent clay in it.

- If the ribbon is 5–9 centimetres (2–3.5 inches) long, it has about 40 per cent clay.

- If the ribbon is greater than 9 centimetres (3.5 inches) long and doesn't break when held up, it is at least 50 per cent clay.

A more accurate test for texture: The jar method

For most gardeners most of the time, knowing the exact texture of your soil is not so important. But once you do know, that information can help explain much of what goes on in your garden. You can then tailor your soil management for maximum effect. Allow several days to carry out the following test.

Here's how to use the jar method:

1. **Put 5 centimetres (2 inches) of dry, crushed garden soil in a tall jar.**

2. **Fill the jar two-thirds with water and add a teaspoon of a dispersing agent, such as a washing up liquid or table salt.**

3. **Shake the jar thoroughly and let the contents settle.**

4. **Measure the depths of the different layers of soil.**

   When the sand settles to the bottom (in about a minute), measure the depth of that layer.

   Silt settles in four to five hours. You should see a colour and size difference between the silt and sand layers; if not, subtract the sand depth from the total to determine the silt depth. The clay takes days to settle, and some of the smallest particles may remain permanently in suspension.

By measuring the depth of each layer, you can figure out the approximate percentages of sand, silt, and clay in your soil. For example, you have loam soil if the 5 centimetres (2 inches) of soil settles down like this: The sand and silt layers are about 2 centimetres (0.75 inches) each, and the clay layer is less than 1.25 centimetres (0.5 inches).

Soil structure

The way in which sand, silt, and clay particles combine or cluster is called the *soil structure*. Structure modifies the influence of texture. Most often, gardeners use additions of organic matter – compost, manure, mulch, and so on – to improve soil structure.

No matter what kind of soil you have, adding organic matter improves the soil structure. Organic matter breaks down to form *humus*, which enables small clay or silt particles to stick together to form larger aggregates; in sandy soils, humus acts like a sponge to catch and hold moisture and nutrients. An easy method of determining your soil structure is the *percolation method*.

The percolation do-it-yourself test evaluates *water drainage* – the ability of water to move through the soil, which is called the *percolation rate*. To evaluate drainage:

1. **Dig several holes 30 centimetres deep x 45 centimetres wide (1 foot x 2 feet) in various places in your garden.**

2. **Cover the holes with sheets of plastic to let the soil dry out.**

3. **When the soil is dry, fill each hole to the top with water and record the time it takes for the water to completely drain.**

   The ideal time is between 10 and 30 minutes.

   - If the water drains in less than 10 minutes, the soil will tend to dry out too quickly in the summer. Amend the soil with moisture-retaining matter such as peat moss and humus.

   - If it takes 30 minutes to 4 hours to drain, you can still grow most plants but you have to water it slowly to avoid runoff and to allow the water to soak in deeply.

- If your soil takes longer than 4 hours to drain, you may have a drainage problem. In sandy soil, dig 30–60 centimetres (a foot or two) deep to see whether a hard layer is blocking water movement. If so, break it up in the area you want plants to grow. You may have to dig down with a post-hole digger, though in some cases, the impermeable layer is too deep even for that. You can also use a nozzle on the end of a pipe to make a water jet bore through an impermeable layer.

- If your soil is waterlogged, the hole may actually fill up with water! If this is the case, you'll need to put in a substantial amount of work to install a drainage system, or take the easier approach of growing moisture-loving 'bog garden' plants such as willows and marsh marigold.

If your soil is clay, create a raised bed and use purchased soil or a homemade soil mix for planting. The goal is to get plant roots up out of the soggy soil and into well-drained, elevated soil rich with organic matter.

One more big thing: Soil pH

The symbol pH represents the relative alkalinity or acidity of the soil. You don't need to know what it means, but in case you're ever asked the question in pub quizzes the symbol *pH* represents the 'negative logarithm of hydrogen ion concentration.' Bet you wish you'd never asked!

Professional soil analysis

For the definitive word on your soil's chemistry and makeup, a professional test is the ultimate truth. The results of these tests can tell you about soil nutrient levels, soil structure, and pH. You also get suggestions on how to make your soil even better.

Keep in mind that the reliability of any soil test depends on the accuracy of the soil sample. Avoid contaminating soil samples with residue from tools, containers, or cigarette ash, for example. The small sample that you send to a lab must also be representative of your garden. Gather soil from several places and mix it together to form a composite picture of the plot. However, don't mix soil from different garden areas where you'll be growing plants with different needs or with soil near foundations or walls where construction residues may remain. Follow the directions from the soil lab for best results.

Soil pH is rated numerically on a logarithmic scale of 1 to 14, but you'll almost never see a soil with a pH of 2 or 13. In practice, soil with a pH of 4.5 is strongly acidic and a pH of 9.5 is strongly alkaline. Most soils in the world range between a pH of 5 and 9. An absolutely neutral pH is 7.0.

Finding out your soil pH is important because certain plants (like rhododendrons and azaleas) need an acid soil in order to thrive, while the ideal pH for most plants is from 6.0 to 7.0. Kits for testing pH are available in garden centres. Or, if you want to be spot-on accurate, send off a soil sample for professional analysis.

Improving Your Soil

If your soil is a nice, fertile blend – one that grows good grass – you may not need to do anything special to it to grow most garden plants. But beefing up the organic content never hurts, because organic matter is constantly being broken down. *Organic matter* – such as well-rotted leaves, hay, grass clippings, compost, and decomposed cow or horse manure – improves soil texture, and releases nutrients and other chemicals that make soil fertile and productive. Organic matter is especially valuable for adding richness to sand and lightness to clay. The organic material makes good gardens great and poor gardens better by making any soil more like the ideal loamy soil. Be careful not to use cat or dog droppings, because this waste can contain parasites.

Before planting, spread and dig in a layer of organic matter (at least 5 centimetres or 2 inches thick), such as garden compost, well-rotted manure, or leafmould. Then, each year, mulch planted areas with another layer of the same. Fallen plant debris is left to rot down naturally in the wild and boosts soil fertility. But, in our gardens, most people like to be tidy gardeners and gather up fallen leaves and grass clippings. Never chuck out this garden waste, but use it to make compost to return all this fertility to your own plot (and reduce the amount of waste going to landfill into the bargain). Dig your way over to Chapter 14 to find out how.

Be prepared to amend the entire planting area so that plant roots can grow freely without encountering a bewildering range of different soil blends. Dramatically different soil types can stop root growth cold.

Here are some tips to improve tough soils:

✔ Add a 5–10 centimetre (2–4 inch) deep layer of compost to compacted soils in perennial beds annually. You don't need to dig it into the soil; worms and other soil organisms do the job for you.

- ✔ Break up a compacted layer and build extra-deep top soil in annual gardens by double digging (see the section 'Double digging' in this chapter) or by deeply cultivating the soil below the hard layer and mixing in generous amounts of organic matter.

- ✔ Build a raised bed if the soil is really poor and doesn't allow for planting. (See 'Simple raised beds' in this chapter.) Build the bed about 20 centimetres (8 inches) high – or even higher if you install a retaining wall. Cover the existing soil with bought-in topsoil that's preblended with about 20 per cent compost.

Top ingredients for scrumptious soil

Organic matter that you add to your soil comes in loads of different forms and varieties. Garden centres offer many kinds, bagged up in 80-litre sacks, but this is the costly approach (unless you have a tiny garden or difficult access, in which case the convenience of bagged materials far outweighs the cost). If you decide to go for the bagged option, take care not to confuse *soil improvers* with more expensive *planting composts* or *potting composts*. Buying in bulk is generally the best approach, either by purchasing loose material by the truck or trailer-load, or in huge cubic-metre bulk bags.

Here are some of the tempting tidbits that can do wonders to improve the texture of garden soil:

- ✔ **Compost.** When different kinds of dead plant material get piled together, dampened, and stirred or turned every week or so to keep air in the mixture, they become compost (after several months). Products labelled as compost can originate from all sorts of stuff. Fallen leaves, shredded Christmas trees, and wood chips left from tree-trimming crews often find their way to compost-manufacturing facilities.

  One place to get lots of compost cheap is from your local waste site. Many councils offer compost and mulch; some charge a modest fee. The only caveat is quality. Expect to find little bits of sticks and other recognizable things in a bag of compost, but mostly judge quality by the texture of the material, which should be soft and springy. If you plan to buy a large quantity of compost, compare products packaged by different companies to find the best texture.

- ✔ **Well-rotted manure.** In addition to its soil-improving properties, horse or farmyard manure also contains a proportion of important plant nutrients. Nutrient content varies with the type of manure. Composted chicken manure is very potent, whereas horse manure is comparatively lightweight. The amount of manure you use depends on your soil type. With bulky manure from large animals (cow, horse, goat, sheep), put on a layer around 7.5–10 centimeters (3–4 inches) thick. Follow package application rates when using stronger manure from chickens and other birds.

If animals are kept locally, you can probably obtain manure free or for a small charge if you 'pick your own' – the big problem here is transporting the stuff home without trashing your car. Sometimes you can buy bagged manure, or you may be able to get a load delivered for a reasonable charge.

Any manure must be well-rotted (that is, at least six months old). Fresher manure is likely to damage and even kill your plants, particularly young ones.

Mushroom compost is another soil improver. This is the discarded compost used after growing mushrooms, the basis of which is top quality manure. Mushroom compost contains some lime, so avoid using it on acid-loving (lime-hating) plants like rhododendrons.

✔ **Topsoil.** Sometimes topsoil is exactly what you might find in bags of compost, and other times it may look more like unbelievably black soil. Whatever the bag contents include, topsoil is almost always fairly cheap – but very heavy, and hence requires delivery (not always cheap). You can use bagged topsoil as a soil improver, or use so much of it that your flower bed is filled with mostly imported topsoil and only a little of the native stuff.

✔ **Peat.** Peat is a very spongy, acidic, brown material harvested from peat bogs. If you're concerned about the sustainability of peat harvesting, a better alternative is coir (shredded coconut husk).

Changing pH

If you're growing pH-sensitive plants, or if you're dealing with very acidic or very alkaline soils, you can adjust pH with specific soil amendments. It's relatively easy to make soil less acidic, by adding ground limestone, but much less easy to make a limy soil acidic. If you want to grow acid-loving plants and your soil is limy, the best approach is to make raised beds and fill them with bought-in topsoil or compost that is suitably acid. The best option is to choose garden plants that grow well in your native soil with its existing pH.

Adding nutrients

If your soil is low in nutrients, which you can determine by having the soil tested or by seeing that plants grow poorly, add extra nutrients. If your soil has been tested, add amendments and fertilisers according to the lab's recommendations. If you haven't tested the soil, add a complete fertiliser according to package directions. A *complete fertiliser* is one that contains nitrogen, phosphorus, and potassium, the major nutrients that all plants need. See Chapter 14 for more on nutrients.

Green manure crops and cover crops

One easy way for gardeners to add organic matter and nutrients to the soil is to grow *green manure crops*. These are plants grown to be chopped and dug into the soil when they are still green (before they blossom and produce seeds). The succulent plant material breaks down quickly, adding nutrients and improving soil texture. These crops are usually grown during the main gardening season – between crops or just after harvesting a crop. Some green manure crops remain standing over the winter and get dug into the soil before spring planting.

Cover crops are often the same plants that are used for green manure crops. However, the primary purposes of a cover crop are to prevent soil erosion and to choke out weeds, usually when the soil is bare of crops before and after the harvest.

The plants used as green manure and cover crops can be divided into two broad categories: *legumes* and *nonlegumes*. Legumes have special nodules on their roots that house nitrogen-fixing bacteria of the genus *Rhizobium*. Examples of legumes are beans, vetches, and clovers. If you incorporate the legumes back into the soil, succeeding crops benefit from the nitrogen that the legumes and its *Rhizobium* absorbed from the air.

Although nonlegumes don't add as much nitrogen to the soil as legumes do, many nonlegumes are very useful as green manure and cover crops simply for the organic matter that they add to the soil. Examples on nonlegumes that are good for green manure are grazing rye and mustard.

Seed of green manure crops is available from some nurseries and garden centres, or you can purchase it by mail order from seed suppliers.

Cultivating the Soil

The depth and techniques that you use to loosen the soil depend on which plants you intend to grow and the condition of your soil. For your average garden of annual flowers and vegetables, for example, you can use a process called *single digging* to break up the top 20 centimetres (8 inches) of soil by using a spade or rotovator.

When to work the soil

Timing your digging is all-important. You need to wait until the soil is in the right condition – lightly moist, but not wet. If it's too wet, clay soil can dry into brick. If too dry, soil can turn into dust and blow away, leaving beneficial soil life to perish. If your soil tends to be wet and clammy in spring when you're ready to plant annual flowers, you can avoid this frustration by preparing your beds in the autumn, when dry conditions often prevail.

Fortunately, the right soil condition is easy to evaluate. Take a handful of soil and squeeze it in your fist. Tap the resulting ball with your finger. If it breaks up easily, the soil is ready. If it stays in a sodden clump, the soil needs to dry out more. Or go down the easy route: if the soil sticks to your boots, it's too wet to dig!

In existing gardens with light, easily worked soil, you may be able to turn the ground with a spade without too much difficulty and minimise organic matter loss. Dig heavier ground in autumn, so the frost can help break up the soil clumps over winter. Then dig again in spring and finish up with a rake.

Single digging

Begin digging by removing a section of soil the width of the bed and the depth of your spade. Place excavated soil in a wheelbarrow, or simply pile the soil to the side temporarily. Soon, you'll have what looks like a shallow grave. Next, slice down into the adjacent portion of soil with the spade and roll that soil into the trench you just made. Continue this process until you have covered the garden width (or length). Finally, haul the soil excavated from the first trench and place it into the last space.

After your first pass with the shovel, break up the clods and add the soil improvers and fertiliser. Then dig through the bed again, rake vigorously to break up clods and to mix in the improvers. Use a garden rake to comb through the soil and remove rocks, clods, and any chunks of vegetation or plant roots that you missed previously. Smooth the soil over the entire bed by raking, and you're ready to plant.

Time for a rotovator

Digging a small flower bed is great exercise that beats going to the gym, but preparing a large area by hand in one day is almost impossible without the help of a rotovator. These handy machines are worth buying if you have a large garden that you want to cultivate regularly (if you grow vegetables, for example), otherwise, borrow or hire one. Lightweight minitillers are sufficient for many cultivating chores. For larger jobs, look to either front- or rear-tined tillers. Professional growers usually favour the latter.

Another option is to have someone else prepare your garden. No matter where you live, you can usually find professional gardeners or landscapers in your area. Look in the classified ads in the newspaper or call local garden centres to find a recommended landscaper. After you or your hired person has cultivated the area and removed any debris, spread out your soil amendments and fertiliser, and cultivate it again.

Rotovators are handy tools for occasional use. Beware, however, that repeated use can create a hard layer below the soil surface. Tillers promote faster breakdown of soil organic matter because of how they stir and mix the soil; and tillers cultivate soil to only one depth, so the soil beneath the tilled layer becomes compacted from repeated pressure.

Double digging

Double digging works the soil more deeply than single digging and is useful for deep-rooted plants or areas where drainage needs improvement. This process takes a lot of work, but the effects last for years.

1. **Mark out the area you wish to dig (not too large, or you'll be barrowing soil a long way).**

2. **Across the width of the bed, remove a layer of the topsoil to create a trench 15–20 centimetres (6–8 inches) deep and 30–60 centimetres (1–2 feet) wide.** Place the soil in your wheelbarrow.

3. **With a digging fork, break up the subsoil at the bottom of the trench to the full depth of the tines – about 15–20 centimetres (6–8 inches). Mix in plenty of soil improvers.**

4. **Step down into the bed and dig the topsoil from the adjacent strip, moving it onto the exposed, loose subsoil of the first trench.**

5. **Break up the newly exposed subsoil with the garden fork, and add improvers.**

6. **Continue in this fashion until you break up upper and lower layers across the entire bed.** The soil from the first trench, held in the wheelbarrow, goes into the last trench.

7. **Spread soil improvers over the entire bed and rake it into the top 15–20 centimetres (6–8 inches) of soil.**

   After you finish, the earth is mounded up high in the bed. Walk on the adjacent ground rather than on the raised bed. When you go to prepare the bed in subsequent planting seasons, you'll be amazed at how little work it takes to loosen the ground.

Simple raised beds

Raised beds are an ideal way to loosen the soil of the garden and define planting areas. To make a raised-bed garden, outline the beds with string. For vegetable gardens, a 1-metre (3-foot) wide bed is best; for ornamental plantings, choose a size that best fits your design. After you define the beds, loosen the soil in the bed by using a spade or a garden fork. Then shovel soil from an adjacent path onto the bed. Figure 11-2 shows a basic raised bed and one edged with wood. Use pressure treated or *tanalised* timber (wood treated with the preservative Tanalith).

Figure 11-2:
Create raised beds by first (A) drawing soil from walkway areas onto loosened soil. You can finish the edges with pressure treated or tanalised timber (B).

The easy approach: no-dig beds

The traditional approach to growing crops is to dig over the ground each year, in winter or spring, incorporating manure or compost to revitalise the soil. Life doesn't have to be like that. The no-dig bed system is a great way to grow vegetables, fruit, or cut flowers with the minimum of work. It works by dividing the ground into beds that are a maximum of one metre (4 feet) wide, accessed from paths either side. These paths can be as smart or as informal as you wish, from neat paving slabs or bricks to simple chipped bark.

The beds can be raised or at ground level. The beds are deeply dug to begin with, with lots of organic matter added. But after that, because the soil doesn't get trodden and compacted, you don't need to dig again. Revitalise the soil by putting on a 5–10 centimetre (2–4 inch) thick layer of manure or compost in late winter to early spring, and leave it to be taken down by soil organisms.

Chapter 12

Raising Plants from Seeds

. . . .

In This Chapter

▶ Shopping tips

▶ Sowing right in the ground

▶ Top choices for direct sowing

▶ Starting seeds indoors

▶ Top choices for indoor sowing

. . . .

Starting some plants from seeds can't be simpler. On a warm spring day, you poke a big fat sunflower seed into moist ground, stand back, and – almost before you know it – a towering plant is looking down on you. But, as you may expect, some plants are not so easygoing – like that Australian wild-flower seed whose first step calls for something like 'Scorch rock-hard seed shell with a blowtorch'.

Naturally, we're going to stay closer to the sunflower camp. The plants that are easiest and most rewarding to start from seeds are annuals (nasturtiums, pot marigolds, love-in-a-mist, and many more), and vegetables (lettuce, rocket, radish, courgette, and many more).

Why start flowers and vegetables from seeds when you can find so many different kinds of young plants at garden centres?

✔ With seeds, you have a greater variety of choices than you find with small plants in a garden centre. One seed catalogue can offer dozens of different nasturtiums, whereas a garden centre can have just two or three.

✔ Seeds save you money. One pack of seeds, which can produce hundreds of plants, can cost less than a six-pack of the same variety of small plants.

✔ Some plants do better or just as well when started as seeds in the spot where you want them to grow to maturity.

✔ Sowing seeds is satisfying and fun.

What Those Needy Seeds Need

Flower seeds come in all shapes and sizes, from begonia seeds the size of dust grains to nasturtium seeds the size of peas. Larger seeds are the easiest to handle, and they often grow into comparatively large seedlings. Be forewarned that tiny seeds usually take longer to grow into big plants.

Growing flowers from seeds is pretty straightforward. You plant them in good soil, add water, and keep them constantly moist until they sprout. Here are the basic necessities for growing seeds:

- **Moisture** triggers the germination process and softens the hard outer covering of the seed, called the *seed coat*, so the sprout can emerge.
- **Soil temperature** affects the speed of the process. For most seeds, the warm side of 21 degrees Celsius (70 degrees Fahrenheit) is just about right.
- **Light** is critical for seedlings from the moment the sprout breaks through the soil. If you want to grow healthy seedlings indoors, you need a warm, sunny windowsill at the very least. A conservatory is even better, and a heated greenhouse is best of all. Another option is using artificial lighting indoors.

Seedlings grow roots as rapidly as they grow leaves, and some annual flowers put a huge amount of energy into roots right from the start. Some flowers spend their infancy developing long, brittle taproots that are difficult or impossible to transplant, so you are best sowing them in their designated garden spot.

Smart Seed Shopping

Every garden centre and DIY shop puts big seed racks where you can't help but see them. Those packets usually contain good-quality seeds. Just to be sure, though, look beyond the beautiful picture on the front of the packet to find other information that reveals much more important data:

- Species and/or variety name
- Mature height
- Packing date (don't purchase if the seeds are more than a year old)
- Special planting instructions

Another popular option is buying seeds by mail order. Suppliers send catalogues free or for a small charge to cover postage, which gives you the great advantage of being able to browse catalogues at your leisure in the comfort of your home (a wonderful winter pastime when it's impossible to get outside and garden). This way you can make considered choices rather than buying on impulse and ending up with the wrong plants.

Mail-order seed companies can maintain huge selections, and they tend to be meticulous about storage conditions. However, because mail-order companies give detailed information about their seeds in their catalogues, the actual packets may give little detail beyond the plant name. As soon as your seeds arrive, read over the packet labels and write the year on the packets if the date isn't stamped on there somewhere so you don't keep the packet longer than a year.

Sowing Seeds Right in the Ground

Direct sowing means planting seeds outdoors in the soil in the place where they are to sprout and mature. This method is the best way to grow many flowers and vegetables that don't transplant well (for example larkspur, Californian poppies, beets, carrots, peas, and radishes) and a very good way to grow many other plants.

Follow these guidelines for successful seed sowing in open soil:

- ✔ **Sow seeds at the right season.** Hardy annuals and vegetables are best if you sow them from early spring to early summer. You can also sow hardy annuals in autumn if you garden in well-drained soil, as the seeds tend to rot in soil that's wet for long periods. Sow half-hardy annuals and frost-tender vegetables outside from late spring onwards. Get a head start with frost-tender vegetables by sowing under cover (see 'Starting Seeds Indoors' later in this chapter)

- ✔ **Prepare the planting bed thoroughly.** Take extra care to rake smoothly – lumpy soil and clods interfere with germination. (Get your hands dirty in Chapter 11, on improving soil.)

- ✔ **Give large seeds a head start.** Moisten large seeds by leaving them overnight in a tray or bowl with moist vermiculite or perlite (a growing medium that looks and feels a bit like crumbled polystyrene), or between layers of a moist towel. But once the seeds are moist, be sure they don't dry out prior to planting. This moistening process really speeds things along when you sow hard-coated seeds like sweet peas.

- ✔ **Sow seeds in a definite pattern.** Sow seeds in rows, so when your seeds and the weeds all germinate at the same time, you know that those baby plants are flowers or vegetables and not weeds. For this reason, even if you want to grow flowers in informally shaped drifts or patches, still sow them in a series of short rows within each patch.

- ✔ **Read the label.** Pay attention to directions for best planting depth. If you plant deeper than indicated on the packet, the seeds may not contain enough energy for seedlings to reach the surface. A light layer of sifted compost is usually sufficient coverage for most seeds, though you're best off using a *dibber* (a small, pointed tool used for making little holes in the ground) or trowel to plant large seeds like beans.

✔ **Water carefully and gently.** Water the ground before sowing, then keep soil damp until seeds sprout. You can water from overhead as long as you do it gently with a fine spray from a hose or sprinkler. The best way to water is with a *soaker hose* or *drip irrigation*. Soaker hoses and drip irrigation systems are ground-hugging tubes that let moisture trickle out without splashing or compacting the soil. (See Chapter 14 for more information about watering systems.)

✔ **Weed early and often.** Take care not to let weeds overwhelm your young plants. If you have trouble weeding around small seedlings, use a table fork to gently pull out awkward little weeds. For more about dealing with weeds, head to Chapter 16.

✔ **Create some elbow room.** When the seedlings have developed two sets of *true leaves*, thin out seedlings that stand too close together. (The first leaves a seedling produces are called *seed leaves* or *cotyledon*, which are followed by the true leaves.) To *thin out* seedlings, gently pull extra seedlings without disturbing the ones you want to keep. You find it easiest to do this if the soil is moist rather than dry, so water a few hours beforehand if necessary.

You have a choice of planting patterns and techniques to use. Here are some tips on arranging your garden:

✔ Plant vegetables, or flowers that you want to transplant later, in rows in 'no-dig' beds (see Chapter 11) that are a metre or so wide. This allows easy access to plants from either side of the bed without you treading on and compacting the soil, so the ground won't need digging each year.

✔ If you like a neat, exact garden, use a grid of wire mesh to calculate your spacing. With carrots, for example, use wire mesh with openings about 2 centimetres (1 inch) square. Lay the wire mesh across the bed and press a few seeds down into the soil through each opening. *Thin* (remove excess seedlings) when the seedlings arise so that each carrot has at least 19 square centimetres (3 square inches) of space. For larger plants, such as lettuce, you can plant a seed every four or five squares to eliminate overcrowding.

You can also scatter seeds in a wide 'drill': a shallow trench about 15 centimetres (6 inches) wide, as shown in Figure 12.1a. Be sure to scatter seed thinly, and if plants look a bit overcrowded, thin seedlings early on.

✔ Larger plants need more space. You can plant them in wide beds, alternating two or three plants across the bed in a diamond or triangle. Another method is to place seeds of larger plants in single rows, as shown in Figure 12-1b. To make the rows straight, tie a string between two stakes. Following the string line, run a hoe through the soil to dig a trench of the proper depth for the seeds you're planting. Set the seeds in the trench at the proper spacing. Then cover the seeds with soil.

✔ In a decorative annual-flower garden, you can plant in rows, as shown in Figure 12-1c, or use wide-bed planting techniques to create clusters or drifts of flowers. Use a trickle of sharp sand to mark the place where you want a mass of seed-grown flowers, such as marigolds or nasturtiums. Set the seeds within that space as you would for a wide bed.

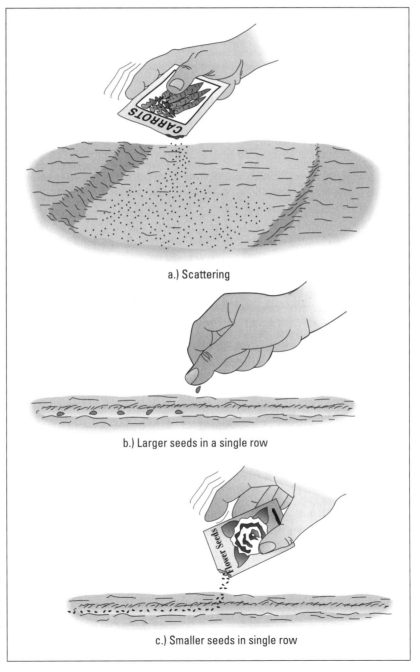

a.) Scattering

b.) Larger seeds in a single row

c.) Smaller seeds in single row

Figure 12-1:
Three ways
to sow
seeds.

A Dozen Easy Plants to Direct Sow

These plants are easy to grow from seeds that you sow directly in carefully prepared beds. The great thing about hardy annual flowers is that they often self-sow and you have plants year after year. Once flowering is over, just leave the seeds to ripen and fall. If in doubt about when to sow, just check the details on the seed packet.

- **Californian Poppy.** *Eschscholzia.* These colourful sun lovers thrive in well-drained soil and even tolerate poor, stony ground, bearing vivid silken-petalled blooms for many weeks. The feathery grey-green leaves look pretty too.

- *Cosmos bipinnatus.* Long-flowering and showy, with large 'daisy' flowers on tall stems up to 1.2 metres (4 feet) high.

- **Larkspur.** *Delphinium elatum.* A favourite old-fashioned flower, with stems of blue, pink, or white flowers and feathery green foliage.

- **Loose-leaf lettuce.** Nothing beats the freshness of salad leaves picked straight from the garden, and lettuce is dead easy to grow. The loose-leaf or cut-and-come-again types are great for picking a handful at a time, rather than having to harvest an entire plant. Some varieties look very attractive too, with frilled or red-tinged leaves.

- **Love-in-a-mist.** *Nigella.* A charming cottage garden favourite with its feathery blooms and foliage. The inflated seed pods are decorative too, and children find them irresistible to 'pop'.

- **Nasturtium.** *Tropaeolum majus.* Carefree and easy to grow, nasturtium leaves look like little green, flat umbrellas. Choose between bushy varieties and climbing or trailing forms – you can leave them to carpet the ground and tumble down banks, or train them up trellis or wire netting. You can eat the flowers, leaves, and seeds.

- **Pot marigold.** *Calendula.* This plant bears glowing orange blooms, either singles or doubles, for many weeks. You can eat the flowers and a scattering of vivid petals makes a lovely garnish for salads.

- **Radish.** One of the fastest vegetable crops to grow, with crunchy roots that are great for adding texture to salads.

- **Statice.** *Limonium.* You can find strains in several soft single colours, including purple, rose, and yellow. The seeds are easy to handle.

- **Strawflower.** *Helichrysum.* Harvested and dried, the flowers are wonderful for indoor arrangements and hold their colour well.

- **Sunflower.** *Helianthus annuus.* You can get sunflowers in a rainbow of hot colours and in all sizes, from dwarf varieties growing less than 60 centimetres (2 feet) tall to towering giants that reach roof height. Plant a row of tall sunflowers to make a wonderful, if temporary, screen. Let the seeds ripen and save them to feed the birds in winter.

✔ **Sweet pea.** *Lathyrus odoratus*. Fragrant and free-flowering, sweet peas are wonderful either in the garden or to cut for the home. Either way, cut off the dead flower heads frequently as, once the plant has set seed, it thinks its role in life is over and stops producing new flowers. Plants that you sow directly bloom from mid-summer on, or, for earlier blooms, sow the seed in a cool greenhouse or cold frame in autumn or early spring. Soaking the seed for a full day before planting aids germination. Sow in late winter or early spring while the soil is still quite cool. In mild winter areas, sow in autumn for winter and early spring bloom. Sweet pea seedlings easily survive spring frosts.

Starting Seeds Indoors

Many vegetables and flowers grow quickly and easily from seed. Many plants get off to a better start when you sow them indoors in containers and later transplant them into the garden. You also harvest crops and enjoy flowers earlier as a result. Remember, if the thought of raising seeds is too much hassle, look in garden centres in early to mid-spring for pots of ready-germinated seedlings, all prepared for you to take them home and transplant them into trays or pots.

Here's one basic seed-sowing method that works for us:

1. **Choose a container with drainage holes to hold the soil.**

   You can plant in seed trays or pots. *Modular seed trays* (those divided into a dozen or more separate sections or 'cells') are particularly good as you won't disturb the roots when planting. You can buy pots and trays from garden centres, or recycle aluminium foil pans, fast food containers, plastic cups, or yogurt pots (well washed, of course – seedlings don't thrive on a diet of leftover food! – and you'll need to make holes in them too).

2. **Buy compost specifically formulated for starting seeds.**

   Garden centres offer several brands of these; they usually say 'seed and cuttings compost' on the bag. This type of compost has a fine texture, ideal for seeds, and also has low levels of fertiliser (high levels can scorch or kill the delicate seedling roots). Pour some in a bucket and, if on the dry side, thoroughly moisten it.

3. **Fill the container to about one centimetre (half an inch) from the top with compost and level it, as shown in Figure 12-2.**

4. **Water the compost thoroughly before sowing, using a watering can fitted with a fine rose.** Leave the containers to drain for an hour or so. Watering after sowing can wash the seed deep into the compost, where it won't germinate.

Figure 12-2:
Level the compost to about one centimetre (half an inch) from the top of the container.

5. **Plant the seeds.**

   • **Small seeds.** Broadcast over the soil surface and cover with a fine layer of the moistened planting mix.

   • **Large seeds.** Plant in shallow drills or furrows scratched or pressed into the soil surface, or poke each seed into the soil individually using a pencil or dibber, as shown in Figure 12-3. Cover these seeds as recommended on the seed packet, usually to a depth equal to twice the seed diameter. Press the mixture gently yet firmly.

A few plants need light in order for their seeds to germinate – check out the instructions on the packet. If so, cover the seed with a thin layer of perlite or horticultural vermiculite or with kitchen clingfilm.

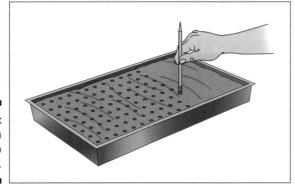

Figure 12-3:
Poke each seed into the soil.

6. **Cover the container with a plastic bag, as shown in Figure 12-4, to conserve moisture.** Place the container in a warm spot (ideally 24–30 degrees Celsius or 75–85 degrees Fahrenheit), such as on a warm windowsill or near a radiator. Buying a heated propagator gives you a much better chance of success.

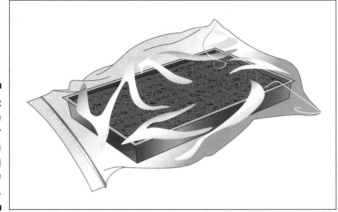

Figure 12-4:
Cover the container with a plastic bag to conserve moisture.

7. **Start checking for growth in about three days.**

   As soon as you see any sign of life, remove the plastic and move the container to a warm, bright site. Water as needed to keep the compost moist. Some seeds take a while to germinate, so be patient! Never let the compost dry out: The best way to water seedlings is from below, by standing the pot or seed tray in a tray of water, for a maximum of an hour. This keeps the delicate leaves and stems dry and helps avoid disease problems.

   If you haven't got a sunny windowsill or greenhouse, you can use *growlights* – fluorescent bulbs specifically designed to provide plants with ideal light for growth. Adjust the height of the lights so that they nearly touch the seedlings (raise the lights as the seedlings grow), and leave the lights on for 16 hours per day.

8. **When the seedlings have a second pair of true leaves, transplant them to small, individual pots filled with potting compost.**

   Use a dibber or pencil to help scoop the plants from their original container. If necessary, gently pull the seedlings apart – hold the plants by the leaves rather than by their fragile stems, and plant them at the same depth they were growing previously. Space them 5 or 7.5 centimetres (2 or 3 inches) apart in larger containers if you have too many for individual pots.

9. **Place the containers in bright, indirect light and keep the compost moist.**

   In most homes, the seedlings should receive the brightest light available as soon as they emerge. Seedlings thrive under fluorescent lights. If you have a fluorescent fixture, set seedlings 2.5 or 5 centimetres (1 or 2 inches) below the tubes. Begin feeding seedlings with liquid fertiliser. Follow label directions or, to be safe, begin feeding at half the recommended rate.

Hardening off seedlings to their new environment

Seedlings and cuttings raised in comfortable indoor conditions need gradual adjustment to the more strenuous outdoor environment. This process of acclimatising plants to the wind, strong light, and cooler temperatures outdoors is called *hardening off.*

1. One week before you begin hardening off your plants outdoors, cut back the amount of water you give them, stop fertilising them, and, if possible, keep temperatures slightly cooler by lowering the thermostat.

2. Starting about ten days before transplanting into the garden, place plants outdoors in bright, indirect light for a couple of hours.

Protect the plants from strong winds and be sure to keep them watered, because the plants dry out more quickly outside.

3. Each day, increase the time that the plants are left outdoors and gradually expose them to more intense light and wind and a range of temperatures.

4. The last few days before transplanting, you can leave them outdoors overnight if weather permits.

A cloudy, windless, warm day is the best time for easing the plants into their new home outdoors.

---

10. **One or two months after potting, and when all danger of frost is past, you can harden off most plants and plant them in the garden.** (See this chapter's sidebar entitled 'Hardening off seedlings to their new environment'.)

A Dozen Easy Plants to Start Indoors

Here are a dozen easy frost-tender flowers and vegetables well worth the trouble of planting early indoors.

- **Ageratum.** Covered in a frothy mass of lavender-blue flowers, ageratums make excellent edging plants.

- **Bidens.** This plant bears masses of golden 'daisies' right through the summer on slender stems among finely divided fresh green leaves. The perfect plant for sun-baked beds and containers.

- **Celosia.** *Celosia cristata, C. plumosa.* The plume types are lovely additions to any garden, but some people really like the cockscomb types, with rippled flower heads that look like brains!

✓ **Cleome (spider flower).** Tall and spectacular, the unusually shaped blooms in rose, pink, or white give borders a real lift.

✓ **Courgette (zucchini).** Just a couple of plants provide a plentiful crop of fruits through the summer. Sow the large seeds on their sides to reduce the risk of rot.

✓ **Marigolds.** *Tagetes.* Incredibly easy to grow, marigold seeds are easy to handle and quick to germinate. Grow alongside tomatoes and roses, because the pungent foliage helps deter insect pests.

✓ **Mexican sunflower.** *Tithonia rotundifolia.* Tall, heat-loving tithonia lights up the background of a sunny garden in late summer. Start seeds in late spring and use the plants as replacements for others that wear out in hot weather.

✓ **Rudbeckia hirta.** For a blaze of summer sunshine, the large yellow and orange blooms of annual rudbeckias are hard to beat. Compact-growing varieties are great for containers too.

✓ **Salvia.** *Salvia.* Fiery red *S. splendens* grows most widely, but experiment with unique colours by growing more unusual varieties from seeds.

✓ **Tobacco plant.** *Nicotiana alata.* This old-fashioned strain of flowering tobacco produces fragrant white flowers on tall spikes that open in the evening and attract night-flying moths. Tobacco plants need a long growing season – sow seeds by early spring.

✓ **Tomatoes.** *Lycopersicum esculentum.* Here's the one 'annual' that's most often planted indoors. Sow seeds in moist soil in early spring.

✓ **Zinnia elegans.** If you're after a vivid display of showy blooms, look no further than zinnias. The dwarf varieties are so free-flowering that you can hardly see any leaves.

Chapter 13

Choosing and Putting in Your Plants

Garden centres and nurseries tend to sell certain types of plants during certain seasons and in certain ways. Some plants are only available in a particular season. Understanding when to shop for your plants and how to plant different plant types is a useful and important gardening skill. We arm you with the knowledge you need in this chapter.

We also take you through the best ways of planting your new shrubs, hedges, or trees, so you can be a green-fingered expert in no time.

A Matter of Timing: Buying Plants in Season

Although you can obtain many plants all year, buying and planting in the 'right' season offer distinct advantages.

You can buy seasonal plants – that is, most summer annuals, perennials, and a few vegetables – from late winter to around mid-spring as *tots* or *starter plants* (also called *plug plants*) to grow yourself. These delicate little babies need immediate potting-up into 7.5–10 centimetre (3–4 inch) pots. Grow them in a warm, frost-free environment (like a sunny windowsill or heated greenhouse) until you can plant them outside.

From mid-spring and well into the summer, you can get these plants as slightly bigger young plants ready to go in the ground from packs or small pots.

Garden centres and nurseries sell plants from early spring, but don't make the mistake of thinking that because they're on sale, you can safely plant them out. Any plant that's *frost tender* is only safe to plant out when all danger of frost is past – this varies from around early May in mild areas to early June in cold regions. Only buy plants early if you have growing space under cover – a greenhouse, conservatory, or porch, for example. Otherwise, wait until the right time to plant and let the garden centres take care of the stock.

From late summer you can find *autumn bedding* – plants to colour your containers until the hard frosts arrive – and at the same time *spring bedding* – plants to put in during autumn to flower next spring. These short-lived plants must be planted in their correct seasons, but hardy plants (listed later in this chapter) are available all year. However, try to plant in autumn, early spring, or during winter if the weather is favourable, because your plants get a far better start in life and you'll have a lot less work to do!

Perennials and ornamental grasses are generally available in different sizes; a limited range of small, cheaper plants in 0.5 litre pots, and a wide selection of larger plants in pot sizes ranging from one to three litres. Small plants are most widely available in spring and autumn.

Larger, permanent plants – shrubs, trees, and climbers, for example – come typically in containers of three litres and upwards. You'll also find plants at both extremes; a limited range of *budget* shrubs in 1 litre pots, and much larger *specimens* in big pots (10 litres is a big shrub, 35 litres is a big tree). The choice is largely down to budget; specimens cost a whole lot more but that's balanced out by the fact that you're 'buying time'.

Shopping tips

As you shop, look for plants that are a vibrant green colour and are relatively short and stocky. Also look around at the display. Has the retailer simply lined everything up in the blazing sun or gone to the trouble of placing shade lovers like fuchsias and impatiens under benches or shade netting? Most bedding plants, including those that grow best in full sun, hold better in small containers when kept in partial shade.

Plants grown in small containers cost less than those in larger ones. Larger plants with more extensive root systems have a head start over smaller plants; however, larger, more developed bedding plants may have one disadvantage. In any container, a plant's roots tend to grow into a thick spiral. If the root system is extremely crowded, the roots may refuse to spread outwards after transplanting. Avoid plants with thick tangles of root searching for a place to grow – like out the bottom of the container's drainage hole.

Shrubs come in two seasonal forms – *bare root* and *balled and burlapped* (plants that are lifted from nursery fields during the dormant season, and supplied either with their bare roots wrapped in protective material, or with a ball of soil held around the roots by a burlap wrapping). You can find these shrubs during autumn and winter, while plants are dormant. Generally, such plants are bigger and cheaper than their container-grown counterparts, although the range of varieties is much more limited. Hedging plants are worth buying in this form because you save a lot of money.

Of course, you can use other ways to get plants started – such as bulbs (see Chapter 9). And roses are so popular that we give special planting directions for them in Chapter 10.

Working Out Spacing for Seasonal Flowers

Flowering annuals vary in how much space they need to grow. Plant spacing tends to be very tight in window boxes and containers, but in open beds your best strategy is to space plants so that they barely touch each other when they reach full maturity. Space very small annuals like sweet alyssum and lobelia only 10–15 centimetres (4 to 6 inches) apart, whereas big coleus and Cosmos may do better 45 centimetres (18 inches) apart. Most other annuals grow best when planted 25–30 centimetres (10–12 inches) apart, more or less. The plant tags stuck into the containers of purchased bedding plants often suggest the best spacing.

Instead of setting your annuals in straight lines, you get better results by staggering them in a concentrated zigzag pattern so that you have two or more offset rows of plants. Better yet, plant different annuals in natural-looking teardrop-shaped clumps (called *drifts*). The clump approach also makes many flowers easier to care for. A closely spaced group of plants that need special care is much simpler than a long row when you need to pinch and prune, or water and feed.

You can estimate spacing with just your eyes if you like, and simply go over the prepared bed, making little holes where you intend to set the plants. Or you can mark the planting spots with short canes or lightly dust each spot with flour or sand. If you purchase plants in individual containers, simply place each one where you intend to plant it, and move them around as needed until you're happy with the arrangement.

Planting Seasonal Flowers, Step by Step

Whether you buy your annuals and tender perennials at the garden centre or grow your own from seeds, follow these steps to ensure a seamless transition from nursery to garden.

1. **A few days before planting, apply a complete granular fertiliser to the prepared bed and rake in. A day or two before transplanting, water the planting bed so that it will be lightly moist when you set out your plants.**

2. **At least one hour before transplanting, water your plants thoroughly. Doing so makes the rootballs much easier to remove from their containers.**

   Ideal planting time is any time that temperatures are moderate, neither too hot nor too cold nor too windy. In mid-summer when the weather is hot, try waiting for a cloudy day. Transplanting under the hot sun causes unnecessary stress to the little plants.

3. **Check to see if small roots are knotting around the outside of the drainage holes.**

   If you find roots knotting in such a manner, break them off and discard them before trying to remove the plants.

4. **Remove the plant from the container by pushing and squeezing on the container bottom so that the entire root ball slips out intact, as shown in Figure 13-1.**

   If the root ball doesn't come out easily, use a table knife to gently pry it out, the same way you might remove a sticky cake from a cake tin. Pull on the plant only as a last resort, and then by holding the stem close to the soil.

5. **Use your fingers or a table fork to loosen any badly tangled roots at the bottom of the root ball.**

   Loosening the roots is important! Otherwise, the roots may make little effort to spread out into the soil.

6. **Make final spacing decisions, and then dig small planting holes slightly wider than the root balls of the plants.**

7. **Set the plants into the holes at about the same depth they grew in their containers.**

   You may need to place a few handfuls of soil back in the hole and then set the plant in place to check the height.

8. **Lightly *tamp* (firm) down the soil around the roots with your hands so that the soil comes in contact with the root ball, as shown in Figure 13-2.**

   Tamping down the soil helps remove some pockets of air, which can dry out roots.

Figure 13-1:
Carefully remove the plant from the container so that the rootball slips out intact.

Figure 13-2:
Tamping down the soil removes pockets of air around the roots.

9. **Water the entire bed until it is evenly moist.**

   Thorough and gentle watering is important to finish settling the soil around the roots.

10. **Water regularly for the next three to four weeks as required.**

    Plants take a while to establish their roots, and until then you need to keep the soil moist. (See Chapter 14 for more on when and how to water.)

11. **After a few days, check to make sure soil has not washed away from the top of the plants' roots.**

    If the root ball is exposed, use a rake or small trowel to add more soil, making sure to cover the root ball.

12. **As soon as new growth shows, mulch around plants with an attractive organic material such as chipped bark, garden compost, or leafmould.**

    A 5–7.5-centimetre (2–3-inch) layer of mulch greatly discourages weeds and radically reduces moisture loss from the soil due to evaporation. It also prevents the soil from forming a crust by cushioning the impact of water drops from rain and sprinklers.

Container-Grown Permanent Plants

These days most permanent plants – that is, long-lived ones like shrubs, trees, climbers, and perennials – are in containers when you buy them. The plants are easy to move around, and you don't have to plant them right away. (But keep them watered until you're ready to plant.)

Choosing container-grown hardy plants

You want plants that have a healthy appearance – with sturdy branches, dense foliage, and other signs of vigorous growth depending on the type of plant. Inspect the root system as well as you can. You don't want a plant that has spent too little or too much time in the container. If recently planted, the root system may not have developed enough to hold the soil ball together; soil can just fall off the roots as you plant. If the plant has been in the container too long, it may become *pot-bound* or *root-bound* – when roots are so tangled and constricted, the roots have a tough time spreading out into the soil and growing normally.

Look for these classic root-bound symptoms:

- ✔ Roots stick out of the container's drainage holes.

- ✔ Roots bulge out above the soil line.

- ✔ Plants are spindly (tall but with few leaves), poorly proportioned in relation to the container, or have a lot of dead growth.

Avoid root-bound woody shrubs and trees (it's not so much a problem with perennials); or, failing this, at least gently loosen and untangle the roots without shattering the ball of soil at planting time.

When to plant

Autumn is the time of year when the garden is getting ready to go to bed for the year – and it's time for us gardeners to wake up and get planting! This is by far the best time of year to put in all *hardy* plants (leave anything of remotely dubious hardiness until spring, so the plant has a whole season to establish before the frosts). In autumn, the soil is lovely and warm, ideal for encouraging root growth, and a plant's top growth is slowing down so that trying to burn the candle at both ends won't stress it. Autumn rain keeps the soil good and moist, making watering unnecessary. During the winter and early spring, plants continue to make root growth during mild spells, and should be well established in time to explode into growth in spring.

You can plant in winter, so long as the ground isn't frozen or waterlogged. If you live in a cold area, delay planting hardy container plants until early spring. Of course, you can plant at any time of year at all, but bear in mind that you need to keep plants that go in during spring and summer well watered, as they won't have put down enough roots to support themselves.

Transplanting permanent plants from containers

Follow these steps for planting container-grown plants:

1. **Prepare the ground beforehand, as Chapter 11 describes.**

   Locate any underground wires, cables, or pipelines before you begin digging and proceed around them carefully. You can easily cut through a wire with a sharp spade or fork.

2. **A couple of hours before, give your plants a thorough watering.**

   Dry rootballs are hard to re-wet. If your plants are really dry (horrid thought), soak the root ball in a bucket of water for at least an hour before planting.

3. **Dig a hole as deep as the original root ball (use a stick to determine depth) and twice as wide as the root ball.**

   Slant the walls of the hole outwards and loosen the sides and base with a spade or garden fork to allow easy root penetration.

   If your soil is especially poor, work compost or organic matter into the base of the hole and the soil that goes back into the hole. If the soil is dry, fill the hole to the brim with water and allow it to drain before planting.

4. **Remove the plant from its container.**

   Most plant containers are plastic and plants slip right out. If they don't, trim away any roots protruding from drainage holes. Tap the bottom or knock the rim of the pot on a hard surface, and then tip the pot upside down (or onto its side, for large plants) and slide the root ball out.

   Save the empty plastic containers; they come in handy for potting up bulbs. Otherwise, you can recycle most plastic pots.

5. **Place the plant into the hole, at the right depth, and fill around the root ball with soil.**

   Stand back and check the plant's position to be sure it faces the way you want, and then begin backfilling. Once you've replaced about half the backfill, tamp down with your hands or the end of a shovel.

6. **Water the plant well by letting a hose trickle into the planting area until the area is soaked.**

   To help direct irrigation and rainwater to the new roots, shape loose surface soil with your hands into a water-holding basin. Make it 7.5–10 centimetres (3–4 inches) high just above and around the root ball.

   Continue to water any time the soil begins to dry out for the next six months or so, only whilst the plant is actively growing. Don't count exclusively on sprinklers or rain to water new plants. To see if soil is dry, dig down 10–15 centimetres (4–6 inches) with a trowel. If it's hard to dig, and if the soil is very dry, the root ball needs water.

7. **Mulch the plant.**

   Cover the excavated soil and several inches beyond (the larger the plant, the wider the circle) with 5–7.5 centimetres (2–3 inches) of mulch. Only put on mulch when the soil is moist, as dry ground is then hard to soak. Keep the mulch clear of the plant stems, or it may cause disease.

8. **Keep well watered.**

   For the next three or four months, keep the roots moist until the plant has put down enough root growth to support itself.

Staking a tree

All but the smallest trees are likely to need support for a year or two until they've put down enough roots to support themselves. Use a short stake (about a third of the tree's height) placed in the ground at an angle of 45 degrees and secured to the trunk using a wide, buckle-type tree tie, as shown in Figure 13-3. For larger specimens, insert two stakes vertically either side of the root ball, with a single horizontal bar attached to them at 30–45 centimetres (1–1.5 feet) high.

Don't use a tall stake (half the height of the tree), because such substantial stakes encourage dependency, like a crutch, and discourage trees from developing a strong root system.

Every couple of months, check the tree ties to make sure they haven't loosened and are rubbing the trunk. As the tree grows, loosen the tie a little as needed.

Figure 13-3:
Staking a tree.

WIND

Digging deeper with clematis

Go in deep when you plant clematis. Whereas you plant other plants at the same depth they were growing previously, plant clematis so that the top of the rootball is 7.5–10 centimetres (3–4 inches) lower than the level of surrounding soil. You need to plant this deep to avoid an irritating disease called *clematis wilt*, where all of the plant can suddenly collapse and die. Deep-planted clematis can regrow from below ground.

Bare-Root Planting

The tried-and-tested method of bare-root planting offers benefits to the plant and to the gardener. During the dormant, leafless season, growers lift plants that are *deciduous* (leaf shedding) from nursery fields and transport them without any soil around the roots. Bare-root plants are easy to transport and handle – which allows for a lower price than the same plants sold in containers. Bare root is also a good way for plants to get off to a good strong start; roots can follow their natural direction better than they can in the confines of a container.

Choosing bare-root plants

The most important factor to look for in bare-root plants is roots that are protected in some way so they're fresh and moist, not dried out and stringy. Check for damaged, soft, broken, mushy, or circling roots and prune them back as necessary to obtain healthy, firm growth. Inspect the top growth for broken branches and damaged buds. Ask a nurseryperson about proper pre-planting pruning for the specific plant. Don't let the roots dry out; soak them in a bucket of water before planting, if necessary.

Planting bare-root plants

Plant bare-root plants by using the same procedure for container-grown plants described in the section 'Transplanting permanent plants from containers'. The only difference between the two procedures is in the shape and depth of the hole you dig.

For bare-root planting, set the base of the roots on a cone of soil in the middle of the hole, as shown in Figure 13-4, adjusting the cone height so that the first horizontal root is just below the soil surface. Spread the roots in different directions and then refill the hole gradually, tamping down soil around roots.

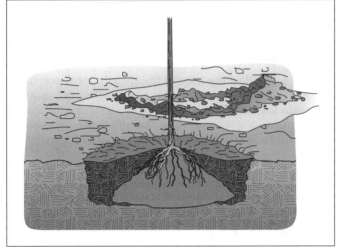

Figure 13-4:
Spread the roots of a bare-root plant around a central cone of soil.

Planting a New Hedge

Groundwork is all-important when you plant a new hedge, because a hedge is a long-lasting feature of the garden, so don't skimp on the soil preparation, planting, and aftercare. Autumn is the ideal time to plant a new hedge because plants establish best at this time of year. Winter or early spring are the next best times to plant (if the ground isn't frozen or waterlogged).

You can save a fair bit of cash by planting in autumn or winter when plants are dormant, because you can buy deciduous plants bare-rooted (field grown), which works out a whole heap cheaper than pot-grown plants. You can buy evergreens like holly and laurel as large, burlapped, or root-wrapped plants for a similar price to smaller container-grown ones. If you want large quantities of hedging plants, buy from mail-order suppliers or from a nearby nursery, because garden centres tend to supply a limited range of bare-rooted hedging plants sold in packs of five or ten, which are expensive.

Preparing the ground

Rather than preparing individual planting holes, tackle the ground for a hedge in one long strip. The width of this strip varies between 60 centimetres (2 feet) wide for a single-row hedge, and 90 centimetres (3 feet) wide for a double row.

Most hedges are planted in single rows, with the exception of mixed native hedges, or unless you want a dense, wide hedge.

Follow these steps to prepare the ground for your hedge:

1. **Mark out the site using canes and string to ensure that the strip is a straight line.**

2. **Double-dig the soil by removing a trench to one spade's depth and putting it to one side.**

3. **Fork over the soil in the base of the trench, incorporating plenty of well-rotted organic matter, which ensures that the roots penetrate deeply into the subsoil.** Work along the strip, moving the top layer of soil onto the area you've just dug, then fill in the first part of the strip with the soil you removed first of all.

Ideally, carry out this preparation in late summer, clearing the weeds first and using weedkiller if necessary to get rid of perennial weeds, then digging the ground in early autumn to allow several weeks for it to settle before planting.

Planting a single-row hedge

1. **Set up a string as a guideline to ensure that you plant in a straight line.** The correct line and spacing are important, as any little errors will stand out like sore thumbs and annoy you for years! Cut a bamboo cane to the length of the spacing between each plant and use this as a spacer when planting.

2. **Take the plants out of their pots and gently unwind any roots spiralling around the bottom of the root ball.** Soak bare-rooted or root-balled plants for an hour or two beforehand. Put in the plants at the same depth as they were growing previously, using the spacer cane to mark the position of the next one in line.

3. **Using your heel, firm the soil all around the roots and water well.**

Planting a double-row hedge of bare-rooted plants

For a dense, wide hedge or a mixed one made up of native plants, plant the hedge in two rows and stagger the plants to offset one another. Within each row of a double hedge, place the plants 50 per cent further apart than the spacings given in the plant list.

1. **Set up two strings 45 centimetres (18 inches) apart as marker lines.** Cut two bamboo canes to the necessary spacings between plants. Soak the plant's roots for a couple of hours before planting. Using secateurs, shorten any long roots and trim off any damaged ones.

2. **Put in the plants at the same depth as they were growing previously.** You can tell the previous depth by the darker colour of the stem that was below ground. Firm the roots thoroughly.

3. **Immediately after planting, cut back all deciduous plants by a third, including shortening long sideshoots.** Water well to settle the soil around the roots.

Aftercare

The care that you give a new hedge in its first year can make the world of difference to how quickly the plants establish. Mulching the soil with a 5-centimetre (2-inch) layer of chipped bark or cocoa shell keeps the roots moist, helps even out the soil temperature, and prevents weed growth that competes with the plants. Apply a general fertiliser in early spring, scattering it onto the soil at the recommended rate, and raking in. Water well during dry spells in the first spring and summer, giving plants a thorough soaking two or three times a week.

Temporary windbreaks

If the site for your hedge is at all exposed, put up a temporary windbreak of plastic netting to help your plants establish well. Evergreen plants really need protection, because they lose moisture through their leaves right through the year. You can buy netting from garden centres. Put up the netting at least as high as the plants themselves.

 If you want to have a hedge but need instant privacy as well, put up an ornamental screen of reed, bamboo, or willow roll with a view to leaving it in place for several years until your hedge is well established. As a bonus, the hedge grows faster in the sheltered environment too.

Burlap-Wrapped Root Balls

Root-balled plants are less common now that most plants grow in containers. During autumn and winter, nurseries dig these plants from their growing fields and wrap the root balls in *burlap*, or rough cloth (sometimes also wrapping both burlap and root ball in a wire cage for the extra support).

Choosing balled-and-burlapped plants

When looking at balled-and-burlapped plants, be sure to check for major cracks or breaks in the root ball. Make sure that the trunk doesn't rock in the soil ball or move. Keep the root ball moist if you can't plant right away; cover it with organic matter such as ground bark, and moisten thoroughly. Keep the plant in a shady spot until you plant it.

Planting balled-and-burlapped plants

Dig a hole with a circumference twice as large and a depth equal to the root ball. Sit the root ball on firm soil to avoid settling. Set the root ball into the hole; check the position of the plant; and then remove all burlap, nails, and any twine or wire to prevent interference with the plant's future growth. If you can't remove all the burlap, use a sharp knife to cut off everything except for what is directly underneath the ball. (See Figure 13-5.)

Figure 13-5:
Remove any metal, burlap, and twine to avoid inhibiting growth.

To get balled-and-burlapped planting height just right, open the root ball and remove some soil from the top until you find the first *root flare* or horizontal root. Position that root just below the soil surface. Many trees are planted too deeply because they have too much soil over the roots in the root ball.

Like many things, burlap isn't quite what it used to be. Don't assume that it will decay in a season or two, where it would be fine to leave in the soil around the root ball. Nowadays, burlap is often a coarsely woven synthetic that can take years to dissolve in the soil, if ever. Cut away and remove as much of the wrapping as possible without breaking up the root ball.

Part V
Caring for Your Plants

"If I could speak a foreign language then
I would know how this exotic plant I bought
will eventually turn out."

In this part . . .

Does your garden need water? How much? What about fertiliser? And what about weeds . . . and pruning or feeding? Oh, and what about pests? What tools do you use to care for your garden?

We answer all these questions in this part. Garden care may sound like a lot of work, but it's really not. And anyway, it's fun. And relaxing. And it keeps you fit. Caring for your garden is, in fact, the essence of gardening.

Chapter 14

Watering, Feeding, and Composting

. . . .

In This Chapter

▶ Looking at the whys and hows of watering

▶ Understanding plant nutrients

▶ Fertilising your plants

▶ Mulching around

▶ Dabbling in the muck and magic of composting

. . . .

*W*hat's the most important thing you can do in your garden? The answer you get depends on whom you talk to and where that gardener lives. Someone with a lot of container plants will put fertilising first. If you have horrid soil, nothing, we mean nothing, is more essential than composting.

So, what do we say? Our answer, of course, is . . . all of the above. But the amount of watering, feeding, and composting (the Big Three of your support system for healthy plant growth) depends on where you live, what you grow, and all sorts of other local conditions. But take our word for it – all of the three are extremely important.

Watering Basics

How much water your plants need to stay healthy depends on a number of factors:

> ✔ **Climate.** If you live in an area like Wales or much of Scotland, you're unlikely to need to water much at all. In dry parts of the country like East Anglia where rain is in short supply, you need to pay much more attention to choosing the right plants for the climate – or spend a lot of time and money watering the wrong ones!

✔ **Weather.** The average weather where you live on a season-to-season, year-to-year basis determines the climate. Weather is what's happening outside right now. Out-of-the ordinary weather can wreak havoc on your plants. Hot, dry winds can dry out plants in double-quick time.

✔ **Soil types.** Different soil types also affect how often a garden needs water.

 • **Sandy soil** holds water about as effectively as a sieve. Water penetrates sandy soils readily and deeply, but tends to filter right on through. Adding organic matter, like compost, leafmould, or well-rotted manure, helps sandy soils retain moisture.

 • **Heavy clay soil** is the exact opposite of sand – the dense particles in clay cause the soil to crust over and deflect water drops. Water applied slowly and in stages soaks in deeply; water applied quickly just runs off. Saturated clay holds water very well – sometimes so well that the plants rot. Adding plenty of organic matter helps break up the soil and improves drainage.

✔ **Location.** In general, shady gardens need less water than those receiving direct sun. However, in places where trees cast the shadows, their roots may greedily hog all the water, leaving little for the flowers.

✔ **Type of plants.** Different plants adapt to a whole range of growing conditions, so if you live in an area where rain is in short supply, or if your soil is free draining, make sure you select plants that tolerate drought and that come up trumps when the sun bakes down. Equally, in areas of heavy rainfall you need moisture-loving plants.

Target the right plants

If you choose plants that thrive in the conditions your garden offers, you won't have too many plants that need regular watering. However, you mustn't ignore these plants and you need to water them well:

✔ New plants that go in during spring and summer. They won't have made enough roots to support themselves.

✔ All plants in containers.

✔ Most summer-flowering annuals and tender perennials (those *planted out* in late spring to mid-summer are more in need of water than direct-sown plants).

✔ Vegetables that produce large fruits or pods, such as courgettes, marrows, tomatoes, cucumbers, beans, and leafy salad crops.

✔ Soft fruit such as strawberries and raspberries, while the fruit is forming.

Different ways to water your plants

The best watering method for you may depend on how large a space you have. For example, with just a small bed of annuals, you may find that watering with a hand-held watering can or hose is effective. If, however, you have lots of flowers and vegetables, watering effectively by hand is well-nigh impossible.

The following sections describe the main watering methods.

Hand watering

If you want to stand among your vegetables with a hose and water the plants by hand, that's fine. Hose-end attachments soften the force of the spray and help apply the water over a larger area. You can control the amount of water each plant gets and even do some pest control at the same time – blast that blanket flower to wash away aphids! Hand watering, however, takes time, especially in large gardens.

Sprinklers

Hose-end sprinklers come in a wide range of styles and sprinkler patterns. The problem with watering with sprinklers is that you have to drag the hose all around and move the sprinkler every so often. Also, most hose-end sprinklers don't apply water very evenly. If you forget to turn off the sprinkler, you waste a lot of water.

If you need help remembering to turn off your sprinkler, check out the various timers you can buy.

One other possible problem with sprinkler watering is the wet foliage that results. In cooler areas, overhead watering can encourage diseases to spread and turn flowers into a mouldy mess.

Drip irrigation

Drip irrigation is a very effective and efficient way to water plants, particularly those growing in containers. Water slowly drips through tiny drip heads fitted to the ends of narrow black plastic pipes. The pipe connects to a tap via a pressure regulator. The pipes weave among and around the plants, applying water directly to the base of the plants. For plants growing in borders, *porous pipe* or *seep hose* is the best way to deliver water. You can either lay the pipe right on top of the soil and cover it with a mulch, or bury it a few inches deep. Most people like to keep the pipe close to the surface so that they can check it for blockages or fix breaks.

Drip emitters can wet an entire planting bed from one end to the other at each watering. (You can either snap the emitters into the pipe or buy the pipes with the emitters already installed.) Space the emitters 30 centimetres

(12 inches) apart along the length of the pipe. Arrange the pipes so that you have no more than 45 centimetres (18 inches) between lengths or loops, as shown in Figure 14-1. The moisture radiates sideways and underground, and wets the soil between emitters.

Figure 14-1:
Drip
irrigation is
an efficient
watering
solution.

Drip systems usually have to run for at least an hour to wet a large area. Watch the soil carefully the first few times you water. Dig around to see how far the water has travelled over a given time and then make adjustments in how long you water in the future.

Most garden centres sell irrigation systems. You can also purchase them by mail order. Drip heads are available with different application rates, varying by the number of litres applied per hour. A container watering starter kit is priced at around £80.

If you live in an area where the soil freezes, don't leave your drip system outside in winter. Instead, to prevent it from bursting, drain the water, roll up the tubing, and store it in the garage.

Automatic watering systems

Automatic watering systems can be real time savers and take the hassle out of leaving your plants for a weekend or while you're on holiday. Not only that, if you love having a beautiful garden but hate watering, just sit back and have the job done for you! You can automate both drip and sprinkler systems. Simply fit a water timer to your system where it attaches to the tap. A whole range of different timers is available, from simple ones that put the water on once a day, to complex water computers that you can program to water for varying periods several times a day. If in doubt, go for simplicity!

How much, how often?

A plant's water needs vary with the weather and the seasons. Even an automated system needs adjusting to water less in spring than in summer, and from week to week as the weather varies. Keep an eye on your garden and make adjustments accordingly.

Irrigation hardware is useless if you don't have a clue how much water your plants need. The answer is to water just enough, but not too much. The best way to water is to replace the moisture the plants use up by watering daily during spring and summer (even twice daily in hot weather), reducing to 3–4 times per week in early spring and autumn.

Plants lose moisture through their foliage because of *transpiration*. The soil also gives up water by *evaporation*. The combination of evaporation and transpiration is *evapotranspiration*. Hot, dry, and windy weather causes plants to use much more moisture than they do on a cool, overcast day. Keep an eye on your plants to see when they're calling out for a drink.

- ✔ **Note the condition of your plants.** When plants start to dry out, the leaves get droopy and wilt. (Just to confuse matters wilting leaves is also a symptom of overwatering or disease, so stick a finger in the soil to check its moisture content.) The plant may also lose its bright green colour and start to look a little drab. Your goal is to water before a plant gets to that point, but the plant will show you when it needs water more often.

- ✔ **Dig in the ground.** Most plants need water when the soil is dry just below the surface, from around 2.5–5 centimetres (1–2 inches) below ground level. Use a small trowel or shovel to dig around a bit. If the soil is dry deep down, you need to water.

Eventually, through observation and digging, you start to develop a watering schedule, and a lot of the guesswork disappears.

Using water wisely

Water shortages are a reality in almost any climate or region. Following are a few things you can do when water is scarce or limited, when you want to reduce your water bill, or when you just want to conserve the precious resource of fresh water.

- ✔ **Use a timer.** Set an egg timer or an alarm clock to let you know when it's time to shut off the water. Or get even more high-tech and use one of the automated timers available from garden centres.

- ✔ **Install drip irrigation.** This watering method applies water slowly without runoff. Drip irrigation is definitely the most frugal watering system you can use.

- ✔ **Mulch, mulch, and mulch some more.** Several centimetres of compost, chipped bark, leafmould, or other material cools the soil and reduces evaporation, thus saving water. And as the mulch breaks down, it improves the soil. For more on mulches, see 'A-Mulching We Will Go . . .' in this chapter, as well as Chapter 11.

- ✔ **Pull weeds.** Weeds steal water meant for your plants. Pull out weeds regularly. For more on weeds, see Chapter 16.

- ✔ **Water deeply and infrequently.** Shallow sprinkling does very little good. Water to a depth of 20–25 centimetres (8–10 inches), then let the soil dry out partially before you water again. This method encourages plants to develop deep roots, which can endure longer periods between waterings.

- ✔ **Water early or late.** Water early in the day or in the evening when temperatures are cooler and it's less windy. That way, less water evaporates into the air and more reaches the roots. Also, watering in hot sun can damage flowers and foliage, because drops of water can act like little magnifying glasses and burn the plants.

- ✔ **Use rainwater.** Put water butts where the drainpipes from your roof empty out. Then use that water on your garden.

- ✔ **Plant at the right time.** By planting in autumn, early spring, or in mild periods during winter, your plants can establish well without any further help from you. However, plants that go in during late spring and summer need regular watering, because they won't have put down enough roots to support themselves.

Providing a Balanced Diet for Your Plants

Before you head for the nursery to pick up a bag of fertiliser, remember that understanding the nutrients that plants need and how plants use them is helpful.

Sixteen elements are known to be essential for healthy plant growth. Plants particularly need carbon, hydrogen, and oxygen in large quantities. Plants also need energy from sunlight for *photosynthesis*, the process by which green plants take carbon dioxide from the air and water from the soil to produce sugars to fuel their growth. Apart from watering plants, gardeners can trust nature to supply these big basic requirements.

Plants also need nitrogen, phosphorus, and potassium in relatively large quantities. These three elements are often called *macronutrients*, or *primary nutrients*. Plants take up these three nutrients from the soil. If they are not present in the soil, you can supply them by adding fertilisers. The percentages of these nutrients are the three prominent numbers on any bag or box of fertiliser, and the nutrients always appear in the same order. For more on fertiliser, see 'Don't Compromise, Fertilise!', later in this chapter.

- **Nitrogen (N).** This nutrient, represented by the chemical symbol N, is responsible for the healthy green colour of your plants. It is a key part of proteins and *chlorophyll*, the plant pigment that plays a vital role in photosynthesis. Plants with a nitrogen deficiency show a yellowing of older leaves first, along with a general slowdown in growth.

- **Phosphorus (P).** Phosphorus is associated with good root growth, increased disease resistance, and fruit and seed formation. Plants lacking in phosphorus are stunted and have dark green foliage, followed by reddening of the stems and leaves. As with nitrogen, the symptoms appear on the older leaves first.

- **Potassium (K).** This nutrient promotes vigorous growth and disease resistance. The first sign of a deficiency shows up as browning of the edges of leaves. The deficiency affects older leaves first.

Plants also need a range of other nutrients such as calcium, magnesium, and iron. Although garden soil contains these nutrients in sufficient quantities, sometimes they're locked up in the soil due to extremes of soil pH (the level of acidity or alkalinity; scoot back to Chapter 11 to find out more), or because the soil is too dry for the nutrients to be taken up.

Don't Compromise, Fertilise!

All plants need feeding in order to perform at their best and remain healthy. In a garden situation plants grow closely in a limited space, which takes more out of the soil than goes back in naturally. Plus, people gather up fallen plant debris and cut grass, which would otherwise rot down and return nutrients to the soil. Although bulky soil conditioners like manure and garden compost do contain some nutrients, these alone aren't enough to keep your plants really healthy. For a balanced diet, your plants need concentrated plant foods, or fertilisers.

Applying fertilisers

You find a bewildering range of fertilisers on the garden centre shelves, so take a quick look at the list below to find out what's what.

Whatever fertiliser you choose, always follow the manufacturers' instructions. Never be tempted to put on too much on the basis that double the feed does twice as much good – overfeeding can do more harm than none at all.

Granular fertiliser

Scatter fertiliser granules or powder on the soil surface around plants and hoe or rake it into the soil. Take care to apply at the recommended rate by weighing the amount per metre on kitchen scales, then marking a pot or small container at this level for future reference. For easy and accurate distribution, make your own applicator using two small plastic pots of the same size, placing them one inside the other with the drainage holes just offset to leave small gaps. Simply shake the pot to distribute the fertiliser evenly.

Plants can only take up fertiliser when it becomes dissolved in water, so either avoid applying granular fertiliser in dry weather or water well after-wards. Ideally, apply when the ground is moist but plants are dry, otherwise fertiliser can stick to and scorch damp leaves. If you do get any fertiliser onto the plant foliage, brush it off and then water thoroughly. Always wear gloves and take care not to breathe in any dust.

Controlled-release fertiliser

These polymer-coated granules or tablets are designed to release nutrients gradually over a set period of months, when conditions are sufficiently warm and moist for the plant to utilise the food. While more expensive than other types, controlled-release fertilisers are also more effective. They are particu-larly useful for feeding plants in containers, because they do away with the time-consuming weekly job of liquid feeding.

Liquid fertiliser

You dissolve soluble or liquid fertiliser in water and then water the liquid onto the soil around the roots. The plants can take up the nutrients rapidly, as they are already dissolved. However, you need to feed regularly with liquid fertiliser because the nutrients quickly leach away through the soil, particularly on light, free-draining ground. You can water liquid fertilisers onto the soil using a watering can. If you apply fertiliser over a large area, a hose-end diluter cuts down a lot of work – simply attach the filled applicator and turn on the hose (see Figure 14-2).

Do not water liquid fertiliser onto dry soil because the fertiliser can scorch the soil; avoid applying before rain, which would wash away the fertiliser; and apply in the morning or evening to avoid risk of sun scorch on splashed foliage.

Foliar fertiliser

This is liquid fertiliser that you spray onto the leaves using a pump-action hand sprayer. The plant can absorb the nutrients extremely quickly, which is particularly useful if the plant is showing signs of nutrient deficiency such as pale, yellowing, or discoloured leaves. Follow the same guidelines for apply-ing liquid fertiliser, and never spray when the sun is on the leaves to avoid severe scorching.

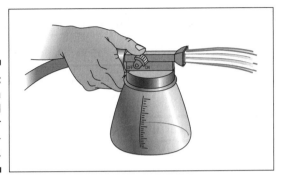

Figure 14-2:
Applying a liquid fertiliser with a hose-end diluter.

Organic

These fertilisers often comprise dead or composted plants and animals. Examples are blood meal, fish emulsion, and manure. Usually organic fertilisers contain significant amounts of only one of the major nutrients; for example, bone meal contains only phosphorus. Nutrients in organic fertilisers are made available to plant roots after soil microorganisms break down the nutrients. Activity of these microorganisms is fastest in summer when soils are warm. The nutrients are released slowly over a period of months.

Specialist fertilisers

Certain fertilisers are well worth using on specific plants in order to achieve the best performance. Lawn fertiliser is usually carries a label indicating the time of year you apply it, which affects the balance of nutrients. Lime-hating or _ericaceous_ plants benefit from an ericaceous fertiliser containing iron, something they often become deficient in. You can use some specific fertilisers for a wide range of plants, such as rose fertiliser on all flowering plants.

Getting completely techy with fertiliser

When you buy a commercial fertiliser, its analysis appears on the label with three numbers. These three numbers are helpful because they let you know the amounts of nutrients (N-P-K) that are in a particular fertiliser.

✔ The first number indicates the percentage of nitrogen (N).

✔ The second number, the percentage of phosphorus (P_2O_5).

✔ The third, the percentage of potassium (K_2O).

Any fertiliser that contains all three of the primary nutrients – N-P-K – is a _complete fertiliser_. The garden term _complete_ has its basis in laws and regulations that apply to the fertiliser industry; it does not mean that the fertiliser literally contains everything a plant may need.

Different fertilisers for various plants

Different kinds of plants need different kinds of fertilisers, and Table 14-1 lists our recommendations. The best advice before using any fertiliser is to have your soil tested. For more about soil testing, see Chapter 11.

Table 14-1	Fertilising at a Glance	
Plant	*Fertiliser*	*Comments*
Annuals	Granular	Apply before planting, supplemented by liquid- soluble applications after planting
Bulbs	Granular	Apply after flowering
Fruit trees	Granular	Apply as necessary in spring only
Hanging baskets	Controlled release	At planting time
	or liquid soluble	Apply every two weeks
Lawns	Granular (specific for each season)	Spring and autumn
Perennials	Granular	Apply in spring, soluble
Roses	Granular	Apply in spring and autumn for good growth
Trees and shrubs	Granular	Apply in spring
Vegetables	Granular	Apply at least a week before planting or sowing

Soil conditioners

Natural fertilisers such as manure and composts are more cumbersome than synthetic fertilisers, but nothing quite takes their place when it comes to improving the soil. These fertilisers provide some nutrient value and, when you incorporate them into the soil, improve soil structure, which increases the soil's ability to hold air, nutrients, and water.

Fresh manure can 'burn' plants (damaging leaves and growth from excess application) just as surely as any chemical fertiliser, whereas woody materials (wood chips, sawdust, leaf piles, and so on) can cause a temporary nitrogen deficiency until they are sufficiently decomposed. The microorganisms that help the decay process may use up all the available nitrogen to break down the woody material. You can counteract this effect somewhat by applying a little extra nitrogen in the spring. A rule of green thumb is that when the material starts to resemble soil, it is ready for the garden.

Piling onto the Compost Bandwagon

A *compost heap* is a collection of plant (and sometimes animal) materials, combined in a way to encourage quick decomposition. Soil microorganisms (bacteria and fungi) do the work of breaking down this organic material into a soil-like consistency.

These organisms need oxygen and water to survive. Turning the pile over provides oxygen, and an occasional watering helps keep it moist. If you make the pile well and the organisms thrive, it heats up quickly and doesn't emit any unpleasant odours. Finished compost that looks and feels like dark, crumbly soil can thus take as little as several months to produce.

Not so long ago, we gardeners hid our compost piles. We witnessed in private the magic of composting, the transformation of garden and kitchen waste into sweet-smelling black gold. We feared that others (especially neighbours) would judge our passion as a waste of time and space.

Attitudes have changed. Landfills are filling up, and composting is now widely recognised as an easy, effective way to reduce solid waste at home.

 More to the heart of gardeners is the fact that compost is a valuable, natural soil improver. Adding compost to garden beds and planting holes enhances nutrients and improves soil texture. Compost helps loosen heavy clay soils, and it increases the water-holding capacity of sandy soils. (See Chapter 11 for more about soils.) Why throw out garden waste and then go and spend good money on packaged soil improvers?

From refuse to riches

Whether you make your compost in an elaborate shop-bought bin or simply in a freestanding pile, the essentials of good composting are the same. To get fast results, follow these steps:

1. **Collect equal parts, by volume, of dried, brown, carbon-rich material (like old leaves or straw) and fresh, green, nitrogen-rich material (fresh-cut grass, green vegetation, and vegetable kitchen wastes).**

2. **Chop or shred larger, woody materials into small pieces, if possible.**

   Pieces that are 2 centimetres (¾ inch) or smaller are ideal because they break down quickly.

3. **Build the pile at least 3 feet × 3 feet × 3 feet (1 cubic yard or 1 cubic metre), mixing together the dry and green waste.**

   Too much dry material and the heap will take years to decompose, whereas too much green material becomes airless, soggy, and smelly.

   Layer a thin covering of soil for every 45 centimetres (18 inches) of depth. The soil carries more microorganisms, which aid in decomposition.

4. **Wet the pile as you build it.**

   Keep the material moist, not soaked, for optimum rotting – about as moist as a wrung-out sponge.

5. **Keep the pile covered.**

   A cover of any description – a tailor-made lid or a piece of old carpet – keeps the heap moist and warm so that the waste rots down faster.

6. **Turn the pile – if you feel like it.**

   If you want perfect compost, empty the material out of the bin and then fork it back in, giving it a good mix as you go. Granted, you end up with beautiful compost, but digging out a load of compost is a heck of a lot of work. If you have time and energy, great, but don't stress if not – your compost will get there all by itself, it'll just take a bit longer and you'll need to dig off the 'uncooked' layer of material to reach the well-rotted compost beneath.

As a general guide, compost takes about six months to produce (it's ready when the material is dark and crumbly in texture, with few recognisable bits of garden waste). However, compost made in an insulated bin during the warmer seasons can be ready in as little as 3–4 months.

Bin there, done that!

Although a simple mound of compost waste rots down in time, a compost bin keeps the pile neat, confines it to a fairly small area, and retains moisture and heat, ensuring that your waste turns into compost in a much shorter time. Depending on its design, a compost bin also keeps out animal pests. For these reasons, especially in urban settings, a bin is a good idea. (See Figure 14-3.) It's worth making or buying two or more bins, so one can be 'cooking' whilst the other fills.

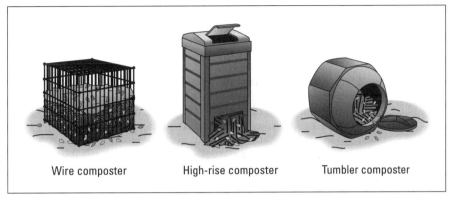

Figure 14-3:
A variety of compost bins.

Wire composter   High-rise composter   Tumbler composter

To build or to buy?

You can buy compost bins from a wide variety of sources – garden centres, DIY shops, by mail order, and sometimes at bargain prices from your local council.

Or you can make your own with scrap materials. Following are a couple of options for designs:

- ✔ **Wooden pallet bin.** The large wooden pallets used for shifting goods make cheap and easily constructed bins, if rather rough and ready. Simply take four pallets, stand them on edge, and tie together with strong wire. Once the waste has rotted down into compost, just untie the wires and let the bin fall apart. You can make this design more effective by filling the gaps in the middle of the pallets with polystyrene to retain more heat in the heap.

- ✔ **Wire bin.** A wire bin is perhaps the easiest type to make. You need a 3.5 metre (11-foot) length of 1-metre (36-inch) wide welded reinforcing wire with a grid of about 5×10 centimetres (2×4 inches). Simply bend the wire to form a hoop and tie the ends together with strong wire. You can line the wire mesh with landscape fabric to help prevent the pile from drying out excessively. This bin holds about a cubic metre when full.

Ready-made bins

You can find many different designs of ready-made compost bins, but the principle is broadly the same. Some designs have a hatch at the bottom. With these plastic units (which usually have air vents along the sides), you make a compost pile by putting a balance of waste materials in the top of the bin and letting the mixture sit. As the waste decomposes, you remove the finished compost from the bottom of the bin and add more waste to the top. This type of bin is the most commonly available, although not necessarily the best. You don't need to do any turning, and you can add waste at any time; however, decomposition is slow, and you get only small amounts of compost at a time. Because the pile does not get very hot, weeds, seeds, and plant diseases may survive.

- ✓ **Containers for hot compost.** Usually made out of recycled plastic, you use these bottomless boxes or cylinders in much the same way as the wire bin. Some of these containers are stackable, which makes removing them and turning the compost easier. With sufficient turning, this type of bin delivers fast results. You completely fill the bin with the right blend of materials and let the pile heat up. To turn the compost, when the bin is full, you lift off the top section of bin and place it on the ground (the section on top now becomes the section on the bottom). Then you reach in with a fork and lift some of the lower compost, making it the top section of compost, and so on.

- ✓ **Tumblers.** With a tumbler, you place your compost inside the container and then turn the entire bin to toss the compost inside. Some tumblers have crank handles for turning. One tumbler system is designed to roll on the ground, tumbling the compost inside as it goes.

   With these units, you make a hot compost by balancing the waste materials and turning the bin frequently. Tumblers are generally the most expensive type of bin, but the ease of turning and the fast results may be worth the money. Choose one with at least a 1 cubic metre (1 cubic yard) capacity and test it for ease of loading and turning before you buy.

- ✓ **Three-bin composters.** The Rolls-Royce of compost bins uses two or even three bins arranged side by side, as shown in Figure 14-4. Though this bin can be time consuming to construct and quite pricey to buy ready-made, it lasts for years and really organises your garden waste. Each bin is for compost at a different stage of maturity. For example, fresh material is added to the far-left bin, turned into the middle one after a few weeks, and then turned into the bin at the far right to finish.

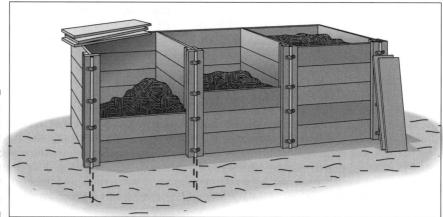

Figure 14-4:
Three wooden compost bins allow for easy turning.

Composting aids for your wish list

You don't need to have any shop-bought gadgets to make compost. With or without accessories, you can create a perfect pile. If you really become fascinated by composting, however, you may want to put a few handy items on your Christmas list. Better than socks, anyhow.

✔ **Compost thermometer.** This thermometer consists of a face dial and a steel probe (about 50 centimetres, or 20 inches, long). You use this tool to accurately monitor the temperature of compqst. The instrument measures temperatures from −18–104 degrees Celsius (0– 220 degrees Fahrenheit) and enables you to know when your pile is cooking and when it is cooling down and ready to turn. After you insert the steel probe

into the pile, you can see the temperature reading on the face dial. If the compost gets hot, meaning up to 60– 71 degrees Celsius) 140–160 degrees Fahrenheit, most of the bad players – weeds, diseases, and insect eggs – get killed.

✔ **Compost aerating tool.** You push a galvanised steel tool, which is about 1 metre (3 feet) long, into the compost pile. As you pull the tool out, two paddles open, creating a churning action that enables oxygen to enter the pile.

✔ **Pitchfork.** This long-handled tool, with tines about 25 to 30 centimetres (10 to 12 inches) long, is great for turning compost.

Heapin' it on

So what else can you put in your compost pile besides the obvious? The following list describes several other materials found around the home and garden that make good additions to any compost pile:

✔ Wood ash (sprinkle it lightly between layers; *don't* add them by the bucketful)

✔ Manure from chickens and small pets such as guinea pigs or rabbits

✔ Coffee grounds and tea bags

✔ Crushed eggshells

✔ Flowers

✔ Fruit and vegetable peels, stalks, and foliage (everything from salad leftovers to old pea shells)

✔ Fruit pulp from a juicer

✔ Cardboard and paper that you don't recycle, such as packaging and toilet roll inners

✔ Vacuum cleaner dust

 ✔ 100 per cent wool or cotton clothing (chopped up small)

 ✔ Grass clippings (mix them thoroughly to prevent clumping)

 ✔ Hedge clippings

 ✔ Shredded woody prunings (a garden shredder is a great tool to have if your garden is likely to generate lots of this sort of waste)

 ✔ Pine needles (use sparingly; they break down slowly)

 ✔ Sawdust

 ✔ Turf and soil

 ✔ Wood chips (chipped very small for faster decomposition)

And what *not* to add . . .

 ✔ Dog and cat faeces, which can contain parasites

 ✔ Cooked food and meat scraps, which can attract vermin

 ✔ Diseased plant material (the diseases are likely to survive in a warm, snug compost heap, unless the waste gets very hot)

 ✔ The roots of perennial weeds (which also thrive)

 ✔ Embers from coal fires

 ✔ Lawn clippings or plants that have been recently treated with weedkiller

Compost activators

Manufacturers of compost activators say that these products accelerate the composting process and improve the quality of the finished compost. While they do speed things up a bit, you have several alternatives that cost nothing at all. Adding a little garden soil for every 30–45 centimetres (12–18 inches) of garden waste introduces bacteria in a similar way. Nitrogen-rich materials speed up decomposition: Grow a clump of comfrey near your compost heap and chuck in handfuls of the leaves from time to time, while nettle tops are also excellent.

Those of a squeamish disposition may want to look away at this point. Urine is a fantastic compost activator, and if the men of the household wee on the compost (if neighbours don't overlook it, obviously!) your heap will benefit enormously. Ladies can have a go, but needless to say it's a bit trickier. If you're contemplating a self-build house, think about installing a composting toilet too – they really do work.

Leafmould

Leaves rot down more slowly than most other garden waste, so if you have lots of fallen leaves littering your garden in the autumn, compost these separately. After a year you end up with *leafmould* – the best soil conditioner of all. Make a simple wire netting bin by banging four posts into the ground, wrapping netting around the outside, and fixing it in place with metal staples. Fill the bin with leaves, squashing them down as you go. Just check the bin a couple of times in dry weather and add some water if the leaves are on the dry side, to speed up the rotting process.

Wiggly wormeries

If you don't have enough space to spare for a compost heap, the smallest of courtyards or balconies gives enough space for a wormery. This is a closed container for kitchen and plant waste, inhabited by worms that rapidly break down the waste into lovely rich compost. You can buy wormery bins and kits from garden centres. Keep your wormery outside apart from in the coldest weather, when you're best off moving the wormery into a shed or garage.

Make a woody pile

Woody plant stems and branches take years to rot down on the compost heap unless you put them through a shredder first. Alternatively, use this woody waste to make a snug retreat for wildlife, by stacking it up in an out-of-the-way corner of the garden. Lots of creatures that are friends to gardeners will use the heap for hibernating and breeding.

A-Mulching We Will Go . . .

Mulch is any material, organic or not, placed over the surface of soil to conserve moisture, kill weed seedlings, modify soil temperatures, or make the garden look more attractive – or all four at once. Mulch was traditionally natural, organic material such as leaves, wood chips, and manure. Now you can get a multitude of plastic-based films or woven materials.

Organic mulches

All mulches described as *organic* rot down (decompose) at a variety of speeds, and improve the soil to a lesser or greater degree. These are:

- Home-made garden compost
- Well-rotted manure
- Grass clippings (from a weed- and pesticide-free lawn)
- Leafmould
- Newspaper (shredded or flat)
- Pine needles (for acid-loving crops)
- Composted bark
- Wood chips (use composted wood chips that can be bought in bulk from a landscape supply company)
- Shredded woody prunings (stacked for at least six months or they'll rob nitrogen from the soil)

Some organic mulches (including well-rotted manure and garden compost) rot down quickly and add nutrients to the soil as well as improving its structure. Other organic mulches decompose slowly and release few nutrients; these are usually dry, woody, and very low in nitrogen. Bark mulches decompose slowest because bark is naturally rot resistant. Use bark mulches for pathways, or around trees and shrubs.

A well-read mulch

Newspapers provide the ultimate organic 'herbicide', a simple and cost-effective way to mulch out weeds. A thin layer of five to ten sheets of newspaper suppresses all sprouting weed seeds, and makes life difficult for runner roots. You can use black-and-white or coloured paper. (Most printers no longer use toxic ink these days.) You're best off using newspapers around woody perennials, shrubs, and trees, but once you're familiar with the process, you can use them around flowers or vegetables.

To apply the newspaper, moisten the sheets so that they don't blow around as you lay them out among the plants. Cover the papers with a thin layer of a weed-free, attractive mulch. The mulch helps the newspaper last for 6 to 18 months, depending on whether you have wet or dry summers, respectively.

Cardboard works even better than newspaper for the really tough weeds.

A common goal of mulching is to reduce weeding, so don't use mulch that's chock-full of weed seeds. Fertile mulches that decompose quickly but are likely to have weed seeds include cow, rabbit, goat, sheep, and horse manure; hay; some poultry bedding; and straw. Fertile mulches that also decompose quickly but have no weed seeds include leafmould and garden compost made by a 'hot' method (which kills weed seeds). Alternatively, use an inorganic mulch to suppress weeds, as explained in the next section.

Inorganic mulches

Inorganic mulch holds in moisture and stops weeds, but doesn't add fertility to the soil. Examples of infertile mulch include gravel, landscape fabric, sand, and stone. Woven plastic materials (called *planting membrane* or *landscape fabric*) act as a weed barrier, but these effective materials are not attractive enough for some situations. Also, sunlight deteriorates these plastic fabric mulches, so cover them with a weed-free organic mulch or gravel to block the sun's ultraviolet rays. The fabric lasts longer and your garden looks better. Newspaper, shredded bark, and wood chips add little fertility to the soil and decompose slowly because they are high in carbon; they have no weed seeds.

Chapter 15

Snip, Snip:
Pruning and Propagating

*O*ne of the images that often comes to mind when you think about gardening is of a wise gardener with a pair of secateurs in her hand carefully clipping and snipping in a knowing way. What are gardeners doing when they snip and clip? Well, they're *pruning* – which usually refers to cutting plants to redirect the plant's growth to where you want it.

In this chapter you also find out about *propagating* – which is the technical term for the fascinating process of making new plants by several different methods. The great thing about propagating is that you can make loads more plants yet spend little or no cash, which is a big deal if you have a new or a large garden to fill. You get a huge kick out of raising your own plants: The enormous satisfaction of watching plants grow from tiny cuttings or seeds and finally admiring a big, blooming plant takes some beating.

In this chapter, you find out how to make the cut as a pruner and propagator. Okay, you won't leave this chapter as Edward Scissorhands, but we do give you the fundamentals that will have you happily snipping and cutting in no time.

Practical Pruning

Pruning is one of the most misunderstood, and therefore neglected, gardening techniques. If you allow plants to grow without interference, everything will be hunky-dory for a while. But in the confines of a garden, some plants start to take up more than their fair share of space, so you have to intervene and take charge.

Pruning can be a big job, such as removing a heavy, damaged branch of a tree or trimming a large hedge; it can mean giving topiary plants a light haircut to maintain their shape, or tackling an overgrown shrub to give it a new lease of life. Pruning is part maintenance, part preventive medicine, and part landscaping. Because plants grow, they change all the time – a branch that was just right last year is now too long. Pruning is nothing more than snipping or cutting or pinching away some part of a plant for some good reason.

Here are some common reasons for pruning plants:

- ✓ **Increasing flowering or fruiting.** Many plants benefit from annual pruning to boost their production of flowers or fruits.

- ✓ **Restricting growth.** Over time, many plants hog more of the garden than you originally intended. Rather than hoicking out a plant and leaving a huge gap, a bit of careful pruning can keep unruly ones in order.

- ✓ **Encouraging growth.** Hard pruning of weak or straggly shoots can encourage the production of vigorous new growth.

- ✓ **Keeping the plant healthy.** By removing dead, diseased, or damaged growth, you can prevent the spread of disease. Thinning out the dense centre of a plant lets light and air through, improving vigour and encouraging healthy growth.

- ✓ **Creating decorative shapes.** This is your chance to be fanciful, by clipping certain plants like yew, box, and privet into distinctive shapes, or *topiary*. There are no rules, but be aware that once you embark on pruning a plant to a specific shape, it's hard to go back.

- ✓ **Creating more planting area.** Mature shrubs and conifers occupy a large area of ground, but you can reclaim some of this space by removing the lowest branches (taking care to enhance the plant's shape rather than ruining it). You reveal an amazingly large patch of soil that you can turn into a tapestry of colour with shade-tolerant ground-cover shrubs, perennials, and bulbs.

Always consider whether the plant really needs pruning rather than taking the shears to everything and ending up with a border of currant-bun-shaped shrubs. Many shrubs, conifers, and ornamental trees grow perfectly fine without pruning (apart from the three 'Ds' – removing anything dead, diseased, or damaged, which applies to all plants). But many plants *do* need regular attention, such as most roses, a fair few shrubs, most climbers and wall shrubs, and fruit trees and bushes.

When to prune is all important. Pruning at the wrong time can mean losing a whole year's crop of flowers or fruit. For example, if you prune a summer-flowering shrub in spring, you take off the stems that would bear that year's blooms. If you trim a shrub in autumn, the soft young shoots that are then produced may be scorched or killed by the winter's frosts. Or you may endanger the health of a plant by pruning at a time when the wounds are slow to heal and hence give an open invitation to disease.

As we only have space to give some general guidelines here, we recommend consulting a plant encyclopaedia or a pruning book for details of exactly what to prune and when. (A good guide is *The Pruning of Trees, Shrubs and Conifers* by George Brown and Tony Kirkham.) If you have an overgrown but unidentified plant in your garden that needs pruning, find out first what you're dealing with. A bit of professional advice can save a lot of heartache.

Table 15-1 gives some general guidelines about when to prune most plants in your garden.

Table 15-1	When to Prune
Type of Plant	*When to Prune*
Shrubs that bloom in spring	Just after flowers fade
Shrubs that bloom in summer or autumn	Early to mid-spring
Climbers and wall shrubs (most)	Early to mid-spring, and tie in regularly as required
Shrubs with coloured stems	Late winter to early spring
Roses (most)	Early spring
Rambler roses	Late summer, after flowering
Clematis (most)	Spring (pruning varies depending on variety)
Formal hedges and topiary	Late spring and again in summer
Fruit trees and bushes	Winter (plus summer for trained fruit trees)
Renovation pruning of overgrown deciduous shrubs	Winter
Renovation of evergreens	Early to mid-spring

How pruning affects plant growth

To understand how and when to prune, you need to know a bit about a plant's biology (and its inner struggles). Like a fast-growing teenager, a mixture of hormones and food controls a plant's growth. Its food consists of carbohydrates that photosynthesis generates in the leaves. Some of the important hormones – growth stimulators or regulators – come from the bud at the tip of each leafy shoot or branch. Biologists refer to this bud as the *apical*, *leading*, or *tip* bud. The tip bud stimulates new, lengthy, vertical growth and stifles the growth of lower potential shoots – called *dormant buds*.

When you clip out any tip bud, you take away the stifling tip hormones and their dominance. The dormant buds below the cut burst into growth and begin to produce the tip hormones themselves.

When a branch is positioned at a 45–60 degree angle, the flow of carbohydrates, hormones, and nutrients naturally favours the formation of flower buds. With many deciduous fruit trees, like apple, almond, and pear trees, the flower buds become long-term fruiting places, called spurs, in the following years.

The kindest cuts

All pruning cuts, whether made with a chain saw or fingertips, fall into one of two categories: *thinning* cut or *shortening* cut. Both kinds are important, but it helps to know the difference and when to use them.

You prune plants using the following techniques:

- ✔ **Thinning cuts.** Thinning cuts remove an entire branch or limb all the way to its origin. You do this with your fingertips when pinching a coleus or tomato seedling; with secateurs for larger plants or shrubs; or pruning shears or a saw for trees. Regardless of scale, the principle is the same. When thinning, you remove a branch or stem completely to create better air circulation or to reduce crowded conditions. Cut at a slight angle and leave about half a centimetre (¼ inch) of the shoot above a bud or main stem – not a long stub that would die and be a potential source of disease.

- ✔ **Shortening cuts.** These cuts shorten a branch or stem. As opposed to thinning, this type of pruning cut shortens a branch and doesn't remove it entirely. Always make shortening cuts to just above a dormant bud.

- ✔ **Pinching.** This action can be either a shortening or a thinning cut. Usually, you pinch soft growth between your thumb and forefinger. Pinching is handy with soft annuals and perennials, but also good for larger plants too, if you do it early enough when their shoots are still young and soft, as it encourages bushy growth. Any pruning done at this early stage is ideal because the plant suffers minimal harm and recovery is quick.

- ✔ **Trimming.** For hedges and large shrubs, use either hand shears or a powered hedgetrimmer. For finely shaped topiary plants, the best tool is a pair of scissorlike pruning shears.

Pruning trees

Usually when pruning trees you use thinning cuts, but don't cut absolutely flush to the remaining limb or branch. Leave the *branch collar* intact. The branch collar is slightly wider than the shoot you're removing, is marked with many compact wrinkles, and is usually a slightly different tone or texture than the shoot. Natural chemicals within the branch collar encourage rapid healing and help prevent rot from entering the heart of the tree. If you make a cut flush to the remaining limb, rot can slip past the collar and invade the very core of the tree or plant.

Consider these pruning tips before you take out your saw:

- ✔ **Sawing a medium-sized limb.** If the limb is small enough to hold so that it doesn't fall while cutting, you can use only one cut with a pruning handsaw. Leave the larger and more noticeable branch collar intact. Don't let the limb drop as you cut through it, or the bark will tear.

- ✔ **Sawing a large limb.** You use three cuts to remove large, heavy limbs, as shown in Figure 15-1. First, about 8 centimetres (3 inches) outside of the branch collar, cut halfway through the limb from the underneath side. Then, a few inches outside of the first cut, make a second cut (from the top), this time going all the way through the limb. If any bark begins to tear, it will stop at the cut underneath. Trim off the remaining stub with a final cut just outside the branch collar.

- ✔ **Treating your tree's wounds.** The old method of covering pruning wounds with tar or asphalt does not really help the tree much. The toxins in the tar may even slow wound healing. Allow the wound to heal naturally.

Pruning in winter

The traditional season for major pruning of *deciduous* (leaf-shedding) plants is while all the buds are dormant – in late winter or very early spring before flowers or leaves open. Such pruning stimulates new vegetative shoots. On fruit trees these shoots produce leaves rather than fruit, so try to keep major pruning to a minimum. Cutting back a dormant branch causes two or more side shoots to emerge below the cut as a result of lost tip dominance (skip back to 'How pruning affects plant growth' in this chapter for more about tip dominance). Winter pruning is especially helpful when you want to force new shoots to fill air space around the trunk with branches.

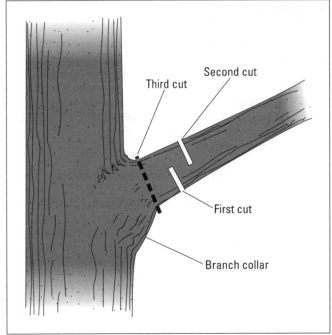

Figure 15-1:
Sawing a
large
branch is a
three-cut
process.

Pruning in spring

Shrubs that bloom in winter or spring bear flowers on growth they make during the coming growing season, so prune as soon as possible when flowering has finished to give the plant the maximum time to develop flower-bearing shoots. Prune winter jasmine (*Jasminum nudiflorum*) and forsythia in spring.

Late-flowering shrubs and climbers also produce flower-bearing growth in the same year, so you need to prune these shrubs in spring too. Examples include butterfly bush (*Buddleja*), tree mallow (*lavatera*), hardy fuchsias, and many varieties of clematis.

Shrubs that bear colourful stems, like dogwoods (*Cornus alba* varieties) and shrubby willows (*Salix*), produce brighter-coloured stems if you prune them hard every year or two – ideally by cutting all growth back to a stump each time (this type of pruning is called *stooling*).

Pruning in summer

Prune some early summer-flowering shrubs as soon as they've flowered, such as mock orange (*Philadelphus*) and Deutzia. Small shrubs, including lavender, rosemary, cotton lavender, and broom, become straggly if you ignore them, so trim them after flowering each year.

Prune trained fruit trees in summer. (Consult a book on growing fruit trees to see exactly how to tackle the different tree forms such as fan, espalier, and cordon.)

Summer pruning is the best time for thinning cuts. The active photosynthesis allows the trees to begin forming a *callus* over the cut. The well-knit callus tissue that forms a ring around the cut resists the sprouting of new shoots in the coming spring.

Pruning too early in the season, during spring's burst of vegetative growth, has a stimulating effect more like dormant pruning. Summer prune after the initial flurry of spring growth, as the weekly growth rate slows down.

Renovating an overgrown shrub

You can give neglected or overgrown shrubs a new lease of life over a period of several years by *renovation* pruning. Stick your head in the middle of a big shrub and you see that lots of space is occupied by a central mass of leafless stems, with all the growth on the outside. The plant simply can't produce any central growth when it has little or no light and not much air movement.

Pruning trees and shrubs

A few 'rules of limb' apply when pruning all trees and shrubs:

✔ Remove dead, damaged, or diseased wood as soon as possible. (Be sure not to spread certain diseases, like fireblight, with the pruning tools; if cutting back diseased shoots, clean the blade with a 10 per cent dilution of bleach after *every* cut.)

✔ Cut out one or two branches or shoots if they rub against each other (which would eventually create wounds in the stems).

✔ Prune in the winter to encourage new shoots and leafy growth.

✔ To remove unwanted shoots or limbs without stimulating too many new shoots, prune in the summer.

Tackle such shrubs using the *one-in-three* method. In winter, remove about a third of all the main branches, cutting as near to the ground as possible. Select the oldest, thickest branches to go first. The following spring, remember to feed the plant and give it a good mulch with well-rotted compost or manure. Take a peek at the plant the next summer, and you should see new shoots emerging in the centre. Repeat the process next winter, then the one after that, and eventually you have lots of fresh, young growth bursting with vitality. (Some really old shrubs don't take kindly to hard pruning and show their disapproval by dying, but at least you tried!)

Pruning Tools

Poorly constructed tools are a hassle and a pain to work with, so select a set of well-made, sturdy pruning tools. Lots of cheap imitations are on the market, so bear in mind that you really do get what you pay for. Here's a brief list of the essentials.

- **Secateurs.** Usually reserved for cuts up to 1.5–2.5 centimetres (½–1 inch) in diameter. You can find heaps of different models in a range of styles, and a vast range of prices. Ask to have a hold of various pairs before you buy – one size certainly doesn't fit all. Adjust your spend according to how much pruning you're likely to do. If you have lots of plants to tackle each year, every penny you spend on a good pair of secateurs is worthwhile.

- **Shears.** Useful for cutting back shrubs like lavender, or for hedge trimming if you only have a small hedge (or if you like lots of arm-toning exercise).

- **Lopper.** Loppers can cut limbs up to several centimetres in diameter. If you're restoring an abandoned tree or shrub, you need a lopper to remove older wood. We suggest choosing a 40–60 centimetre (16–24-inch) or 75-centimetre (30-inch) lopper. Aluminium- or fibreglass-handled loppers are easy to handle.

- **Hand saw.** The one hand saw you need is a short bladed, folding saw. Make sure that you get one with a locking mechanism for the open position.

  If you're working on a tree with large limbs slated for removal, you may want a large, 60–90 centimetre (24–36-inch) long curved pruning saw with large 2. 5–5 centimetre (1–2-inch) saw teeth. The bigger the saw's teeth and the wider the space between the teeth, the faster the saw cuts.

Powered saws are a real boon if you have a lot of pruning to do, or perhaps if your muscles aren't quite as strong as they used to be. You can find different sizes of power saw, so make sure that the model you buy can cope with the largest branches you need to cut. *Always* use a power-breaker device with any electrically powered tool: It cuts off the power supply immediately when any break or damage occurs with the tool or cable, and can, quite literally, save your life. Rechargeable saws are safer to use than those powered directly from the mains.

✔ **Hedgetrimmer.** Choose between models powered by electricity, petrol, or rechargeable battery, depending on your budget and the amount and size of hedge to cut. You can buy models that have collecting boxes for the trimmings; ideal if you're regularly cutting small-leaved, formal hedges such as box and yew, where clearing up is a pain.

Safety First

On any weekend – and particularly the first fine one of spring – the casualty department of any hospital is guaranteed to contain a few people with gardening-related injuries. It's a dangerous jungle out there! Avoid being one of the casualties by checking out these essential safety tips.

✔ Take extra care with power tools and follow the manufacturer's instructions to the letter. Always use a powerbreaker device when using any electrical tool outside (that includes the lawnmower).

✔ Always wear appropriate protective clothing. One of the most useful items to have in your shed is a couple of pairs of plastic safety glasses to protect your eyes during pruning.

✔ Danger lurks on high. When pruning tall trees or hedges, make sure that your footing is safe and that ladders are secured (hopefully by another person). If in doubt, call in a professional to do the job. Okay, it costs, but a spell in hospital with a broken leg is worse . . .

Plants for Free: Down-to-Earth Propagating

When people speak of propagating, mostly they mean *taking cuttings* – using pieces of stems, roots, and leaves to start new plants. The best technique for most gardeners to know is how to take stem cuttings, which you can use to propagate perennials and shrubs. Other methods of propagation include *seed* (using the seeds from an existing plant to grow new plants), *division*, and *layering* (both described in the following sections).

Sometimes the best sources of plant material for propagating are your neighbours and friends. If your neighbour has a plant you want to grow (maybe a splendid fuchsia or a geranium that you can't find at the nursery), just ask to take cuttings. (Gardeners love to share.)

Softwood cuttings

Softwood stem cuttings, taken from spring until midsummer, root the quickest. During this time, plants are actively growing, and the stems are succulent and flexible. Here's how to take a softwood stem cutting:

1. **Select a healthy, non-flowering stem or side shoot. Use a sharp knife to cut a 7.5–10-centimetre (3–4-inch) shoot just below a leaf, and remove all but two or three leaves at the top.**

2. **Dip the cut end into *rooting hormone*.** Decant a bit into a small pot rather than spoil a whole jar.

   Rooting hormone is a powder or liquid containing growth hormones that stimulate root growth on cuttings. They also contain a fungicide to control root rot.   You can buy rooting hormone from your garden centre.

3. **Insert the cutting into a small pot filled with moistened seed and cuttings compost.** This has a finer texture than potting compost, and also contains little or no fertiliser, which can scorch the delicate new roots. Alternatively, mix potting compost with equal parts by volume of perlite or horticultural vermiculite (an expanded volcanic aggregate, rather like crumbly polystyrene, which is available from garden centres).

4. **Slip the container into a self-sealing plastic bag.**

   Prop up the bag with short canes so that the plastic doesn't touch the leaves. Seal the bag to minimise water loss. A popular plant that *doesn't* like to be covered is geranium (*pelargonium*).

5. **Place the covered container in indirect light.** A windowsill out of direct sun is fine.

6. **When the cutting is well rooted (starting in four to eight weeks, for most plants) and is putting on new growth, water well and then transplant it into an individual container of potting compost.** As the cutting continues to grow, gradually expose it to more light.

7. **When the plant is well established in the pot and continues to put on top growth, *harden it off* (see Chapter 12) and plant it in the garden.**

Half-ripe cuttings are the easiest to take, as you can root them outdoors (or in pots, if you prefer). You take this type of cutting in midsummer, from shoots produced this year that are just starting to harden up and become woody. Take cuttings as described above, and place them either in pots or in the ground (choose a shady but well-lit spot for a nursery bed, and improve the soil by mixing in some potting compost first). A cold frame is an ideal place for rooting cuttings.

Layering

Although a slow method of getting new plants, layering is a good way to produce plants that don't grow well from cuttings (including many evergreen shrubs and some climbers).

Look round the lowest branches of a plant and find some healthy, flexible shoots that can bend down and touch the ground. You need to select shoots that are around a year old, not the softest new growth. At the point where the shoot touches the soil, use a sharp knife to remove a sliver of bark from the underside (this helps stimulate root production). Peg the shoot down into the soil, using stout wire bent into a U-shape or large metal staples. If the soil is very poor, mix in some potting compost, and water from time to time.

After a year or so you should find lots of new roots formed where the shoot meets the ground. You can detach the rooted shoot, or layer, from its parent plant and pot it up (using potting compost). Grow the layer on for another six months or so before planting out.

Division

Another great way to get new plants is through *division*, the process of pulling apart clumps of herbaceous perennials or ornamental grasses to create new clumps. (See Figure 15-2.) As plants (like daylilies and Michaelmas daisies) become established in a garden, most develop into larger and larger clumps made up of small plants. Dividing these clumps and replanting is the easiest means of spreading and increasing them. Dividing works great with all but a handful of perennials that dislike disturbance (such as hellebores and peonies). You can divide plants by using the following techniques:

- ✔ Use a spade or digging fork to lift out a mature clump (usually three to five years old).
- ✔ Divide fine-rooted types, such as lamb's ears, by hand, gently teasing apart the clump into separate plants.
- ✔ Divide tough or fleshy rooted types with a spade by cutting down through the roots, or use two garden forks back to back to pry the clumps apart.

In both cases, ensure that each new section for replanting should include several buds. Discard the older central section and replant the divisions as soon as possible.

Figure 15-2:
Divide by pulling apart the root ball or by using a spade.

Knowing the best season to divide plants is important – and it varies by plant and climate. As a general guideline, divide spring-flowering plants in very late summer or early autumn so that the new divisions can establish before winter. Divide summer- and autumn-flowering plants in early spring, while new top growth is just 5 to 8 centimetres (2 or 3 inches) high.

Chapter 16

Fighting Pests, Diseases, and Weeds

*W*hen you begin creating that little piece of paradise that is your garden, you may envision picture-perfect plants with no weeds at their feet or holes in their leaves or half-eaten flowers. The reality can be startling, prompting some discouraged gardeners to run to the garden centre for the most potent insect-disease-weed killer they can find. As we explain in this chapter, bringing out the big guns early on can be a big mistake, yet completely understandable from an emotional point of view.

The key to a healthy garden may sound a bit strange to some of you, but here it is: Don't sweat the small stuff. The more you try for a perfect, pest-free garden, the more likely you are to invite problems. You can find lots of natural pest controllers that can keep things in hand for you, so adapting your gardening methods to suit the beneficial bugs and beasties makes a whole lot of sense. Accepting a certain amount of damage is not only realistic, it also makes gardening more fun and less frustrating. Don't try to vanquish all enemies and leave them decimated, but do try to outsmart them, perhaps losing a battle but winning the war. In addition, when you learn more about insect and animal pests, diseases, and weeds – and the conditions that invite them – you arm yourself with new techniques to reduce damage while promoting a healthier garden.

This chapter gives you a start in that direction. However, so many pests, diseases, and disorders are out there that we can only give broad guidelines to the most common ones. A good plant encyclopaedia or pest and disease guide can help you identify problems with pictures in glorious, gory technicolour.

Prevention Is Better than Cure

Keeping your plants healthy can save on all sorts of problems in the first place. Research suggests that plants emit a chemical signal when they are under stress, and insects home in on this chemical signal like a landing pattern from air-traffic control. Diseases are similarly opportunistic, causing the most problems when plants are already weakened. So, what can you do to give your plants the best possible chance at a good life? Here are some suggestions:

- **Right plant, right place.** Make sure you're growing plants in the conditions that they really like and do well in. That means paying attention to the amount of sun or shade a plant likes, and its preferred soil type. For example, planting shade-loving plants in a baking hot site, or putting blueberries or azaleas in alkaline soil – instead of the acid soil they require – guarantees poor performance. (See Chapter 11.)

- **Avoid planting the same vegetables or flowers in the same location year after year.** Crop rotation prevents pests and diseases that are specific to certain crops from accumulating in the soil. If you're replacing shrubs or other long-lived plants, don't put the same type in exactly the same spot. Roses in particular are likely to suffer from rose replant disorder.

- **Plant several small patches of the same type of vegetable rather than one large patch.** This approach makes it more difficult for insects to home in on and decimate their favorite crop.

- **Practise good garden hygiene.** When diseases do occur, gather up affected leaves or fruits and chuck them in the bin – not on the compost heap where the disease spores survive to fight another day. If you prune a diseased plant, clean the secateurs before moving on to another. If a virus infects a plant, harden your heart and throw it out before the disease spreads. Some insect pests – such as aphids – can spread virus diseases. Keep them under control, and you help prevent disease.

- **Choose resistant plants when possible.** Many plants (or varieties of plants) are less attractive to plant pests and less susceptible to certain diseases. To reduce carrot fly damage, for example, choose a variety like 'Flyaway' or 'Resistafly' that has some natural resistance. Many varieties of roses, particularly newer ones, have good natural pest and disease resistance. Look for this information in plant and seed catalogues.

✔ **Take steps to encourage beneficial insects and useful wildlife into your garden.** See 'Encouraging "good" insects and creatures', later in this chapter.

✔ **Cultivate the vegetable garden soil in the autumn and early spring.** Loosening the soil exposes insect eggs, larvae, and pupae that provide a tasty treat for birds.

✔ **Look after your soil.** Healthy soil that is rich in organic matter holds on to water and nutrients, keeping plants growing strongly. Prepare the ground thoroughly before planting. In late winter or early spring, mulch the soil with well-rotted garden compost or manure. Keep mulch several inches away from trunks and stems to discourage collar rot. Lightly rake the mulch once or twice a season to expose and kill pests' eggs. Though mulch may provide a safe haven for slugs, you can use baits and traps to reduce their numbers. Provide for good soil drainage to discourage root rot.

✔ **Space plants to provide good air circulation.** Spacing plants correctly is particularly relevant in a greenhouse or cold frame. Leaves that dry quickly prevent spores of some fungus diseases from growing.

✔ **Water the soil, not the plants.** Early-morning watering is best because the sun evaporates any water on the leaves. Avoid evening watering in the greenhouse, as the foliage stays wet overnight and provides ideal conditions for disease to spread.

✔ **Feed your plants.** Discoloured foliage is often a symptom of a *nutrient deficiency* and means that your plant is hungry for fertiliser (see Chapter 14). Take a look at the pictures in a good pest and disease book or a plant encyclopaedia to find out the symptoms of nutrient deficiency in your plants. However, take care not to overdo the feed, because too much can be as bad as none at all.

Identifying Damage

When a problem with your plants does occur, correctly identifying the cause is essential. Finding out what's wrong can require some sleuthing unless you happen to witness the damage in the making. You can make more reliable guesses about what's going on in your garden if you visit it often. Taking a stroll just before sunset or in the early morning can reveal insects that hide during the heat of the day. Many pests feed under cover of darkness, so an investigative tour with a torch (and gloves) after dark can yield a bucketful of slugs and snails for the birds to appreciate the next day.

One of the most frustrating experiences is to care for seeds and seedlings and then have them die or fail to appear at all. Table 16-1 offers a listing of common problems and causes.

Table 16-1	Common Pests of Seedlings
What the Problem Looks Like	*Probable Cause*
Seeds fail to germinate or seedlings fail to appear	Damping-off disease, birds
Seedling collapses	Damping-off disease, heat, planted too early, planted in soil that is too cold or wet
Stems eaten at soil line	Cutworms
Leaves and stems chewed, torn	Snails, slugs, caterpillars, rabbits
Severely wilted plant (roots eaten)	Vine weevils
Small, round pits in leaves	Flea beetles
Threadlike, twisting lines in leaves	Leaf miners
Clusters of small, pear-shaped insects	Aphids
Plants completely removed	Slugs and snails, animal pests such as rabbits or deer

Common Insect Pests

Do bugs drive you barmy? Do weevils give you the willies? In this section we describe some of the common pests and give you some tips on how to deal with them.

✔ **Aphids.** These tiny, soft-bodied, pear-shaped pests (shown in Figure 16-1) suck plant sap with their needlelike noses. Colours vary: They may be black, green, red, or even translucent. Aphids leave behind sticky sap droppings, called *honeydew*, that may turn black if covered with sooty mould (this can happen after the aphids have gone). Aphids can proliferate quickly on weakened plants. Blast them off with a hose; control with beneficial insects such as green lacewings and ladybirds that eat the aphids (under cover in the greenhouse or similar) or sticky yellow traps from your garden centre; or, as a last resort, spray with insecticide. The drawback to spraying with insecticide is that you're likely to kill the beneficial insects too.

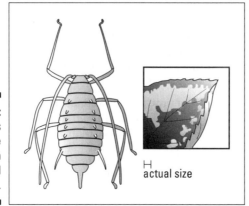

actual size

✔ **Caterpillars.** Moth and butterfly larvae are avid eaters that can cause damage to a variety of plants. However, you may decide to overlook the activities of some butterfly caterpillars so that you can enjoy the handsome butterflies later. (See Chapter 20 for more about gardening for butterflies.) The main pest for gardeners is the cabbage white butterfly, which lays its eggs on brassica crops such as cabbages and nasturtiums. You can squash the eggs and young caterpillars (peer under the leaves to find them), or spray them with the parasitic bacterium *Bacillus thuringiensis* from your garden centre.

✔ **Codling moth.** Slightly smaller than houseflies, these pests overwinter in soil, then come out to tunnel into apples. You can achieve a reasonable level of control with pheremone traps, which lure the males in to be caught on sticky pads. Put traps up after the apple trees have flowered: One trap is sufficient for up to five trees. Alternatively, spray with insecticide.

Pheromones are the perfumes of the insect world. Undetectable to us, female butterflies and moths release tiny amounts of these chemicals, which are a siren song to a wandering male of the right type. Professionals use synthetic pheromones to monitor pest populations; you can use them to trap and disorient the codling moth.

✔ **Cutworms.** These 1 centimetre (½ inch) long, greyish caterpillars emerge on spring and early summer nights to eat the base of young seedling stems, cutting the tops off from the roots. Surround seedlings with a barrier that prevents the cutworms from crawling close and feeding. Use an empty cardboard toilet paper roll or a collar made from aluminium foil – just make sure that the collar encircles the stem completely and you set it 2.5 centimetres (1 inch) deep in the soil.

✔ **Flea beetles.** These tiny black beetles feed on vegetable plants such as rocket, radish, and broccoli, sometimes riddling the entire leafy area of seedlings with tiny holes. Cover susceptible plants with floating crop covers (horticultural fleece or polythene) as soon as the seedlings emerge or are transplanted. Keep them covered until the plants get fairly large and can withstand a few beetle bites.

✔ **Leaf miners.** The larval form of tiny flies, these maggots tunnel randomly through leaves of plants such as columbine, peppers, beans, and lilacs, plus trees such as holly. Leaf miners disfigure plants and are hard to eliminate because they are protected inside the leaf. Although leaf miners are unlikely to severely damage a plant's health, infested leaves do look unsightly. Limit their spread by squishing the larvae in their tunnels within the leaves.

✔ **Mealybugs.** These small sucking insects cover their bodies with a white, cottony substance that makes them easy to identify. Plus, they usually feed in groups. Mealybugs are common on houseplants. You can wash off small numbers with cotton buds dipped in methylated spirits. Spray indoor plants with an oil-based 'leaf-shine' product from your garden centre.

✔ **Scale.** Looking like bumps on plant stems and leaves, these tiny sucking insects cling to plant branches, hiding under an outer shell that serves as a shield. These pests suck plant sap and can kill plants if present in large numbers. Look for sticky, honeylike sap droppings, one clue that scale may be present. Indoors or on small plants, clean off light infestations with a cotton ball soaked in methylated spirits. For chemical control, use a systemic insectide.

✔ **Snails and slugs.** These soft-bodied molluscs (see Figure 16-2) feed on tender leaves during the cool of night or in damp weather. Sometimes they're hard to spot: All you see is the slime trail they leave behind. They proliferate in damp areas, hiding and breeding under rocks, mulch, and other garden debris. Clean up dark, damp hiding spots to relocate slugs elsewhere. Catch the ones that remain by setting a saucer with the rim at ground level. Fill the saucer with beer. Slugs crawl in and can't get out. Refill regularly. Or surround plants with copper barriers – metal strips that seem to shock slugs if they attempt to crawl across. Other barriers that repel slugs include bran, charcoal, sharp grit, and crushed eggshells. Set out traps, commercial or homemade. If you opt for chemical slug pellets, use sparingly according to the manufacturer's instructions to minimise their impact on beneficial garden wildlife. Look for new, nontoxic baits (nontoxic to other creatures, that is, but toxic to slugs!) that contain aluminium sulphate.

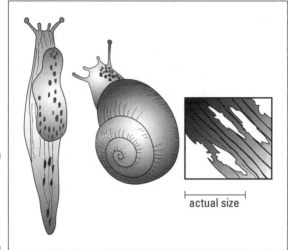

Figure 16-2:
Slugs and snails like to live in cool, damp areas.

actual size

Make your own slug trap by placing a few boards or rolled-up newspaper in the garden, because slugs hide in cool, moist places during the day. In the early morning, lift the board and destroy the slugs (excellent fast food for birds) or toss out the newspaper if it has slugs.

✔ **Spider mites.** These tiny arachnoids (shown greatly enlarged in Figure 16-3) are almost microscopic, but when they appear in large numbers, you can begin to see the fine webs that they weave. They suck plant sap, causing leaves to discolour and plants to lose vigour. They are especially active in dry conditions. You find spider mites on fruit trees, miniature roses, potted begonias, and many houseplants. Treat with a biological control or systemic insecticide (but not at the same time, because the insecticide can kill the biological predators).

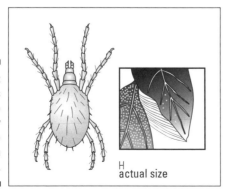

Figure 16-3:
Spider mites are easier to identify by the damage they do than by sight.

actual size

✔ **Vine weevil.** Particularly troublesome in containers and greenhouses, the larvae that live in the soil cause the most damage. These creamy-white, brown-headed grubs munch their way through a plant's roots, and often go unnoticed until the plant starts to die. The flightless adult beetles, steely-grey in colour, come out at night and chew holes in the edges of leaves, particularly of evergreen shrubs (vine weevils are one of the few pests with strong enough jaws to bite through tough evergreens). Combat with a biological control or a systemic chemical insecticide.

✔ **Whiteflies.** Whiteflies look like small, white gnats, but they suck plant sap and can proliferate in warm climates or greenhouses, and especially like tomatoes. They can also spread diseases with their sucking mouth-parts. Trap whiteflies with yellow sticky traps or use a biological control under cover. The strong smell of marigolds helps deter whitefly, so plant a few marigolds or tagetes along with your tomatoes.

Pest Control: Organic vs Chemical

Think of pest management as a staircase. On the first step you can find the least disruptive, innocuous actions, and on the top step are the most toxic and the most potentially harmful measures. The best way to control pests is to start at the bottom and move up the stairs only when absolutely necessary. This strategy is called *integrated pest management*, or IPM. This approach takes advantage of the complex interrelationships between insects and plants to find the least toxic ways to reduce damage to crops.

Organic means gardening without synthetic chemicals or, if you want to be totally organic, also using only natural fertilisers. The drawback of spraying to control pests (and this goes for some 'organic' sprays too) is that they're indiscriminate, killing both the pests and the beneficial insects that feed on them. The best approach is to avoid spraying wherever possible, to allow a balance of nature to establish in your garden. Be patient, because it can take a year or two for this to happen completely.

Changes in legislation mean that manufacturers are withdrawing many garden chemicals because of the soaring costs of rigorous testing. Fortunately, the range of biological controls (using a specific environmentally friendly organism to target a pest) is increasing. Companies that supply products by mail order include Green Gardener (www.greengardener.co.uk, or call 01603 715096) and The Organic Gardening Catalogue (www.OrganicCatalog.com, or call 01932 253666).

Identify which pest or disease you need to deal with and ask for advice at your local garden centre. Chemical control is no longer available for some pests and diseases, which makes it even more important to avoid problems in the first place by providing good growing conditions. Also check out if a biological control exists, which is the most environmentally friendly solution.

The following list outlines the actions you can take in your garden to keep a pest from getting the upper hand. The measures move from the least aggressive and potentially harmful to the most aggressive.

- **A strong blast from a hose** that knocks small pests such as aphids and spider mites off your plants. Spraying daily can provide reasonable control but can damage delicate plant growth. Don't spray plants in hot sun because you can scorch plants.

- **Barriers** such as floating crop covers (such as *horticultural fleece*, translucent, lightweight fabrics that cover plants) that keep flying insects from reaching plants; collars placed around brassica seedlings to prevent cabbage root fly; grease bands on fruit trees to catch winter moths; and copper strips that encircle plants and give slugs an electric shock.

- **Insect traps** that use chemical attractants and colours to lure pests, such as pheremone traps for codling moths.

- **Bacterial insecticides,** such as *Bacillus thuringiensis* (Bt) for caterpillars.

- **Least toxic controls,** such as insecticidal soaps, horticultural oils, and rotenone insecticides, which kill pests with less impact on the environment.

- **Chemical controls,** such as *systemic* ones (the strongest chemicals), which you spray onto leaves or mix into the compost. The chemicals are taken right into the plant so the pests suck the poisoned sap. Be sure to select the right chemical to tackle the problem and spray as little as possible. Never spray open flowers because you can kill bees; and spray in the early morning or late evening when fewer insects are around (and you won't scorch your plants, which can happen if you spray in sunlight). *Always* read the label thoroughly and follow the manufacturer's instructions. Many chemicals aren't suitable for edible crops, so do take note of the manufacturer's recommendations.

Encouraging 'good' insects and creatures

A garden contains numerous insects and small animals. Some insects are plant pollinators, some help break down organic matter, and some prey on other more damaging insects. Only a small proportion of the insects cause much damage to your plants. Make your garden into a user-friendly place for wildlife, and you not only get all the pleasure and enjoyment from their company, but they control many of your garden pests – what a fantastic deal! There are loads of different ways of attracting wildlife – see more in Chapter 20.

Beneficial insects prey on or *parasitise* garden pests. In nature, beneficial insects keep plant-eating pests under control.

Here are some beneficial creatures, bugs, and insects that you'll want to keep around your garden:

- **Ladybirds.** You're probably aware of the ladybird's voracious appetite for aphids. Both larva and adults prey on pests. One ladybird can dine on 40 to 50 aphids a day. Ladybirds also prey on mites and other soft-bodied insects.

- **Green lacewing.** Larval stage lacewings feed on aphids, thrips, mites, and various other insect eggs; overall, the most useful insect in home gardens. Both larva and adult stages are beneficial, but the larva much more so.

- **Hoverflies.** The larvae can munch their way through masses of aphids. Encourage these wasplike but harmless insects by providing pollen-rich flowers.

- **Ground beetles.** Most beetles are good guys, feeding on many different insects, usually at night.

- **Birds.** Many different birds feed on insects of varying sizes, from aphids to slugs and snails.

- **Hedgehogs.** After dark, you may be lucky enough to get these spiny slug and snail munchers visiting your garden.

- **Frogs and toads.** These feed mainly on slugs.

Buying biological controls

You can buy a wide range of predatory insects and *nematodes* (microscopic creatures invisible to the naked eye) from mail-order gardening companies such as the ones listed in this chapter. Some garden centres also sell order cards that you can post off for direct delivery to your home (as you're buying living organisms, garden centres can't stock them on the shelf). Whether you choose to buy beneficial insects or rely on the ones already present in your garden, you can take these steps to encourage them to stick around:

- Avoid indiscriminate pesticide spraying, which kills beneficials as well as pests. If you must spray, choose a product that specifically targets the pests you want to eliminate, and use it when it will be least harmful. For example, sprays that are harmful to bees can be used in the evening after bees have returned to the hive.

- Make sure that the beneficials have plenty to eat by allowing small numbers of pests to reside in your garden. If you release ladybirds before you've even spotted aphids, they may move elsewhere to find food.

✔ Provide beneficials with shelter. Grow a variety of plants – tall, short, spreading, and upright – to give the insects many potential homes.

✔ Many beneficials also feed on nectar and pollen, so grow flowers such as evening primrose and poached egg flower. Lacewings love fennel, caraway, and dill.

✔ Keep beneficial insects housed in winter. Many insects need a place to hibernate, so don't keep your garden too tidy. Delay cutting back perennials and ornamental grasses until spring. A number of companies sell tailor-made 'homes' for a variety of insects and creatures.

Preventing Plant Diseases

You can't cure diseases – you can only check them and prevent them spreading further. If you suspect that a certain disease is going to show up on your prized plant, such as black spot on roses, you can take steps to prevent infection. Find out when that disease is most likely to strike. Then identify the best product to use and apply it according to recommendations on the label.

When you spot a disease on your plants, try to identify it with the help of reference books or staff at a local garden centre, or by using a plant advisory service. Occasionally, you can get products to prevent further spread of the disease.

Here are some tips on how to prevent, identify, and – if possible – treat a dozen dirty diseases:

✔ **Anthracnose.** These fungi can attack dwarf and runner beans as well as many trees, including dogwoods and sycamores. It begins by producing small, discoloured leaf spots or dead twigs, which can spread to become serious. Avoid by choosing resistant plants. Destroy fallen diseased leaves and dead branches and twigs. Consider removing susceptible trees and replanting with resistant varieties.

✔ **Apple scab.** This fungus attacks apple and crab apple trees, producing discoloured leaf spots and woody-brown fruit lesions. Avoid by planting scab-resistant varieties. Rake up and destroy leaves in autumn to reduce the number of overwintering spores. Susceptible varieties need a preventive spraying programme during wet spring weather to prevent reinfection.

Spray sulphur, copper, or Bordeaux mixture (a mixture of copper sulphate, lime, and water) as a protective spray at the beginning of scab season (after flowers bud in spring), then two or three more times at approximately weekly intervals.

✔ **Bacterial canker.** This bacterial disease attacks woody stems on susceptible plants, such as fruit trees and ornamental cherries, forming cankers that can kill infected branches. If possible, remove and destroy infected branches. Take care to prune trees at the correct time to minimise reinfection.

✔ **Black spot.** This rose disease causes black spots on foliage and can spread, causing complete defoliation. Avoid problems by growing disease-resistant roses and cleaning up and destroying any diseased leaves that fall to the ground. To prevent black spot on susceptible roses, use a preventive fungicide spray. Start spraying at regular intervals from early to mid spring as recommended on the product, because you need to spray before symptoms appear.

✔ **Botrytis blight.** This fungus attacks a wide variety of plants, including peonies, tulips, geraniums, and strawberries. It causes discoloured patches on foliage; browning and droopy stalks on flowers; and premature rotting of fruits. Discourage botrytis by allowing air to circulate freely around susceptible plants. Remove and destroy any infected plant parts.

✔ **Brown rot.** This fungus disease is common on apples and plums. Brown rot can attack flowers and fruit, ultimately coating the infected parts with brown spores. The fruit rots and shrivels. Remove and destroy infected plant parts, and be sure to check trees after leaf fall and remove mummified fruits still on the branches.

✔ **Coral spot.** This disease can affect all woody plants, entering the plants through wounds and dead wood. Bright red spots appear and that part of the plant eventually dies. The only treatment is to remove the affected parts, cutting back well into healthy wood. Diseases such as this are the reason you must remove dead, diseased, and damaged stems from plants (see Chapter 15).

✔ **Damping-off.** This fungus disease attacks the base of seedling stems, cutting the stem off from the roots. Avoid damping-off by sowing seeds in sterile seed-sowing mix and spacing the seeds so that they don't come up in a crowded mass. Keep the soil moist but not soggy, and water from below by standing trays and pots of seedlings in water for about half an hour, rather than watering from above.

✔ **Mildew (downy and powdery).** These two fungi produce similar symptoms – a white, powdery coating on leaves. A variety of plants are susceptible, including roses and honeysuckles. The fungi disfigure plants but may not kill them outright. Instead, they weaken plants, making them unattractive and susceptible to other problems. Downy mildew attacks during cool, wet weather; powdery mildew (shown in Figure 16-4) comes later in the season during long dry spells. Avoid downy mildew by planting resistant plants and by not getting the leaves wet. Avoid powdery mildew by improving the growing conditions through mulching to improve the water-holding capacity of the soil, and by occasional but thorough watering during dry spells.

✔ **Phytophthora blight.** This bacterial disease attacks a variety of plants, including some conifers and rhododendrons. It causes leaves to discolour and stems to die, often killing the entire plant. Another form can cause root rot and rapid plant death. Start with healthy plants and provide them with well-drained soil. Improve drainage on heavy ground by working bark into the soil; it seems to discourage the fungus. Take care not to plant too deep as this can cause the stems to rot. If mulching the ground, make sure the mulch doesn't touch the stems or leaves. Try not to wet the foliage in the afternoon or evening. When watering tomatoes, do so gently to avoid soil splashing onto the plant.

✔ **Rust.** This fungus disease is easy to identify: It forms a rusty coating on the foliage of susceptible plants such as roses, snapdragons, hollyhocks, and blackberry (see Figure 16-5). Avoid susceptible plants, select disease-resistant varieties, and apply a preventive spray of fungicide early in the season before the problem occurs. Provide good air circulation. Remove and destroy infected parts.

✔ **Sooty mould.** Insect pests that release sticky drops of honeydew, such as aphids, encourage this harmless but unattractive fungus disease. The black-coloured mould grows on the honeydew, a sure sign that sucking insects are at work. Rinse off the mould and sap with soapy water and then control the insect pests.

Figure 16-4: Powdery mildew thrives during long periods of dry weather.

Figure 16-5:
Rust is an easily identified fungus.

Outwitting animals

If rabbits have ever decimated your newly planted garden, you know just how infuriating some wildlife can be. Whether it be greedy rabbits, browsing deer, or tunnelling moles and burrowing badgers, you may not always welcome wildlife in your garden. The irony is that the nearby woods or fields or open space that attracted you to living in your home in the first place also provide a habitat for many of the animals that plague you. You may, in fact, have moved into their territory.

When trying to coexist with wild animals, the first priority is to keep your sense of humour. Beyond that, you can use a few techniques to protect some of that garden produce for you to enjoy. If you don't succeed with one method, try another.

✔ **Deer.** Unless you spend a fortune on a fence up to 3 metres (10 feet) high, deer are almost impossible to keep out of a garden if you live in woodland where they roam. Deer avoid some plants, although they are notorious for changing their minds about what they want for dinner. In general, pungent or fuzzy-leafed plants are safe.

✔ **Rabbits.** Rabbits are less keen on plants with prickly or aromatic leaves, but in a hard winter the little blighters are likely to eat just about anything. Secure fencing is the only remedy, using wire netting 1 metre (3 feet) high and sunk a further 30 centimetres (12 inches) underground. Put individual guards around trees to prevent rabbits nibbling the bark. Rabbit pie is said to be tasty . . .

✔ **Cats.** An emotive one, this. Cat lovers don't, of course, consider that their pets come under the pest category, but non-cat owners can be driven demented by neighbouring moggies using their borders and freshly sown seed beds as toilets, and catching garden birds. By law, cats are recognised as free-roaming animals, so their owners can't be held guilty of trespass. So, what do you do (apart from getting a dog, that is)? First, block their main entrance points, filling hedge gaps with prickly plants or prunings. Within the garden, cover seed beds with netting or a scattering of prickly prunings. If cats are using your trees as scratching posts, wrap the trunks in wire netting. Strong-smelling deterrents have limited effect and need to be reapplied regularly. The scaredy-cat plant, *Coleus canina*, gives off a strong aroma that many cats dislike. It's frost-tender, so you need to overwinter it under cover. At the other extreme, don't plant catmint (Nepeta spp.) which will have cats flocking to your garden! Ultrasonic devices, although costly, are fairly effective, and you can also buy a motion-sensitive device that squirts water at passing animals (and at passing people too, so warn your visitors!).

Weeding Out Weeds

The challenge of combating insects, disease, and animal pests is fraught with unknowns: What works today might not work tomorrow. Weeds, however, have an element that is much more predictable and comforting: Weeds don't change their minds. You can always count on weeds to behave in a certain way.

Most people dislike weeding, though it's satisfying to tackle a weedy bed and create order out of chaos. Trouble is, you can't have a garden to enjoy without having to do at least a little bit of regular weed control too. Weeds are immensely successful simply because they have evolved to grow best in your locality, so they can nearly always outperform garden plants.

However, bringing a weedy patch under control need not be a hard slog, and indeed may take hardly any work at all if time is on your side (see 'Weedkilling the slow and easy way', later in this chapter). And, once the garden is clear, you can employ plenty of labour-saving ways to reduce the amount of regular weeding. But first, get to know your weeds and the best way to combat them.

Know your enemy

Weeds divide into two groups, annuals and perennials. Annual weeds grow fresh from seed every year and aren't too much of a problem, because you only need to kill them once. Perennial weeds are the real nightmare because they regrow from even a tiny piece of root left in the soil. Left unchecked, perennial weeds run riot and become very hard to get rid of, particularly if they grow through a border of plants. Getting to know which weeds are which may look hard at first, but an easy test is to slice off the top of a weed and see if it grows again or not. That tells you if you're dealing with annual or perennial pests. Alternatively, ask a gardening friend – they're bound to know the major enemies in your area.

Clear the ground thoroughly of weeds *before* you do any planting.

Choose your method of control from the following list.

Controlling weeds

The fewer chemicals you use in your garden, the better it is for the whole environment, but in really dire situations weedkiller is the only resort. In many cases the best approach is to use a combination of methods – hand weeding first and then applying chemicals to any tenacious perennial weeds that continue to grow. With all garden chemicals, it's vital to read and follow the instructions carefully.

- ✔ **Hoeing.** Catch weeds young. A hour's session with a good sharp hoe on a dry breezy day in spring while seedlings are small saves you a day or two's hard weeding later on. Choose a type of hoe that you find easy to use.

- ✔ **Digging/hand weeding.** When clearing weedy ground, dig out every scrap of perennial weed root and then bin or burn the roots. In borders, use a trowel or hand fork to dig out weeds between plants, and a small *onion hoe* (a short-handled hoe with a curved blade) to cultivate small areas of soil around delicate plants or seedlings.

- ✔ **Flame guns.** While the name of this method may stir the action hero within us, the reality is really quite dull (though effective). You cook your weeds to death. With a propane torch in hand, you can kill weeds in a tenth of a second by boiling the water in the plant's cells until they burst. Flaming is most effective against annual weeds in spring and early summer. Perennial weeds may require several treatments. Follow the manufacturer's instructions; safety precautions depend on the size of the flame gun although protective gloves and goggles are always a good idea. Particularly good for weeds in awkward spots like paving crevices.

- ✔ **Non-toxic weedkillers.** Non-toxic, that is, unless you're a weed. Non-chemical weedkillers contain fatty acids that kill weeds by creating a smothering coating to the leaves.

✔ **Residual (soil-acting) weedkillers.** Only suitable for use on uncultivated ground, such as pathways, or on bare ground between large, woody plants such as shrubs and trees. This type of weedkiller controls weeds as they germinate.

✔ **Contact weedkillers.** Only effective against annual weeds, as these chemicals kill the growth they touch, but not the roots. These weedkillers do not discriminate between weeds and your plants, so take care not to get any on your plant foliage! Home-made shields of cardboard, or an inverted dustbin lid, make good shields to protect plants while you're applying chemicals.

✔ **Systemic weedkillers.** Used to combat perennial weeds, as you spray the chemical onto the leaves and the plant then takes the poison right down to the roots. Glyphosate is the most widely available chemical. Apply on a windless day and shield nearby plants with wood or cardboard, because the weedkiller kills plants too. You can treat perennial weeds that grow among garden plants with this weedkiller in gel form. Either paint the gel onto the leaves, or put on a pair of tough rubber gloves, smear the weedkiller over the palms, and simply pull the stems through your hands, but take care that newly treated weeds don't come into contact with your plants.

Weedkilling the slow and easy way

Almost no work is required to get rid of weeds by the cover-up method – just time and patience. Even the toughest weeds eventually die when deprived of all light.

1. **Choose any readily available light-excluding material** such as old carpet, carpet underlay, or sheets of cardboard. You can buy landscaping fabric (also known as *planting membrane*) or heavy-duty black polythene, both of which work out much cheaper if bought in bulk.

2. **Mow or cut down the worst of the weeds, then cover the ground with your chosen material.** Make sure you have a good overlap at any joins, and weigh down or bury the edges to keep out every scrap of light.

3. **Ignore for at least a year.** After that, everything underneath will be well dead and the ground should be in reasonable condition to dig over. If time permits, leave the ground bare for a couple of months after digging and before planting so annual weed seeds can germinate and you can hoe off the seedlings.

Weed Prevention

The old saying of prevention being better than cure is never truer than when you apply it to weeds. You can save hours and hours of work by putting down a weed-stopping barrier in the form of a mulch or planting membrane. Your plants will look a whole load better too, as they can concentrate on growing rather than doing battle with weeds.

In the following sections we give you a selection of materials to keep weeds at bay. Some are fairly costly and very effective, while others are cheap or entirely free but are not long lasting. You pays your money and you takes your choice!

Mulches and membranes

Before putting any mulch or membrane around your plants, make sure that the ground is clear of weeds, especially perennial ones, and give the ground a good soaking. Take care not to pile mulch around plant stems because this can cause rot. Choose mulches and membranes from this list:

- **Chipped bark.** An attractive material that makes a really good contrast to border plants. Apply in a layer at least 5 centimetres (2 inches) thick. Bark can encourage slugs so you may need preventive measures, particularly if you use chipped bark around hostas and lilies, their favourite plants.

- **Cocoa shell.** Similar in appearance to chipped bark, but repels slugs into the bargain. Don't use cocoa shell mulch if you have a dog, because the material is toxic to them and a few dogs find the taste of fresh mulch attractive.

- **Garden shreddings.** You can shred woody prunings to make your own bark mulch. Apply as for chipped bark, but stack for four to six months before use because freshly shredded material takes nitrogen, a vital nutrient, from the soil.

- **Garden compost or well-rotted manure.** Compost or manure suppresses weeds when you apply them in a 10-centimetre (4-inch) layer and rots down to improve the soil and feed plants. However, most compost and manure contains some weed seeds!

- **Mushroom compost.** Mushroom compost is high-quality horse manure that has been used for growing mushrooms. It often contains lime, so is not suitable for use on lime-hating (ericaceous) plants such as rhododendrons and azaleas.

- ✔ **Planting membrane or landscaping fabric.** You cut out the holes for plants through this woven plastic matting. Very effective but looks ugly, so disguise it with a thin layer of chipped bark. Excellent for use on slopes because it helps stop soil washing away. See 'Planting through membrane' for more.

- ✔ **Black polythene.** Although cheaper than planting membrane, polythene doesn't let water through, so you need to water your plants regularly.

- ✔ **Newspaper or cardboard.** Lay whole newspapers or sheets of cardboard with the edges overlapping, and keep in place with a thin layer of soil or bark to stop weeds from popping up. Dig the paper or card into the ground after one season.

Planting through membrane

Landscaping fabric or planting membrane is tough, woven plastic sheeting that stops weeds from growing but still lets water through to the roots. However, it must be put down before you do any planting and you can't add it later!

First, prepare the ground really thoroughly by digging over, clearing weeds and mixing in organic matter (see Chapter 11 for advice on improving your soil). Spread the membrane over the border and bury the edges in the ground.

Gather all the plants for a particular area and stand them out, still in their pots, moving them around until you're completely happy with the positioning. Then, for each one, cut a cross in the membrane just large enough to be able to peel back the corners and put in each plant. After planting, tuck the membrane back.

Planting membrane works well but isn't attractive to look at, so it's worth adding a thin layer of chipped bark or something similar, just to cover it up.

One year's seeding is seven years' weeding

This old saying is not far off the truth! Let those oh-so-innocent little weed seeds float around your garden, and you'll be pulling up the results for years. If you have lots of big weeds that are about to seed, but no time to pull up all the weeds themselves, go round and quickly snap off the seed heads. Bag them up and put them in the bin, unless your compost heap heats up enough to kill weed seeds. Even if you pull up your weeds in flower, before they set seed, remember that some sneaky weeds like dandelions and groundsel can mature their flowers into seeds.

Space invaders

Few things are more infuriating than your own weed-free (well, weed-free*ish*) garden space becoming infested by perennial weeds creeping under the fence from next door. The solution is to sink a permanent barrier into the soil between the gardens. Dig a trench 45 centimetres (18 inches) deep and line it with a strong material such as root barrier membrane, corrugated iron, or paving slabs, making sure that it butts up to the base of your fence as snugly as possible. The barrier should protrude around 2.5 centimetres (1 inch) above ground. Replace the soil, and you have a permanent and almost-invisible barrier to repel invaders.

Ten wicked weeds

If you remember nothing else about controlling weeds, keep this strategy in mind at all times: Remove perennial weeds as soon as you spot them, and pull annual weeds before they flower. Here are a few of our least-favourite weeds:

- ✔ **Bindweed.** Perennial. Spreading from underground roots, this twining perennial can snake sneakily around your garden and wrap itself around your plants. The leaves are shaped like an arrowhead and the flowers resemble morning glories, a more appreciated cousin. Beware, however, that if you allow bindweed to flower, you greatly compound your problem.

  Use a digging fork to remove the plants rather than a spade, which can divide the roots into pieces, each of which grows new plants.

- ✔ **Chickweed.** *Stellaria media.* Annual. You can easily spot this densely matting annual weed in late winter and early spring, when the stems of 1-centimetre (½-inch), oval leaves reach towards the sun. The tiny white flowers open fully on sunny days. Broken stems can root if you drop them on the ground.

- ✔ **Couch grass.** Perennial. This sneaky weed is adept at getting itself well established in borders among your plants before you notice it. Couch grass differs from annual grasses in that it forms wide-spreading, wiry, underground stems with sharp, white, pointed, growing tips.

- ✔ **Creeping buttercup.** Perennial. While more charming in appearance than many other weeds, with its bright golden yellow flowers, don't be fooled! In a lawn, you can keep creeping buttercup within bounds by regular mowing, particularly if you rake the lawn occasionally to bring up the runners and cut them with the mower. In borders, however, it's a different story and buttercup fast assumes thug-like tendencies.

✔ **Dandelion.** Perennial. The first leaves, which emerge in early spring, are low and oval. Later leaves are arrow shaped with deep lobes. The unmistakable yellow flowers quickly go to seed, so pick them early. (Only let your kids blow dandelion clocks on country walks!) The edible flowers are apparently tasty when battered and fried. Long-handled weeders seem made to remove this common weed from lawns and gardens. Remove as much of the taproot as possible, because the plant regrows from any portion that's left.

✔ **Dock.** Perennial. Dock leaves may be useful for taking the pain out of nettle stings, but they give you a lot of pain if they take hold in your garden. Left alone, dock grows to over 1 metre (4 feet) tall with clusters of heart-shaped, reddish-brown seed pods. The taproot can extend 60 centimetres (2 feet) underground, but if you can remove just the top 12.5 centimetres (5 inches), the root dies.

✔ **Ground elder.** Perennial. Once used as a treatment for gout, which is no consolation whatsoever if you're unfortunate enough to suffer from this tenacious weed. Dig out, smother, or poison it with weedkiller – stop it spreading further as a matter of urgency!

✔ **Groundsel.** Annual. Although easy to eradicate by hoeing or pulling, groundsel spreads itself with great alacrity if you allow it to seed. Even if you pull this weed in flower, before seeding, the flowerheads mature into seeds just when you think you're safe – so get it young!

✔ **Japanese knotweed.** Perennial. A real nightmare of a plant, which is becoming an increasing problem in the wild because it is well-nigh impossible to eradicate and takes over from native wild plants. It has tall, arching, woody stems with oval, mid-green leaves. Tackle this weed at the first signs, for it forms a colony as soon as you turn your back.

✔ **Oxalis.** Perennial. This is a weed notable for its clover-like leaves and bright yellow flowers. Control by repeated cultivation or flaming and applications of systemic herbicide from your garden centre. Use a residual herbicide to minimise or prevent seed germination on uncultivated ground.

Chapter 17

Tools of the Trade

In This Chapter

▶ Looking at the handiest hand tools

▶ Finding the right lawnmower

▶ Using garden power tools

*G*ardening really doesn't require a shed full of tools. In fact, we recommend starting with just a few essential tools and then building your collection as specific jobs call for more specialised tools. But having the right tool for the job often makes the difference between a pleasurable experience and a frustrating chore, or between a job well done or not. That's what this chapter is all about: Choosing the right tool for the job.

Hand Tools

To save money in the long run, buy high-quality, durable tools. Remember that with garden tools, you really do get what you pay for. Garden centres, hardware shops, and DIY stores usually offer a good selection, while mail-order suppliers offer more specialised tools for keen beans.

Ten top tools

Which tools you need to own depends entirely on the jobs that you're trying to accomplish. If, for example, you've just moved into a home with a garden that includes overgrown shrubs, buy secateurs before a trowel. If making a vegetable garden is your top priority, a fork and spade are essential. Have a good think before you buy.

Here are our top ten hand tools.

✔ **Fork.** Buy a full-width fork for digging over the ground, making planting holes, and moving bulky materials such as garden compost. Narrower border forks (sometimes still called 'ladies' forks' even in these days of political correctness) are good if you just want to dig the soil lightly between existing plants. Forks sometimes come with handles of varying lengths, so choose one to match your height.

✔ **Spade.** Use as for a fork. It's possible to manage without a spade on heavy soils, but not if you garden on light sandy or stony soil, which runs through the prongs of a fork. A spade is also good for moving finer materials like mulch.

✔ **Flat-headed rake.** The best first rake to buy is a *flat-headed* rake, often just called a garden rake, as shown in Figure 17-1. This rake is an important tool for spreading and levelling soil and for gathering organic materials.

The rake is a good tool for preparing seedbeds by breaking up small clods of earth. Use both the *tines* (the thin, pointed prongs) and the back edge of the rake for building and smoothing raised garden beds. Keep the tines facing downward when breaking up lumps of soil or collecting stones, and keep the flat edge of the head downward when levelling.

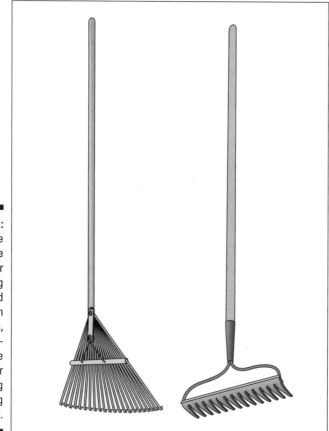

Figure 17-1:
A lawn rake is effective for gathering leaves and lawn clippings, and a flat-headed rake is useful for spreading and levelling the soil.

✔ **Lawn rake.** Nothing works better than a bamboo, polypropylene, or metal rake with long, flexible tines for gathering up lawn clippings, leaves, and even small rocks on both paved and natural surfaces. (See Figure 17-1.)

✔ **Hoe.** Unless your garden is really tiny, invest in a hoe. A hoe is great for keeping on top of weeds and saves lots of wear and tear on your back too. A Dutch hoe is the best type for general weeding. Hoe when the soil is dry, preferably on a sunny day so weeds die quickly and you can spot any missed ones. Sweep the blade of the hoe over the soil surface, severing the top growth from the roots.

✔ **Secateurs.** Once you own a pair of secateurs that you can hold comfortably and that produce a clean cut with little effort, you find it hard to imagine gardening without them. Most gardeners favour *by-pass secateurs*, which cut like scissors. *Anvil secateurs*, which cut by pressing a blade into a soft metal anvil, are less expensive. Use either type to cut soft and woody stems up to about 1.5 centimetres (½ inch) thick. Use this tool to clip flowers, harvest vegetables, cut back perennials, and prune shrubs. Secateurs are easy to lose, so buy a belt holster too.

✔ **Trowel.** Use for planting and weeding. A trowel sees loads of use, so don't even consider getting a cheap one.

Trowels are small and easy to lose among your plants, so cover the handle with brightly coloured tape to make it easy to spot.

✔ **Watering can.** Metal is fashionable but plastic cans are much easier to use. Buy a full-size long-spouted can (unless you can't lift it when the can is full). To reach up and water hanging baskets, use a large plastic mineral water bottle instead of buying another, smaller can.

✔ **Garden hose.** Buy a top-quality hose with a lifetime guarantee. A good hose coils easily, resists kinking, and remains flexible even in cold weather. Choose one long enough to reach all corners of your garden.

✔ **Wheelbarrow, bucket, or garden carry bag.** These tools are for moving rubbish and garden materials. The choice depends on the size of your garden, because in a small plot you can manage with a builder's bucket or stout plastic carrying bag designed for garden use. If, on the other hand, you have lots of heavy jobs to do in a bigger garden, buy a large, strong model from a builders' merchant rather than a lightweight garden barrow.

Hand-tool maintenance

Take care of your hand tools – they last longer and work better if you do.

Clean and dry your tools each time you finish your gardening chores, but also know that primary maintenance consists of keeping

- ✔ Wood handles smooth and sound
- ✔ Metal tool heads rust free
- ✔ Blades sharp

Try to give your tools a thorough overhaul every winter (the dark days are a great time for sorting out your shed and tools – a good New Year's resolution!). When wooden tool handles show wear, sand off the factory varnish and apply linseed oil. Apply several coats, allowing the oil to soak in each time. Clean metal tool heads with a wire brush and sharpen edges with a file. Many by-pass secateurs have replacement cutting blades that are easy to install. You can also sharpen secateurs (the bevelled side of the curved blade only) with a fine-grit diamond file. You can even send off good-quality secateurs for servicing.

Replace worn hand-tool grips with a liquid plastic, sold in most hardware stores. The best tool lubricants are synthetic oils that lubricate, repel dust, protect against rust, and leave only a light film.

Powering Up Your Tools

Does anyone really *need* power equipment? In our experience, most gardeners use at least one of the following tools from time to time.

Lawnmowers

One of the reasons that people get fed up with lawns is that lawns require this regular, monotonous maintenance called *cutting the grass*, which, for some people, conjures up memories of noisy, dirty, hard-to-start engines. We're here to tell you that times have changed! New lawnmowers are quieter, better working, less polluting, and safer to use.

Choose a lawnmower according to the size of your lawn, the type of grass, your tolerance (or not) of noise, and your desire for exercise.

Table 17-1 sums up the pros and cons of the different types of mowers.

Table 17-1	The Pros and Cons of Different Mowers	
	Advantages	*Disadvantages*
Manual (push) lawnmowers	Cheap and quiet. Great exercise – a session with the mower is as good as a trip to the gym. Require little maintenance. Useful for small lawns.	Can be hard to manoeuvre, particularly when cutting edges and awkward corners. Hard work if your lawn is large.
Electric	Convenient because you just plug in and go. Easy to use. Small models in particular are very reasonably priced. Potentially dangerous; always, *always*, use a powerbreaker device that cuts off the electrical supply should you damage or sever the cable.	The inconvenience of having to mess about with cables, particularly in a larger garden. Can overheat if cutting a large or long lawn.
Petrol	Can use it anywhere, unlike electrically powered mowers that need to be near a power source. Quick and powerful; larger models can tackle long or rough grass with ease. The best type of mower if you want a fine lawn.	Heavier and more awkward to handle. Older types can be hard to start. More polluting on the immediate environment (although electricity creates pollution where tricity creates pollution where it's generated).

You may come across different types of mowers: *hover*, *cylinder*, and *rotary*. Broadly, cylinder types cut the grass finely, like scissors, and leave those lovely stripes on your lawn (lovely, that is, as long as the lines aren't wonky), whereas rotary mowers are fine for general-purpose lawns and for cutting long or rough grass. Hover mowers are easiest to manoeuvre and so are best for cutting banks and other awkward areas. You cut grass to varying lengths according to the time of year, so check that the height of cut is easy to adjust.

Picking up cut grass is another key decision when buying a mower. Many mowers have a detachable grass box in which to collect clippings, so you can change your mind at will. Clippings left lying on the lawn aren't too much of a problem, although they can be a pain if you tread them indoors or if the kids have a grass fight. More recently available are *mulching* mowers, which finely chop the clippings and return them to the base of the grass where they rot down into the soil.

If you have vast swathes of lawn, you're likely to want a *ride-on* mower, which is far quicker at doing the job than one you walk behind. If you have older kids, they're likely to be far keener to cut the grass with one of these.

Mower safety and maintenance

Bear these safety guidelines in mind when you mow the lawn:

✔ Follow the manufacturer's instructions.

✔ Always wear stout shoes.

✔ Always use a powerbreaker device with an electric mower. A few lives are lost every year for want of a device that costs less than £20.

✔ If blockages or problems occur, switch off or disconnect the mower before investigating.

✔ Old or second-hand mowers may not be fitted with the same safety devices as newer models. These include features such as a *deadman's handle* (that you hold when mowing and stops the engine if you let it go) and a *blade brake* that stops the blades from rotating within seconds of switching off the mower.

Follow these tips for keeping your mower in tiptop condition:

✔ After mowing, switch off or disconnect, then brush off grass and clean as necessary.

✔ Lubricate moving parts regularly.

✔ Check blades occasionally and sharpen or replace as required.

✔ Check electrical cables for breaks or damage.

✔ Check the oil level if applicable.

✔ With petrol mowers, drain the tank before putting the mower away for the winter.

✔ Service your mower every year or so. If you send the mower in for servicing, do so in autumn or winter to avoid a long wait in the spring. In spring the repair shops are packed and you may have to wait for weeks while watching your beautiful smooth lawn develop into a meadow.

Strimmers

The nylon-line *trimmer*, or *strimmer*, is (after a lawnmower) the most widely used power tool, and is very useful for cutting awkward areas that the mower can't reach. Some are electric (power cord or battery), and some are powered by petrol; the same pros and cons apply here as with mowers (see Table 17-1).

Most strimmers cut soft grass and weeds with a spinning nylon cord. Some use a solid nylon disk, and some can accept other, heavy-duty cutting blades. For a basic string trimmer, look for one with an automatic or semiautomatic 'feed' system for the nylon string (not standard with older models). Petrol-powered trimmers are ideal for larger gardens, but they cost more and need more maintenance. They're also heavier and so harder to use.

Brushcutters

A *brushwood cutter*, usually known as a brushcutter, is an excellent machine for tackling long grass, tough weeds, and undergrowth. A brushcutter is usually fitted with a metal blade; some models have plastic blades but these aren't quite as tough and don't last as long. Most models are petrol driven and are quite heavy and tiring to work with, although very robust and efficient. Electric models are lighter and easier but less efficient.

Rotovators

If you regularly cultivate a quarter acre or more, a rotovator may be a smart investment. A *rotovator* is a powered cultivator with sharp blades for digging, and it turns over the soil in a fraction of the time it would take you to dig the same area. A rotovator consists of an engine that provides the power to a transmission that channels the power to the wheels and the tiller. Tillers with the tines in front don't have powered wheels, so the transmission only has to drive the tiller.

If you only need a rotovator to cultivate neglected ground in order to create a lawn, border, or vegetable garden, buying your own may not make good economic sense (and where would you store it?). Renting one for a day or two is a sensible option. You can hire a large, powerful model that can tackle the job with ease.

Check the features of a cultivator before hiring or buying. All rotary tillers are categorised according to the location of the engine. Heavy-duty tillers have the engine in front and the tines in the rear. Expert gardeners prefer rear-tine tillers because they're much easier and less jarring to operate (but heavier). The tines dig down into the soil rather than force the machine to lurch forward, and you don't need to walk through freshly tilled soil. Mid-engined cultivators are good for deep cultivation, because the engine weight is directly over the rotors. However, they can be a little difficult to control. Rear-engined models are best for manoeuvring into awkward places.

The higher the tine speed, the more easily and more finely you can prepare the seedbed. You also need a higher tine speed to adequately chop up crop residues or compost and incorporate them into the soil. Commercial rotovators often allow you to vary the tine speed for different uses. The throttle setting also affects tine speed.

Garden shredders

A shredder is useful for all but very small gardens, because it's a great way of dealing with your woody garden waste. The size of shredder you go for depends on how much waste you have to deal with, and how often.

Garden shredders chop up woody garden waste into small pieces suitable for composting, or for stacking and using as a mulch. You feed material – branches or stalks for instance – to it via a narrow tube. The shredder chops the material up inside and the shreddings come out of the bottom, where you can gather them in a bucket or bag. From a safety point of view, don't allow the inlet tube direct access to the blades.

When you buy a shredder, check the diameter of branches that the machine can deal with. Smaller machines can only take a small amount of material at a time, so it can take ages to feed through a load of prunings. Hiring a large, powerful shredder may be a better option if you only do a garden tidy-up once or twice a year.

Garden shredders are among the most dangerous tools that gardeners regularly use. Wear goggles or protective glasses at all times and avoid loose-fitting clothing. Follow all the safety precautions carefully, and always turn the engine off and wait for it to stop completely before reaching in to unclog it. Shredders for garden use are powered by electricity, so do not use them outside in wet conditions.

Aerators, rakes, sweepers, and blowers

Why stop at mowers and strimmers? A few more power tools can make your life easier, depending on the size and content of your garden.

Aerators and *raking machines* are useful for tackling poorly drained lawns. If you have a large area to tackle, hiring a powered machine avoids a lot of sweat and hard work. A hollow-tine aerator pulls out cores of soil, which you can replace with sharp sand to improve drainage. A raking machine, or scarifier, rakes out moss and the layer of *thatch* or dead grass from a lawn.

Powered leaf sweepers and blowers can save a lot of time in a large garden with lots of trees and large shrubs. Use a sweeper to collect up leaves from a large lawn, and a blower to blow leaves into heaps where they're easy to pick up. A blower is particularly useful for clearing up leaves from gravel or shingle areas – but do this job regularly, before leaves become soggy and cling to the stones.

Hedge trimmers and powered saws can be very handy. For more on these useful tools, snip your way to Chapter 15 on pruning.

Part VI
Special Gardens

"My gardener told me to go away for two or three days & when I come back I'll have a genuine alpine garden."

In this part . . .

Your garden may be in a tablecloth-sized plot or it may cover an acre or more. What makes a garden is the interest and intent of the gardener, not grandeur or super plantsmanship.

Inevitably, many gardeners adopt specialties. Some like to grow their own food; others cultivate only flowers. For some, a garden must be neat and orderly; for others, the more natural, the better. Of course, there's nothing to stop you incorporating a bit of everything into one garden.

Here are five of our favourite ways of adding variety to your garden: gardening in containers; growing your own produce; gardens that attract wildlife; scented gardens, and how to squeeze the most into a small plot.

Chapter 18

Food Gardens

Absolutely nothing beats watching your own crops grow, then harvesting them and feasting on the results. And nothing beats the flavour – and satisfaction – of home-grown veggies. Great for your health (exercise and fresh air); great for kids or grandkids (encourages them to try lots of healthy produce); and great for the environment and your conscience (no food miles and, depending on your choice, organic, without any harmful chemicals). You also get a great insight into the natural world as you attempt to stay one step ahead of the bugs and beasties that try to munch the harvest before you do!

Most edible plants (especially vegetables) are easy to grow. You don't need a lot of space either. Gardening has no rule that you must lay out vegetables in long rows – many of them grow better in beds. You can even mix vegetables, herbs, fruits, and flowers together and end up with a garden that pleases all your senses.

Planning a Vegetable Garden

Vegetable gardening can be downright simple if you follow a few guidelines. Planting at the right time is key, and to do that, you need to know a little about both the vegetables you want to grow and your climate.

Pay especially close attention to the seasons. (Why do you think farmers are always talking about the weather?) Most vegetables are annuals. Their lives begin and end within the scope of one 'season'. Exactly when that season begins and ends is the rub.

Seasonal preferences

Regarding season, you broadly categorise vegetables as either hardy or tender. *Tender* vegetables like warmth and they don't like cold. Their season is pretty much bracketed by frosts – the last one in spring and the first one in autumn. The days or months between those two markers are the season for warmth-loving vegetables such as sweetcorn, peppers, courgettes, cucumbers, and tomatoes. (See Figure 18-1.)

Figure 18-1:
Plant tender vegetables after all danger of frost has passed.

Hardy vegetables (see Figure 18-2) such as peas, carrots, lettuce, and radishes can withstand a little bit of frost. You can also plant *winter-hardy* vegetables such as cabbage, Brussels sprouts, and leeks, which can stand hard frosts and you can harvest them during winter.

Figure 18-2:
Hardy vegetables stand up to colder weather.

Use lots of canny ways to extend your growing and harvesting season. A covered growing area such as a greenhouse or polythene tunnel is biggest and best, not only protecting your crops but also providing a great place to potter under cover so you can garden while protected from the elements. Heating a greenhouse extends the length of the growing season even further.

Small-scale crop covers such as cloches and cold frames are extremely useful too. *Cloches* are lightweight and moveable covers, whereas *cold frames* are a bit like mini-greenhouses: heavier and designed to stay in one place. Cloches come in a number of sizes and materials, from small domes to cover individual plants to long tunnels to place over crop rows. During late winter, place the cloches over prepared soil for several weeks so the soil warms up a bit, then you can sow hardy crops like lettuce, carrots, spring onions, radishes, and peas. In late spring you can move the cloches to cover newly planted tender vegetables, including beans, courgettes, and sweetcorn. Then, at the back end of the year, you can cover summer-sown crops with cloches in autumn as the temperature falls. You can also cover overwintered crops – those you sow in late summer to stay in the ground for a spring or early summer harvest – to keep off the worst of the weather.

Choose the right location

Most vegetables need six to eight hours of direct sun daily for best results. Leafy greens, like spinach and lettuce, can thrive with a bit less. Fruit-producing vegetables including tomatoes, peppers, pumpkins, and squash need more. Be mindful of nearby trees. Deciduous trees allow much light to pass through in winter and early spring, and cast increasingly dense shade as the season progresses.

If possible, locate your vegetable garden so that access to and from the kitchen is easy and convenient – you're more apt to notice what needs to be tended and to take full advantage of the harvest.

Make the garden the right size

Even the smallest space can become productive. You can use large containers and growing bags to raise a mini-feast if you have no garden at all. If you have the luxury of choosing how much space to dedicate to crops, a 3 × 6 metre (10 × 20 foot) plot is sufficient for a garden sampler that will yield a variety of greens, some herbs, a few tomatoes and peppers, beans, cucumbers, and even edible flowers such as nasturtiums for garnishes.

A 6 × 9 metre (20 × 30 foot) garden gives you room to grow a wide range of crops, including some tasty space hoggers like sweetcorn and pumpkins. If you grow plants in succession and using 1-metre (4-foot) beds with 45-centimetre (18-inch) paths, you should have plenty of luscious vegetables for fresh eating – even extras for friends.

Designing the garden

The process of designing a vegetable garden is both practical and creative. You need to give plants enough room to grow and arrange them so that taller vegetables don't shade lower-growing types. You also need to be aware of the appropriate planting techniques that fit the growth habits of different kinds of vegetables. How you water your garden is also a strong influence on the garden design. And you also need to think about access – how you get to your plants to harvest, weed, or water. How can you keep out creatures like rabbits, if they are a problem in your area?

Following are three basic planting arrangements for vegetables:

- **Rows.** You can plant any vegetable in rows, but this approach works best with plants that need quite a bit of room, such as tomatoes, cabbage, sweetcorn, potatoes, onions, and courgettes.

- **Beds.** Beds are wide, flat-topped rows of soil, usually at least 60 centimetres (2 feet) wide and at least 15 centimetres (6 inches) high. Beds are great if you want crops with the minimum of work, because if you make each one about 1 metre (4 feet) wide, you won't need to tread on and compact the soil – so you won't need to dig it every year!

  You can install permanent borders of wood or other material, which makes maintaining edges easy. You can also concentrate all your soil improvers and fertilisers in the bed more easily and without waste. Beds are ideal for smaller vegetables that don't mind living in close quarters – such as lettuce, carrots, radishes, and turnips – but any vegetable can thrive. Plant the vegetables in a random pattern in the bed or in closely spaced rows.

- **Containers.** Containers are ideal if you live in a flat and only have a patio or balcony to use for outdoor living. You can find more about container gardening in Chapter 19.

Proper plant spacing is a compromise of sometimes competing needs. You want to squeeze as many plants into the available space to maximise harvest or appearance. Plants need enough physical room (in soil for roots, too) to grow and spread. You need to leave enough space between plants for you to get in to inspect, water, and harvest. Check the catalogue or seed packet for mature plant size and planting distance recommendations.

Sketching out your plan on paper can help you purchase the right amount of seeds or transplants and use space more efficiently.

Drawing out the design is a good way to see the possibilities for *succession planting* (following one crop with another) and *interplanting* (planting a crop that matures quickly next to a slower-maturing one and harvesting the two before they compete for space). For example, you may see that you can follow your late peas with a crop of broccoli, and be ready with young plants to transplant in July. Or you may see that the garden still has space for you to tuck in a few lettuce plants among your tomatoes while the toms are still small.

Improving the soil

The ideal garden location has fertile, moisture-retentive soil that drains well. If you haven't had your soil tested to determine the pH, do so now. Most vegetables require a pH between 6.0 and 6.8. (See Chapter 11 for more on soil testing and adjusting the pH.)

In most gardens, vegetable garden soil can stand some improvement. Apply several inches of well-rotted manure or garden compost and work it into the soil with a fork.

If your soil is hopeless or if you like convenience, consider growing vegetables in a raised bed – a planting area that rises above the surrounding ground level. The bed can simply be a normal bed with the soil piled about 15 centimetres (6 inches) high (higher if you prefer), or construct a large containerlike structure with wood, stone, or masonry sides. Make wooden raised beds from timber that has been pressure treated with preservative, or recycled plastic 'timbers'.

Planting Your Vegetable Garden

Many vegetables are best started from seeds sown directly in the ground (*direct sown*); others go in as young plants called *seedlings*. You can grow your own seedlings or buy them. (See Chapter 12 for specifics on raising your own seedlings and transplanting.)

Two of your best sources of information about seeds and seedlings are free – seed packets and seed catalogues. To acquire several seed catalogues for free, you can subscribe to a garden magazine; you begin receiving a selection of catalogues almost immediately. Or you can request catalogues via the adverts inside gardening magazines.

All in the timing

The key date in vegetable planting timing is the average date of the *last spring frost* (when all danger of frost has passed). Though frost may not always kill your young plants, it damages tender vegetables. As a general rule of thumb, mild areas such as the south and west coasts usually see their last frost around early May; inland areas up to the north of England are around the middle to end of May, going up to early June in the coldest parts of the country. Of course, weather does vary tremendously from year to year – and sadly no hard-and-fast rules exist. Keep a close eye on the weather forecasts if you've just put out some frost-tender plants, and have some horticultural fleece or old net curtain handy to cover up tender plants if a late frost threatens.

Potatoes are frost tender, so plant them out around mid-spring and then protect from frost by drawing soil up around the developing shoots (a process called *earthing up*).

Table 18-1 lists some popular 'tough' crops that tolerate frost.

Table 18-1	Frost-Resistant Crops
Direct Sow	*Transplant*
Beetroot	Broccoli *
Carrots	Brussels sprouts *
Onions *	Cabbage *
Spinach and chard *	Lettuce and salad greens
	Peas
	Radishes
	Leeks

* You can sow these crops again later in the season: in midsummer for an autumn harvest; and, in the mildest areas, in autumn for a winter garden. These plants also are some of the easiest and best for autumn vegetable gardens.

Table 18-2 shows examples of 'tender' crops to start off under cover – in the greenhouse or on a sunny windowsill (or buy ready-grown plants from garden centres) – that can go into the garden after the danger of frost is past:

Table 18-2	Frost-Tender Crops
Basil	Aubergines *
French and runner beans **	Peppers *
Cucumbers *	Tomatoes *
Melons *	Courgette/marrow **
Squash	Sweetcorn **

These plants also do well grown under cover if you have a greenhouse or polytunnel.
** You can also direct sow these plants outside for a late crop.

Raise them right

Successfully planting seeds in the ground hinges on two factors – depth and moisture. The general rule: Plant the seeds twice as deep as they are wide. So you plant really big seeds such as beans around 2.5 centimetres (1 inches) deep; medium-sized seeds like sweetcorn 1–2 centimetres (½–1 inch) deep; small seeds like beets and spinach 1 centimetre (½ inch) deep; and itty-bitty lettuce, carrot, and turnip seeds no more than 0.5 centimetre (¼ inch) below the surface. Sow seeds in rows or wide drills, and make sure that you label each variety. You can also buy strips of paper with small seeds glued on at exactly the right spacing. You plant these strips, called *seed tapes*, and eliminate thinning. Some seed catalogues offer seed tapes, although in a very limited range of varieties.

Keep the seeds moist. Water helps soften the seed's coat or shell so that the sprout can break through more easily. Start by sowing into moist ground, watering the ground thoroughly beforehand and allowing it to drain for several hours first. Afterwards, either water with a can or hose fitted with a fine rose, or set up a sprinkler to help keep newly seeded beds moist.

Whether you set out plants or sow seeds, weeds will appear all over your garden. This is a natural occurrence, but you do have to stifle those wild invaders. This is also why it's important to sow seeds in rows or distinct spacings – so you tell the weeds apart from the crops. Get a comfortable pad to sit on and hand weed right around your plants. Then use a hoe to clear weeds from large areas of bare soil.

After you finish weeding, mulch over the weeded space to keep more weeds from taking the places of the ones you killed. You can use chipped bark, leafmould, composted manure, or newspapers covered with enough leaves or grass clippings to keep them from blowing away. (See Chapter 16 for more on mulching.)

Have a happy harvest

If you plant what you like to eat, you have to hold yourself back to keep from picking your vegetables too early. Fortunately, most veggies are best when you pick them on the young side, especially leafy greens, sugar-snap peas, radishes, and cucumbers. With some other vegetables, especially root vegetables, the old-timers taste better. Wait for carrots to reach full size – that's when they're full of flavour; and tomatoes and peppers are best when you allow them to hang on the plants until they're very ripe.

When in question, take a bite! If you don't like what you taste, spit it out, wait a few days, and try again. You'll probably be enthralled with the superior taste of really fresh, ripe vegetables from your own garden, compared with those on the supermarket shelves that are picked long before they're ripe.

The Best of the Crop

Following is a top ten list of popular vegetables, along with a few tips on planting and cultivation. Seed packets give details of planting times and spacing, which can vary according to individual varieties.

- ✓ **Carrot.** Plant seeds several times throughout the growing season; early spring into late summer for a continuous harvest. Soil needs to be fertile and deep; avoid planting into freshly manured soil, which can cause the roots to fork.

  Carrot root fly is a troublesome pest that you're likely to encounter. The fly is attracted by the smell of carrots, so sow the seed thinly and avoid the need for further thinning. Growing crops in mini-tunnels of horticultural fleece keeps this pest at bay. Certain varieties also have some natural resistance to carrot fly.

- ✓ **Courgette/marrow.** These crops both come from the same plants – the difference is that courgettes are picked when small, and marrows are what you get if you forget to harvest your courgettes! Certain varieties produce better fruits when small or mature, which is why you find some seeds called courgettes and others marrows. Harvest courgettes regularly because the fruit develops fast in summer. Sow seeds in small pots under cover in warmth in mid to late spring, and plant out in early summer.

✔ **Cucumber.** Varieties divide into those for greenhouse cultivation and for outdoors, so be sure to choose the right one for you. Sow seeds in pots under cover in a warm, frost-free place during early to mid-spring, or buy ready-grown plants.

✔ **French and runner beans.** For an early crop, sow seeds in pots under cover in a warm, frost-free place, then harden off and plant out once all danger of frost is past. Bush types are easier to manage (particularly French beans), but climbing types are more productive in an equal space (because they're taller!) – but remember to put up stakes or other supports.

✔ **Lettuce.** Sow seeds outdoors from early spring onwards, as soon as the soil is workable, and continue sowing at three- to four-week intervals for a constant supply. You can also grow lettuce under cover during winter, and raise plants under cover in spring for planting out in late spring/ early summer. Your main choice is between those types of lettuce that you harvest in one go (like 'Little Gem'), and loose-leaf or cut-and-come-again varieties where you can pick a few leaves at a time.

✔ **Onion.** The easiest way to get a good crop of onions is by planting the miniature onion bulbs called *sets*. Most onion sets need to be planted in the spring, although some are suitable for autumn planting.

✔ **Peas.** Sow seeds early in spring, as soon as you can work the soil.

✔ **Radish.** Sow seeds at three- to four-week intervals from early spring onwards. Radishes are probably the easiest and fastest vegetable to grow.

✔ **Sweetcorn.** Although a space-hungry plant, the taste of fresh-picked sweetcorn is so delectable that it's well worth growing your own. You can always fill the spaces between with short-lived crops like lettuces or salad leaves. The sweetness of the corn declines rapidly as soon as you harvest it, so don't leave the cobs sitting around waiting to be cooked. Sow seed in pots under cover, in warmth, and plant out in early summer.

✔ **Tomato.** You can choose from numerous varieties of tomato, so decide which ones to go for – such as little, sweet-tasting cherry tomatoes, larger salad ones, or the great big plum tomatoes. Unless you want a particular and less common variety, don't bother raising your own plants from seed, as you find plenty of ready-grown plants on sale in late spring/early summer. Tomatoes do well under cover, and also in a sheltered, sunny site outside.

Tomatoes are one of those rare plants that actually benefit if you plant seedlings deeper than they grew in the nursery pot. Plants are more anchored and sturdier, and roots develop along the buried portion of the stem. Pinch off lower leaves before planting.

Getting Technical: Hybrids, Heirlooms, and AGM Varieties

As you look through seed catalogues or read seed packets, you may notice the words hybrid and heirloom, or a trophy symbol that denotes an Award of Garden Merit (AGM) variety. *Hybrid* vegetables are the result of a cross of selected groups of plants of the same kind (where pollen from one flower fertilises another, resulting in seed). Hybrid plants may show what's called *hybrid vigour* – a significant increase in qualities such as early and uniform maturity and increased disease resistance. The increased vigour and predictably good performance make hybrids worth the extra cost to many gardeners.

If you choose hybrid seeds, you need to buy a new batch every season rather than save your own. When hybrid plants cross with themselves and form seeds, these seeds lose the specific combination of genetic information that gave the hybrid its predictable qualities. If you plant seed from hybrids, you end up with a very mixed bag of plants.

At the other end from hybrid varieties are *open pollinated varieties*. These plants are basically inbred lines that are allowed to pollinate each other in open fields. The resulting seeds are pretty predictable, but you won't have the consistency of hybrids.

Heirloom vegetables, like the varieties your grandparents grew, have been open pollinated for years. Heirlooms are enjoying quite a revival because of the variety of fruit colours, tastes, and forms. Neither hybrid nor heirloom is necessarily better than the other. Try all kinds of vegetables, especially those that sound promising to you. Then see what works best, what you like most, and plant more of them.

Those plants awarded the Royal Horticultural Society's Award of Garden Merit (AGM) are definitely worth selecting, as these plants are trialled in different locations around the country and given this coveted award for good performance. However, not all the varieties listed in books or catalogues are trialled, so the award doesn't mean that these are the *only* good varieties.

Squeezing in Herbs

A few fresh herbs are invaluable in the kitchen, so always try to squeeze a few into a vegetable garden – or into pots or even a flower garden. Herbs look attractive and smell superb (well, *most* of them, anyway), so they make great companions to ornamental plants in a border.

A few herbs are best treated as annuals (such as basil, which requires full sun and a long warm season). Some, like parsley, are best grown as biennials and chucked out after their second year; and many, such as oregano and thyme, are perennials. The majority of herbs grow best in soil that is not too rich and that drains freely, although this doesn't apply to all herbs.

The following are among the most useful herbs to grow. However, as with vegetables, grow what you like to eat (or like the look of). You can raise many herbs from seed, but unless you want loads of one particular herb, the easiest way to get plants is simply to buy ready-grown ones. They're not expensive and are easy to get hold of.

- ✔ **Basil.** Sow seeds indoors in early to mid-spring. Plant outdoors, in full sun, only after the danger of frost has passed. Plants grow 15–30 centimetres (6–12 inches) high. Pick leaves as you need them.

- ✔ **Chives.** Start plants from seeds or clumps. Plant in early spring as soon as the soil is workable, in full sun or partial shade. Plants grow about 30 centimetres (12 inches) high and produce round, pinkish flowers in early summer. Chives make good edging plants for borders, and are excellent companions to roses (where they can help discourage black spot disease). Use scissors to snip leaves as needed. Divide slowly expanding clumps every three years or so.

- ✔ **Garlic.** Start with bulbs from the garden centre or mail-order supplier (the latter can provide extensive variety selection and although you can use bulbs from the greengrocer, the results aren't guaranteed because the variety of garlic may not suit your climate). Plant in autumn. Separate bulbs into individual cloves, leaving the papery membrane in place. Set cloves pointed end up with the tips just below the soil, then check them a couple of times a week, because birds often pull up newly planted cloves. Allow 8–10 centimetres (3–4 inches) between plants. Harvest all types in midsummer when the leaves are mostly brown.

- ✔ **Mints.** These tremendously varied plants all have leaves that are rich with aromatic oils, and all share a love of moist soil. Peppermint (*Mentha piperita*) is a favourite. You can snip the tip of a branch, pour hot water over it, and have instant peppermint tea. Many mints, however, are real thugs and spread themselves with enthusiasm. Avoid the hassle in the first place by planting mint in a large container or, if you want to put mint in the ground, in a sunken bucket with the bottom removed. Plants grow about 30–60 centimetres (1–2 feet) high.

- ✔ **Oregano and marjoram.** We place these two plants together here because they are so closely related and so often confused. Oregano (*Origanum vulgare*) is a 60-centimetre (2-foot) tall hardy perennial, and marjoram (*O. majorana*) is a 30-centimetre (1-foot) tall half-hardy annual.

Both are strongly aromatic and flavourful, but marjoram is a little sweeter and milder.

✔ **Parsley.** This herb is so familiar as a restaurant garnish that you can overlook how attractive and useful it is in the garden. The rich green of the leaves is a perfect foil to spring daffodils or pansies, and to summer marigolds. Snip or pinch a few leaves whenever you need them for a recipe. Start from plants, because gardeners often have trouble starting the seeds.

✔ **Rosemary.** Gardeners anywhere can grow this resinous, aromatic shrub in summer. In all but the coldest areas, rosemary is a perfectly behaved garden shrub that you can also harvest for the kitchen and barbecue. Many named varieties of rosemary are available, but all have flavourful leaves and stems. They differ primarily in growth habit: Some trail and some are upright. Most have blue flowers and need full sun and well-drained soil. Buy rosemary plants at your local garden centre.

✔ **Sage.** This plant is a hardy perennial (*Salvia officinalis*) that you can have in your garden for years no matter where you live. Sage is ornamental: Several kinds have variously coloured leaves, but all have the same distinctive flavour. Sage grows 60–75 centimetres (24–30 inches) high and produces violet flowers in early summer. Plant in full sun and well-drained soil. Start with young plants from your local garden centre.

✔ **Thyme.** These hardy perennials are mostly low growing (a few very low growing). Some are ornamental, with just a faint flavour. Most, however, have leaves and stems that are rich with fragrant oils. Common thyme (*Thymus vulgaris*) grows 15–20 centimetres (6–8 inches) high and is the form that cooks prefer. Lemon thyme (*T. citriodorus*), with its citrus scent, runs a close second. Thymes are excellent growing between stepping-stones where an occasional step releases the wonderful scent.

Fruity Harvests

Even if you don't have space for a good-sized fruit garden, you can still pack in a few fruit trees or bushes in even the smallest of spaces.

Fruit trees come in many shapes and sizes. The *rootstock* on which the tree grows determines the size, so for all but large gardens, ask for trees on a *dwarfing rootstock*, which tend to be the norm these days. The best space savers of all are *trained* fruit trees that you can grow flat against walls, fences, or supports within the garden.

Then you have a whole range of mouthwatering berry and currant fruits – raspberries, blackberries, blackcurrants, and of course the ever-popular strawberries. Simply grow what you like to eat!

Six tips for a fruit tree harvest

You don't have to be an expert to grow fruit trees. Just take a look at the following general tips:

- ✔ **Be patient.** Most fruit trees require several years from planting to the first harvest. If you're in a hurry, stick to fruit bushes and berry fruits.

- ✔ **Provide pollinators.** Many fruit trees need the pollen from a different but compatible variety – called *cross-pollination* – to produce a crop of fruit. Apples, pears, sweet cherries, and plums are in this category, although some varieties are *self-fertile*, which means that they set a crop with their own pollen. Apples need cross-pollination, but ornamental crab apples can serve too, so you can get by with only one apple tree if you live where apples and crab apples are abundant.

- ✔ **Plant in the right place.** A good site means full sun and fertile, well-drained soil. If you live in an area with strong winds, plant trees in protected locations. If spring frosts threaten developing buds and flowers, plant on a gentle slope so that cold air travels downhill and away from the trees.

- ✔ **Keep trees well watered and fertilised.** Water trees thoroughly at least once a week during dry weather during spring and summer. Use mulch, such as compost or well-rotted manure, to help maintain a fertile soil that can hold moisture and nutrients. Apply a general fertiliser with a high potash content, in early spring.

  Too much fertiliser can cause bland, soft fruit that is susceptible to brown rot.

- ✔ **Prune and thin.** The primary objectives of pruning fruit trees is to create a strong tree form and maximise the harvest. Thin the number of fruits that the tree sets after flowering to get larger, higher-quality fruit and to encourage steady, year-to-year production. The best time to thin most fruit trees is in July, after what is known as the 'June drop' when trees naturally shed their surplus fruits. Consult a fruit tree book for details of how to prune different shapes and varieties of tree.

- ✔ **Extend the season.** Plan for as long a harvest season as you can by planting different kinds of fruit, and by selecting a range of varieties that fruit at different times. Berries give you the earliest fruit.

Fruits for the home garden

The following sections describe some good choices for a fruit garden.

Apples

One of the easiest fruit trees to grow, apples come in a huge range of varieties. First decide on whether you want an eater or a cooker, then decide which varieties you prefer the most. A good way to give your taste buds a treat is to go to an 'apple day', which a number of large gardens and organisations around the country run in autumn. Here you can find out loads more about apples and taste a selection of different fruits. Check your local newspaper for details.

Apple trees are widely available in *bush* form (which is actually a small tree), the size of which is determined by the rootstock, as well as miniature varieties. However, if you're really pushed for space, you can buy apple trees that are *fan trained* and *horizontal trained*, or *espalier* shapes and *cordons*, which are single-stemmed trees grown at an angle of 45 degrees.

Make sure you choose two varieties that flower at the same time so that they pollinate each other. In colder areas, select varieties that flower late to avoid the blossom being damaged by frost.

Pears

Pears are not as easy to grow as apples, partly because they flower earlier and so the blossom is more likely to be damaged by frost. In most areas pears prefer growing against a sunny, sheltered wall that gives extra warmth and protection, in fan-trained or espalier shapes. The same rules of pollination apply as for apples.

Cherries

Cherries are relatively easy to grow and make attractive garden trees in spring when smothered in blossom. However, although producing a crop of fruit isn't too tricky, keeping the birds off it so you can get some of the harvest certainly is! A free-standing tree is almost impossible to protect, so the best approach is to buy a fan-trained cherry to grow against a wall or fence, where you can cover it with netting or horticultural fleece if you need to. Some varieties of cherry are self-fertile whereas others require a pollinator.

Plums

Plums and the closely related damsons are fairly easy to grow and make nice small to medium-sized trees for a garden. While many varieties need a pollinator, one of the most popular plums, 'Victoria', is self-fertile. You can also buy plums as miniature or fan-trained trees. Avoid pruning trees in winter because they're susceptible to a disease called silver-leaf, which can enter wounds more easily during that season.

Raspberries

Raspberries are easy to grow and summer-fruiting raspberries crop from early to late summer, depending on the variety. Early to midsummer ones include 'Glen Clova', 'Glen Moy', 'Glen Prosen', and 'Malling Delight'. You can find several autumn-fruiting varieties, most popular of which is 'Autumn Bliss'. Grow raspberries on a supporting framework of posts and wires 1.5 metres (5 feet) high with the wires spaced horizontally 30 centimetres (12 inches) apart. Raspberries thrive in cool climates, preferring partial shade in hot areas, and tolerate a range of soils. Plant the dormant canes in autumn or early winter with the topmost roots not more than 5 centimetres (2 inches) below soil level, and cut back the canes to 15 centimetres (6 inches) high immediately after planting. Plant single canes 40 centimetres (16 inches) apart in the row. After harvest, cut out the old canes at ground level and tie in new ones, spaced 10 centimetres (4 inches) apart.

Currants

Easy and reliable to grow, these bushes are grown for their coloured currants that are black, red, or white. Red varieties include 'Jonkheer van Tets' and 'Laxton's No 1', while only one white variety is widely available, 'White Versailles'. 'Versailles Blanche' has pale yellow fruit. Blackcurrant 'Ben Sarek' is a compact variety for small spaces. Grow in a warm, sheltered site. Plant bushes 1.2 metres (4 feet) apart with 1.5 metres (5 feet) between rows.

Strawberries

The taste of ripe strawberries, eaten while still warm from the sun, is one of the greatest pleasures of growing your own fruit. If you have room to plant patches of different varieties that fruit from early to late in the season, you can be harvesting strawberries for over a month. Grow them in 90–120 centimetre (3–4-foot) wide beds and be ready to lay netting over the plants to keep out the birds. After harvest, cut back and rake off all the foliage, to allow the sun to reach the crowns of the plants.

Blueberries

Blueberries are well known for being packed with healthy antioxidants. Blueberries like an acid and moisture-retentive soil, so they aren't suitable for all gardens. If your soil isn't suitable but you still long for a home-grown crop, plant the bushes in large wooden half-barrels using *ericaceous* (lime-free) compost. For container growing, choose a compact variety such as 'Sunshine Blue' or 'Top Hat'. You need two varieties for cross-pollination, unless you choose a self-fertile variety – three or more are better and can extend the blueberry harvest to two months.

Looking further afield – renting an allotment

If you love growing your own produce but just haven't enough space at home, consider renting an allotment. Nearly all cities, towns, and villages have varying amounts of land set aside for allotments, where you can rent a plot of ground for an amazingly low annual rent. Here you not only have the space to grow stacks of vegetables and fruit (plus cut flowers or whatever your heart desires), but you also benefit from loads of fresh air and exercise, and make new friends into the bargain. Contact your local council for details.

Briar fruits

Fruits such as blackberries, loganberries, and hybrid ones such as tayberries are vigorous climbers and are best grown on a stout post-and-wire framework (good for boundaries in small gardens, or as dividers within a large plot). Most varieties are viciously thorny, so grow them well away from paths and other places where people pass. Fortunately several thornless varieties are available, which are much less painful to grow in the average-sized garden.

Chapter 19

Container Gardens

Some people grow plants in containers (or pots or planters) because that's the only suitable place they can find – maybe their garden soil is too horrible or their space too limited. Others who have abundant garden space are just as motivated to grow plants in pots – container plants can add height, charm, and surprise to a garden.

One of the best aspects of containers is that they're the nearest thing to instant gardening in reach of us ordinary folk (not the ones with huge bank balances who call in the makeover brigade to bring in a ready-grown jungle). A couple of hours planting and bingo, you have a great garden in miniature. You need never be bored with containers either; they're a real moveable feast and can be juggled around to create a fresh look in minutes. Using containers is also a great way to experiment with different plant and colour combinations without the sweat of putting plants in the ground.

And, most fun of all, you can *cheat*. Have a corner of the garden for growing plants on, ready to bring centre stage to your patio in their prime, and where you can hide plants past their best. If your borders look a bit colourless or gappy – well, just drop in a few pots full of container-grown summer annuals or bulbs. Welcome to the world of container gardening!

Choosing the Right Containers

Containers come in a huge variety of materials – especially if you start making your own or finding them. As you look, be sure you consider at least two key factors – porosity and drainage.

- ✔ **Porosity.** Some materials used to create containers are more *porous* than others and allow moisture and air to penetrate more readily. For example, unglazed terracotta, wood, and paper pulp dry out faster than nonporous material, but also allow soil to cool by evaporation and to *breathe* (roots need oxygen). Porosity has the effect of drawing away excess water, thereby preventing waterlogged soil. Nonporous materials such as glazed terracotta, plastic, and cans hold soil moisture better, which helps to reduce watering frequency. That characteristic, however, may make the plants vulnerable to waterlogged soil.

- ✔ **Drainage.** For healthy root development, soil must drain water properly and have enough space for air. Soil that is too heavy or dense can slow drainage – so can lack of a drain hole or a blocked drain hole. If drainage is slow or nonexistent, water may collect at the bottom (where it can stagnate and smell bad); roots can rot, and the plant can die. Look for drain holes when selecting containers. If you have a container you love but it has no drainage hole, you can *double-pot* (place a container within a larger container) so that the inner pot can drain into the larger one; or drill drain holes by using a carbide-tipped drill.

The following list contains the materials used most often for making containers these days. Each has its strengths and weaknesses.

- ✔ **Terracotta.** Unglazed clay, or *terracotta* (which means *baked earth* in Italian), is usually reddish orange but comes in other colours as well. These pots come in many shapes and sizes. Higher-quality pots – those with thick walls and fired at high heat – last longer. Pots fired at low heat have a more grainy texture and weather away more quickly. If your pots remain outside all year, choose *frost-proof* terracotta containers. Otherwise, empty the container and store it in a garage or shed until spring.

  Terracotta pots generally offer good value for money. Their earthy colours and natural surface make the pots look comfortable in almost any garden situation, from rustic to formal. The porosity in unglazed clay enables plant roots to breathe and excess moisture to evaporate – both desirable for many plants. However, porosity also means that soil dries out quickly, so plants in such pots are likely to need more frequent watering.

✔ **Glazed clay.** Usually inexpensive, these pots come in many more colours than unglazed ones – bright to dark, and some with patterns. Many are made in Asia and fit nicely in Japanese-style gardens. Glazed clay containers are great in formal situations and can liven up a grouping of plain clay pots.

✔ **Wood.** Square and rectangular boxes and round tubs come in many styles and are usually made of treated wood to resist rot. Wood containers are heavy, durable, and stand up well to cold weather. Wood provides good soil insulation, keeping roots cooler in summer and warmer in winter than terracotta. Evaporation is also slower than with clay pots. Thicker timber is better – at least 2.25 centimetres (⅞ inch).

Wooden bottoms can rot if the containers stay too moist; raise containers at least a couple of centimetres off the ground, and line the inside with stout polythene (with drainage holes in the bottom, of course).

✔ **Plastic.** Many plastic pots imitate the look of standard terracotta pots. Plastic is less expensive, easier to clean, and weighs less than terracotta. Plastic is nonporous, so soil doesn't dry out as quickly as with terracotta – be careful that you don't overwater. Don't buy poor-quality plastic pots, which can fade in the sun and become brittle.

✔ **Metal pots.** Their sleek lines and polished finish make metal containers especially good for contemporary gardens. Check quality carefully when buying, as cheaper pots are made of thin materials that are liable to damage. Unless your containers are double-walled, always line the insides of the pot (but not the base) with an insulating material or your plants' roots will roast in summer and freeze in winter. Sheets of polystyrene or bubble polythene do the job nicely. Look for iron, aluminium, and other metal containers at car boot sales and antique shops.

✔ **Other materials.** *Cast concrete* is durable, heavy, and cold resistant. *Stone* looks superb, particularly in formal gardens, but it is expensive and very heavy. *Paper pulp* is compressed recycled paper that degrades in several years. You can actually plant pot and all directly in the ground, and the roots grow through the sides as the paper decomposes. Inexpensive and lightweight but not particularly handsome, paper pulp pots are also candidates for slipping into larger, more attractive containers. Use pulp pots where looks don't matter.

✔ **Improvised containers.** Turning mundane items – wheelbarrows, mop buckets, old butler sinks, old boots – into plant containers is fun and may not cost anything at all. If your proposed container is less than smart, simply plant masses of trailing plants such as ivies to tumble over the sides. The only thing a plant container absolutely *must* have is a drainage hole in the bottom.

Designing with Container Plants

Does *designing* sound pretentious for determining what plants to put in which pots, how to combine different plants in the same pots, and how to combine different types of pots? Whatever designs you create, be sure to combine plants or pots that have similar maintenance requirements. For example, you wouldn't plant a water-loving plant with a *succulent* (a plant with thick, fleshy leaves), nor a shade lover with a plant that needs eight hours of sun.

One plant in a container standing alone can be stunning – it had better be if that's all you have space for. However, combining several or many container plants creates a fuller, lusher effect, almost like a garden growing in the ground. Containers can do all the things that a whole garden can: Announce the seasons, flash bright colour, and create miniature slices of nature. Once you have a feel for which plants work well together, you can combine plants in larger pots. But if in doubt, go for the simple option of planting one type of plant per pot, with several of the same plant if they're small, or if the pot is big. Then, simply group your containers together to create the effect of mixed planting.

Style points

Talking about style and taste is never easy – you seldom find any definite answers. We give you a few reminders about style anyway, to keep in mind when creating container plantings:

✔ **Work with what you already have.** Use container plants to complement your home or garden. In an informal setting, for example, you may want to use tubs of mixed summer annuals or herbaceous perennials. Succulents in shallow bowls, ornamental grasses, and architectural shrubs lend a dramatic note to a contemporary setting.

✔ **Think about colour.** Mixing lots of different colours doesn't always work. Restrict the number of colours for a much better overall effect. Using mostly green or white creates a cooling effect. Bright, hot colours (red or pink dahlias, for instance) heat things up.

✔ **Consider the different shapes of the plants you're using** – whether they're in individual containers, mixed plantings, or multiple containers. Think about the shapes of the plants and use shape to complement and contrast with each other. Plant shapes fall into several categories. For example:

  • **Tall, spiky plants with a bold architectural shape:** Coryline, yucca, New Zealand flax

  • **Round, mounded shapes:** Busy lizzies, geraniums, lavender

  • **Trailers:** Lobelia, ivy

✔ **Think about formality.** Topiary is formal. So are symmetrical plantings –
a pair of identically planted containers flanking the front door or box
pyramids lining a path, for instance. Containers with flowers all in the
same colour are formal. A more casual look would be mixed-colour annuals, or groups of containers of different sizes, materials, and shapes.

✔ **Decide on something old or something new.** A sleek, contemporary
atmosphere in your garden calls for uncluttered, geometric lines in the
shapes of your containers and plants. A few boldly shaped containers
can be effective filled with succulents, New Zealand flax, or clipped box.

If you prefer an always-been-there look, choose used containers that
show a bit of wear and tear. Or make your pots grow old fast. One
speedy way to 'age' a new stone or terracotta pot is to paint buttermilk
or yogurt onto the outside. The buttermilk or yogurt helps promote
green algal growth, quickly creating a nice 'old' patina.

✔ **Remember the value of repetition.** Repeat the same colours or plants.
For example, use yellow marigolds in a cluster of pots near the beginning of a front path and again on the front porch. Of course, moderation
is important. Going overboard on repetition – for instance, a long border
of alternating red and white busy Lizzies – can end up looking like a
giant stick of rock.

✔ **Scale is a big subject.** Big spaces demand large containers. If you cluster
pots, make sure to include at least one good-sized container with a taller
plant in it (or stand one on a stack of bricks to make it look taller).

Combining plants in containers

Mix annuals or tender perennials with shrubs, perennials with bulbs – you
can combine different types of plants in the same container.

Start with one dominant plant (Japanese maple, clipped Box, or yucca), and
then place compatible mounding or trailing plants (lobelias, busy Lizzies, and
many others) around it.

Arranging containers

Arranging groups of container plants is like hanging pictures or moving furniture. Don't be afraid to experiment, to move around your plant-filled containers again and again. Remember the most important thing: The results should
look good to you.

The most visually effective groupings use a minimum of three plants and up
to a dozen. (As a rule of composition, an uneven number of items usually
looks better than an even number, unless you want a formal layout.)

A few basic rules apply for grouping container plants:

- ✔ Start by using matching types of containers (for example terracotta) in different sizes and shapes. Make one or two pots a lot larger than the others.

- ✔ For a big patio, which can seem bleakly spacious, create a homely feel by using lots of pots, and mix sizes, styles, and shapes (but not more than one or two different materials).

- ✔ Mix plants of different textures, colours, and heights, as shown in Figure 19-1. Think about the basic categories of shapes described in 'Style points', earlier in this chapter.

Figure 19-1:
Vary the height, colour, and texture in container planting.

- ✔ Group identical pots with identical plants. Nothing looks more smashing in spring than a set of identical pots stuffed to the gills with red tulips.

- ✔ Raise some containers higher than others. Provide a lift with a couple of bricks underneath or use plant stands. The height adds emphasis and puts the plants at a better viewing level.

✔ Be careful when placing small plants by themselves. People can over-look or trip over them. Use small containers to accompany bigger ones, or place on low walls.

✔ Try to place containers where people gather – a seating area, for instance – and can view plants up close and appreciate their beauty and fragrance.

✔ In large gardens, place containers near the house where you can easily notice them often. Selectively scatter container plants along garden paths. Another good spot is in the transition zone between a patio and lawn or between lawn and wild garden.

✔ Head upwards. The easiest and quickest way to get favourite plants up to eye level is by using hanging baskets, window boxes, or wall pots. Make sure that supports are strong, because a plant gains weight as it grows, not to mention the weight after watering. See Figure 19-2.

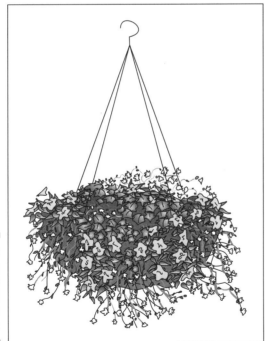

Figure 19-2:
A hanging basket adds colour and height to an empty spot.

Putting It All Together

As you think about the possibilities of designing with containers, consider the following suggestions for growing and displaying them effectively in your garden – making use of the principles we discuss in 'Designing with Container Plants', earlier in this chapter.

- ✔ Circle a small tree, where roots don't allow anything to grow, with eight or so terracotta containers overflowing with white busy Lizzies (*impatiens*).

- ✔ On a balcony, create a privacy screen with containers of bamboo or New Zealand flax.

- ✔ By your front door, where shade can make growing conditions tough, use a pair of topiary box or ivy balls in matching containers to greet visitors in a formal way.

- ✔ Announce spring with a window box full of sun-loving, early-blooming primulas and violas.

- ✔ For Christmas, buy container-grown plants of spruce, pine, or other conifer trees available in your area, transplant them to terracotta or glazed pots, and decorate them with tiny glass balls for tabletop or porch decorations. These plants also do well indoors for a few weeks.

- ✔ If you live where Japanese maples thrive (shade and shelter from wind), you can't find a better choice for a striking specimen tree in a container. For all-year good looks, choose colourful-leaf types (like 'Dissectum' varieties), or even colourful-bark varieties (such as 'Sango-Kaku').

- ✔ Lead the way up front steps by flanking steps with big pots of white marguerites for the summer – one plant per 30–33-centimetre (12–14-inch) pot.

- ✔ On a blank, shady wall, attach wire half-baskets – at least three, staggered at different heights – filled with blooming fuchsias, busy Lizzies, and lobelia, plus ferns for greenery.

Favourite Container Combos

Wondering what to plant in containers? Because summer annuals and bulbs are downright easy to grow in pots, why not start with one or both of them? We throw in some edible ideas as well.

Annuals all summer

The flowers in Table 19-1 are team players that also make good solo performers if planted alone. Match numbers to find plants that combine well in containers. For example, combine alyssum (number 1 in this table) with fibrous begonia, celosia, lobelia, and pansies (numbers 2, 3, 7, and 8, respectively). If you're combining different plants, place the tallest, most upright ones in the centre and surround them with lower-growing or trailing plants.

Table 19-1		Annuals to Combine in Pots	
Number	*Flower*	*Combinations*	*Uses*
1	Alyssum	(2, 3, 5, 7, 8, 10)	Pots, boxes, baskets
2	Begonia (fibrous)	(1, 4, 7)	Pots, boxes
3	Celosia (plume)	(1, 9, 10)	Pots, boxes
4	Coleus	(1, 2, 6, 7)	Pots, boxes, baskets
5	Geraniums	(1, 7, 9, 10)	Pots, boxes, baskets
6	Impatiens	(4, 7)	Pots, boxes, baskets
7	Lobelia	(1, 2, 4, 5, 6, 7, 8, 9)	Pots, boxes, baskets
8	Pansy	(1, 7)	Pots, boxes, baskets
9	Petunia	(3, 5, 7)	Pots, boxes, baskets
10	Verbena	(1, 3, 5)	Pots, boxes, baskets

Easy-care permanent plants

To have year-round fun in a container garden, you need some evergreens to hold the fort from autumn to spring. As long as you use big pots (more than 35 centimetres or 14 inches wide at the top), dwarf conifers, camellias, pieris, Euonymus, box, and other small shrubs are happy to serve as permanent features. Around the base of the evergreens plant a few little bulbs (such as crocus or grape hyacinth) or 'pave' over the soil with ivy.

For great low-maintenance spring- and summer-interest plants, take a look at herbaceous perennials and ornamental grasses. Pick out those with a compact habit and long-lasting good looks, and you can have fantastic foliage and structure year after year with very little input. See Chapter 8 for more info.

Get an exotic look by growing tender plants outdoors in containers during warm weather and then winter them indoors, near a bright window, in a conservatory, or in a heated greenhouse. The plants you can grow depend on how warm a winter environment you can provide.

Delectable edibles

Your adventures in containers don't need to stop with flowers and ever-greens. Try some tastier side trips – carrots, red- and green-leaf lettuces, dwarf or cherry tomatoes, peppers, and radishes are some suggestions. Herbs – chives, marjoram, parsley, and thyme – are also good choices for containers.

Growing just about any vegetable in a container is possible, but a giant pumpkin or something similarly huge may not be worth the effort (although it is possible!). Look for 'container-friendly' vegetable varieties, described as 'patio', 'compact', or 'bush type'.

With containers, you can have a vegetable garden on a balcony, patio, or even a rooftop. Maintaining a few vegetables in some pots is much easier than a traditional garden, and you can move the containers out of the way after harvest.

Container Plants for Four Seasons

Depending on your climate, you can find appealing container plants at almost any time of year. Table 19-2 lists just a few of the many annuals, perennials, bulbs, and permanent plants that perform particularly well outdoors at various seasons.

Table 19-2	Container Plants for Various Seasons
Season	*Container plants*
Spring	Azalea, double daisy (*Bellis*), camellia, crocus, narcissus, primula, tulip, dwarf rhododendron, viola
Summer	Bidens, cosmos, diascia, geranium, fuchsia, heliotrope, busy Lizzie (*impatiens*), nemesia, petunia, roses (patio varieties), scaevola, sutera, verbena
Autumn	Japanese maple (*Acer palmatum*), aster, chrysanthemum, dwarf cyclamen, *Erica gracilis*, ornamental cabbage, kale
Winter	Box, *Camellia sasanqua*, dwarf conifers, holly, winter heather (*Erica carnea*), Euonymus, ivy

The big no-no: when garden soil is out of bounds

Why not use ordinary garden soil to grow your prize plants in containers? After all, many of the plants that you grow in containers on your patios and decks also grow successfully in the open ground. Why can't you just take a shovelful of soil and dump it in a pot?

As garden soil settles in a shallow container (which is much different from the natural depth of the soil in your garden), it forms a dense mass that roots can't penetrate. The soil drains poorly, saturating the roots. As a result, not enough oxygen reaches the root zone, and the roots suffocate. Plus, garden soil may harbour disease-causing organisms that can devastate container plantings; and it could have weed seeds and insect eggs as well.

Choosing the Right Compost

Plants in containers are especially dependent on the soil or growing mix in which they grow, simply because the roots have so much less soil area to explore in the confines of the pots. So to keep your plants happy and healthy, you need first to take care of the roots – and that means growing them in the right stuff. (To get a better understanding of what all plants need from soil, dip into Chapter 11.)

Plants in containers have different soil and water requirements than plants in the ground, and they need a special soil mix that meets those needs. The following list provides a rundown of the particular needs of container plants:

✔ **Fast water infiltration and optimal drainage.** In garden soil, water gets pulled down to the roots by gravity, a process called *capillary action*; and the way water attracts small clay particles also dictates how water moves in soil. The water keeps moving through the soil in a continuous column, acting in the same manner that a hose siphon works or a blotter of ink. Each drop needs another drop of water behind it to continue the flow. Because the soil in a container is so confined, the soil needs to have a loose, open structure to encourage this flow of water.

✔ **Plenty of air spaces in soil.** This soil condition goes hand in hand with the requirement for good drainage. Air space is actually the most important requirement for a good container mix. Container plantings must have plenty of air in the soil after drainage because they require air for growth and to keep roots healthy. Disease organisms abound in the absence of oxygen.

✔ **Water retention.** You're probably thinking, 'Hey, you just said that container plants need plenty of air and good drainage. Doesn't that go against holding on to moisture?' This point is where mixtures get tricky. This last requirement is a tradeoff, because the soil mix that holds on to the most water and drains slowest also has less room for air.

Don't 'improve' drainage in pots by adding a layer of pea gravel. A drainage layer may sound logical, but using pea gravel in the bottom of a pot actually results in *less* air for the plant's roots and *more* water in the bottom of the pot. Instead, cover the drainage hole at the bottom with a layer of *crocks* (broken pots and small rocks), plus a bit of fine mesh or disposable cloth.

Use potting compost for your container plants because it is specifically designed to retain water while being well aerated so the roots don't go short of oxygen. However, you find different types of compost for a range of purposes, so choose the right one for the job to be sure of success. Don't confuse *potting composts* with *soil conditioners*, *planting composts*, or *mulches* (described in Chapter 11). Trouble is, they're often sold side by side in similar brightly coloured bags, so beware.

Soil-less potting compost

Usually sold as multipurpose compost, much soil-less compost is based on peat, although you can also find an increasing range of alternatives that incorporate materials such as coir (coconut fibre) and composted chipped bark. Lightweight and clean to use, soil-less compost is excellent for short-lived seasonal plants such as summer annuals. It's also the best choice where weight is an issue, such as with hanging baskets and window boxes. However, soil-less compost is not a good choice for long-lived plants because the structure of this compost breaks down rapidly. Regular watering is vital, because soil-less composts dry out fast and are hard to re-wet. However, waterlogging can be a problem during very wet weather or if you overwater plants. Fertiliser levels are short lived, so feed your plants about six weeks after potting.

Hanging basket compost

Hanging basket compost is basically soil-less compost with added water-retaining gel, because hanging baskets dry out extremely quickly as the whole rootball is exposed to the drying effects of sun and wind.

Soil-based potting compost

This is the compost to use for all permanent plants including shrubs, grasses, and perennials. Compost that contains soil, also called *loam*, has much more 'body' than soil-less types. The loam provides a good buffer against drought and this type of compost is less liable to suffer from waterlogging than soil-less types. Soil-based composts include those made to the John Innes formula that are numbered according to the amount of fertiliser in them. JI No. 1 is suitable for propagation, while Nos 2 and 3 are suitable for established plants.

Soil-based potting compost is much heavier and also more expensive than soil-less potting compost, but is the best to use if you want your plants to look great for you, year after year.

Lime-free potting compost

Certain plants dislike lime and need to be grown in *ericaceous* or lime-free potting compost. Popular lime-hating plants include camellias, rhododendrons, azaleas, and pieris.

Planting Up Your Containers

Ready to get your green fingers dirty? Follow these steps to plant a pot, one step at a time. The procedure is the same whether you're planting bedding plants (annuals and perennials sold as small seedlings), vegetables, herbs, or permanent plants.

1. **Cover the drainage holes in your container.**

   If you cover the holes with a small section of crocks or chunks of polystyrene, water can't puddle up in the bottom of the pot, and the soil won't gush out through the holes. Simply *cover* holes; don't plug them up entirely.

2. **Fill the container about two-thirds full with compost.**

3. **Remove the plant from its container.**

   If you're working with lightweight plastic containers, simply push on the bottom of the container until the plant pops out. Or use one hand to turn the container upside down while supporting the plant with the other hand. If the plant is reluctant to come out, tap the pot against a wall or step to loosen the roots. Whatever method you use to remove a plant from its container, try to keep the root ball intact. A moist root ball doesn't fall apart as easily as a dry one, so water the plant at least an hour before you plant.

4. **Plant plants at the same depth they grew in their previous pots, adding more soil almost to the top of the pot.**

   Don't add soil up to the brim of the pot. Leave some space at the top of the pot (about 2.5 centimetres or 1 inch) to hold water.

5. **Place the container in its final position and water the plant thoroughly.** The water causes the plant to get a whole lot heavier.

6. **Wait 15 minutes and then water your plants again.** If any gaps appear in the compost as it settles, add a bit more compost as required.

Planting a Hanging Basket

Hanging baskets broadly divide into two types: *Solid* ones, which you plant as for containers, with the exception of adding drainage material; and *open-mesh* ones, which you plant as outlined below. The open-mesh type is more versatile because you can pack the sides as well as the top with plants to create globes of glorious colour.

1. **Line the basket with a suitable liner,** such as one made of coir, foam, or wool, and sit it on an empty bucket or a large pot for stability.

2. **Put a little compost in the base and, starting at the bottom and working upwards, plant through the sides, making holes in the liner where necessary.** Depending on whether the plant's root ball is small or large, either push the root ball in from outside or gently pull the plant through from inside.

3. **Plant round the basket, spacing plants evenly apart and alternating different varieties.** Add more compost as you go.

4. **When it comes to planting the top layer, use plants with a short, bushy habit in the centre.** Fill with compost to within a couple of centimetres of the rim to allow room for watering, and hang the basket up before watering it gently but thoroughly.

Keeping Your Containers Happy

Plants growing in containers can't let their roots wander about in search of food and water, so you must take care of these needs. It's a bit like having a pet, dependent on you for everything (but at least you don't have to walk the pots every day).

In mild spring or autumn weather you probably don't need to water your plants more than once or twice a week, but as temperatures rise and the plants get bigger you may need to water every day – maybe even twice a day in scorching hot, breezy weather for quick-drying containers such as hanging baskets. Big plants need more water than little ones do (but big containers hold more water, too).

Fertilising

Plants growing in containers need more water than those growing in the ground. The more you water, the more you flush nutrients from the soil, and the more often you have to fertilise.

You can offset some of this continual loss of nutrients by mixing controlled-release fertilisers into the soil mix before planting, which will feed your plants for most of the season. You only need to top up with a few liquid feeds for annual flowers in late summer and autumn. But the best-looking container plants we've seen are on a *constant-feed programme*. In other words, you give plants a little liquid fertiliser every time, or every other time, you water. Of course this means using less, sometimes a lot less, fertiliser with each watering. Some fertiliser products include directions for *constant* (same as *every time*) feeding, which you need to follow. Wait until you see the results!

Repotting

The time comes when a permanent plant outgrows its container, and it needs repotting (this doesn't apply to seasonal flowering plants that only last for a few months). How can you tell when to repot?

Any plant that has restricted roots obviously needs more space. If you see lots of roots coming through the drain hole or find matted roots near the soil surface, it's time for a move. How often do plants need repotting? A general rule is to repot every two or three years with permanent plants. Seasonal plants such as annuals and most vegetables don't need repotting because they don't stay in the container that long.

Repot permanent plants when growth is slow or when the plant is dormant – usually well before or after flowering. (Camellias are one notable exception: They're most dormant when in bloom.) With this timing, plants have a chance to recover from these rather dramatic changes. Repot spring-blooming permanent plants in autumn, evergreens in spring, and spring-flowering bulbs in autumn. For summer-flowering bulbs, repot in spring.

If you want to increase the growth of your container plants, you need to give plants more room for roots by transplanting into larger pots. How much larger do the pots need to be? Move up little by little to a new pot that's about 5 centimetres larger in diameter, as shown in Figure 19-3.

Figure 19-3:
Place your plant in a new container that measures about 5 centimetres more in both depth and diameter than its previous pot.

If you want to control growth and keep the plant from getting too big, you can trim the roots and return the plant to a pot of the same size.

To repot a plant, simply follow these steps:

1. **Turn the container upside down, tap the rim, and slide the plant out.**
   If you're repotting something prickly or otherwise unwieldy, such as a cordyline, wrap the plant with heavy cloth so that you can handle it safely.

2. **Inspect the roots; then separate and trim the roots (if needed).**

   You may have to trim off large roots poking through the drain hole. For plants going into larger containers, gently pull apart tangled roots.

3. **Prune roots (if needed).**

   Some permanent plants require *root pruning*, which refers to using hand pruners to cut away root growth. This step is necessary if, once exposed, you can see that roots are a dense, circling mass. Prune the roots of plants that have reached a desired size and have become pot bound. Root pruning controls growth and forces plants to grow new roots, leading to limited but healthy new growth.

To root prune properly, remove about a quarter of the soil and untangle as much of the root mass as you can. Using shears, cut between a quarter and a third of the roots. For tightly balled roots, slice off half a centimetre (a quarter of an inch) all around the outside of the root ball, and make vertical cuts from the top to the bottom of the root ball in several places. After root pruning, lightly prune top growth to help maintain some balance between leaves and roots.

4. **Set the plant in its new pot or in its newly filled existing pot.** Add compost to the height of the original root ball, and make sure to allow at least 1.25 centimetres (½ inch) from soil to pot rim (more for larger plants).

Chapter 20

Gardens for Wildlife

. . . .

In This Chapter

▶ Understanding why you want to attract wildlife

▶ Making a wildlife-friendly garden

▶ Taking in some bird-friendly tips

▶ Boosting the butterfly population

▶ Encouraging pollinators

. . . .

*F*or most of us, the appeal of a garden goes far beyond just good looks. All the creatures that visit and come to live in your garden add enormously to the enjoyment you get from your surroundings. Listening to the varied melodies of birdsong, watching the antics of birds as they feed and bathe, seeing the flittering beauty of butterflies, and listening to the soothing hum of bees is all part and parcel of the attraction of a garden. Getting in touch with nature via your own backyard is the perfect way of de-stressing too.

Yet wildlife is under threat like never before, as development and pollution destroy habitats. But unlike watching a gloom-and-doom documentary on television that leaves you feeling depressed and powerless, gardeners really *can* do something to make a difference. The United Kingdom is home to 15 million gardens that together make up an area greater than all the National Nature Reserves in the country, and every garden is part of a great patchwork. Every garden, however small, is home to at least some wildlife. Plan your garden to be wildlife friendly, and you can attract a greater number of creatures.

Because birds, bees, butterflies, and other creatures mostly hang around places where they can meet their needs for food, water, and shelter, providing these three necessities is your primary means of attracting them.

After you manage to attract these friendly visitors, you're likely to notice some other changes. Your garden comes closer to the balance found in nature, which means that the creatures start to take charge more and you have less work to do in controlling unfriendly pests. You won't achieve this balance overnight, but be patient and eventually you'll see a real difference.

Head to Chapter 24 for ten great tips on creating a wildlife garden.

Pampering Your Feathered Friends

You can help solve birds' housing and food shortage by planting or preserving bird-friendly trees and bushes, particularly native species that host native birds. From a bird's-eye point of view, here are some of the best trees and shrubs that provide food and shelter.

- ✔ **Trees.** Conifers such as Lawson and Leyland cypress, yew, and Western red cedar (*Thuja plicata*), cotoneaster (tall varieties such as *C. lacteus* and *C. 'Cornubia'*), wild cherries, birch, willows, hawthorns, blackthorn, crab apples, and mountain ash.

  Be careful not to plant trees that produce juicy berries close to your house, decking, and pathways, or you'll get berry goo all over your shoes.

- ✔ **Shrubs.** Berberis, hollies, firethorn (*Pyracantha*), native viburnums, and cotoneaster.

- ✔ **Climbers.** Honeysuckle, ivy, firethorn (*Pyracantha*).

- ✔ **Annuals and biennials.** Seed of cornflower (*Centaurea*), sunflower (*Helianthus*), forget-me-not (*Myosotis*), evening primrose (*Oenothera*), and wallflower (*Cheiranthus*).

As well as providing natural nest sites, putting up some bird boxes is likely to boost residency levels. Choose a selection of boxes in different sizes and designs to suit a variety of birds. Buy bird boxes sold or approved by the Royal Society for the Protection of Birds (RSPB) or the British Trust for Ornithology (BTO).

Bird-table banquets

Even in the best-planted wildlife gardens, birds really benefit from an extra supply of food right through the year. During the bleak winter months, the food and water you put out can mean the difference between life and death for them. On a lighter note, the displays and antics around the bird table are fascinating to watch and highly entertaining. For anyone who is ill or housebound, a bird table and feeders can be the best present ever. And when birds get used to finding a regular supply of good food, they go to great lengths to find acceptable nesting sites in or near your garden.

Hungry birds are not finicky eaters, but putting out a selection of food attracts a greater variety of birds. Feeding birds is big business and you find an amazing range of bird food and feeders available. Peanuts are always popular, but put them out in feeders with mesh fine enough to prevent birds pulling out whole nuts (or young birds could choke). Supply seed and fat balls in a special feeder too. A fresh coconut cut in half and hung upside-down is a favourite with tits. You can put out most food scraps, including cooked potatoes, fruit, grated cheese, cereal, bacon rind, and soaked bread (dry bread can swell up in the bird's stomach). Avoid spicy or salty food.

Make sure you buy nuts from a reputable source, because mouldy ones can contain a fungus called aflatoxin that can be fatal to birds.

A bird table is an ideal place to put out food because it gives the birds somewhere to feed out of reach of cats, and gives you a grandstand view of their antics. Although all sorts of elaborate designs are on sale, all you really need is a table area with a raised lip at the edge to stop food being blown away, and with a roof to keep the food dry. Avoid bird tables that also include a nest box, or any poor birds that do take up residence will be driven demented by other feathered visitors.

When summer comes, you can ease up on the food supply; most birds crave protein-rich insects while raising their young, and they can probably find plenty of palatable creatures in and around your garden. On the other hand, if you want to attract woodpeckers year round, keep a supply of commercial suet in your garden, as shown in Figure 20-1.

Figure 20-1:
Suet attracts insect-eating birds such as wood-peckers.

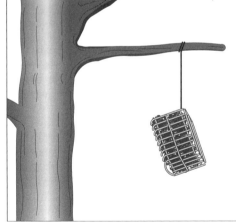

Bird baths going cheep

Provide a year-round supply of water for birds either in a birdbath or in shallow dishes of water. Replace the water and clean the containers frequently, to avoid the spread of disease. If your house is near a pond, stream, or river, don't worry too much about putting out water – the birds will know where to go.

Depending on how cold it gets in your region, you can keep the water in the birdbath ice free either by changing it frequently or by using a pond heater (shown in Figure 20-2), powered by electricity and designed for outdoor use.

Figure 20-2:
Birds need water year round. In cold winter areas, keep the water thawed in the birdbath by using a pond heater.

Keep feeders and watering sites for birds out of reach of cats and squirrels. Your beloved kitty is probably adept at assassinating birds, and you don't want to be an accomplice to such crimes. Suspend feeders from secure tree limbs or place them atop a smooth, stout pole that kitty can't climb. A cat collar with a bell helps warn birds that a cat is close by.

Squirrels are another matter – cute in their own right, but downright confounding when it comes to keeping them from emptying a bird feeder. Either use a bird feeder that includes an attached *baffle* (a barrier that prevents squirrels from climbing up a pole), or that has a funnel-shaped top, or that is enclosed within a larger metal frame that lets small birds through but keeps squirrels out. When you have the right feeder, be sure to hang or support the feeder with wire or something the squirrels can't chew. For good measure, situate the feeder 2.5–3 metres (8–10 feet) from buildings and tree branches – just further than squirrels are likely to jump.

Keeping pesky birds at bay

The pleasing sounds and movements that birds bring to your garden sometimes come at a cost. If you plan to grow fruit, you must take precautions to keep birds from devouring it. Birds especially love strawberries, and brassicas in winter. Effective deterrents include the following:

✔ Polyester bird netting. Sold at most garden centres, this barrier is by far the most reliable way to protect fruits and vegetables. Fix the netting over fruit-bearing plants as soon as fruits begin to ripen. Make sure that the netting is tightly stretched, or birds and hedgehogs could become fatally entangled

✔ Fake predators. These fool-the-eye figures include artificial snakes, owls, and good old scarecrows. Rearrange these phony spooks often to keep the birds baffled.

✔ Noisemakers. These devices include wind chimes, bells, rattling aluminium pans, and other items that make sounds when bumped by birds or jostled by the wind (just use your imagination).

Beckoning Butterflies to Your Garden

Inviting butterflies and moths into your garden is as easy as growing flowers. Butterflies and moths find your garden no matter what kinds of flowers or plants you grow, but you can choose from many easy ways to make sure they flit in your direction.

First, you need some sun. Butterflies can feed in shade, but they must have sun to charge their energy batteries. On cool mornings, have you noticed how butterflies stand around, slowly opening and closing their wings, and how they don't fly away when your 6 year old grabs at them? This inactivity is called *basking*, and it's how cold-blooded butterflies gather solar energy. If your garden is basically shady, put some flat, dark-coloured stones in a spot that gets morning sun and watch the butterflies use the sun-warmed stones as their warm-up room.

Next, grow flowers that produce nectar. Butterflies and moths consume the juices of flowers, and flower nectar is becoming a rare commodity these days. Like native birds, native butterflies and moths are struggling amid burgeoning urbanisation. The weeds, clovers, and wildflowers they used to find everywhere are in increasingly short supply. You can help set things right by growing flowers that butterflies like a lot and by planting the flowers in ways that make it impossible for butterflies to miss them.

Plants that are native to your region not only are more likely to grow and survive, but also provide the specific foods that native birds and butterflies rely on. By using native plants, you help sustain native wildlife.

A butterfly sips flower nectar by sticking its long tongue (properly called a *proboscis*) down the throats of nectar-rich flowers. Some flowers are much more slurpable than others, both because they have a lot of nectar and because the flowers are shaped just right. Here are several of the best plants to tempt butterflies into your garden.

- ✔ **Butterfly bush.** *Buddleia davidii*. Vigorous and easy to grow, this shrub is top of the list. The flowers come in many shades of purple, pink, and white; and, depending on variety, grow 90–300 centimetres (3–10 feet) tall.

- ✔ **Michaelmas daisy.** *Aster*. Late-summer perennial with flowers in shades of blue, pink, and purple.

- ✔ **Ice plant.** *Sedum spectabile*. Late-summer perennial with heads of flowers in shades of pink and red.

- ✔ **Heliotrope** and **Lantana.** *Lantana camara*. These tender perennials are best if you buy bedding plants in the spring and grow them as summer annuals. Plant in full sun.

As long as your garden includes plenty of flowers you'll see plenty of butterflies.

Try to plant a good selection of flowers to bloom right from spring to autumn. Although summer is the main time for attracting butterflies, bulbs and early-flowering perennials like hellebores, honesty, *Lunaria*, primroses, and *Pulmonaria* provide vital food supplies in spring.

Butterflies prefer single flowers (as opposed to the double-petal type) because when a blossom is jam packed with petals, butterflies have a hard time getting to the nectar hidden in the middle. Single flowers that are relatively flat give butterflies a solid place to land and easy access to nectar. These five easy annuals are of great interest to butterflies: Single cosmos, viper's bugloss, *Echium vulgare*, marigolds, and zinnias. Where you can use more height, try *Tithonia*, also known as Mexican sunflower or torch flower.

Some other good plants to incorporate into your butterfly haven include any type of verbena, salvia, cosmos, phlox, globe thistle, *Echinops*, and hebe. Always keep your eyes peeled for flowers that attract butterflies in your area.

Night-scented plants attract moths, which in turn provide food for bats. Jasmine, honeysuckle, evening primrose, and tobacco plant will enhance your garden's perfumes after dark.

Designing for butterflies

If you splash flower colour around in broad strokes, butterflies have an easier time finding the flowers. The colour of the flowers is not as important as the size of the clump, which should include at least three plants of any individual flower.

The key is to keep similar colours more or less together. Butterflies are not very smart. A big jolt of colour or fragrance is often necessary to get their attention.

Most buddleias produce lavender or purple flowers, so use that hue as a starting point for choosing the colours of your other flowers. Orange or yellow contrasts nicely with purple, and many butterfly gardens use either purple and yellow or purple and orange as the basic colour scheme.

Mixing a butterfly cocktail

If you're a butterfly, you don't want to hang out around deep or moving water, where a good gust of wind may turn your beautiful wings into a sopping mess. But you and your friends like to get together for a drink, so you're always on the lookout for a nice watering hole. Your idea of a friendly bar is an almost-puddle of soaked soil, where you can stand firmly (without getting your feet too wet) and slurp up soupy water by sticking your proboscis in the ground.

One fact of butterfly life is that males (and an occasional female) like to drink together in puddle clubs. To create such a pub in your butterfly garden, mix some sand, soil, and pebbles and use the mixture to fill a small, shallow basin lined with smooth stones. From time to time, fill the basin with water until it's puddly. Neon signs are not necessary – the butterflies will find the water on their own.

Catching up with caterpillars

When winter comes, most butterflies have already ensured the welfare of the next generation: Some lay dormant eggs (which become caterpillars); others migrate south to warmer countries; and some wait out winter as adults, hidden away in tree crevices or perhaps your shed or attic.

The long-time favourite pesticide of organic gardeners, *Bacillus thuringiensis* (Bt), is deadly to all caterpillars – pest and nonpest. That's why we think handpicking selected caterpillars is the best control method. (Most pesticides are toxic to butterflies, which is one reason to use gentle biological controls for pest management and to use them only when absolutely necessary. See Chapter 16 for more information on wise use of garden pesticides.)

Buzzing Bees and Pollination

When you make your garden more favourable to birds and butterflies, you're also making it friendlier to honeybees and other pollinators. These insects are important (especially for gardeners who grow vegetables and fruit) because insect pollination sets abundant and healthy crops. Moreover, the numbers of the most familiar pollinator, honeybees, have declined in recent years.

Pollination occurs when insects move pollen from the (male) *anther* of one flower to the (female) *stigma* of another flower. All adult bees eat protein-rich pollen and feed it to their young.

Although the honeybee is an extremely valuable pollinating species, wild bees and other insects that we don't often recognise as pollinators are also vital to your garden's wellbeing. Spraying pesticides destroys all insects – harmful, beneficial, and pollinating – so think twice before using such sprays.

You can encourage the proliferation of the beneficial and pollinating insects by providing nesting sites. You can buy different designs of nest ready made, or you can have a go at making your own, as follows.

- ✔ **Set out blocks of wood or logs drilled with holes** to attract mason and leafcutter bees to your garden. Use a ⁵⁄₁₆-inch drill and space the holes about 2 centimetres (¾-inch) apart. Drill 7.5–15 centimetres (3–6 inches) deep. The wood provides convenient nesting sites when placed in a protected area.

- ✔ **Bundle a dozen or so plant stems,** like raspberry canes or stiff stems of herbaceous perennials, to lure solitary bees into your garden. Secure the stems with twine and place the bundles in protected locations such as under a fence or in a hedge.

Chapter 21

Gardening in Small Spaces

. . . .

In This Chapter

▶ Designing in a limited space

▶ Making small seem big

▶ Discovering hidden growing spots

▶ Getting the most from your front garden

▶ Choosing the best small-space plants

. . . .

*J*ust because your outdoor space is small doesn't mean you have to give up your dreams of having a truly satisfying garden. In fact, if you've ever lingered in a small garden that is well planned and carefully put together, you've probably noticed that the garden has a sense of intimacy and enclosure that most large, sprawling designs lack.

Smallness need not dictate the type of gardening you do. Whether you are aiming for a serene, Japanese-style meditation garden or the country charm of a cottage garden, the basic techniques for successful small-space gardening are the same.

The following tips and techniques can help you on your way; but before you start digging, review Part I of this book on garden planning. Because all available space is critical in small gardens (and every element is seen close-up), starting with a cohesive plan is doubly important.

And think about container gardening too (see Chapter 19) – often the best answer for growing plants on a patio, deck, balcony, or any place where every centimetre counts.

Simple Pleasures: Small Garden Design

A small garden feels most spacious and harmonious when the design is simple and all the elements work together. Choose a single style or theme for your garden and use this style to connect all the parts, from paving to plants and from structures to ornaments. Just imagine how distracting a spewing Goliath of a fountain would be in a tiny, contemplative Japanese-style garden. In contrast, a bamboo spout trickling water onto stone would feel soothing and appear quite natural in such a setting.

To help keep things simple and avoid a hodgepodge, repeat garden elements. For example, rather than planting a wide assortment, use a few types of plants repeatedly in different areas of the garden. Rely on two or three colours that best express the garden's mood. Choose one or two types of paving for the patio and paths and use those same materials throughout the garden to create a visual, as well as physical, connection.

Details make the difference

In a little garden, everything shows. Each plant, ornament, structure, and surface becomes an integral part of the whole. One goal of small-garden design is to create interest and intrigue without adding extraneous *stuff*.

One of the advantages of smallness is that it encourages you to focus on quality rather than quantity. Just a few carefully chosen and well-placed plants or ornaments can transform an otherwise bland plot into an evocative haven. With a limited number of plants to buy, it's worth considering splurging on one or two expensive ready-grown specimen plants to give the instant 'wow' factor to your garden. Consider using the following lures (and invent some of your own) to attract attention and to keep the viewer from taking in your entire garden in one glance:

- ✔ Decorative chair flanked by a large pot of tulips in bloom
- ✔ Wall-mounted fountain (saves more space than a freestanding one) flowing onto a pebble surface or into a trough
- ✔ Small pond in a large ceramic pot
- ✔ Stone sculpture
- ✔ Clipped box topiary
- ✔ Single raised urn set in brick paving and filled with white daisylike marguerites and geraniums at the urn's base
- ✔ Apple tree trained to a decorative pattern against a fence or wall

Creating illusions

Visual trickery lies at the very heart of successful small-space gardening. Employ the following strategies to help defy garden boundaries and make your small space feel larger:

✔ **Use plants to blur walls and fences.** Doing so ensures that your eye doesn't abruptly stop at the garden's boundaries.

✔ **Construct gently curving paths.** By curving your paths, you can make them 'disappear' at the garden's edge (perhaps at a false gate in a fence) to suggest that more lies beyond.

✔ **Vary levels.** Add vertical texture to the garden by using raised beds, steps, or terraces. Changes in levels add dimension and lengthen the route through the garden, which makes the space appear bigger. Level changes also divert the eye from the garden's boundaries and add an element of surprise as you move through the garden.

✔ **Create depth.** Layer plants at the garden's periphery. Put light-coloured or variegated plants in front of taller, darker-green ones. Or place shrubs or small trees in front of a creeper-clad wall.

✔ **Crafty use of colours.** Use cool colours, such as blue, cream, mauve, and violet, toward the farthest edges of the garden. These colours tend to recede and give an impression of distance, whereas bright ones such as red, pink, and orange shorten the view by leaping forward to catch the eye.

✔ **Install a wall-mounted mirror.** A mirror reflects an intriguing view or, if placed at the end of a path, makes the path appear to continue onwards. Keep safety in mind and use a tough mirror suitable for outdoor use (plastic ones are best), and fix it very firmly to its support. You can even buy false windows or doors complete with mirror.

✔ **Draw attention inwards and downwards.** Use decorative paving or an eye-catching living ground cover.

✔ **Borrow a view.** Expand the boundaries of your garden visually to incorporate a view beyond your property line into your garden design. If, for example, your neighbour has a gorgeous flowering tree, situate a bench in your garden to take advantage of the view.

Finding Space Where It Doesn't Exist

Take a cue from dandelions: They make room for themselves in the cracks of tarmac! If you feel as though you have no growing space, then create some – on walls and overhead, in containers and window boxes, between paving slabs, and in raised beds. Here's how.

✔ **Plant in gaps.** Gardening in the crevices between bricks or stone not only gives you more growing space but also softens the hard look of these surfaces. Plants growing between paving create a visual link, connecting the hard surfaces with adjacent flower beds or other plantings.

Good gap-plant choices provide a thick, low carpet of greenery that stands up to some foot traffic. Certain ground covers add flowers or fragrance, as well. See the sidebar 'Top plants to fill gaps' in this chapter for information about plants best suited for gaps.

- **Plant in tiers.** Get the most from your borders with careful planning and planting. Start high with a small tree – like a mountain ash, birch, or crab apple – that doesn't cast a dense shade. Underneath, plant medium-sized shrubs that don't mind a little shade, such as many viburnums or mock orange blossom (*Philadelphus*). Then, cover the ground with shade-tolerant, spreading shrubs and perennials such as *Euonymus*, *Ajuga*, and *Heuchera*. Later, when the shrubs are well established, thread in even more colour with a well-behaved flowering climber like *Clematis viticella*.

- **Pack in bulbs.** You can pack in ultra-versatile bulbs almost anywhere to give bursts of superb seasonal colour. The spring bulb season can last from late winter to early summer if you choose a range of varieties, then move on to summer bulbs such as lilies and alliums, finishing off with autumn crocus and colchicum.

- **Put up window boxes and hanging baskets.** These wall-hung mini gardens provide a view from inside and outside your window. Mix in a few sweet-scented plants and enjoy the wafting fragrance as well. (See Figure 21-1.)

Figure 21-1:
Space-saving window boxes add charm to your home.

✔ **Build raised beds.** When space is at a premium, room for large flower beds and borders may be unavailable. Rather than plant large beds and borders, squeeze in a few raised beds spilling over with annuals, perennials, or even vegetables. Around a patio, raised beds made with broad tops make excellent informal seating, or you can even build a proper seat into a raised bed.

✔ **Make the most of verticals.** Save valuable ground space by growing plants on walls and fences, and on introduced vertical features including arches, trellis screens, and obelisks. Use annual or perennial climbers or use *wall shrubs* – shrubs you can prune until they are nearly flat against a wall. For ideas on how to choose and train climbers and wall shrubs, see Chapter 6.

✔ **Plant overhead.** Encourage plants up and over arbours and pergolas to create a cool, green ceiling or a dramatic canopy of blooms. Deciduous plants provide welcome filtered shade in summer and let the warming sun shine through in winter.

Start with simple, sturdy structures that can support the weight and bulk of heavy, woody climbers at maturity. A classic plant for garden ceilings is wisteria with its fragrant violet flowers in 45-centimetre (1.5-foot) long clusters. Check out Chapter 6 for additional ideas.

Use lightweight containers to suspend plants from tree branches or overhead structures. Chapter 19 explains container gardening in detail.

Getting the Most from Your Front Garden

Even if your back garden is large, your front garden is likely to be small. First impressions really do count, yet the front garden is all too often neglected. However, an attractive and well-planned front garden is a real asset, presenting a warm and welcoming face to your home as you go in and out every day.

Small is beautiful: Garden style

The best-looking front gardens have a style matching that of the house, so take your cue from the building to achieve a really successful look. If you're not sure where to start, take a walk around the houses in your immediate area and see how your neighbours tackle their plots. A smart town house calls for a neat, formal garden with a symmetrical layout, containing features such as low clipped hedges and strongly architectural plants. On a modern estate, the planting can be more informal but with plenty of form and structure. A country cottage suits a really informal and colourful style, with lots of flowers as well as some structure planting, and with low-growing plants spilling out onto curving paths.

Here are our favourite ideas for great-looking front gardens.

- ✔ Unless the garden is large, cut down on maintenance by doing away with the lawn. Replace it with a hard surface such as paving slabs, brick pavers (the same shape as bricks but suitable for surface), stone setts (square blocks), gravel, stone chippings, or glass 'gravel'.

- ✔ Combine two or three different hard materials for lots of interest. For example, you can surround gravel with edging tiles or bricks, or you can intersperse paving with sections of stone chippings and plants.

- ✔ A fence made to an open design looks more welcoming than a solid fence. From a security point of view, an open design is much harder for would-be intruders to hide behind.

- ✔ Make your gate the same height as the boundary fence or wall. If you have young children or pets, fix a self-closing spring so that the gate shuts automatically.

- ✔ Finishing touches really count. A pair of containers flanking the doorway always look good and give a touch of real style. Either choose permanent plants for all-year structure or go for changing displays of seasonal flowers, but take care to match the planting to that of the garden.

- ✔ Add interest at eye level with hanging baskets, wall pots, and climbing plants.

- ✔ If your garden contains a flight of steps, place containers on every alternate step for extra colour. Choose simple planting and repeat similar or identical plants in each container.

- ✔ In a small garden, keep the colours low key to avoid foreshortening distances and making the space look even smaller.

- ✔ Choose climbing plants to contrast with the colour of the wall – pale flowers and foliage on red brick, for example, and deep, rich colours on white or pale stone.

Picking a path

The path is the main element of a front garden. Be sure to make it sufficiently wide – the absolute minimum practical width is 60 centimetres (2 feet), while 90–120 centimetres (3–4 feet) is necessary if you want plants to spill over the edge of the path. If you want a hard surface to take the place of a lawn, simply extend the path material to unify the whole garden.

Choose materials that pick out the colour of the building in order to create a harmonious impression, or at least make sure that the colours don't clash. Paving slabs, brick pavers, or stone setts all make excellent paths. Avoid both lumpy materials such as cobbles, and very smooth surfaces such as concrete slabs that become dangerously slippery in the wet. Avoid gravel for a path too, because the stones are a nuisance when you tread them indoors.

Design the path to take a reasonably direct route to the front door, though it need not take an absolutely straight line. The path can be diagonal or slightly angled in a formal garden, or curving in an informal design. Don't make the angles or curves too severe or you find that visitors take a short cut to the door.

Choosing the Best Small-garden Plants

In a small garden, every plant has to earn its keep and look good for as long as possible. A plant with the right style, fit, size, and colour has the potential to dazzle, just as an inappropriate choice looks and feels awkward. When you select plants, consider the big picture – consider how each plant will contribute to the whole. Bear in mind the following tips when making your choices.

- ✔ Choose plants that fit your soil type, site (shady, sunny, wet, dry), and climate.
- ✔ Choose plants in proportion to your house and garden.
- ✔ Consider the mature size of plants so that, eventually, you don't have to face either constant shearing or a huge tree devouring the entire garden.
- ✔ Select plants with well-mannered roots that won't rob their neighbours of garden space, water, and nutrients.
- ✔ Because flowers are transitory, use them as colour accents in a garden well clothed in trees, shrubs, and climbers that remain attractive year round.
- ✔ Foliage has much longer-lasting good looks than flowers. Take a look at the many plants with attractively shaped leaves, and with foliage in colourful shades such as gold, red, and purple, such as golden *Euonymus* 'Ovatus Aureus' and purple elder, *Sambucus nigra* 'Black Lace'.
- ✔ Consider plant forms. Rounded shrubs are good backdrops for spiky accent plants such as New Zealand flax, *Phormium*, and yuccas. Pendulous or weeping plants such as crab apple 'Red Jade' direct attention downward. Use pyramidal or columnar plants for height, such as slender junipers and *Sorbus* aucuparia 'Fastigiata'.

✔ Limit the number of plant varieties and plant forms, and plant in groups to give your garden order.

✔ At the garden's edges, group plants of different sizes, shapes, and textures to create a sensation of depth.

✔ Because too many plants with strong personalities can make the garden's space appear cluttered, choose a few show-offs as accents such as the larger bamboos and evergreens clipped to formal shapes.

Even with room for only a few containers and a chair, your garden can be inspiring and satisfying. So go forth and seek out the nooks and crannies.

Top plants to fill gaps

Excellent plants for planting in crevices are ajuga (*Ajuga reptans*), creeping speedwell (*Veronica peduncularis*), crane's bill, creeping Jenny (*Lysimachia nummularia*), sandwort (*Arenaria montana*), and Mexican daisy (*Erigeron karvinskianus*).

For fragrance underfoot, thymes are reliable as long as they are only gently bruised, not frequently trampled. Plant grey-green woolly thyme (*Thymus pseudolanuginosus*), lemon thyme (*T. citriodorus*), or creeping thyme (*T. serpyllum*). Other fragrant choices include chamomile (*Chamaemelum nobile*), Corsican mint (*Mentha requienii*), and pennyroyal mint (*Mentha pulegium*).

Chapter 22

Gardening for Fragrance

. . . .

In This Chapter

▶ Planning to make the most of scent

▶ Discovering the most fragrant annuals and perennials

▶ Creating a fragrant evening garden

▶ Deciding which trees, climbers, and shrubs to grow for fragrance

▶ Exploring sweet-scented bulbs

▶ Enjoying the essence of roses

. . . .

*G*rowing fragrant plants is a sure way to lift your spirits and stir good memories. Our world is dominated by sight to such an extent that even in the garden, a place that really should please all the senses, people all too often overlook the power and pleasure of scent. Yet fragrance adds enormously to your enjoyment of a garden.

Sweet scents come with all types of plants – from annuals to shrubs, and from climbers to trees. Many garden plants have luscious-smelling leaves as well as flowers – certainly the fragrant foliage of lemon verbena or a mint-scented geranium rivals that of many a rose. Although flower fragrances waft on high, you often need to seek out leaf fragrances. Only when you rub or crush the leaves of such fragrant delights as Corsican mint or rosemary do they release their aromas.

Think of your favourite flower and foliage fragrances when you plan and plant your garden. Including them is easy.

Discovering Fragrant Plants

Generally, older varieties of plants pack the most perfumed punches because most modern hybrids are selected for looks and improved garden performance. But with gardeners now rediscovering the appeal of fragrance, you can find new plants on the scene that combine the best of both worlds.

Why are plants scented?

Plants are scented for their own survival – the fact that you benefit too is a happy coincidence. Flowers are fragrant in order to attract insects such as moths and butterflies to transfer pollen and fertilise their blooms, with those that night-flying moths pollinate giving off their sweetest fragrance after dark. Blooms that bees pollinate are brightly coloured, because bees find flowers mainly by sight, and scent plays a much lesser role. Plants that are wind pollinated or self-fertile have no need to be fragrant at all.

Not *all* scents are pleasant – beware of the few flowers that stink of rotten meat to lure flies to their blooms, and watch out for tell-tale common names such as skunk cabbage!

The amount of fragrance given off by plants depends to a great extent on their environmental conditions, which affect the speed and strength at which the oils in the plant evaporate to create scent. This varies according to conditions such as the time of day, the age of the flower, air temperature, and humidity level. Most flower scents are strongest when the air is mild and still and the moisture level high. Drought and heat cause the greatest reduction in flower fragrances, although these conditions are when plants with aromatic foliage smell their strongest. Some plants give off their perfume early in the day – roses, for example, smell sweetest in the morning and peak in the afternoon – whereas others save their scent until evening. Choose plants to match areas of the garden and the time of day when you're out there.

Plants from hot, drought-prone areas have developed aromatic foliage. To protect themselves from the baking sun, plants give off an oily vapour from their leaves – hence the wonderfully evocative aromas of Mediterranean plants such as lavender and rosemary.

Fragrance is a very personal matter and perfumes that appeal to one person may be too strong or weak for another. Quite simply, trust your nose and choose plants when in flower – either at the garden centre, or by visiting gardens and making a note of your favourites for ordering later.

Planning a Scented Garden

To enjoy fragrance to the full calls for a bit of careful planning. Creating shelter and still air is top priority, because wind whisks away scent instead of letting it hang on the air to be inhaled. Exposed gardens benefit from windbreaks in the form of hedges or slatted wooden panels that filter the wind, rather than solid screens that create turbulence on the lee side.

Within any garden, not just exposed ones, create small enclosed areas where you can contain scent and inhale it luxuriantly. As most flowers need warmth to bring out the full depth of their scent, get the most bang for your buck by earmarking the sunniest spots on patios, seating areas, or covered arbours where you can enjoy fragrance at your leisure. Bear in mind that walls, and paving to a lesser extent, have a storage-heater effect, retaining the sun's warmth and radiating it into the evening to prolong comfort and scent, so make full use of any building or boundary walls and add panels of hazel, bamboo, willow, or sturdy trellis for extra shelter as required.

Much current garden literature encourages readers to cluster fragrant plants together in a collection. But the most sensual gardens of all are infused with perfumed plants through and through. Cultivate sweet-scented plants in prime locations so that you are certain to catch their drift. Target the following areas:

- **Locate potted plants under windows or on your balcony so that you can enjoy the aromas indoors and out.** Perfumed annuals (such as sweet alyssum, carnations, and stocks) or bulbs (such as lilies and narcissus) are excellent choices.

- **Frame your front door or garden entrance with a sweet-smelling climber such as summer jasmine or honeysuckle.** Or plant the strongly perfumed thornless climbing rose 'Zephirine Drouhin'.

- **Cover a sturdy arbour, pergola, or wall with a robust climber like the old-fashioned wisteria.** Its fragrant blooms in 30–60-centimetre (1–2-foot) pendulous clusters are legendary.

- **Edge pathways with fragrant herbs such as lavender and rosemary that release their scent when you brush against them.** Similarly, fill gaps in paving with creeping aromatic plants like thyme, Corsican mint, and pennyroyal mint.

Flowers Most Possessed with Scent

In a single gardening season, you can work perfume magic simply by planting fast-growing annuals and perennials. Enjoy their instant fragrance gratification while your slower-growing perfumed trees and shrubs become established. Here are our favourite scented plants.

- **Sweet sultan.** *Centaurea moschata.* Annual. This plant has erect branching stems to 60 centimetres (2 feet) with thistlelike, 5-centimetre (2-inch), musk-scented flower heads. Common colours include lilac, rose, yellow, and white.

✔ **Chocolate cosmos.** *Cosmos atrosanguineus.* Perennial. Dark red flowers, like those of tiny dahlias, adorn this perennial, and give off a mouthwatering scent of dark chocolate. Although perennial, this plant isn't hardy and you need to move it into a greenhouse or conservatory for the winter. Height 45 centimetres (18 inches).

✔ **Pinks.** *Dianthus.* Perennial. Several kinds of strongly fragrant perennial pinks, or border carnations, are available. Tops for fragrance are cheddar pink (*D. gratianopolitanus*), cottage pink (*D. plumarius*), maiden pink (*D. deltoides*), and many modern pinks such as 'Doris' and 'Haytor White'.

✔ **Carnations.** *Dianthus caryophyllus.* Perennial. Choose spicy-sweet border carnations, which are bushier and more compact than the florist type. Height to 60 centimetres (2 feet).

✔ **Cherry-pie plant, heliotrope.** *Heliotropium arborescens.* Perennial. This plant's delightful sweet fragrance comes from clusters of rich purple flowers on 30–60-centimetre (1–2-foot) stems. Like the chocolate cosmos, this plant won't tolerate frost and needs winter protection.

✔ **Sweet pea.** *Lathyrus odoratus.* Annual. This much-loved climbing annual is easy to grow and produces masses of sweetly scented blooms. Grow in rich soil and deadhead regularly (or cut the blooms for the house).

✔ **Stock.** *Matthiola incana.* Annual. Spicy-sweet flowers cluster along erect stems, which are 30–100 centimetres(1–3 feet) tall, depending on variety. Stock is good for cutting.

✔ **Mignonette.** *Reseda odorata.* Annual. Old-fashioned and considered one of the most fragrant of all flowers, mignonette possesses a sweet pea–raspberry–tangerine scent. The plant reaches from 30–45 centimetres (12–18 inches) with inconspicuous flowers in dense, spikelike clusters. Compact forms are the most fragrant.

✔ **Sweet violet.** *Viola odorata.* Perennial. This plant is cherished for its sweet oils, which were extracted for perfumes. It has dark green, heart-shaped leaves and, depending on the variety, grows from 5–30 centimetres (2–12 inches). Sweet violet spreads by runners near the soil surface.

Some types of flowers are not usually sought after for fragrance, yet particular species or varieties among them are quite nicely scented. So if you're planting peonies, for example, look for hybrids of *Paeonia lactiflora* such as 'Duchesse de Nemours' or 'Sarah Bernhardt'. Daylilies noted for fragrance include the lemon daylily (*Hemerocallis lilioasphodelus*) and hybrids such as 'Hyperion' and 'Citrina'. Among tulips, some single early types have a sweet scent. Examples are butter-yellow 'Bellona' and golden-orange 'Generaal de Wet'. Also, *Tulipa sylvestris* has a pleasant, sweet fragrance.

Creating a Fragrant Evening Garden

As the day reaches its end, there's no better way to wind down and relax than out in the garden, surrounded by sensuous scents. While the scent of many day-scented blooms intensifies late in the day, the star performers are those that only open their flowers or give off their perfume in the evening.

Choose a sheltered spot for your evening garden, west facing if at all possible to catch the last of the sun's light and warmth. To make a truly enchanting evening garden calls for a few accessories, particularly if you use your garden for entertaining. Outdoor lighting – tealights in glass jars, candle lanterns, or rope lights wreathed around a parasol or arch – create a magical atmosphere. Heating encourages you and your guests to linger for much longer too.

The flowers are the stars of the evening garden, and lots of nature's night-clubbers give off their best scents in the evening. Plant them near the spots where you hang out on summer nights – close to porches and bedroom windows, and next to your most comfy garden bench.

- **Dame's rocket.** *Hesperis matronalis.* Biennial. This plant is excellent for an informal or cottage-style garden where it often self-sows. Its branching stems reach 1.2 metres (4 feet) high with rounded clusters of richly fragrant phloxlike blooms in white, lavender, or purple.

- **Lily** (*Lilium* species and varieties). Bulb. Huge, exotic-looking blooms with a powerful scent, strong during the day but stronger at night. (Not all varieties are scented, though.) Our favourites include the easily grown and gloriously perfumed regal lily (*Lilium regale*) and *L. longiflorum* for early to mid-summer, followed later by hybrids such as 'Black Dragon', 'Casa Blanca', 'Kyoto', and 'Stargazer'. Their ideal site is to have roots in the shade and heads in the sun – great for bringing height to a collection of containers – but lilies tolerate almost total shade.

- **Summer jasmine** (*Jasminum officinale*). Climber. This popular twining climber needs little introduction, although you can find some excellent newer varieties of this easily pleased and vigorous plant, suitable for sun or shade. These include the large-flowered 'Clotted Cream', red-tinged 'Inverleith', and the attractive golden-foliaged 'Fiona Sunrise' (though 'Fiona Sunrise' bears fewer flowers than green-leaved forms).

- **Honeysuckle.** *Lonicera* species. Climber. Not all honeysuckles are scented so choose with care: Good ones include all *L. periclymenum* varieties, particularly the splendid 'Graham Thomas' and 'Sweet Sue'; also *L. x americana, L. caprifolium, L. heckrottii* 'Goldflame', and *L. japonica* 'Halliana'.

✔ **Night-scented stock.** *Mathiola longipetala bicornis.* Annual. This hardy annual is so easy to grow that you often find it in children's seed selections. Scrappy and untidy this plant may be, but its dainty little lilac flowers give off the most delectable clove scent. Sow a few seeds here and there among other plants in your borders, and enjoy. Height 15–30 centimetres (6–12 inches).

✔ **Tobacco plant.** *Nicotiana alata.* Annual. You can find many varieties of this popular annual, but not all are scented. When in doubt, go for white-flowered forms. Height 60–90 centimetres (2–3 feet).

✔ **Night phlox.** *Zaluzianskya capensis.* Annual. Clusters of white flowers with a sweet, bubblegum scent. Height 30 centimetres (12 inches).

The Most Aromatic Herbs

Following is a sampling of some of the best herbs for fragrant foliage. In addition to smelling great, thyme, lavender, and rosemary are extremely useful garden plants that tolerate dry soil.

✔ **Lemon verbena.** *Aloysia triphylla*

✔ **Chamomile.** *Chamaemelum nobile*

✔ **Lavender.** *Lavandula*

✔ **Lemon balm.** *Melissa officinalis*

✔ **Corsican mint.** *Mentha requienii*

✔ **Pennyroyal mint.** *Mentha pulegium*

✔ **Scented geraniums.** *Pelargonium* species, including *P. citrosum, P. grave-olens, P. nervosum, P. odoratissimum, P. quercifolium,* and *P. tomentosum*

✔ **Rosemary.** *Rosmarinus officinalis*

✔ **Thyme.** *Thymus*

Heavenly Scented Shrubs and Climbers

So many shrubs and climbers are scented to a greater or lesser degree, and in so many different ways, that it's hard to pick out a few of the best. Here are some of the most special plants to flood your garden with fragrance.

✔ **Chocolate vine.** *Akebia quinata.* Climber. This attractive twining climber blooms in spring, bearing dark red flowers that have a chocolate scent (though not as strong as that of the chocolate cosmos). The fresh green, lobed leaves look handsome too. Grow in sun or partial shade. Height to 2.4 metres (8 feet).

✔ **Butterfly bush.** *Buddleia davidii.* Shrub. Deciduous and fast-growing, soon reaching 3–3.5 metres (10–12 feet) high. In summer, fragrant flowers develop in arching, spikelike clusters to 30 centimetres (1 foot) long. Butterflies flock to its flowers. Grow in full sun.

✔ **Pineapple broom, also called Moroccan broom.** *Cytisus battandieri.* Shrub. A tall, rather rangy, silvery-leaved plant that does best against a wall where you can tie in its stems. A sheltered, sunny site is essential in cold areas. In mid-summer, it produces large, golden-yellow clusters of flowers, which have a sweet, pineapple scent. Prefers well-drained soil. Height to 4.2 metres (15 feet).

✔ **Warminster broom.** *Cytisus x praecox.* Shrub. This fast-growing though short-lived shrub is smothered with creamy-yellow, powerfully fragrant flowers in spring. You find white and deep gold varieties. Grow in sun and well-drained soil. Height 1.2 metres (4 feet).

✔ **Daphne.** *Daphne* species. These spring-flowering shrubs can be a bit temperamental (as well as being pricey and slow growing), but the flowers' seductive scent encourages serious fragrance fanciers to persist. You can choose from several species, including *D. burkwoodii* (white flowers fading to pink), *D. cneorum* (rosy-pink flowers), and *D. odora* (flowers pink to deep red with creamy pink throats). Grow in sun and in a sheltered spot.

All parts of the daphne are safe to handle but poisonous if ingested.

✔ **Honeysuckle and jasmine.** Head to the section 'Creating a fragrant evening garden' in this chapter.

✔ **Mahonia.** Shrub. This tough evergreen thrives in sun or shade. Mahonias bear showy clusters or spikes of sweetly scented, bright yellow flowers in late winter or early spring. *Mahonia aquifolium* and its varieties are the most compact, growing to around 1.2 metres (4 feet), while hybrids such as *M.* 'Charity' reach around 2.4 metres (8 feet).

✔ **Sweet box.** *Sarcococca* species. This unassuming little evergreen shrub provides a welcome midwinter boost with a rich vanilla scent given off by masses of tiny white, tassel-shaped flowers. Easily grown in sun or shade. Height 60–90 centimetres (2–3 feet).

✔ **Lilac.** *Syringa vulgaris.* This large and much-loved spring-flowering shrub includes many named varieties, with flowers in white, pink, purple, blue, and pale yellow. Prefers sun or light shade. Grows up to 4.5 metres (15 feet).

✔ **Wistera.** *W. floribunda*, *W. sinensis*. In spring this handsome climber is smothered with long, dangling , fragrant flower heads that are made up of many small blooms. They come in white, lavender blue, pink, or purple. *W. sinensis* is vigorous, eventually spreading for many metres, while *W. floribunda* is more compact. In cold or exposed sites, grow wisteria against a sunny, sheltered wall; elsewhere you can grow it over a pergola (but allow extra head room so that the long blooms don't bash you on the head!).

Best Bulbs for Fragrance

You can find some of the most highly scented flowers among bulbs. For more information about bulbs, see Chapter 9.

✔ **Naked lady.** *Amaryllis belladonna*. Evocatively named because 60-centimetre (2-foot) flowering stalks emerge in late summer, but not leaves. Its pink, trumpet-shaped flowers are about 7.5 centimetres (3 inches) in diameter.

✔ **English bluebell.** *Hyacinthoides non-scripta*. The most glorious of all spring sights is that of a bluebell wood in full flower, carpeted in deep azure blue blooms and filled with a delectable fragrance. If you have a little wooded corner or wild area to your garden, bluebells are ideal. Never plant Spanish bluebell, which is causing a serious threat to our native bluebells by taking over in the wild. Height 30 centimetres (12 inches).

✔ **Lily-of-the-valley.** *Convallaria majalis*. The tiny, hanging, bell-shaped flowers that appear in early spring are wonderfully scented. A tough little bulb that can spread to form dense patches if it likes your garden, but on occasions can be hard to establish. Grow in part or full shade. Height 15 centimetres (6 inches).

✔ **Hyacinth.** *Hyacinthus orientalis*. A spring favourite for its large, showy, powerfully scented flowers. You can easily force these large bulbs indoors if you buy specially treated bulbs in late summer and early autumn (see Chapter 9 for details on forcing bulbs), but you need to get special vases to fit the bulbs. You can find several colours of hyacinth, and all are equally fragrant. One flowering hyacinth is enough to perfume an entire house. Or plant outdoors in clumps or in containers. Height 23 centimetres (9 inches).

✔ **Lily.** See the section 'Creating a fragrant evening garden' in this chapter.

✔ **Grape hyacinth.** *Muscari azureum*. Put your nose up to the blue flower spikes and smell a glass of fresh grape juice! Height 15 centimetres (6 inches).

✔ **Narcissus.** Many, especially *Narcissus jonquilla* and *N. tazetta*. Jonquils are the shorter narcissi that produce two to four flowers per flowering stalk. The tazettas include the pure white paperwhites and the golden 'Soleil d'Or'. Tazettas are popular for growing indoors in pots. A single paperwhite can perfume a whole room or more, but it's not a universally loved scent. Try it for yourself. Height 30–60 centimetres (12–24 inches).

✔ **Tulip.** Several hybrids of this popular, showy spring bulb are scented. These include 'Bellona' (bright yellow), 'Generaal de Wet' (orange), and 'Prince of Austria' (orange-red). Height to 60 centimetres (24 inches).

Redolent Roses

Nothing is quite like sniffing a powerfully scented rose for the most intense floral fragrance experience. Old-fashioned roses are nearly all strongly scented, and fragrance aficionados can even identify the class of old rose – Tea, China, Damask, and Bourbon, for example – by its characteristic perfume. Although not all modern roses are scented, many varieties have powerful perfumes. Some dedicated rose lovers, however, have managed to develop garden rose varieties with the attributes of a modern rose *and* a delicious fragrance, notably the English rose series, so you're spoilt for choice when it comes to scent. Whatever variety of rose you fancy, it's best to check them out in summer and let your nose do the choosing. See Chapter 10 for lots more on roses.

The following varieties are all strongly perfumed. This is just a selection of scented roses – far more exist than we can list here.

✔ **Cornelia.** Shrub. Apricot-pink.

✔ **'Crimson Glory'.** Hybrid tea. Deep crimson ageing to purplish.

✔ **'Fragrant Cloud'.** Hybrid tea. Orange-red.

✔ **Gertrude Jekyll.** English rose. Deep pink.

✔ **Graham Thomas.** English rose. Yellow.

✔ **Korresia.** Floribunda. Clear yellow.

✔ **'Papa Meilland'.** Hybrid tea. Bright, dark crimson.

✔ **'Sutter's Gold'.** Hybrid tea. Yellow with red shading on outer petals.

✔ **William Lobb.** Shrub. Crimson.

✔ **Zephirine Drouhin.** Climber. Deep pink.

One last note on experiencing your favourite floral fragrance: A flower's perfume is usually strongest on warm and humid days and weakest when the weather is hot and dry. For an intense rush of flower fragrance, bring the blossom to your face and lightly breathe into it before inhaling. The warmth of your breath releases the flower's volatile oils.

Part VII
The Part of Tens

"Living near a nuclear power station
can be worrying but at least we don't
get any slugs or snails."

In this part . . .

Throughout this book, we give you lots of lists: lists of can't-miss annuals; lists of our favourite perennials; and lists of our favourite trees, shrubs, and more. Well, here we are in a part dedicated mostly to lists.

In this part are a couple more useful lists. You can find a list of great garden projects and a quick scoot through easy ways to attract wildlife to your garden.

We hope you enjoy our part of gar-tens.

Chapter 23

Ten Quick Projects

*W*e can't say it enough: Gardening is fun. And the more you learn and do, the more fun it is. If you have gardening fever, the easy projects we describe here will enable you to enjoy the plants you are growing now or inspire you to grow even more.

Cooking Up Herb Vinegars

Herb vinegars are so easy to make at home that it should be illegal for food companies to sell them. You can flavour and mellow vinegars with many kinds of fresh garden herbs – fennel, sage, rosemary, garlic, and chives, to name a few. Our favourite herb vinegar is made with purple basil. In addition to its spicy basil flavour, this vinegar turns a gorgeous orchid pink.

As a general guide, use 1 cup of fresh-picked herbs to flavour 1 litre of vinegar. Depending on your taste, use white, cider, or wine vinegar. White vinegar works best with purple basil.

Here's all there is to it, though the variations are endless:

1. **Loosely fill a clean glass jar with fresh, clean herbs.**

2. **Fill with vinegar to cover the herbs, and cap with plastic or a cork.**
   (Don't use metal.)

3. **Store in a cool, dark place for two to six weeks.** The longer the time period, the stronger the herb flavour.

4. **Strain to remove the herbs when the flavour satisfies your taste.**

Use flavoured vinegars any way you would a wine vinegar, but consider reserving them for salads. The herb flavours make a subtle and very effective accent to any vinaigrette dressing. Add a whole sprig of the herb to the bottle for visual interest and to help identify the flavour; its presence won't hurt anything. Before presenting as a gift, wrap a bit of ribbon or raffia around the neck. Consider, too, a pretty, hand-printed label that identifies the flavour, date, and maker.

Making Cut Flowers Last

If you're cutting flowers for arrangements, care in harvesting and handling helps them last. Remember the following tips:

- Use sharp secateurs or scissors and cut the flowers in the early morning (before too much moisture has *transpired*, or been lost, from the plant).

- As you cut, put stems directly into water – carry a water-filled bucket into the garden with you.

- As soon as you bring the flowers indoors, remove the lower leaves that will be below the water in your vase. Submerged leaves rot, not only clouding the water and often giving off an unpleasant odour, but also shortening the life of your cut flowers.

- If a flower has hollow stems, recut them under water before placing in the vase to avoid air locks developing (which prevents water being taken up).

- Adding a cut-flower food to the vase water provides nutrients and lengthens the life of the flower.

- Change the vase water every couple of days.

- Place your bouquet in a cool spot, out of direct sunlight and away from heaters or radiators.

Some large flowers with hollow stems, such as delphiniums and amaryllis, last longer if you first hold the stems upside down and pour water into them. Then plug the base of the stem with cotton wool.

Certain flowers, including Iceland poppies, euphorbias, and hollyhocks, need to have their stems sealed by searing to prevent them from drooping. Immediately after cutting, hold each stem over a flame for a few seconds or dip the stems in boiling water for a minute. (Take care with euphorbias, as the milky sap can cause skin irritations.)

For roses, fill a clean sink or large baking dish with lukewarm water and lay the roses in flat. Soak the roses for 10–20 minutes before arranging or to revive fading flowers. The process can even restore drooping flower heads.

Plants with woody stems, such as lilacs, forsythias, and pussy willows, require special treatment. You need to split the stems to help with the uptake of water. Use a sharp knife or clippers to cut several times into the base of the stem.

Drying Flowers

You can easily preserve the essence of summer when you pick a bunch of flowers and hang them to dry for winter bouquets.

Air-dry the annuals listed here simply by hanging them upside down in bundles, from the ceiling, or from a clothes-drying rack. Remove the foliage, group them in small bunches, and secure the bunches with a rubber band. Keep the drying flowers in a warm, dark place with good ventilation. Most flowers are dry when the stems snap. Store dried flowers in covered boxes or paper bags (away from dust and light).

Some dried flowers, such as strawflowers, have weak stems and you need to wrap the stem with florist's wire to provide additional support if you want to use them in arrangements.

Following are a dozen annuals that you can count on to hold their shape and colour:

- ✔ **Winged everlasting.** *Ammobium alatum*, 'Grandiflorum'. Flowers are white and yellow with yellow centres. Cut when buds start to open.

- ✔ **Safflower.** *Carthamus tinctorius*. Cut yellow-orange flowers in bud or just at peak colour.

- ✔ **Cockscomb.** *Celosia argentea*. Colours are intense and warm. Cut when heads reach full colour.

- ✔ **Larkspur.** *Consolida ambigua*, 'Giant Imperial' series. Colours are pink, blue, purple, and white. Cut stems when about two-thirds of the flowers are open and one-third are in bud.

- **Globe amaranth.** *Gomphrena globosa*. Colours are orange, white, pink, purple, and red. Cut when heads are plump and in full colour.

- **Strawflower.** *Helichrysum bracteatum*, 'Bright Bikini' hybrids. Colours are mixed and vibrant. Cut when buds start to open.

- **Pink paper daisy.** *Helipterum roseum* (also called *Acrolineum roseum*). Colours in shades of pink and white. Cut partially open blooms.

- **Statice.** *Limonium sinuatum* varieties. Colours range from purple to orange. Cut when most of the florets are open.

- **Love-in-a-mist.** *Nigella damascena*, 'Miss Jekyll' hybrids. Grown for attractive seedpods. Cut when mature.

- **Pink pokers (or Russian statice).** *Psylliostachys suworowii*. Cut lavender pink flowers when fully open.

- **Starflower.** *Scabiosa stellata*, 'Drumstick'. Cut decorative seedpods as soon as petals fade.

- **Immortelle.** *Xeranthemum annuum*. Colours are lavender, white, and shades of pink and purple. Cut open flowers after they show full colour.

Making a Flowering Centrepiece

For a picnic table in summer, consider mixing begonias, ageratum, and sweet alyssum, the combination that we've based this set of steps on. A winter centrepiece for indoor decoration could include moth orchids and African violets with ivy and diminutive ferns. You may need a small bag of potting compost to fill in gaps between plants. If need be, put loose perlite or vermiculite (that light, popcornlike soil amendment you can get at garden centres) underneath plant pots to raise them up in the basket.

1. **Choose an oblong basket** about 38–50 centimetres long, 20–25 centimetres wide, and 10 centimetres high (15–20 inches long, 8–10 inches wide, and 4 or so inches high).

2. **Line the basket with a heavy plastic carrier bag and trim the edges.**

3. **Fill the basket with a combination of flowering and foliage plants in small 5–10 centimetre (2–4-inch) containers.**

   Place the tallest plants (like begonias) in the centre and the lower-growing plants (like ageratum and sweet alyssum) toward the outside. At the edges, you can squeeze in trailing plants, including small-leafed ivies. Fill all gaps with potting soil. Use moss to hide the pots.

4. **To maintain the centrepiece, water plants individually, using a narrow-spouted watering can.**

   Feed the plants regularly using a liquid fertiliser, especially during summer when most plants grow fastest. Refresh the centrepiece with new plants as needed.

 For a very full look, squeeze in more plants by removing some of the smaller ones from their containers and slipping the root ball of each plant into a zipped sandwich bag (partially close the bag around the base of the plant). Then gently squeeze the bagged plants between the potted plants. Water the plants just enough to keep them moist.

Creating an Autumn Harvest Wreath

You don't need to be an artist to pull off this craft project successfully. After just a couple of hours of collecting and arranging leaves, seedpods, and fruit from your garden and greengrocers, you have a beautiful wreath. It lasts anywhere from several days to several months, depending on the plants you use.

The object is to cover a polystyrene foam wreath base (available at craft and floral supply stores) with garden goodies. You need about two large carrier bags full of plant material to cover a 30-centimetre (1-foot) wreath. Combine foliage such as magnolia, eucalyptus, and cineraria leaves with colourful accents like rose hips, seedpods, and pyracantha berries. If you're short on home-grown plants, use accent material like baby corn, apples, and miniature pumpkins or gourds purchased from your greengrocers.

Here's what you do:

1. **Attach a wire to the wreath base to hang the wreath.**

   Slide the wire through the base, leaving a looped hook on top; twist and cut the ends of the wire.

2. **Cover the wreath base with dry leaves, using hairpins to hold it in place.**

   Work in one direction around the base from the inside of the wreath outwards. Attach thin-stemmed leaves in clusters and large leaves individually. For pizzazz, combine foliage of different colours and textures.

3. **After you cover the base, add accents.**

   Secure small fruit and berries with hairpins or glue. Secure larger fruit, such as baby pumpkins or apples, by using floral picks (available at craft and floral supply shops). Place these larger items sparingly as focal points.

Forcing Narcissus Indoors

On blustery winter days when the garden is dull and quiet, a pot of home-grown bulbs gracing the dining room table is truly gratifying. Setting up narcissus to bloom takes little effort. All they need are water and several weeks to work their magic.

The two varieties of narcissus that are most available and reliable for water culture are varieties of Narcissus tazetta – 'Paperwhite' and yellow 'Soleil D'Or'. Paperwhites flower only five to six weeks after planting; 'Soleil D'Or' takes a bit longer.

Here's what you do:

1. **Choose a fairly shallow waterproof bowl or pot, at least twice as deep as the size of the bulbs.**

2. **Fill the container to within several inches from the top with pebbles.**

3. **Set the bulbs on the pebbles about 1 centimetre (½ inch) apart with the broad ends down.**

4. **Fill the container with water so that the water just touches the bottom of the bulbs.**

5. **To hold the bulbs in place, fill the spaces between them with more pebbles.**

6. **Put the planted container in a cool, dark place to encourage root growth.**

7. **In two to three weeks, when the shoots are about 7.5 centimetres (3 inches) high, move the container to a warmer, bright location.**

8. **As the plants develop, add water from time to time, keeping it at the base of the bulbs.**

For Christmas blooms, start them in mid-November. For continuous flowering throughout winter, start the first pot of bulbs in late October and continue planting at two- to three-week intervals.

Creating a Water Garden in a Tub

The thought of building a traditional garden pond can be overwhelming, but creating a soothing water feature in a tub is quite achievable. This garden is a functioning ecosystem, meaning that you don't need to filter or change water, as for a fish tank. Though small in scale, your tub garden will teem with life – water insects and possibly even frogs or toads may take up residence, and even birds come to drink. Attach a piece of wood to the inside rim, so birds can perch and hedgehogs, if they come to drink and fall in, can climb out easily.

Display the water garden where it can receive two to three hours of shade during the hottest part of the day. For the winter, unless you live in a mild area, you need to drain the pond, because the water is likely to freeze solid. Empty the pond and keep the plants in a porch, greenhouse, or conservatory, standing in plastic bowls or trays containing a little water to keep them moist. Here are the materials you need for your water feature:

✔ Sturdy plastic or glazed ceramic pot without a drainage hole, or:

✔ Durable plastic 'terracotta' container. Choose one about 75 centimetres (30 inches) in diameter and about 50 centimetres (20 inches) high.

✔ An assortment of water plants:

- One water iris

- One water lily (a dwarf variety such as one of the Nymphaea pygmaea varieties)

- One free-floating water hyacinth

- A clump of oxygenating plant

✔ An empty 10 or 20 litre plastic pot from a tree or large shrub.

Here's what you do:

1. **Fill the large tub about ⅔ full with water and place the plastic tree pot, upside-down, to one side of the tub under the water.**

2. **Place the iris on top of the upside-down pot.**

3. **Place the water lily, in its own container, on the bottom of the tub.**

   The water lily's leaves and flowers will rise above the water surface.

4. **Plant the clump of oxygenating plant in a mesh pot using aquatic compost, and place on the bottom of the tub next to the water lily.**

5. **Add the floating water hyacinth and fill the tub with water.**

Preparing a Salad Basket

Many salad leaf plants germinate just a few days after planting and are ready for harvesting in two to four weeks. If you choose cut-and-come-again varieties, they grow back for a repeat harvest.

You can buy a seed blend or mix your own by combining your favourite greens. Typical ingredients include loose-leaf lettuces, chicories, mizuna, and curly cress.

Here's how to grow a basket of succulent salad that you can harvest after several weeks:

1. **Choose a large, sturdy basket that can support the weight of wet soil.**

   Line the basket with a heavyweight black plastic bin bag. To provide drainage, use scissors to poke holes through the plastic at the bottom of the basket.

2. **Fill the basket with multipurpose compost to 5 centimetres (2 inches) below the rim.** Trim off any plastic that extends beyond the rim. Water thoroughly and allow to drain.

3. **Scatter seeds thinly over the soil surface, cover with about half a centimetre (¼ inch) of potting mix, and then water gently.**

4. **Cover the basket with a piece of water-retaining plastic or food wrap and keep in a 18–21 degrees Celsius (65–70 degrees Fahrenheit) location until the seeds germinate.**

5. **When seeds sprout, remove the plastic and move the basket to a sunny location.**

   Keep the soil moist as the plants grow, and fertilise weekly with a complete liquid fertiliser.

6. **Start harvesting when the seedlings are about 8 centimetres (3 inches) tall by cutting with scissors 1.5 centimetres (½ inch) above the soil surface.**

Finding Treasures from Twigs

Consider yourself lucky if you are trimming a climber, clipping a hedge, or pruning a tree and find yourself with a few piles of twigs and branches. These bits of woody materials have many uses in the home and garden, both utilitarian and aesthetic. However, do make sure all your prunings are free of pests and diseases.

✔ **Twiggy shrub prunings.** Use prunings that are about 0.5–1.5 centimetres (¼–½ inch) thick at the base to support peas and lightweight herbaceous perennials.

✔ **Straight branches.** Branches about 1 metre (3 feet) long and about a centimetre or so wide make sturdy plant supports. To keep blooms of large-flowering perennials such as peonies from toppling over, drive stakes into the ground to form a ring around the plant. Connect the stakes with twine tied at the appropriate height to support top-heavy stems.

You can also make your own rustic trellises from straight, sturdy branches. Allow 45 centimetres (18 inches) at the base to push into the soil for support. Weave rope or twine to connect the branches and provide supports for plants.

✔ **Tall stems.** Use wispy, branching stems about 60 centimetres (2 feet) long to support stems of paperwhite narcissus growing in pebbles and water.

✔ **Twigs.** Use thin twigs to support cut flowers in arrangements. Place groups of twigs at different angles in the vase and then insert flowers.

✔ **Flexible stems.** To form decorative wreaths, bend and weave together fresh-cut stems from dormant grapes or willow. Bind the ends together with wire and let the stems dry out.

Cleaning Containers

By cleaning used containers before replanting, you help prevent the spread of plant diseases and pests. Because they are porous, terracotta containers need cleaning more often than plastic.

Using a stiff wire brush, scrape off soil and fertiliser residue, algae, and salt crust inside and outside the pot. Then scrub the pot with hot water and rinse well.

If you've had a perennial or a shrub growing in the same container for several seasons, the outside surface of the container may be dirty and discoloured. To freshen it up, brush the surface and, using an old rag, rub on linseed oil.

On the other hand, if the container has acquired the attractive patina of age and the plant inside it is growing well, you can leave the container as is.

Chapter 24

Ten Tips for Creating a Wildlife Garden

*H*ere are our favourite tips on how to roll out the welcome mat for wildlife in your garden. If you want to know more about creating a wildlife haven, head to Chapter 20.

Choose the Right Plants

Of the tens of thousands of different plants available to you, only a relatively small amount are useful to wildlife. You often hear that 'native' plants are best simply because wildlife has evolved to make use of the plants in its own country, but many non-native ones are extremely good too. Plants can be wildlife-friendly in a number of ways: bearing fruits and berries to feed birds and other creatures in autumn and winter; with flowers that provide nectar for butterflies; host or food plants on which butterfly caterpillars feed; and pollen-producing flowers to feed bees.

Plant a Tree

All but the teeniest of gardens have room for at least one tree, and often more. Birds like to sing from a high vantage point as well as building nests up there. Choose a tree that has other wildlife benefits too, such as crab apple (*Malus*) or mountain ash (*Sorbus*) with flowers that attract insects and berries to provide food for birds; or birch, which attracts insects. These three trees are ideal for small gardens. More space means more choice; you need a large garden for vigorous native trees including pine and alder, and a very big plot for an oak or beech tree. Read Chapter 4 if you can't see the wood for the trees.

Plant Up Walls and Fences

You can transform bare vertical features into food supplies and shelter for wildlife by clothing walls and fences with climbing plants. Ensure that any plant supports such as trellis or wires are spaced at least 5 centimetres (2 inches) away from the wall or fence, to make good nesting sites. Top wildlife climbers include firethorn (*Pyracantha*), herring-bone cotoneaster (*C. horizontalis*), ivy (*Hedera* species), honeysuckle (*Lonicera*), summer jasmine (*J. officinale*), and flowering quince (*Chaenomeles*). Chapter 6 covers climbers.

Choose Hedges Instead of Fences

Hedges make superb wildlife-friendly boundaries, providing better and more dense cover where birds can nest and roost. Berry-bearing plants such as holly, hawthorn, and blackthorn provide much-needed winter food. Hedge your bets: A mixed hedge made up of a mixture of these plants is the best type for wildlife.

Create a Pond

Water is essential for life and a pond is the best way to attract a huge range of wildlife. Birds, hedgehogs, and other creatures come to drink and bathe; frogs, toads, and even newts may take up residence; a host of other insects will live in and around your pond. Make an ideal wildlife pond using a flexible liner that can fit whatever size and shape of hole you wish. Ensure that one side at least is shallow and sloping to allow easy access for birds and animals, and make a proportion of the pond at least 60 centimetres (2 feet) deep to prevent the water freezing completely in winter.

Avoid having a pond if you have young children, or even if they visit regularly. Tragically, several toddlers drown each year in garden ponds, so it's just not worth the risk. Instead, put out water in shallow bowls or bird baths or create a water feature in a tub (Chapter 23 shows you how).

Convert Your Lawn to a Meadow

If your lawn is large, consider developing part of it into a meadow that only needs cutting once or twice a year. Not only do you have lots more flowers to enjoy, but you also attract a great variety of bees, butterflies, and other insects. See Chapter 5 for more.

Bear with the Bugs

Instead of blasting greenfly and other bugs with harmful chemicals, grit your teeth and wait for wildlife to do the job for you. Although it can take months or even a year or more for a balance of nature to establish, eventually the wait is worth it. After all, bugs are food for wildlife – if you don't have any slugs in your garden, you won't find any hedgehogs snuffling around either.

If you have really nasty bugs that you need to tackle, such as vine weevil, use an environmentally friendly zapper such as a biological control. Zip over to Chapter 16 for the lowdown on pest control.

Compost Your Waste

Recycle your garden and kitchen waste by composting. As well as being great for your plants and the environment, a cosy compost heap is home to insects and invertebrates, and is a rich feeding ground for birds. Although all waste rots down eventually if you just leave it in a heap, having a couple of compost bins speeds up the process into months rather than years, and keeps your garden much tidier.

Chapter 14 gets down and dirty with more composting tips.

Don't Be Too Tidy

Leaves, dead wood, and piles of plant material become home and food for insects and other creatures. Instead of giving your garden a thorough clear-up in autumn, be selective and just pick out the weeds, and delay cutting back the dead stems of perennials and grasses until spring. Loads of beneficial insects such as ladybirds will be snug and safe for the winter. When you do cut back plants, tuck bundles of prunings in out-of-sight spots at the base of hedges and under large shrubs, to become important mini-habitats.

Be Environmentally Friendly

Whatever plants or products you purchase, make sure they won't endanger the environment either directly, in the case of harmful chemicals, or indirectly, by endangering another habitat, such as timber from threatened forests. Imported hardwoods from illegally logged forests are a particular problem. Look for the logo of the Forestry Stewardship Council (FSC), which shows that the timber has come from responsibly managed forests. Buy products made from recycled materials wherever possible, and use your own throwaway items too (which saves you cash in the bargain). A few examples are cardboard and newspaper as mulches, large glass jars as mini-cloches and candle holders, and old CDs as bird scarers.

Index

• *M* •

• S •

• *V* •

• *W* •

Notes

Notes

Notes

Notes

Notes

Notes

Notes

Notes

FOR DUMMIES®

Do Anything. Just Add Dummies

HOME

UK editions

Buying and Selling a Home For Dummies
0-7645-7027-7

Renting Out Your Property For Dummies
0-7645-7016-1

DIY & Home Maintenance All-In-One For Dummies
0-7645-7054-4

PERSONAL FINANCE

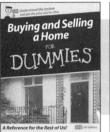
Investing For Dummies
0-7645-7023-4

Paying Less Tax 2005/2006 For Dummies
0-7645-7053-6

Sorting Out Your Finances For Dummies
0-7645-7039-0

BUSINESS

Starting a Business For Dummies
0-7645-7018-8

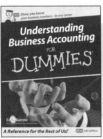
Understanding Business Accounting For Dummies
0-7645-7025-0

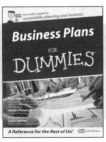
Business Plans For Dummies
0-7645-7026-9

Other UK editions now available:

Building Confidence
For Dummies
(0-4700-1669-8)

British History
For Dummies
(0-7645-7021-8)

Buying a Home On A
Budget For Dummies
(0-7645-7035-8)

Buying a Home in Spain
For Dummies
(0-7645-7057-9)

Cleaning and Stain
Removal For Dummies
(0-7645-7029-3)

Cognitive Behavioural
Therapy For Dummies
(0-4700-1838-0)

CVs For Dummies
(0-7645-7017-X)

Diabetes For Dummies
(0-7645-7019-6)

Divorce For Dummies
(0-7645-7030-7)

DIY & Home
Maintenance
For Dummies
(0-7645-7054-4)

eBay.co.uk For Dummies
(0-7645-7059-5)

Formula One Racing
For Dummies
(0-7645-7015-3)

Golf For Dummies
(0-4700-1811-9)

Irish History
For Dummies
(0-7645-7040-4)

Marketing For Dummies
(0-7645-7056-0)

Neuro-Linguistic
Programming
For Dummies
(0-7645-7028-5)

Nutrition For Dummies
(0-7645-7058-7)

Pregnancy For Dummies
(0-7645-7042-0)

Retiring Wealthy
For Dummies
(0-4700-2632-4)

Rugby Union
For Dummies
(0-7645-7020-X)

Small Business
Employment Law
For Dummies
(0-7645-7052-8)

Su Doku For Dummies
(0-4700-189-25)

Sudoku 2 For Dummies
(0-4700-2651-0)

Sudoku 3 For Dummies
(0-4700-2667-7)

Wills, Probate and
Inheritance Tax
For Dummies
(0-7645-7055-2)

FOR DUMMIES®

A world of resources to help you grow

HOBBIES

0-7645-5232-5

0-7645-5137-X

0-7645-5476-X

Also available:

Art For Dummies
(0-7645-5104-3)
Aromatherapy For Dummies
(0-7645-5171-X)
Bridge For Dummies
(0-7645-5015-2)
Card Games For Dummies
(0-7645-9910-0)
Chess For Dummies
(0-7645-5003-9)
Crocheting For Dummies
(0-7645-4151-X)

Improving Your Memory
For Dummies
(0-7645-5435-2)
Massage For Dummies
(0-7645-5172-8)
Meditation For Dummies
(0-7645-5116-7)
Photography For Dummies
(0-7645-4116-1)
Quilting For Dummies
(0-7645-5118-3)
Woodworking For Dummies
(0-7645-3977-9)

EDUCATION

0-7645-7206-7

0-7645-5581-2

0-7645-5422-0

Also available:

Algebra For Dummies
(0-7645-5325-9)
Astronomy For Dummies
(0-7645-8465-0)
Buddhism For Dummies
(0-7645-5359-3)
Calculus For Dummies
(0-7645-2498-4)
Christianity For Dummies
(0-7645-4482-9)
Forensics For Dummies
(0-7645-5580-4)

Islam For Dummies
(0-7645-5503-0)
Philosophy For Dummies
(0-7645-5153-1)
Religion For Dummies
(0-7645-5264-3)
Trigonometry For Dummies
(0-7645-6903-1)

PETS

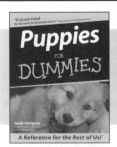

0-7645-5255-4

0-7645-8418-9

0-7645-5275-9

Also available:

Labrador Retrievers
For Dummies
(0-7645-5281-3)
Aquariums For Dummies
(0-7645-5156-6)
Birds For Dummies
(0-7645-5139-6)
Dogs For Dummies
(0-7645-5274-0)
Ferrets For Dummies
(0-7645-5259-7)

German Shepherds
For Dummies
(0-7645-5280-5)
Golden Retrievers
For Dummies
(0-7645-5267-8)
Horses For Dummies
(0-7645-5138-8)
Jack Russell Terriers
For Dummies
(0-7645-5268-6)
Puppies Raising & Training
Diary For Dummies
(0-7645-0876-8)

FOR DUMMIES®

The easy way to get more done and have more fun

LANGUAGES

0-7645-5194-9

0-7645-5193-0

Italian

0-7645-5196-5

Also available:

Chinese For Dummies
(0-4717-8897-X)

Chinese Phrases
For Dummies
(0-7645-8477-4)

French Phrases For Dummies
(0-7645-7202-4)

German For Dummies
(0-7645-5195-7)

Italian Phrases For Dummies
(0-7645-7203-2)

Japanese For Dummies
(0-7645-5429-8)

Latin For Dummies
(0-7645-5431-X)

Spanish Phrases For
Dummies
(0-7645-7204-0)

Hebrew For Dummies
(0-7645-5489-1)

MUSIC AND FILM

0-7645-9904-6

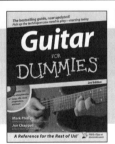

0-7645-2476-3

Piano

0-7645-5105-1

Also available:

Bass Guitar For Dummies
(0-7645-2487-9)

Blues For Dummies
(0-7645-5080-2)

Classical Music For Dummies
(0-7645-5009-8)

Drums For Dummies
(0-7645-5357-7)

Jazz For Dummies
(0-7645-5081-0)

Opera For Dummies
(0-7645-5010-1)

Rock Guitar For Dummies
(0-7645-5356-9)

Screenwriting For Dummies
(0-7645-5486-7)

Songwriting For Dummies
(0-7645-5404-2)

Singing For Dummies
(0-7645-2475-5)

HEALTH, SPORTS & FITNESS

0-7645-7851-0

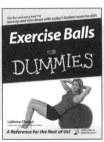

0-7645-7851-0

Asthma

0-7645-4233-8

Also available:

Controlling Cholesterol For
Dummies
(0-7645-5440-9)

Dieting For Dummies
(0-7645-5126-4)

High Blood Pressure For
Dummies
(0-7645-5424-7)

Martial Arts For Dummies
(0-7645-5358-5)

Menopause For Dummies
(0-7645-5458-1)

Power Yoga For Dummies
(0-7645-5342-9)

Thyroid For Dummies
(0-7645-5385-2)

Weight Training For Dummies
(0-7645-5168-X)

Yoga For Dummies
(0-7645-5117-5)